T0156101

Lecture Notes in Computer Science 14285

Founding Editors

Gerhard Goos
Juris Hartmanis

The series Lecture Notes in Computer Science (LNCS), including its subseries Lecture Notes in Artificial Intelligence (LNAI) and Lecture Notes in Bioinformatics (LNBI), has established itself as a medium for the publication of new developments in computer science and information technology research, teaching, and education.

LNCS enjoys close cooperation with the computer science R & D community, the series counts many renowned academics among its volume editors and paper authors, and collaborates with prestigious societies. Its mission is to serve this international community by providing an invaluable service, mainly focused on the publication of conference and workshop proceedings and postproceedings. LNCS commenced publication in 1973.

Antonio Parziale · Moises Diaz · Filipe Melo
Editors

Graphonomics in Human Body Movement

Bridging Research and Practice from Motor Control to Handwriting Analysis and Recognition

21st International Conference
of the International Graphonomics Society, IGS 2023
Évora, Portugal, October 16–19, 2023
Proceedings

 Springer

Editors
Antonio Parziale 🆔
University of Salerno
Fisciano, Italy

Moises Diaz 🆔
Universidad de las Palmas de Gran Canaria
Las Palmas de Gran Canaria, Spain

Filipe Melo 🆔
University of Lisbon
Lisbon, Portugal

ISSN 0302-9743 ISSN 1611-3349 (electronic)
Lecture Notes in Computer Science
ISBN 978-3-031-45460-8 ISBN 978-3-031-45461-5 (eBook)
https://doi.org/10.1007/978-3-031-45461-5

This Springer imprint is published by the registered company Springer Nature Switzerland AG
The registered company address is: Gewerbestrasse 11, 6330 Cham, Switzerland

Paper in this product is recyclable.

Preface

On behalf of the organizing committee, we are very pleased to present the proceedings of the 21st International Graphonomics Society Conference (IGS 2023), held at the Comprehensive Health and Research Center - University of Évora, in Portugal.

The biennial conference of the International Graphonomics Society promotes the advancement of research in the transdisciplinary and multidisciplinary field of graphonomics, which encompasses motor control, experimental psychology, neuroscience, pattern recognition, and artificial intelligence. The aim of graphonomics research is to understand how handwriting is learned and executed, and even more how the writer's neural, psychological, and biomechanical conditions affect the handwriting's features.

IGS has always been an open international event, and this year's edition received submissions from authors affiliated with the institutions of 17 different countries. The five most represented countries were Portugal, Spain, Italy, France, and Czechia.

IGS 2023 adopted a double-blind review model, i.e. both the reviewers' identities and the authors' identities remained anonymous. The review process involved 51 reviewers, including Program Committee members and subreviewers, who spent significant time and effort in the evaluation of the papers. The 47 Program Committee members were selected on the basis of their expertise in the area, and they could invite subreviewers if they needed.

The conference received 35 submissions, including 14 extended abstracts and 21 regular papers. Only the regular papers were eligible for publication in this proceedings book, while accepted extended abstracts were collected separately. Each regular paper received at least three double-blind reviews, while extended abstracts received at least two reviews. We carefully assigned regular papers and extended abstracts to the Program Committee members avoiding any kind of conflict of interest we were aware of. The same review process was applied to all submitted contributions. Objective guidelines based on the reviewers' scores were adhered to in order to prevent any bias in favor of the organizers' papers. In the end, 13 regular papers were accepted for publication in this volume of Lecture Notes in Computer Science, with an acceptance rate of almost 62%.

This proceedings book also includes two regular papers submitted upon invitation by the organizers of the Special Sessions "Movement Variability Analysis" and "Lognormality: an open window on neuromotor control". These two papers were reviewed by the volume editors.

The IGS 2023 conference lasted three days. The final program included a single track with five oral sessions, one poster session, two special sessions, three keynotes, and a session devoted to scientific dating and the doctoral consortium in an effort to foster a high degree of interaction among attendees. The three keynote sessions were devoted to the main topics of the conference, which were motor control, forensics, and computer science, and were held respectively by three distinguished speakers: Rui Alves, Tomasz Dziedzic, and Hans-Leo Teulings.

We express our sincere gratitude to all the people who spent time and effort to make this possible: the authors of the papers, the Program Committee members, the subreviewers, the Organizing and Steering Committees, and the IGS community at large.

August 2023

Antonio Parziale
Moises Diaz
Filipe Melo

Organization

General Chairs

Ana Rita Matias   Comprehensive Health and Research Center,
University of Évora, Portugal

Filipe Melo   University of Lisbon, Portugal

Steering Committee

Claudio De Stefano   Università di Cassino e del Lazio Meridionale,
Italy

Angelo Marcelli   Università degli Studi di Salerno, Italy

Réjean Plamondon   Polytechnique Montréal, Canada

Hans-Leo Teulings   NeuroScript LLC, USA

Arend Van Gemmert   Louisiana State University, USA

Céline Rémi   Université des Antilles, France

Andreas Fischer   University of Applied Sciences and Arts Western
Switzerland (HES-SO), Switzerland

Ana Rita Matias   Comprehensive Health and Research Center,
University of Évora, Portugal

Erika Griechisch   Cursor Insight, Hungary

Sara Rosenblum   University of Haifa, Israel

Heidi H. Harralson   East Tennessee State University, USA

Moises Diaz   Universidad de Las Palmas de Gran Canaria,
Spain

Publication Chairs

Antonio Parziale   Università degli Studi di Salerno, Italy

Moises Diaz   Universidad de Las Palmas de Gran Canaria,
Spain

Filipe Melo   University of Lisbon, Portugal

Local Organizing Committee

José Marmeleira	Comprehensive Health and Research Center, University of Évora, Portugal
Guida Veiga	Comprehensive Health and Research Center, University of Évora, Portugal
Graça Santos	Comprehensive Health and Research Center, University of Évora, Portugal
José Parraça	Comprehensive Health and Research Center, University of Évora, Portugal
João Paulo Sousa	Comprehensive Health and Research Center, University of Évora, Portugal
Ana Rita Silva	Comprehensive Health and Research Center, University of Évora, Portugal
Andreia Santos	Comprehensive Health and Research Center, University of Évora, Portugal
Hugo Folgado	Comprehensive Health and Research Center, University of Évora, Portugal
Jorge Bravo	Comprehensive Health and Research Center, University of Évora, Portugal

Program Committee

Ali Reza Alaei	Southern Cross University, Australia
Gabriela Almeida	Comprehensive Health Research Centre, Universidade de Évora, Portugal
Eric Anquetil	INSA Rennes/IRISA, France
Jorge Calvo-Zaragoza	University of Alicante, Spain
Yury Chernov	Institute for Handwriting Sciences, Switzerland
Giuseppe De Gregorio	Università degli Studi di Salerno, Italy
Claudio De Stefano	Università di Cassino e del Lazio Meridionale, Italy
Vincenzo Dentamaro	Università degli Studi di Bari Aldo Moro, Italy
Moises Diaz	Universidad de Las Palmas de Gran Canaria, Spain
Peter Drotar	Technical University of Košice, Slovakia
Jagoda Dzida	Adam Mickiewicz University, Poland
Mounîm A. El Yacoubi	Institut Polytechnique de Paris, France
Marcos Faundez-Zanuy	Universitat Pompeu Fabra, Spain
Carina Fernandes	NCForenses Institute, Portugal
Andreas Fischer	University of Applied Sciences and Arts Western Switzerland (HES-SO), Switzerland
Alicia Fornés	Universitat Autònoma de Barcelona, Spain

Sonia Garcia-Salicetti	SAMOVAR, Télécom SudParis, France
Rajib Ghosh	National Institute of Technology Patna, India
Nathalie Girard	CNRS - IRISA – University of Rennes, France
Erika Griechisch	Cursor Insight, Hungary
Heidi H. Harralson	East Tennessee State University, USA
Donato Impedovo	Università degli Studi di Bari Aldo Moro, Italy
Josep Lladós	Universitat Autònoma de Barcelona, Spain
Francesca Lunardini	Inntegra, Spain
Angelo Marcelli	Università degli Studi di Salerno, Italy
Ana Rita Matias	Comprehensive Health and Research Center, University of Évora, Portugal
Jiri Mekyska	Brno University of Technology, Czech Republic
Filipe Melo	University of Lisbon, Portugal
Momina Moetesum	Bahria University, Pakistan
Linton Mohammed	Forensic Science Consultants Inc., USA
Ján Mucha	Brno University of Technology, Czech Republic
Marie Anne Nauer	Institute for Handwriting Sciences, Switzerland
Antonio Parziale	Università degli Studi di Salerno, Italy
Michael Pertsinakis	Chartoularios Institute of Questioned Document Studies and MBS College of Crete, Greece
Réjean Plamondon	Polytechnique Montréal, Canada
Ioannis Pratikakis	Democritus University of Thrace, Greece
Céline Rémi	Université des Antilles, France
Sara Rosenblum	University of Haifa, Israel
Adolfo Santoro	Natural Intelligent Technologies Srl, Italy
Rosa Senatore	Natural Intelligent Technologies Srl, Italy
Anna Scius-Bertrand	University of Applied Sciences and Arts Western Switzerland, Switzerland
Imran Siddiqi	Xynoptik Pty Ltd., Australia
Arend Van Gemmert	Louisiana State University, USA
Gennaro Vessio	Università degli Studi di Bari Aldo Moro, Italy
Nicole Vincent	Université Paris Cité, France
Annie Vinter	University of Bourgogne, France
Elias Zois	University of West Attica, Greece

Subreviewers

Francesco Castro	Università degli Studi di Bari Aldo Moro, Italy
Vincenzo Gattulli	Università degli Studi di Bari Aldo Moro, Italy
Gianfranco Semeraro	IUSS Pavia, Italy
Alessandra Scotto di Freca	Università di Cassino e del Lazio Meridionale, Italy

Contents

Handwritten Historical Documents

Special Session on Movement Variability

Special Session on Lognormality

Handwriting Learning and Development

A Short Review on Graphonometric Evaluation Tools in Children

Belen Esther Aleman[✉], Moises Diaz, and Miguel Angel Ferrer

Universidad de Las Palmas de Gran Canaria, Las Palmas, Spain
belen.aleman103@alu.ulpgc.es, {moises.diaz,
miguelangel.ferrer}@ulpgc.es

Abstract. Handwriting is a complex task that involves the coordination of motor, perceptual and cognitive skills. It is a fundamental skill for the cognitive and academic development of children. However, the technological, and educational changes in recent decades have affected both the teaching and assessment of handwriting. This paper presents a literature review of handwriting analysis in children, including a bibliometric analysis of published articles, the study participants, and the methods of evaluating the graphonometric state of children. The aim is to synthesize the state of the art and provide an overview of the main study trends over the last decade. The review concludes that handwriting remains a fundamental tool for early estimation of cognitive problems and early intervention. The article analyzes graphonometric evaluation tools. Likewise, it reflects on the importance of graphonometric evaluation as a means to detect possible difficulties or disorders in learning to write. The article concludes by highlighting the need to agree on an evaluation methodology and to combine databases.

Keywords: Survey · Handwriting · Children · Assessment

1 Introduction

Handwriting is a complex skill that develops during childhood and involves coordination between sensory, motor, and cognitive systems [12]. The evaluation of handwriting is crucial in both clinical and educational fields, as it can reveal information about the neuromotor and cognitive state of the individual, detect alterations or difficulties in these systems, and evaluate the learning and teaching methods of handwriting [16]. Graphonometric analysis is a useful tool in clinical and educational contexts for diagnosing developmental or learning disorders, such as dysgraphia, which affects the process and product of handwriting [67]. Is it also useful for monitoring the evolution and recovery of patients with brain or neuromuscular injuries [25] and adapting or developing strategies to facilitate the learning of writing [7]. The objective of this paper is to present the current state of graphonometric analysis in children over a 10-year period.

This review article is divided into the following sections. The Sect. 2 provides a bibliometric analysis of the articles in the literature, while Sect. 3 examines the age of the participants and the trend in the studies. Section 4 discusses the evaluation methods

A. Parziale et al. (Eds.): IGS 2023, LNCS 14285, pp. 3–20, 2023.
https://doi.org/10.1007/978-3-031-45461-5_1

of each article divided into 4.1 Objective evaluation methods, 4.2 Subjective evaluation methods and 4.3 Objective and subjective evaluation methods. Finally, Sect. 5 closes the manuscripts with the conclusions.

2 Bibliometric Analysis

This section includes the bibliometric analysis of the articles published in the last 10 years on graphonometric evaluation of children handwritten. The objective of this analysis is to identify the trends, patterns and the most relevant authors included in this sample. In total, 77 articles published between 2013 and 2023 have been analyzed. It has been tried that the selected articles represent different studies within the study area. The sample was obtained from the Scopus, IEEE Xplore and Google Scholar databases using the concepts "handwriting in children", "handwriting evaluation children" and "method evaluation handwriting children". In addition, the International Graphonomic Society (IGS) proceedings of the years 2013, 2015, 2017 and 2021 have been consulted. The variables have been extracted from the select papers: number of articles published per year, authors, institutions, countries, and journals.

Figure 1 shows the number of articles published per year on handwriting in children between 2013 and March 2023. It is observed that the average number of papers is approximately seven with peaks on the odd years corresponding to the IGS, indicating interest in this area.

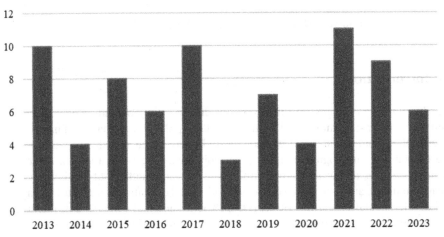

Fig. 1. Number of publications per year until March 2023.

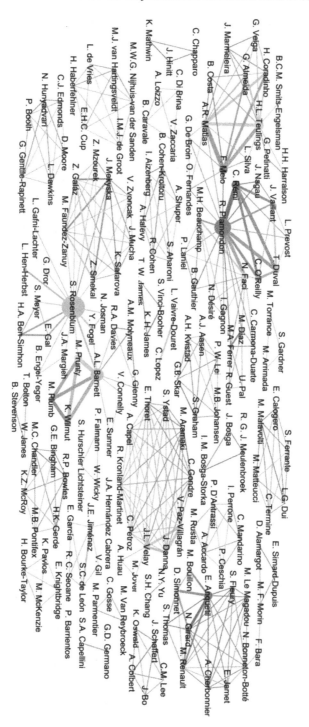

Fig. 2. Author collaboration network of articles revised in this contribution.

Figure 2 shows a network of authors and their collaboration, where the 172 authors of the different articles are gathered and interconnected. These networks are a useful tool to simplify the analysis of the degree of collaboration, the influence, productivity, internationalization, and the researchers engaged on, understanding how knowledge about handwriting develops in children.

The size of the nodes in the graph are proportional to the number of published articles in which the author has appeared. The thickness of each edge that connects the different authors is proportional to the number of collaborations in the various articles included in this work.

Upon analysis of the different papers, it was found that a total of 87 institutions have collaborated on different studies related to handwriting in children, as evidenced by the 77 articles included in the review. Figure 3 shows the 10 most repeated institutions of the 87 that have investigated handwriting in children and Fig. 4 shows a map with the countries that have published more articles among those included in the sample.

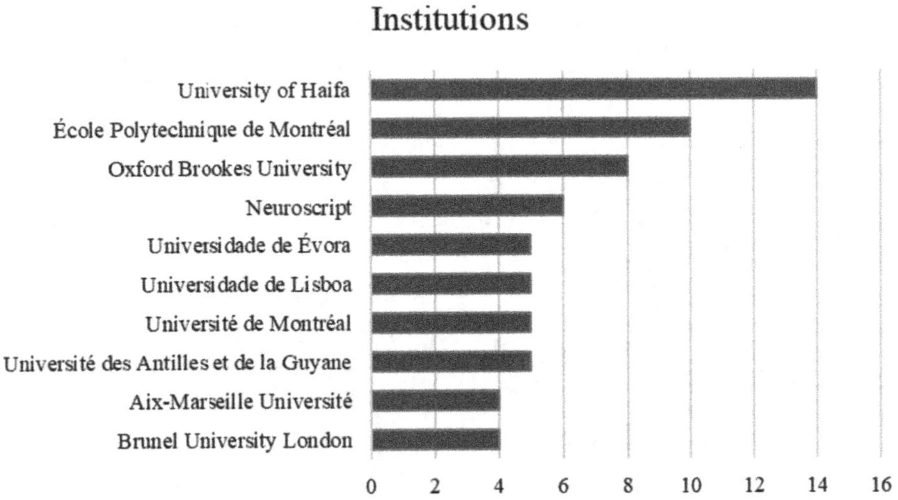

Institutions

Fig. 3. Bar chart of the 10 institutions with more published articles.

Analyzing Fig. 3, the University of Haifa is the one that is most repeated, with 14 papers from the 87 institutions in the articles of the last 10 years included in the sample. However, Fig. 4 shows how France is the country that has led research on handwriting in children with 19 articles, followed by Israel with 15 papers. It is also observed that Canada, the United States, the United Kingdom, and Spain are relevant in graphonometric research in children, although of these countries only two institutions from Canada, one from the United States and two from the United Kingdom appear in Fig. 3.

Countries of articles

Fig. 4. Organizations and countries with the highest number of publications.

Finally, Fig. 5 shows the 10 journals with the highest number of articles published out of the different articles analyzed. Note that the different articles analyzed have been presented in conferences, books, and journals, highlighting biennial conferences of the IGS. In this analysis, only articles that have been published in Peer review journals have been considered.

Journals

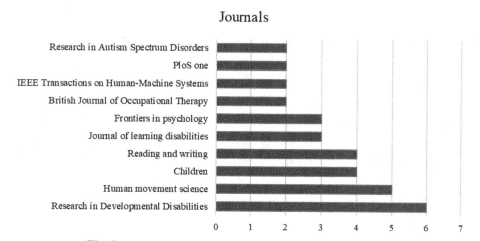

Fig. 5. Bar chart of the 10 journals with more published articles.

3 Participants

The children participating in the studies of the different papers we have collected have an age range between 3 and 18 years. In Danna et al. (2013), Plamondon et al. (2013) and Paz-Villagrán et al. (2014) included children and adults in their studies, the ages of these adult participants are not included in Fig. 5 as the review focuses only on graphonometry in children.

Figure 6 shows that the studies conducted have focused on children between the ages of 6 and 12, with 9-year-olds standing out. After the age of 12, a notable decrease is observed in the studies that include participants between 13 and 18 years of age, on the other hand, as the ages of 3 to 5 years increase, the article number also rises. Therefore, there is a clear increase in the studies carried out from 3 years of age until reaching the peak at 9 years and from this age a decrease, highlighting 18 years as the age with the least studies in the articles of the sample.

Upon analysis of the data, it was observed that the studies primarily focus on evaluating handwriting in children during their primary education, with less emphasis on those who have moved beyond this stage. Additionally, it was found that children in kindergarten are predominantly the subject of evaluation in their final year before transitioning into primary education with tests according to their educational level.

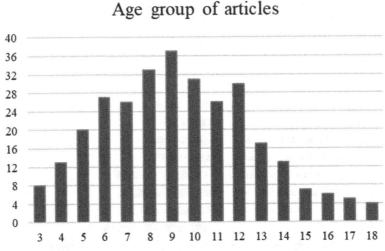

Fig. 6. Bar chart of age group of the study participants.

4 Methods of Evaluation of the Graphonometric State in Children

A classification method based on the type of evaluation performed in each study is presented in this paper. The articles have been categorized as objective, subjective, and objective-subjective evaluation methods. The objective method pertains to evaluations where only software has been utilized for graphonometric evaluation/analysis. The subjective method refers to those articles where the evaluation has been carried out through tests in which human evaluators intervened in their evaluation. Finally, the objective and subjective method pertains to articles in which both software and standardized tests provided by evaluators were employed for evaluation.

4.1 Objective Evaluation Methods

The objective methods present the articles that have evaluated the graphonomy of children only through software. Some studies used in their tasks the standardized tests of Concise the Assessment Scale for Children's Handwriting (BHK) [46], Detailed Assessment of Speed of Handwriting (DASH) [5], Early Grade Writing Assessment (EGWA) [4] and the figure drawing test Beery–Buktenica Developmental Test of Visual-Motor Integration (VMI) [46, 47] but these were not used to assess according to the assessment instructions. These tasks were evaluated by means of software, which collected the data and later the kinematic theory among others was evaluated. In [18] a new variable is proposed, the Signal-to-Noise velocity peaks difference (SNvpd) together with the variables number of inversion of velocity (NIV) and the averaged normalized jerk (ANJ) to calculate the fluency of handwriting in children with dysgraphia. The sigma-lognormal model ($\Sigma\Lambda$) is used to evaluate in numerous studies [20, 22–25, 46, 51, 55, 60, 61] that objective measures through this model.

In the different papers revised in Table 1, the sigma-Lognormal model has been used in the most of them. This model parameterizes the movement following the kinetic theory of fast human movements. This may indicate the subject's ability to control fine motor skills approaching lognormality. In Bouillon and Anquetil (2015) present IntuiScript, a digital handwriting book project to support teaching that allows the teacher to customize the exercises according to the child's difficulties [10] and making it possible to benefit from instant feedback [70].

Table 1. Manuscripts proposing objective evaluation methods.

Article	N	Tasks	Evaluation
Danna et al. (2013) [18]	64	Write 'lapin'	SNvpd, NIV and ANJ
Duval et al. (2013) [22]	66	Write patterns	Sigma-Lognormal
Molyneaux et al. (2013) [50]	98	Handwriting exercises	Letters, word length and frequency
Plamondon et al. (2013) [55]	15	Write patterns, drawing	Sigma-Lognormal
Prunty et al. (2013) [56]	56	Five tasks from DASH	Duration, speed, execution and pause
Paz-Villagrán et al. (2014) [53]	81	Write 'lapin'	Handwriting performances

(continued)

Table 1. (*continued*)

Article	N	Tasks	Evaluation
Prunty et al. (2014) [57]	56	Free writing from DASH	Handwriting pauses
Bouillon & Anquetil (2015) [10]	1000	Writing exercises	IntuiScript
Rémi et al. (2015) [61]	60	Draw scribbles	Classical dynamic and $\Sigma\Lambda$ set
Duval et al. (2015) [23]	48	Write patterns	Classical dynamic and $\Sigma\Lambda$ set
Vinci-Booher et al. (2016) [75]	20	Write letters and shapes	Functional connectivity of the brain
Barrientos (2016) [4]	120	EGWA	Dynamics movement
Rosenblum & Dror (2016) [66]	99	Write, drawing	Dysgraphia
D'Antrassi et al. (2017) [17]	257	Draw	Kinematic parameters
Girard et al. (2017) [31]	100	Handwriting exercises	IntuiScript
Petinatti et al. (2017) [54]	24	Handwriting exercises	Dynamics movement
Rémi et al. (2017) [60]		Draw doodles	Sigma-Lognormal
Simonnet et al. (2017) [70]	952	Handwriting exercises	IntuiScript
Teulings & Smits-Engelsman (2017) [74]	335	Copy	Handwriting quality and speed
Simonnet et al. (2019) [71]	231	Handwriting exercises	Handwriting quality
Díaz et al. (2019) [20]	15	Copy	Sigma-Lognormal
Bonneton-Botté et al. (2020) [7]	233	Copy	Spatiotemporal characteristics
Faci et al. (2021) [25]	32	Draw strokes	Neuromotor system integrity by $\Sigma\Lambda$
Lopez & Vaivre-Douret (2021) [43]	70	Loops	Postural, gestural, spatial-temporal, and kinematic parameters
Faci et al. (2022) [24]	780	Draw triangles	Sigma-Lognormal
Matias et al. (2022) [46]	96	VMI-6, BHK	Sigma-Lognormal
Matias et al. (2022) [47]	110	VMI	Process variables

(*continued*)

Table 1. (*continued*)

Article	N	Tasks	Evaluation
O'Reilly et al. (2022) [51]	780	Draw triangles	Sigma-Lognormal
Germano & Capellini (2023) [29]	95	Write words	Latency, gaze, movement duration, fluency

N* denotes the number of participants in each study.

In most of the papers the number of participants is less than 100 participants. Among the different tasks proposed, the writing tasks designed for each study stand out. The evaluation of the different papers has evaluated quantitative measures of writing [51, 56, 57] among others, but highlights the Sigma-Lognormal parameters [20, 22, 23, 25, 55, 60, 61].

4.2 Subjective Evaluation Methods

The subjective methods present articles assessing children's graphonomy only through rater-administered assessments. The articles in the Table 2 have been evaluated on tasks with BHK [2, 42], DASH [3, 28, 58], EGWA [38], Handwriting Legibility Scale (HLS) [3], Head-Toes-Knees-Shoulders (HTKS) [11], Instructional activities for early writing improvement (IAEWI) [40], Indicadores de Progreso de Aprendizaje en Escritura (IPAE) [30, 40], Just Write! (JW) [6], Perceive, Recall, Plan and Perform (PRPP) [45], Standardized Test for the Evaluation of Writing with the Keyboard (TEVET) [38], VMI [6] and Wechsler Objective Language Dimensions (WOLD) [45]. The Movement Assessment Battery for Children-2 (MABC-2) [58] was included to assess the motor status of the participants. These tests incorporate some tasks and are evaluated according to the instructions of each evaluation. In addition, some articles have provided tasks that have been evaluated by several of the standardized assessments or complemented with other evaluation parameters.

In [38] EGWA is studied, a new method of evaluation of writing in children that includes 10 copying and writing tasks. EGWA was compared with TEVET for its validation carried out by evaluators in which the results were analyzed by the theories of current writing models.

In [40] presented a level 2 intervention. The fidelity of the assessment scale (FAS) and fidelity of the intervention scale (FIS) were used. With FAS, the administration of IPAE teachers was evaluated and FIS evaluated the administration of IAEWI teachers. FAS and FIS were assessed by self-report and direct observation.

Table 2. Manuscripts proposing subjective evaluation methods.

Article	N	Tasks	Evaluation
Bara & Morin (2013) [2]	332	BHK	Handwriting style and speed, BHK
Prunty et al. (2016) [58]	56	Free writing from DASH	WOLD, DASH, MABC-2
Jiménez (2017) [38]	1653	EGWA	EGWA comparing with TEVET
Barnett et al. (2018) [3]	150	Free writing from DASH	HLS
Cohen et al. (2019) [13]	49	Write a story	Graphological analysis
Bolton et al. (2021) [6]	37	JW, VMI	JW comparing with VMI
Chandler et al. (2021) [11]	738	HTKS, write	Fine motor skills, HTKS, performance on writing tasks
Gil et al. (2021) [30]	231	IPAE, EGWA	IPAE, EGWA
Pavlos et al. (2021) [52]	50	HKWSA-V2, VMI	HKWSA-V2
Skar et al. (2021) [72]	4950	Copy, write	Writing fluency and quality
Fogel et al. (2022) [28]	148	DASH	HLS
Jiménez et al. (2022) [40]	164	IPAE, IAEWI	Teacher knowledge, intervention
Loizzo et al. (2023) [42]	562	BHK	BHK
Mathwin et al. (2023) [45]	10	Write the alphabet	PRPP

N* denotes the number of participants in each study.

The tasks performed by the participants in most of the articles are from standardized tests, highlighting the DASH assessment, but the writing task stands out. The evaluation of the tasks does not highlight an evaluation that has been most used, in each study different aspects have been evaluated, some studies with standardized tasks were evaluated with other standardized evaluations [3, 28] and have even been evaluated by three evaluations at the same time. Time [58]. The number of participants in these studies highlights one study with 4,950 [72], but most groups range from 150–738 [2, 3, 11, 28, 30, 40, 42].

4.3 Objective and Subjective Evaluation Methods

The objective and subjective methods expose articles in which their studies were assessed both using software and peer-administered tests. As shown in Table 3, one of the software used for the evaluation was the Computerized Penmanship Evaluation Tool (ComPET) a handwriting assessment consisting of online data collection and analysis software via a pen tablet [68]. Added to previous evaluator-administered assessments, this section adds Adult Developmental Coordination Disorders/Dyspraxia (ADC) [35], Behavior Rating Inventory of Executive Function (BRIEF) [63, 64], Hebrew Handwriting Evaluation (HHE) [63, 64, 67, 68], Handwriting Proficiency Screening Questionnaire (HPSQ) [35,

49, 63, 64], (HPSQ-C) [64], Movement Assessment Battery for Children (MABC) [5, 62, 68], Minnesota Handwriting Assessment (MHA) [5], Questionnaire for assessing students' organizational abilities-teachers (QASOA-T) [62], Lecture in a Minute (LUM) [32], Test of Visual Perceptual Skills (TVPS) [59] and World Health Organization Quality of Life Questionnaire, Brief Version (WHOQOL-BREF) [35].

Table 3. Manuscripts proposing objective and subjective evaluation methods.

Article	N	Tasks	Evaluation
Bosga-Storka et al. (2013) [9]	32	Loops, copy	BHK and Kinematic performance
Danna et al. (2013) [19]	7	Loops, copy a phrase	Kinematic variables, BHK
Rosenblum et al. (2013) [68]	58	Copy a paragraph	Background, MABC, HPSQ, ComPET, HHE
Bo et al. (2014) [5]	41	Write letters and shapes	MABC, VMI, MHA, spatial, temporal
Sumner et al. (2014) [73]	93	Two tasks from DASH	DASH, pause time
D'Antrassi et al. (2015) [16]	40	Drawing, write	Qualitative and kinematic parameters
Huau et al. (2015) [36]	20	Handwriting, learning, BHK	Spatial, spatiotemporal, dynamic variable, pen pressure, BHK
Rosenblum (2015) [62]	42	Write and copy	MABC, ComPET, QASOA-T
Rosenblum (2015) [63]	64	Copy a paragraph	HPSQ, HHE, ComPET, BRIEF
Rosenblum&Gafni-Lachter (2015)[67]	230	Copy a paragraph	HPSQ-C, HHE, ComPET
Mekyska et al. (2016) [49]	54	Write	HPSQ, Feature selection, intrawriter
Prunty et al. (2016) [59]	56	VMI, TVPS and DASH	Perception and handwriting measure
Rosenblum et al. (2016) [69]	60	Write, copy	Handwriting product and process
Hen-Herbst & Rosenblum (2017) [34]	80	Copy, write an essay	Writing, body functions and background measures

(*continued*)

Table 3. (*continued*)

Article	N	Tasks	Evaluation
Matias et al. (2017) [48]	30	Copy a text	BHK and letter formation
Hurschler Lichtsteiner et al. (2018) [37]	175	Write, copy, VMI, phonological loop task	Fluency, automaticity, writing measures and intervention
Rosenblum (2018) [64]	64	Copy a paragraph	HPSQ, HHE, ComPET and BRIEF
Fogel et al. (2019) [27]	81	Copy a paragraph	Handwriting process, daily functions, EF
Jiménez & Hernández (2019)[39]	1124	EGWA, TEVET	EGWA, TEVET
Rosenblum et al. (2019) [65]	60	Story-writing	Production process and EF
Zvoncak et al. (2019) [77]	55	Write the Czech alphabet	HPSQ-C, conventional and FD*
Alamargot et al. (2020) [1]	45	Write the alphabet and name	Background measure and handwriting performance
Coradinho et al. (2020) [15]	97	VMI-6, MABC-2	VMI-6, MABC-2, graphomotor characteristics
Laniel et al. (2020) [41]	24	Draw, BHK and Purdue Pegboard	Intellectual functioning, graphomotor skills, BHK, neuromuscular system, behavior
Bara & Bonneton-Botté(2021)[26]	64	Copy	Handwriting product, process, and quality
Dui et al. (2021) [21]	52	BVSCO-2	BVSCO-2, SUS*, satisfaction, tilt, in-air time
Gosse et al. (2021) [32]	117	Chronosdictées, BHK	Chronosdictées, BHK, LUM
Torrance et al. (2021) [76]	179	Copy, write	Spelling, fluency, letters, phonetic, accuracy, reading, reasoning
Booth et al. (2022) [8]	85	Hand tasks, write	Kinematics and handwriting quality

(*continued*)

Table 3. (*continued*)

Article	N	Tasks	Evaluation
Chang & Yu (2022) [12]	641	Copy	Geometric, spatiotemporal measures
Hen-Herbst&Rosenblum(2022)[35]	80	Copy, WHOQOL-BREF, ADC	HPSQ, HLS, ComPET, ADC, WHOQOL-BREF
Coradinho et al. (2023) [14]	57	BHK	Handwriting product and process
Haberfehlner et al. (2023) [33]	374	Drawing	Handwriting readiness
Lopez & Vaivre-Douret(2023)[44]	35	BHK, loops	BHK, spatial temporal and kinematic

N* denotes the number of participants in each study. FD*: Fractional Order Derivatives. SUS* System Usability Scale

In [77] children were evaluated with HPSQ-C, conventional features, and Fractional Order Derivatives (FD) based feature. FD is used as a replacement for the conventional differential derived from the extraction of the features. In this study, it was developed as a new approach for the parameterization of handwriting. With FD the basic kinematic functions (velocity, acceleration, jerk, and the horizontal and vertical variants) were extracted.

The tasks of the different studies highlight the copy tasks proposed for each study. The number of participants in most studies is in the range of 30–80 participants. Task assessment highlights the BHK [9, 19, 32, 36, 41, 44, 48] and HPSQ [35, 64, 77] assessments, as well as analysis of the handwriting process.

5   Discussion and Conclusion

In conclusion, the evaluation of handwriting in children is a complex process that requires appropriate methods and instruments that must be systematic, objective, and sensitive to the different factors involved. There are various ways to evaluate handwriting, including software and expert evaluation, each with its advantages and disadvantages. While software evaluation is fast, accurate, and objective based on pre-defined parameters, it may not capture some qualitative or contextual aspects of the written product. Conversely, expert evaluation may be more flexible and responsive to the characteristics of the written specimen but may introduce a subjective bias or evaluator fatigue, which could affect the reliability and validity of the results.

Furthermore, it is essential to recognize that the emotional factor can influence the written process and product, as handwriting is not only a means of communication and learning but also an expression of personality, emotions, and feelings. Thus, factors such as children's self-esteem, motivation, and academic performance should also be considered in the evaluation of handwriting [12].

In [9, 25, 30, 32] longitudinal studies are carried out, these studies allow to observe the evolution in time of the handwriting of the participants in tasks. Increasing these studies with longitudinal databases would allow a better understanding of the evolution of handwriting in children and be able to apply tools for learning this skill or new methods for diagnosing different learning problems.

These tools will enable accurate and reliable evaluations, which will ultimately lead to improved interventions and outcomes for children's cognitive and academic development.

On the other hand, the different studies have seen that of graphonomic evaluation under the kinetic theory using the Sigma-Lognormal parameters in different writing and drawing tasks, evaluating the dynamic movements that these tasks imply. Different standardized evaluations have been used, but the use of some more than others stands out, such as the case of BHK and DASH. The BHK and DASH evaluations have been used in several articles, in some only their tasks were applied, and they were evaluated by other criteria. It should be noted that although these evaluations used their tasks in the subjective and objective-subjective methods, there is a lack of consensus between authors for a common task to evaluate the same aspects, especially in the papers included in objective methods.

Evaluations with human involvement and software provide different measures depending on the evaluation to be carried out and the proposed tasks. To address these challenges, it is necessary to agree on the development of an evaluation methodology that is partly common in the recording protocols, allowing faster progress by being able to combine the databases, increasing their size and making it possible to compare the different algorithms on the databases. Considering the different assessments and alphabets used in each task to better understand the way in which handwriting is taught and acquired depending on the type of alphabet and the cultural context. This could lead to a better analysis of the advantages and challenges of the systems, as well as intervention strategies to improve the learning of handwriting in different contexts.

References

1. Alamargot, D., Morin, M.F., Simard-Dupuis, E.: Handwriting delay in dyslexia: children at the end of primary school still make numerous short pauses when producing letters. J. Learn. Disabil. **53**(3), 163–175 (2020)
2. Bara, F., Morin, M.F.: Does the handwriting style learned in first grade determine the style used in the fourth and fifth grades and influence handwriting speed and quality? A comparison between French and Quebec children. Psychol. Sch. **50**(6), 601–617 (2013)
3. Barnett, A.L., Prunty, M., Rosenblum, S.: Development of the handwriting legibility scale (HLS): a preliminary examination of reliability and validity. Res. Dev. Disabil. **72**, 240–247 (2018)
4. Barrientos, P.: Handwriting development in Spanish children with and without learning disabilities: a graphonomic approach. J. Learn. Disabil. **50**(5), 552–563 (2017)
5. Bo, J., Colbert, A., Lee, C.M., Schaffert, J., Oswald, K., Neill, R.: Examining the relationship between motor assessments and handwriting consistency in children with and without probable developmental coordination disorder. Res. Dev. Disabil. **35**(9), 2035–2043 (2014)

6. Bolton, T., Stevenson, B., Janes, W.: Assessing handwriting in preschool-aged children: feasibility and construct validity of the "Just Write!" tool. J. Occup. Ther. Schools Early Interv. **14**(2), 153–161 (2021)
7. Bonneton-Botté, N., et al.: Can tablet apps support the learning of handwriting? An investigation of learning outcomes in kindergarten classroom. Comput. Educ. **151**, 103831 (2020)
8. Booth, P., Hunyadvari, N., Dawkins, L., Moore, D., Gentile-Rapinett, G., Edmonds, C.J.: Water consumption increases handwriting speed and volume consumed relates to increased finger-tapping speed in schoolchildren. J. Cogn. Enhancement **6**(2), 183–191 (2022)
9. Bosga-Storka, I.M., Bosgaa, J., Meulenbroekb, R. G., Bosga-Stork, P., Beaufortweg, D.: Age-related changes in regularity statistics of loop-writing kinematics. In: Recent Progress in Graphonomics: Learn from the Past, pp. 109–114. IGS (2013)
10. Bouillon, M., Anquetil, E.: Handwriting analysis with online fuzzy models. In: 17th Biennial Conference of the International Graphonomics Society (2015)
11. Chandler, M.C., Gerde, H.K., Bowles, R.P., McRoy, K.Z., Pontifex, M.B., Bingham, G.E.: Self-regulation moderates the relationship between fine motor skills and writing in early childhood. Early Child. Res. Q. **57**, 239–250 (2021)
12. Chang, S.H., Yu, N.Y.: Computerized handwriting evaluation and statistical reports for children in the age of primary school. Sci. Rep. **12**(1), 15675 (2022)
13. Cohen, R., Cohen-Kroitoru, B., Halevy, A., Aharoni, S., Aizenberg, I., Shuper, A.: Handwriting in children with attention deficit hyperactive disorder: role of graphology. BMC Pediatr. **19**(1), 1–6 (2019)
14. Coradinho, H., et al.: Relationship between product and process characteristics of handwriting skills of children in the second grade of elementary school. Children **10**(3), 445 (2023)
15. Coradinho, H., Melo, F., Teulings, H.L., Matias, A.R., Matias, A.: COMPETÊNCIA MOTORA E COMPETÊNCIAS GRAFOMOTORAS EM CRIANÇAS NO ÚLTIMO ANO DO PRÉ-ESCOLAR (2020)
16. D'Antrassi, P., Ceschia, P., Mandarino, C., Perrone, I., Accardo, A.: Evaluation of different handwriting teaching methods by kinematic and quality analyses. In: 17th Biennial Conference of the International Graphonomics Society (2015)
17. D'Antrassi, P., Rustia, M., Accardo, A.: Development of graphomotor skills in school-age children. In: Graphonomics for e-Citizens: e-Health, e-Society, e-Education, pp. 205–208. Claudio De Stefano and Angelo Marcelli (2017)
18. Danna, J., Paz-Villagrán, V., Velay, J.L.: Signal-to-Noise velocity peaks difference: a new method for evaluating the handwriting movement fluency in children with dysgraphia. Res. Dev. Disabil. **34**(12), 4375–4384 (2013)
19. Danna, J., et al.: Handwriting movement sonification for the rehabilitation of dysgraphia. In: 10th International Symposium on Computer Music Multidisciplinary Research (CMMR)-Sound, Music & Motion-15–18 October 2013-Marseille, France, pp. 200–208 (2013)
20. Diaz, M., Ferrer, M., Guest, R., Pal, U.: Graphomotor Evolution in the Handwriting of Bengali Children through Sigma-Lognormal Based-Parameters: A Preliminary Study (2019)
21. Dui, L.G., Calogero, E., Malavolti, M., Termine, C., Matteucci, M., Ferrante, S.: Digital tools for handwriting proficiency evaluation in children. In: 2021 IEEE EMBS International Conference on Biomedical and Health Informatics (BHI), pp. 1–4. IEEE (2021)
22. Duval, T., Plamondon, R., O'Reilly, C., Remi, C., Vaillant, J.: On the use of the sigma-lognormal model to study children handwriting. In: Recent Progress in Graphonomics: Learn from the Past. IGS 2013, pp. 26–30 (2013)
23. Duval, T., Rémi, C., Plamondon, R., Vaillant, J., O'Reilly, C.: Combining sigma-lognormal modeling and classical features for analyzing graphomotor performances in kindergarten children. Hum. Mov. Sci. **43**, 183–200 (2015)

24. Faci, N., Carmona-Duarte, C., Diaz, M., Ferrer, M. A., Plamondon, R.: Comparison between two sigma-lognormal extractors with primary schools students handwriting. In: Carmona-Duarte, C., Diaz, M., Ferrer, M.A., Morales, A. (eds.) Intertwining Graphonomics with Human Movements. IGS 2022. Lecture Notes in Computer Science, vol. 13424, pp. 105-113. Springer, Cham (2022). https://doi.org/10.1007/978-3-031-19745-1_8

25. Faci, N., Désiré, N., Beauchamp, M.H., Gagnon, I., Plamondon, R.: Analysing the evolution of children's neuromotor system lognormality after mild traumatic bain injury. In: The Lognormality Principle and its Applications in e-Security, e-Learning and e-Health, pp. 143–160 (2021)

26. Florence, B., Nathalie, B.B.: Handwriting isolated cursive letters in young children: effect of the visual trace deletion. Learn. Instr. **74**, 101439 (2021)

27. Fogel, Y., Josman, N., Rosenblum, S.: Functional abilities as reflected through temporal handwriting measures among adolescents with neuro-developmental disabilities. Pattern Recogn. Lett. **121**, 13–18 (2019)

28. Fogel, Y., Rosenblum, S., Barnett, A.L.: Handwriting legibility across different writing tasks in school-aged children. Hong Kong Journal of Occupational Therapy (2022). https://doi.org/10.1177/1569186122107570

29. Germano, G.D., Capellini, S.A.: Handwriting fluency, latency, and kinematic in Portuguese writing system: pilot study with school children from 3rd to 5th grade. Front. Psychol. **13**, 1063021 (2023)

30. Gil, V., de León, S.C., Jiménez, J.E.: Universal screening for writing risk in Spanish-speaking first graders. Read. Writ. Q. **37**(2), 117–135 (2021)

31. Girard, N., Simonnet, D., Anquetil, E.: IntuiScript a new digital notebook for learning writing in elementary schools: 1st observations. In: 18th International Graphonomics Society Conference (IGS2017), pp. 201–204 (2017)

32. Gosse, C., Parmentier, M., Van Reybroeck, M.: How do spelling, handwriting speed, and handwriting quality develop during primary school? Cross-classified growth curve analysis of children's writing development. Front. Psychol. **12**, 685681 (2021)

33. Haberfehlner, H., de Vries, L., Cup, E.H., de Groot, I.J., Nijhuis-van der Sanden, M.W., van Hartingsveldt, M.J.: Ready for handwriting? A reference data study on handwriting readiness assessments. PLoS ONE **18**(3), e0282497 (2023)

34. Hen-Herbst, L., Rosenblum, S.: Executive functions, coordination and developmental functional abilities as predictors of writing capabilities among adolescents. In: 18th International Graphonomics Society Conference (IGS2017), pp. 6–10 (2017)

35. Hen-Herbst, L., Rosenblum, S.: Handwriting and motor-related daily performance among adolescents with dysgraphia and their impact on physical health-related quality of life. Children **9**(10), 1437 (2022)

36. Huau, A., Velay, J.L., Jover, M.: Graphomotor skills in children with developmental coordination disorder (DCD): handwriting and learning a new letter. Hum. Mov. Sci. **42**, 318–332 (2015)

37. Hurschler Lichtsteiner, S., Wicki, W., Falmann, P.: Impact of handwriting training on fluency, spelling and text quality among third graders. Read. Writ. **31**, 1295–1318 (2018)

38. Jiménez, J.E.: Early grade writing assessment: an instrument model. J. Learn. Disabil. **50**(5), 491–503 (2017)

39. Jiménez, J.E., Hernández-Cabrera, J.A.: Transcription skills and written composition in Spanish beginning writers: pen and keyboard modes. Read. Writ. **32**(7), 1847–1879 (2019)

40. Jiménez, J.E., de León, S.C., García, E., Seoane, R.C.: Assessing the efficacy of a Tier 2 early intervention for transcription skills in Spanish elementary school students. Read. Writ. **36**, 1227–1259 (2022)

41. Laniel, P., Faci, N., Plamondon, R., Beauchamp, M.H., Gauthier, B.: Kinematic analysis of fast pen strokes in children with ADHD. Appl. Neuropsychol. Child **9**(2), 125–140 (2020)

42. Loizzo, A., Zaccaria, V., Caravale, B., Di Brina, C.: Validation of the concise assessment scale for children's handwriting (BHK) in an Italian population. Children **10**(2), 223 (2023)
43. Lopez, C., Vaivre-Douret, L.: Influence of visual control on the quality of graphic gesture in children with handwriting disorders. Sci. Rep. **11**(1), 23537 (2021)
44. Lopez, C., Vaivre-Douret, L.: Concurrent and predictive validity of a cycloid loops copy task to assess handwriting disorders in children. Children **10**(2), 305 (2023)
45. Mathwin, K., Chapparo, C., Hinitt, J.: Children with handwriting difficulties: impact of cognitive strategy training for acquisition of accurate alphabet-letter-writing. Brit. J. Occup. Ther. **86**, 451–461 (2023). https://doi.org/10.1177/03080226221148413
46. Matias, A.R., Melo, F., Coradinho, H., Fernandes, O., de Broin, G., Plamondon, R.: Effects of a graphomotor intervention on the graphic skills of children: an analysis with the sigma-lognormal model. In: Carmona-Duarte, C., Diaz, M., Ferrer, M.A., Morales, A. (eds.) Intertwining Graphonomics with Human Movements. IGS 2022. Lecture Notes in Computer Science, vol. 13424, pp. 114-128. Springer, Cham (2022). https://doi.org/10.1007/978-3-031-19745-1_9
47. Matias, A.R., Melo, F., Costa, B., Teulings, H.L., Almeida, G.: Copy of geometric drawings in children from 4 to 6 years old: a kinematic analysis. In: 20th Conference of the International Graphonomics Society (IGS2021) (2022)
48. Matias, A.R., Teulings, H.L., Silva, L., Melo, F.: Measuring handwriting stability versus context variations. Presentation at IGS2017 (2017)
49. Mekyska, J., Faundez-Zanuy, M., Mzourek, Z., Galaz, Z., Smekal, Z., Rosenblum, S.: Identification and rating of developmental dysgraphia by handwriting analysis. IEEE Trans. Hum. Mach. Syst. **47**(2), 235–248 (2016)
50. Molyneaux, A.M., Barnett, A.L., Glenny, G., Davies, R.A.: The association between handwriting practice and lexical richness: an analysis of the handwritten output of children aged 9–10 years. In: Recent Progress in Graphonomics: Learn from the Past. IGS 2013, pp. 38–41 (2013)
51. O'Reilly, C., Plamondon, R., Faci, N.:. The lognometer: a new normalized and computerized device for assessing the neurodevelopment of fine motor control in children. In: 2022 26th International Conference on Pattern Recognition (ICPR), pp. 952–958. IEEE (2022)
52. Pavlos, K., McKenzie, M., Knightbridge, E., Bourke-Taylor, H.: Initial psychometric evaluation of the hartley knows writing shapes assessment version 2 with typically developing children between the ages of 4 and 8. Aust. Occup. Ther. J. **68**(1), 32–42 (2021)
53. Paz-Villagrán, V., Danna, J., Velay, J.L.: Lifts and stops in proficient and dysgraphic handwriting. Hum. Mov. Sci. **33**, 381–394 (2014)
54. Petinatti, G., Harralson, H.H., Teulings, H.L.: Does Exercise in Children with Learning Disabilities Improve Cursive Handwriting? (2017)
55. Plamondon, R., O'Reilly, C., Rémi, C., Duval, T.: The lognormal handwriter: learning, performing, and declining. Front. Psychol. **4**, 945 (2013)
56. Prunty, M.M., Barnett, A.L., Wilmut, K., Plumb, M.S.: Handwriting speed in children with developmental coordination disorder: are they really slower? Res. Dev. Disabil. **34**(9), 2927–2936 (2013)
57. Prunty, M.M., Barnett, A.L., Wilmut, K., Plumb, M.S.: An examination of writing pauses in the handwriting of children with developmental coordination disorder. Res. Dev. Disabil. **35**(11), 2894–2905 (2014)
58. Prunty, M.M., Barnett, A.L., Wilmut, K., Plumb, M.S.: The impact of handwriting difficulties on compositional quality in children with developmental coordination disorder. Br. J. Occup. Ther. **79**(10), 591–597 (2016)
59. Prunty, M., Barnett, A.L., Wilmut, K., Plumb, M.: Visual perceptual and handwriting skills in children with developmental coordination disorder. Hum. Mov. Sci. **49**, 54–65 (2016)

60. Rémi, C., Nagau, J., Vaillant, J., Plamondon, R.: Preliminary study of t0, a sigma-lognormal parameter extracted from young children's controlled scribbles. In: 18th Conference of the International Graphonomics Society, IGS2017, pp. 109–113 (2017)

61. Rémi, C., Vaillant, J., Plamondon, R., Prevost, L., Duval, T.: Exploring the kinematic dimensions of kindergarten children's scribbles. In: 17th Biennial Conference of the International Graphonomics Society, pp. 79–82 (2015)

62. Rosenblum, S.: Do motor ability and handwriting kinematic measures predict organizational ability among children with developmental coordination disorders? Hum. Mov. Sci. **43**, 201–215 (2015)

63. Rosenblum, S.: Relationships between handwriting features and executive control among children with developmental dysgraphia. Drawing Handwriting Process. Anal. New Adv. Challenges 111 (2015)

64. Rosenblum, S.: Inter-relationships between objective handwriting features and executive control among children with developmental dysgraphia. PLoS ONE **13**(4), e0196098 (2018)

65. Rosenblum, S., Ben-Simhon, H.A., Meyer, S., Gal, E.: Predictors of handwriting performance among children with autism spectrum disorder. Res. Autism Spectrum Disord. **60**, 16–24 (2019)

66. Rosenblum, S., Dror, G.: Identifying developmental dysgraphia characteristics utilizing handwriting classification methods. IEEE Trans. on Hum. Mach. Syst. **47**(2), 293–298 (2016)

67. Rosenblum, S., Gafni-Lachter, L.: Handwriting proficiency screening questionnaire for children (HPSQ–C): development, reliability, and validity. Am. J. Occup. Ther. **69**(3), 6903220030p1–6903220030p9 (2015)

68. Rosenblum, S., Margieh, J.A., Engel-Yeger, B.: Handwriting features of children with developmental coordination disorder–results of triangular evaluation. Res. Dev. Disabil. **34**(11), 4134–4141 (2013)

69. Rosenblum, S., Simhon, H.A.B., Gal, E.: Unique handwriting performance characteristics of children with high-functioning autism spectrum disorder. Res. Autism Spectrum Disord. **23**, 235–244 (2016)

70. Simonnet, D., Anquetil, E., Bouillon, M.: Multi-criteria handwriting quality analysis with online fuzzy models. Pattern Recogn. **69**, 310–324 (2017)

71. Simonnet, D., Girard, N., Anquetil, E., Renault, M., Thomas, S.: Evaluation of children cursive handwritten words for e-education. Pattern Recogn. Lett. **121**, 133–139 (2019)

72. Skar, G.B., Lei, P.W., Graham, S., Aasen, A.J., Johansen, M.B., Kvistad, A.H.: Handwriting fluency and the quality of primary grade students' writing. Read. Writ. 1–30 (2021)

73. Sumner, E., Connelly, V., Barnett, A.L.: The influence of spelling ability on handwriting production: children with and without dyslexia. J. Exp. Psychol. Learn. Mem. Cogn. **40**(5), 1441 (2014)

74. Teulings, H.L., Smits-Engelsman, B.C.: objective measurement of handwriting learning outcomes at elementary schools suggest instruction improvements. In: 18th International Graphonomics Society Conference (IGS2017), pp. 1–5 (2017)

75. Vinci-Booher, S., James, T.W., James, K.H.: Visual-motor functional connectivity in preschool children emerges after handwriting experience. Trends Neurosci. Educ. **5**(3), 107–120 (2016)

76. Torrance, M., Arrimada, M., Gardner, S.: Child-level factors affecting rate of learning to write in first grade. Br. J. Educ. Psychol. **91**(2), 714–734 (2021)

77. Zvoncak, V., et al.: Fractional order derivatives evaluation in computerized assessment of handwriting difficulties in school-aged children. In: 2019 11th International Congress on Ultra Modern Telecommunications and Control Systems and Workshops (ICUMT), pp. 1–6. IEEE (2019)

Assessment of Developmental Dysgraphia Utilising a Display Tablet

Jiri Mekyska[1]([✉])(iD), Zoltan Galaz[1](iD), Katarina Safarova[2](iD),
Vojtech Zvoncak[1](iD), Lukas Cunek[2], Tomas Urbanek[2](iD),
Jana Marie Havigerova[2](iD), Jirina Bednarova[2], Ján Mucha[1](iD),
Michal Gavenciak[1], Zdenek Smekal[1](iD), and Marcos Faundez-Zanuy[3](iD)

[1] Department of Telecommunications, Faculty of Electrical Engineering and
Communication, Brno University of Technology, Brno, Czech Republic
mekyska@vut.cz
[2] Department of Research Methodology, Institute of Psychology,
The Czech Academy of Sciences, Brno, Czech Republic
[3] Tecnocampus, Universitat Pompeu Fabra, Mataro, Barcelona, Spain

Abstract. Even though the computerised assessment of developmental dysgraphia (DD) based on online handwriting processing has increasing popularity, most of the solutions are based on a setup, where a child writes on a paper fixed to a digitizing tablet that is connected to a computer. Although this approach enables the standard way of writing using an inking pen, it is difficult to be administered by children themselves. The main goal of this study is thus to explore, whether the quantitative analysis of online handwriting recorded via a display/screen tablet could sufficiently support the assessment of DD as well. For the purpose of this study, we enrolled 144 children (attending the 3rd and 4th class of a primary school), whose handwriting proficiency was assessed by a special education counsellor, and who assessed themselves by the Handwriting Proficiency Screening Questionnaires for Children (HPSQ–C). Using machine learning models based on a gradient-boosting algorithm, we were able to support the DD diagnosis with up to 83.6% accuracy. The HPSQ–C total score was estimated with a minimum error equal to 10.34%. Children with DD spent significantly higher time in-air, they had a higher number of pen elevations, a bigger height of on-surface strokes, a lower in-air tempo, and a higher variation in the angular velocity. Although this study shows a promising impact of DD assessment via display tablets, it also accents the fact that modelling of subjective scores is challenging and a complex and data-driven quantification of DD manifestations is needed.

Keywords: Developmental dysgraphia · Handwriting difficulties ·
Handwriting proficiency · Online handwriting · Computerised
assessment · Machine learning · Display tablet

This study was supported by a project of the Technology Agency of the Czech Republic no. TL03000287 (Software for advanced diagnosis of graphomotor disabilities) and by Spanish grant of the Ministerio de Ciencia e Innovación no. PID2020-113242RB-I00.

A. Parziale et al. (Eds.): IGS 2023, LNCS 14285, pp. 21–35, 2023.
https://doi.org/10.1007/978-3-031-45461-5_2

1   Introduction

Handwriting is a complex perceptual-motor skill combining precise graphomotor movements, visual perception, visual-motor coordination, motor planning and execution, kinesthetic feedback, and orthographic coding [29]. It is a crucial skill that children acquire during their early years of schooling. Typically, around the ages of 8 to 10 [39], after 3–4 years of education and letter formation practice, handwriting becomes automatic, and children effortlessly and accurately produce letters.

Developmental dysgraphia (DD) refers to a condition where children experience difficulties in acquiring proficient handwriting skills, despite having normal cognitive abilities, ample learning opportunities, and an absence of neurological issues [7,10,25]. The occurrence of DD varies between countries, assessment methods, and raters, with prevalence rates ranging from 7% to 34% [21,27]. Furthermore, studies have shown that boys tend to be diagnosed with DD more frequently than girls [19,36]. DD can have a detrimental impact on various aspects of a child's daily life. This includes lower self-esteem, poor emotional well-being, as well as problematic communication and social interaction. In order to provide timely and effective therapy, and enhance the quality of life of children with DD, psychologists, special education counsellors, and other experts need a robust framework that enables accurate diagnosis and assessment.

Nowadays, psychologists or special education counsellors assess DD mainly subjectively using scales such as Handwriting Proficiency Screening Questionnaire (HPSQ) [30], Handwriting Legibility Scale (HLS) [5], or the shortened version of the Concise Assessment Methods of Children Handwriting (SOS: BHK) [38]. Moreover, some scales, such as Handwriting Proficiency Screening Questionnaires for Children (HPSQ–C) [33], were developed for children's self-evaluation. Nevertheless, approaches based on these scales could have several limitations, e.g. they are subjective, they rely on the perceptual abilities of a rater, they do not provide a complex assessment of the product/process of handwriting, etc.

One possible way of overcoming these limitations is to use decision-support systems that process online handwriting recorded by digitizing tablets [11,26]. Such technology proved to bring interesting results and insights in both binary diagnosis [3,14] and assessment [26,40] of DD or graphomotor difficulties. For a comprehensive review, we refer to [20]. In all these studies the children performed handwriting/drawing tasks on a paper using a special inking pen. In a few works, the authors utilised protocols, where children wrote on displays/screens using plastic nibs (this way of writing has already been proven to be different when compared to writing on a paper [1]). In 2022, Asselborn et al. employed the Apple iPad to overcome the conventional binary diagnosis procedure and to assess handwriting difficulties on a scale, from the lightest cases to the most severe [2]. This revolutionary approach provided a global score, as well as four specific scores for kinematics, pressure, pen tilt and static features. The authors also highlighted that although two children could be diagnosed with DD, they could have different manifestations (e.g. kinematic vs. spatial). In the same year,

Dui et al. introduced an Android app for handwriting skill screening at the preliteracy stage [15]. Using the Samsung Galaxy Tab A, the authors proved that the app, and generally drawing on a screen, could facilitate the detection of graphomotor disabilities in children attending a kindergarten. Lomurno et al. used the same app in a longitudinal study, where the authors monitord the development of graphomotor/handwriting skills in children starting in the last year of kindergarten and ending in the second class of a primary school [22]. In a sample of 210 children, they predicted a risk of dysgraphia with 84.62% accuracy.

To the best of our knowledge, the three above-mentioned studies are the only ones where the authors used screen/display tablets to quantitatively analyse handwriting or graphomotor difficulties. Thus although writing/drawing on display tablets has increasing popularity, this relatively new field still contains some knowledge gaps. Asselborn et al. demonstrated that a display tablet could be used to assess the severity of DD [2]. Nevertheless, for that approach, they developed their own scale (in a data-driven way). The main goal of this study is to explore, whether the quantitative analysis of online handwriting recorded via a display tablet could sufficiently emulate children's self-assessment (which has not been explored before), and how well it models the diagnosis made by special education counsellors.

2 Materials and Methods

2.1 Dataset

For the purpose of this study, we enrolled 62 children (12 intact girls, 23 intact boys, 13 girls with DD, 14 boys with DD; age $= 9.2 \pm 0.5$ years) and 82 children (12 intact girls, 15 intact boys, 12 girls with DD, 43 boys with DD; age $= 10.2 \pm 0.5$ years) attending the 3rd and 4th class of a Czech primary school, respectively. The children were assessed by a special education counsellor who stratified them into two groups: intact and dysgraphic. In addition, children assessed themselves by the Czech version of the HPSQ–C questionnaire [35], more specifically, they addressed 10 items (on a 5-point Likert scale ranging from 0 to 4, where a higher value means worse performance) that could be grouped into three factors: legibility (max value $= 12$), performance time (max value $= 12$), and physical and emotional well-being (max value $= 16$) [33, 35]. An overview of the HPSQ–C scores in both classes could be found in Table 1.

During the acquisition, the children were asked to perform a paragraph copy task on a display tablet Wacom Cintiq 16 (DTK1660K0B) using a stylus with a felt nib. Before the acquisition of this task, the children had time to get familiar with the tablet, e.g., by drawing a random picture. The content of the paragraph was selected depending on the class a child attended. Regarding the 3rd class, children were asked to copy the following text (printed using capital letters) on the display using cursive letters:

Maminčina třešňová marmeláda je nejsladší.
Nejoblíbenějším pamlskem našich návštěvníků jsou škvarky.
Babiččiny rozbité hodiny netikají.

Table 1. Overview of the HPSQ–C scores in both cohorts.

3rd class						
Score	Mean	Std	Min	Q1	Median	Q3	Max
legibility	2.98	2.37	0	1	2	5	11
performance time	5.47	2.18	2	4	5	7	11
well-being	3.87	2.75	0	2	4	6	10
total	12.31	5.66	4	7	11.5	17	29

4th class						
Score	Mean	Std	Min	Q1	Median	Q3	Max
legibility	3.71	2.20	0	2	3	5	10
performance time	5.66	2.26	1	4	6	7	11
well-being	5.05	2.91	0	2	5	7	12
total	14.41	4.96	5	11	14	18	27

Examples of this task performed by an intact boy and a boy diagnosed with DD could be seen in Fig. 1. Children attending the 4th class followed the same instructions, but copied the following text:

Uprostřed náměstí se tyčil stříbrný sloup.
Pod střechou babiččiny chaloupky se uhnízdila vlaštovčí rodinka.
Tetička mi dala pestrobarevné odstřižky látek.
Nejbližší tramvajová zastávka je u víceúrovňové křižovatky.

Parents of all children enrolled into this study signed an informed consent approved by the Ethics Committee of the Institute of Psychology of the Czech Academy of Sciences. Throughout the whole study, the Ethical Principles of Psychologists and Code of Conduct released by the American Psychological Association [4] were followed.

2.2   Feature Extraction

The handwriting was sampled with frequency $f_s = 200$ Hz and represented by a set of time-series: x and y position; timestamp; a binary variable, being 0 for the in-air movement (recorded up to 1.5 cm above the tablet's surface) and 1 for the on-surface one; pressure exert on the tablet's surface; pen tilt; and azimuth. Consequently, these online handwriting signals were processed by the freely available Python library handwriting-features (v 1.0.5) [17]. More specifically, we extracted these conventional features [3, 14, 20, 27]:

1. temporal – duration of writing, ratio of the on-surface/in-air duration, duration of strokes, and ratio of the on-surface/in-air stroke duration
2. kinematic – velocity, angular velocity [24], and acceleration
3. dynamic – pressure, tilt, and azimuth

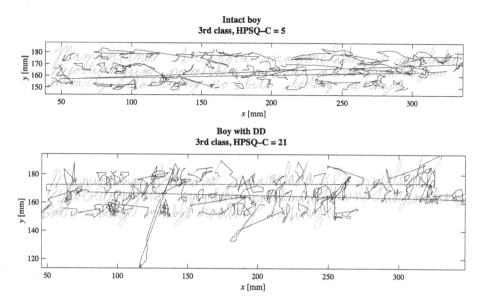

Fig. 1. Examples of the paragraph copy task performed by an intact boy and a boy diagnosed with DD (blue colour represents the on-surface movement, red colour the in-air one). (Color figure online)

4. spatial – width and height of strokes
5. other – number of interruptions (pen elevations), relative number of interruptions, number of pen stops [28], tempo (number of strokes normalised by duration), Shannon entropy [8]

   In this study, we consider the stroke as an on-surface/in-air trajectory between two pen elevations. Since some of these features are represented by a vector, we transformed them into a scalar value using statistics such as median, ncv – non-parametric coefficient of variation (defined as the median divided by the inter-quartile range), 95p – 95th percentile, and slope. The Shannon entropy, tempo, kinematic, and temporal features were calculated from the in-air movement as well. In addition, the Shannon entropy, velocity and acceleration were considered globally, but also in the horizontal/vertical projection.

2.3   Statistical Analysis and Machine Learning

Since the dataset is not balanced in terms of sex, before any further processing, we have regressed out [37] this confounding factor from the feature values. Next, in order to get a first insight into the features' discrimination power, we calculated the Mann-Whitney U test comparing the intact and dysgraphic groups. To have an intuition whether a feature has generally higher/lower value in the intact group, we calculated Spearman's correlation between the feature values and the diagnosis performed by the special education counsellor. The same correlation was employed to explore the relations between feature values and the HPSQ–C scores (i.e. the total score and those evaluating the legibility, performance time and physical and emotional well-being). In this exploratory statistical analysis, the p values were adjusted using the FDR (false discovery rate) correction [6]. The significance level was set to $\alpha = 0.05$.

Next, we built binary classification (modelling the diagnosis) and regression (modelling the HPSQ–C scores) models using XGBoost algorithm [9]. The classification test performance was evaluated using balanced accuracy (BACC), Matthew's correlation coefficient (MCC), sensitivity (SEN), and specificity (SPE). The regression test performance was evaluated using mean absolute error (MAE), mean squared error (MSE), root mean squared error (RMSE), and estimation error rate (EER). EER is defined as MAE normalised by the theoretical range of values in the given score (to provide the error in terms of percentage).

In both cases, we optimized the models' hyperparameters using 500 iterations of randomized search strategy via stratified 10-fold cross-validation with 10 repetitions. The following hyperparameters were optimised: the learning rate [0.001, 0.01, 0.1, 0.2, 0.3], γ [0, 0.05, 0.10, 0.15, 0.20, 0.25, 0.5], the maximum tree depth [6, 8, 10, 12, 15], the fraction of observations to be randomly sampled for each tree (subsample ratio) [0.5, 0.6, 0.7, 0.8, 0.9, 1.0], the subsample ratio for the features at each level [0.4, 0.5, 0.6, 0.7, 0.8, 0.9, 1.0], the subsample ratio for the features when constructing each tree [0.4, 0.5, 0.6, 0.7, 0.8, 0.9, 1.0], the minimum sum of the weights of all observations required in a child node [0.5, 1.0, 3.0, 5.0, 7.0, 10.0], and the balance between positive and negative weights [1, 2, 3, 4]. Finally, the models were interpreted via the SHAP (SHapley Additive exPlanations) [23] values of the top ten features.

3   Results

The results of the Mann-Whitney U test and Sperman's correlation with the diagnosis are reported in Table 2 (in each class we show the top 5 most discriminative features). In both cases, these top 5 features were significant ($p < 0.05$) even after the FDR correction. The most significant feature is the in-air movement duration, where children diagnosed with DD reach significantly higher values. The global duration plays a significant role as well (with the same direction). Moreover, the ratio of the on-surface/in-air movement duration suggests that children with DD spent significantly higher time in-air than on-surface. Children with DD also manifested a higher number of pen elevations, a bigger height of on-surface strokes, a lower in-air tempo, and a higher variation in the angular velocity.

The results of the correlation analysis could be found in Table 3 and Table 4. In this case, for each HPSQ–C sub-score and the total score, we report the top 3 most significant features. Except for the correlation with the total score in the 4th class, none of the results passed the FDR correction, thus they must be considered critically. The legibility sub-score positively correlated with, e.g., increasing duration of in-air strokes (3rd class) or increased height of on-surface

Table 2. Results of the exploratory statistical analysis (the top 5 features).

Feature	p (MW)	$\hat{p}$ (MW)	ρ (DG)	p (DG)	$\hat{p}$ (DG)
3rd class					
duration of writing (in-air)	0.0001	0.0043	−0.51	0.0000	0.0017
duration of writing	0.0001	0.0043	−0.49	0.0000	0.0017
median height of stroke (on-surface)	0.0002	0.0044	−0.48	0.0001	0.0019
number of interruptions	0.0007	0.0104	−0.44	0.0004	0.0062
ratio of on-surface/in-air duration	0.0008	0.0104	-0.43	0.0005	0.0062
4th class					
duration of writing (in-air)	0.0001	0.0056	−0.42	0.0001	0.0030
ratio of on-surface/in-air duration	0.0002	0.0056	−0.42	0.0001	0.0030
duration of writing	0.0007	0.0162	−0.38	0.0005	0.0111
tempo (in-air)	0.0013	0.0213	-0.36	0.0009	0.0157
ncv of angular velocity (on-surface)	0.0022	0.0294	−0.34	0.0017	0.0230

[1] p – p value; $\hat{p}$ – p value after the FDR correction; ρ – Spearman's correlation coefficient; MW – results of the Mann-Whitney U test; DG – Spearman's correlation with the diagnostic value

strokes (4th class). In terms of the performance time, we observed positive correlations with, e.g. higher maximum on-surface velocity/acceleration (3rd class) or increased duration (4th class). Regarding physical and emotional well-being, this sub-score positively correlated with, e.g., increased values of kinematic features (in both classes). Finally, concerning the HPSQ–C total score, we observed positive correlations with, e.g., higher on-surface strokes or higher values of vertical on-surface velocity (in both classes).

The results of the classification analysis are reported in Table 5. In the 3rd class, a model performed the diagnosis of DD with 74.3% balanced accuracy (SEN = 88.6%, SPE = 60.0%), while in the 4th class, the model reached BACC = 83.6% (SEN = 92.7%, SPE = 74.6%). The associated SHAP values could be found in Fig. 2. The top 3 most important features in the first case were the slope of the duration of on-surface strokes, the slope of horizontal in-air velocity, and the slope of pressure (the directions suggest that DD children had increased slope in all three features). Regarding the 4th class, the top 3 most important features were the slope of angular on-surface velocity (higher in the DD group), the ratio of the on-surface/in-air movement duration (lower in the intact group), and the variation of angular on-surface velocity (lower in the intact group).

Results of the regression analysis could be found in Table 6. The legibility sub-score was estimated with 17.96% and 14.90% error in the 3rd and 4th class, respectively. In terms of the performance time, we reached 16.48% (3rd class) and 16.31% (4th class) errors. Regarding the physical and emotional well-being, this sub-score was estimated with 15.34% and 16.69% error. The HPSQ–C total

Table 3. Results of the correlation analysis (3rd class).

Legibility	ρ	p	$\hat{p}$
slope of duration of strokes (in-air)	0.29	0.0238	0.7767
ncv of altitude	0.29	0.0247	0.7767
ncv of duration of pen stops	−0.26	0.0377	0.7767
Performance time	ρ	p	$\hat{p}$
median height of strokes (on-surface)	0.40	0.0012	0.0832
95p of vertical velocity (on-surface)	0.33	0.0085	0.2749
95p of vertical acceleration (on-surface)	0.31	0.0152	0.2749
Well-being	ρ	p	$\hat{p}$
95p of vertical acceleration (on-surface)	0.33	0.0094	0.3550
95p of vertical velocity (on-surface)	0.31	0.0137	0.3550
median of vertical velocity (on-surface)	0.31	0.0157	0.3550
Total	ρ	p	$\hat{p}$
ncv of duration of pen stops	−0.32	0.0126	0.5101
95p of vertical velocity (on-surface)	0.28	0.0253	0.5101
median height of strokes (on-surface)	0.28	0.0274	0.5101

[1] ρ – Spearman's correlation coefficient; p – p value; $\hat{p}$ – p value after the FDR correction

Table 4. Results of the correlation analysis (4th class).

Legibility	ρ	p	$\hat{p}$
median height of strokes (on-surface)	0.36	0.0008	0.0557
ratio of on-surface/in-air duration	−0.32	0.0035	0.0936
95p of vertical velocity (on-surface)	0.31	0.0041	0.0936
Performance time	ρ	p	$\hat{p}$
median of angular velocity (on-surface)	−0.23	0.0382	0.6137
duration of writing	0.22	0.0461	0.6137
ncv of duration of strokes (in-air)	0.22	0.0489	0.6137
Well-being	ρ	p	$\hat{p}$
median of vertical velocity (on-surface)	0.33	0.0025	0.0871
median of velocity (on-surface)	0.33	0.0026	0.0871
ncv of tilt	−0.30	0.0055	0.0963
Total	ρ	p	$\hat{p}$
median height of strokes (on-surface)	0.35	0.0013	0.0363
95p of vertical velocity (on-surface)	0.34	0.0020	0.0363
95p of velocity (on-surface)	0.33	0.0022	0.0363

[1] ρ – Spearman's correlation coefficient; p – p value; $\hat{p}$ – p value after the FDR correction

Table 5. Results of the classification analysis.

Class	BACC [%]	MCC	SEN [%]	SPE [%]
3rd	74.3	0.5068	88.6	60.0
4th	83.6	0.6841	92.7	74.6

[1] BACC – balanced accuracy; MCC – Matth ew's correlation coefficient; SEN – sensitivi ty; SPE – specificity

score was in the 3rd class estimated with 14.00% error (MAE = 5.60) and in the 4th class with an error equal to 10.34% (MAE = 4.13). The SHAP values of models estimating the total score are shown in Fig. 3. E.g., in the 3rd class, the model mostly relied on the 95p of vertical in-air velocity (higher in the DD group), the variation of horizontal in-air velocity (lower in the intact group), and the 95p of vertical on-surface acceleration (higher in the DD group). In the 4th class, the most important features were the 95p of vertical/horizontal/global on-surface acceleration (higher in the DD group).

4 Discussion

The results of the exploratory analysis showed that children with DD spent significantly higher time in-air. This result is in line with findings of previous studies [3,34] and could be probably explained by difficulties recalling a correct letter shape, which is linked with a poor orthographic coding process [27]. Children with DD also manifested higher strokes. Rosenblum et al. assume that this is the effect of trying to write legibly because oversized letters do not require so big precision of handwriting [32]. In addition, in accordance with other studies, we observed that DD children manifested a higher number of pen elevations [27,31]. To sum up, even though in our study we acquired handwriting using a display tablet, the most discriminative features were identical or similar to those reported in studies employing the paper and digitizer setup. Nevertheless, in order to precisely explore differences in features that discriminate between intact children and children with DD who write on paper or display, we would need to have tasks performed by a child on both types of devices. This point deserves further attention in future studies and research.

An interesting finding was done when we correlated the features with the HPSQ–C sub-scores and with the total score. In many cases, we identified that the scores positively correlated with the median or 95th percentile of on-surface velocity meaning that children with the less proficient handwriting achieved higher velocities. On the one hand, this is against the findings of many studies (please see the review in [27]), on the other hand, a couple of teams reported that experts should rather focus on the speed-accuracy trade-off meaning that

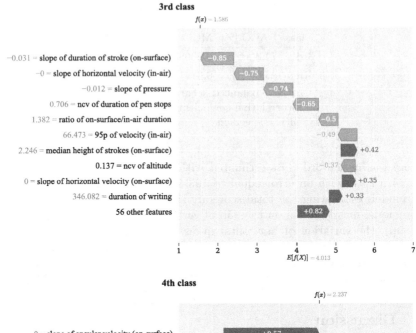

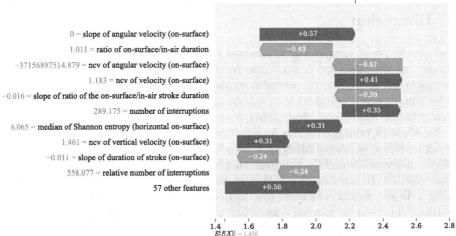

Fig. 2. SHAP values of the classification models.

the low velocity does not have to be linked with the less proficient handwriting, but it could be associated with better accuracy of writing [16,21].

When performing the binary diagnosis, we achieved BACC = 74.3% and BACC = 83.6% in the 3rd and 4th class, respectively. These accuracies are not high and we think there is still a place for improvement. On the other hand, most of the available studies reported diagnostic accuracy in a range between

Table 6. Results of the regression analysis (mean ± std).

3rd class				
Score	MAE	MSE	RMSE	EER [%]
legibility	2.16 ± 0.40	7.23 ± 2.17	2.65 ± 0.43	17.96 ± 3.34
performance time	1.98 ± 0.44	6.48 ± 2.19	2.51 ± 0.45	16.48 ± 3.70
well-being	2.45 ± 0.46	8.90 ± 3.30	2.94 ± 0.53	15.34 ± 2.86
total	5.60 ± 1.10	44.23 ± 19.85	6.50 ± 1.41	14.00 ± 2.74
4th class				
Score	MAE	MSE	RMSE	EER [%]
legibility	1.79 ± 0.31	5.31 ± 1.71	2.27 ± 0.37	14.90 ± 2.58
performance time	1.96 ± 0.42	6.09 ± 2.46	2.43 ± 0.46	16.31 ± 3.53
well-being	2.67 ± 0.36	10.46 ± 3.48	3.19 ± 0.51	16.69 ± 2.25
total	4.13 ± 0.18	27.35 ± 2.34	5.22 ± 0.23	10.34 ± 0.46

[1] MAE - mean absolute error; MSE – mean squared error; RMSE – root mean square error; EER – equal error rate

70% and 90% [13,14,18,20] suggesting that we cannot fully rely on the scores provided by special education counsellors, because their assessment is subjective, inconsistent (e.g. one rater focuses more on the product and another one more on the process [27]), and with a questionable inter- and intra-rater variability [12]. Thus we believe that rather than performing a binary diagnosis and rather than modelling unreliable scores depending on human perception, we must introduce a concept that would be semi-data driven (i.e. less dependent on a human) and that would provide a detailed and objective assessment of manifestations associated with DD (because with this, we can even discriminate between several sub-types of dysgraphia and introduce a more focused therapy). For this purpose, we have developed the Graphomotor and Handwriting Disabilities Rating Scale (GHDRS), a first scale of its kind addressing the above-mentioned requirements [27].

Finally, we explored whether display tablets could be used to emulate children's self-assessment. The errors in the sub-scales ranged between 14.90% and 17.96%. The HPSQ–C total score was estimated with 14.00% error in the 3rd class and with 10.34% error in the 4th class. This is close to the results reported by Zvoncak et al. [40], however, who used the paper and digitizer setup.

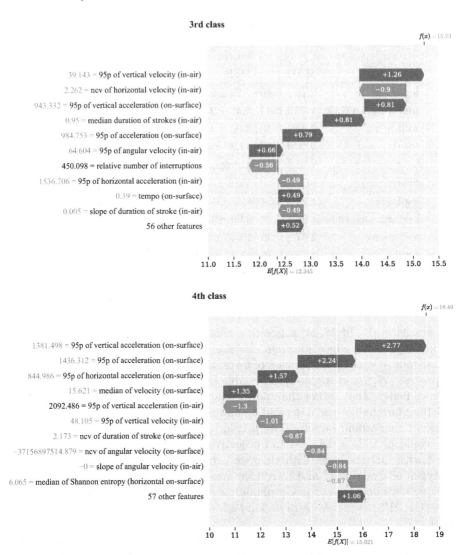

Fig. 3. SHAP values of the regression models.

5   Conclusion

The aim of this study was to explore, whether the easy-to-administer acquisition
of online handwriting via display tablets could be used for a supportive diagnosis
and assessment of DD. Our findings suggest that this approach could provide
results comparable to those based on the paper and digitizer setups. Even though
we used a display tablet connected to a laptop, which is still less comfortable,
we proved that writing on a display/screen has a good potential in DD screening
and further steps, such as transfer to e.g. iPad or Samsung Galaxy Tab tech-

nologies, could make the whole process even more comfortable and easy-to-use. In addition, we recommend using scales less dependent on human perception, while providing a complex overview of manifestations associated with DD (e.g. the GHDRS scale).

This study has several limitations. Firstly, the experiments were conducted on a database with a relatively small sample size. In order to generalize the conclusions, further studies should be performed. Additionally, although the effect of sex was regressed out, a more in-depth analysis of the impact of this confounding factor would be beneficial. Lastly, the diagnostic scores were provided by only one special education counselor. Having multiple raters would enhance the reliability of these scores.

References

1. Alamargot, D., Morin, M.F.: Does handwriting on a tablet screen affect students' graphomotor execution? A comparison between grades two and nine. Hum. Mov. Sci. **44**, 32–41 (2015)
2. Asselborn, T., Chapatte, M., Dillenbourg, P.: Extending the spectrum of dysgraphia: a data driven strategy to estimate handwriting quality. Sci. Rep. **10**(1), 3140 (2020)
3. Asselborn, T., et al.: Automated human-level diagnosis of dysgraphia using a consumer tablet. NPJ Digit. Med. **1**(1), 42 (2018)
4. Association, A.P., et al.: Ethical principles of psychologists and code of conduct. Am. Psychol. **57**(12), 1060–1073 (2002)
5. Barnett, A.L., Prunty, M., Rosenblum, S.: Development of the handwriting legibility scale (HLS): a preliminary examination of reliability and validity. Res. Dev. Disabil. **72**, 240–247 (2018)
6. Benjamini, Y., Hochberg, Y.: Controlling the false discovery rate: a practical and powerful approach to multiple testing. J. Roy. Stat. Soc.: Ser. B (Methodol.) **57**(1), 289–300 (1995)
7. Blöte, A.W., Hamstra-Bletz, L.: A longitudinal study on the structure of handwriting. Percept. Mot. Skills **72**(3), 983–994 (1991)
8. Brabenec, L., Klobusiakova, P., Mekyska, J., Rektorova, I.: Shannon entropy: a novel parameter for quantifying pentagon copying performance in non-demented Parkinson's disease patients. Parkinsonism Relat. Disord. **94**, 45–48 (2022)
9. Chen, T., Guestrin, C.: XGBoost. In: Proceedings of the 22nd ACM SIGKDD International Conference on Knowledge Discovery and Data Mining - KDD 2016. ACM Press (2016)
10. Chung, P.J., Patel, D.R., Nizami, I.: Disorder of written expression and dysgraphia: definition, diagnosis, and management. Transl. Pediatr **9**(Suppl 1), S46 (2020)
11. Danna, J., Paz-Villagrán, V., Velay, J.L.: Signal-to-noise velocity peaks difference: a new method for evaluating the handwriting movement fluency in children with dysgraphia. Res. Dev. Disabil. **34**(12), 4375–4384 (2013)
12. Deschamps, L., et al.: Development of a pre-diagnosis tool based on machine learning algorithms on the BHK test to improve the diagnosis of dysgraphia. Adv. Artif. Intell. Mach. Learn. **1**(2), 114–135 (2021)
13. Devillaine, L.: Analysis of graphomotor tests with machine learning algorithms for an early and universal pre-diagnosis of dysgraphia. Sensors **21**(21), 7026 (2021)

14. Drotár, P., Dobeš, M.: Dysgraphia detection through machine learning. Sci. Rep. **10**(1), 21541 (2020)
15. Dui, L.G., et al.: A tablet app for handwriting skill screening at the preliteracy stage: instrument validation study. JMIR Serious Games **8**(4), e20126 (2020)
16. Feder, K., Majnemer, A., Synnes, A.: Handwriting: current trends in occupational therapy practice. Can. J. Occup. Ther. **67**(3), 197–204 (2000)
17. Galaz, Z., Mucha, J., Zvoncak, V., Mekyska, J.: Handwriting features (2023). https://github.com/BDALab/handwriting-features
18. Galaz, Z., et al.: Advanced parametrization of graphomotor difficulties in school-aged children. IEEE Access **8**, 112883–112897 (2020)
19. Katusic, S.K., Colligan, R.C., Weaver, A.L., Barbaresi, W.J.: The forgotten learning disability: epidemiology of written-language disorder in a population-based birth cohort (1976–1982), Rochester. Minnesota. Pediatr. **123**(5), 1306–1313 (2009)
20. Kunhoth, J., Al-Maadeed, S., Kunhoth, S., Akbari, Y.: Automated systems for diagnosis of dysgraphia in children: a survey and novel framework. arXiv preprint arXiv:2206.13043 (2022)
21. Kushki, A., Schwellnus, H., Ilyas, F., Chau, T.: Changes in kinetics and kinematics of handwriting during a prolonged writing task in children with and without dysgraphia. Res. Dev. Disabil. **32**(3), 1058–1064 (2011)
22. Lomurno, E., Dui, L.G., Gatto, M., Bollettino, M., Matteucci, M., Ferrante, S.: Deep learning and Procrustes analysis for early dysgraphia risk detection with a tablet application. Life **13**(3), 598 (2023)
23. Lundberg, S.M., Lee, S.I.: A unified approach to interpreting model predictions. In: Guyon, I., et al. (eds.) Advances in Neural Information Processing Systems, vol. 30, pp. 4765–4774. Curran Associates, Inc. (2017)
24. Luria, G., Rosenblum, S.: A computerized multidimensional measurement of mental workload via handwriting analysis. Behav. Res. Meth. **44**, 575–586 (2012)
25. McCloskey, M., Rapp, B.: Developmental dysgraphia: an overview and framework for research. Cogn. Neuropsychol. **34**(3–4), 65–82 (2017)
26. Mekyska, J., Faundez-Zanuy, M., Mzourek, Z., Galaz, Z., Smekal, Z., Rosenblum, S.: Identification and rating of developmental dysgraphia by handwriting analysis. IEEE Trans. Hum. Mach. Syst. **47**(2), 235–248 (2016)
27. Mekyska, J., et al.: Graphomotor and handwriting disabilities rating scale (GHDRS): towards complex and objective assessment (2023)
28. Paz-Villagrán, V., Danna, J., Velay, J.L.: Lifts and stops in proficient and dysgraphic handwriting. Hum. Mov. Sci. **33**, 381–394 (2014)
29. Rosenblum, S., Parush, S., Weiss, P.L.: Computerized temporal handwriting characteristics of proficient and non-proficient handwriters. Am. J. Occup. Ther. **57**(2), 129–138 (2003)
30. Rosenblum, S.: Development, reliability, and validity of the handwriting proficiency screening questionnaire (HPSQ). Am. J. Occup. Ther. **62**(3), 298–307 (2008)
31. Rosenblum, S., Chevion, D., Weiss, P.L.: Using data visualization and signal processing to characterize the handwriting process. Pediatr. Rehabil. **9**(4), 404–417 (2006)
32. Rosenblum, S., Dvorkin, A.Y., Weiss, P.L.: Automatic segmentation as a tool for examining the handwriting process of children with dysgraphic and proficient handwriting. Hum. Mov. Sci. **25**(4–5), 608–621 (2006)
33. Rosenblum, S., Gafni-Lachter, L.: Handwriting proficiency screening questionnaire for children (HPSQ-C): development, reliability, and validity. Am. J. Occup. Ther. **69**(3), 6903220030p1-6903220030p9 (2015)

34. Rosenblum, S., Weiss, P.L., Parush, S.: Product and process evaluation of hand-writing difficulties. Educ. Psychol. Rev. **15**, 41–81 (2003)
35. Safarova, K., et al.: Psychometric properties of screening questionnaires for children with handwriting issues. Front. Psychol. **10**, 2937 (2020)
36. Snowling, M.J.: Specific learning difficulties. Psychiatry **4**(9), 110–113 (2005)
37. Todd, M.T., Nystrom, L.E., Cohen, J.D.: Confounds in multivariate pattern analysis: theory and rule representation case study. Neuroimage **77**, 157–165 (2013)
38. Van Waelvelde, H., Hellinckx, T., Peersman, W., Smits-Engelsman, B.C.: SOS: a screening instrument to identify children with handwriting impairments. Phys. Occupa. Ther. Pediatr. **32**(3), 306–319 (2012)
39. Ziviani, J.: The development of graphomotor skills. In: Hand Function in the Child, pp. 217–236. Elsevier (2006)
40. Zvoncak, V., et al.: Effect of stroke-level intra-writer normalization on computerized assessment of developmental dysgraphia. In: 2018 10th International Congress on Ultra Modern Telecommunications and Control Systems and Workshops (ICUMT), pp. 1–5 (2018)

Analysis of Eye Movements in Children with Developmental Coordination Disorder During a Handwriting Copy Task

Raphaël Lambert[1,2], Jérôme Boutet[1], Etienne Labyt[1], and Caroline Jolly[2]([✉]) [iD]

[1] Univ. Grenoble Alpes, CEA, Leti, 38000 Grenoble, France
[2] Univ. Grenoble Alpes, UMR CNRS 5105 Laboratory of Psychology and NeuroCognition, Grenoble, France
caroline.jolly@univ-grenoble-alpes.fr

Abstract. Little is known concerning eye movements during handwriting, especially for children with handwriting disabilities (dysgraphia), because of head movements which limit this kind of analysis. In this paper we present an exploratory study analyzing eye movements during a handwriting copy task using eye-tracking glasses in children with comorbid dysgraphia and Developmental Coordination Disorder (DCD), and in Control (CTL) children. We found that children with DCD spent less time looking at what they were writing than CTL children. Moreover, children with DCD made shorter fixations when writing and these fixations tend to be more numerous, suggesting distinct oculomotor strategies during handwriting copy tasks in these children.

Keywords: Developmental Coordination Disorder · Eye-tracking · Dysgraphia

1 Introduction

Handwriting is a complex activity involving cognitive, perceptual and motor skills. Because of its prominence at school, handwriting difficulties, or dysgraphia, can lead to many hardships for children, including lower academic success and loss of self-esteem [16]. Several neurodevelopmental disorders are associated with dysgraphia, namely Developmental Coordination Disorder (DCD), dyslexia, and Attention Deficit Hyperactivity Disorder (ADHD) [16].

DCD is a developmental disorder affecting fine and gross motricity, and concerns 5–6% of school-aged children [6]. Different school activities are impacted by the disorder, such as mathematical learning [7], but handwriting is often the most visible: 50–88% of children with DCD display comorbid dysgraphia [3]. A lot of work has focused on the qualitative and kinematics aspects of handwriting in DCD children, unraveling their underlying motor impairments [3]. Visual motor skills and visuomotor integration are other essential aspects of handwriting playing a key role in the automation of fine movements [4]. Whereas abnormal eye movements have been reported in DCD children in different tasks such as a high number of fixation before a lifting task [2], unstable fixations [9], less accurate and slower to counting tasks [7] or slower eye-hand coordination when reaching a target [11], little is known concerning the visual strategy implemented by these children during handwriting. This lack of studies is due to the difficulty of studying eye movements during a writing task because of head movements, of posture variations and of the need for visual correction. Several solutions to overcome this problem have been tested [1,5,8]. Among them, eye-tracking glasses were chosen, because they allow to follow eye movements during natural head and torso movements in a copy task with a distant model, and can include corrective lenses without issue for the tracking of gaze [5].

In this pilot study, we set up an experiment aiming at comparing eye movements during a handwriting copy task using eye-tracking glasses in children with DCD and dysgraphia, and in typically developing children (CTL). We had two hypotheses concerning children from the DCD group: (i) a greater number of looks at the model, and (ii) a longer time spent reading the text model, due to the greater need for rereading. More specifically, we analyzed normalized metrics to allow comparison between groups, and we expect a greater number of glances per second, and a higher percentage of time spent looking at the model. These hypotheses rely on the fact that handwriting is not automated in children with dysgraphia in the context of DCD, often leading to dual-task situations. Since handwriting takes more time in DCD children, we hypothesized that the amount of text kept in the working memory will be lower for these children, leading to a quicker forgetting of the text to copy and thus a need for rereading.

2   Materials and Methods

2.1   Participants

Twenty children were included in the study, divided into two groups: the 'DCD' group of 9 children with DCD and dysgraphia, and the 'CTL' group of 11 children without motor or handwriting difficulties. All children were right-handed, and French native speakers. There was no age difference between the groups (p = .676; Table 1). As reported in the literature [6], boys were overrepresented in the DCD group compared to the control group (p = .017; Table 1). All parents reported that their child had normal hearing, and normal or corrected-to-normal vision. Demographic and clinical profiles of each group are presented in Table 1.

Children from the DCD group underwent complete medical and psychological screening, and all had normal intellectual functioning level (French-language version of the WISC-V [10]) and normal reading skills (Alouette test [17]). Three of them displayed comorbid ADHD, and 2 of them had a suspicion for ADHD (DSM-5 checklist [14]). Motor skills were evaluated using the MABC 1 or 2 (Movement Assessment Battery for Children 1st or 2nd Ed. [18]). Children with DCD scored below the 10th percentile at the MABC1 or 2. Dysgraphia was diagnosed using the French version of the BHK scale (Brave Handwriting Kinder [15]). Children with DCD all scored below -1.5 SD in at least one of the two scores (i.e. handwriting quality or speed), while both scores were in the norms for the children from the CTL group (Table 1).

Table 1. Demographical and clinical profiles of each group of participants, and comparison of the different means between the two groups. Kruskall-Wallis ANOVAs were used to compare BHK scores and age, and a chi^2 test was applied for the comparison of boys/females ratios between the two groups. Age is shown in years.

Group	N (female)	Mean Age (SD)	MABC Percentile Mean (SD)	Mean BHK Speed Score (SD)	Mean BHK Quality Score (SD)
CTL	11 (7)	10.62 (1.9)	NA	−0.09 (1.17)	1.61 (0.81)
DCD	9 (1)	10.22 (1.39)	4.21 (3.17)	−0.87 (0.93)	−2.2 (1.84)
p-value	0.017*	0.676	NA	0.119	< .001***

Children from the DCD group were recruited via therapists or by mean of public announcement. Children of the CTL group were recruited by mean of public annoucements in schools of the Grenoble suburbs. The parents gave written informed consent to participate in the study, and the children gave oral consent just before the beginning of the experiment. This project has been approved by the University Grenoble Alpes Ethics Committee Review Board (CER Grenoble Alpes-Avis-2020-02-18-2).

2.2   The Experiment

Eye-Tracking Apparatus. Each subject was equipped with eye-tracking Tobii Pro Glasses 3, tracking gaze by pupil tracking with two cameras per eye, and a sampling rate of 100 Hz. The children who needed visual correction had additional corrective lenses directly on the Tobii glasses. The recordings were analyzed using the Tobii Pro Lab software to compute the different metrics. As the lighting levels could not be properly controlled during the experiment, no accurate pupil size analysis could be performed.

Task. Children were asked to perform the BHK, a task during which they have to copy a short text during 5 min on a blank paper [15]. The text model was printed on a third of an A4 sheet, and placed close to the child, vertically, so that they can read it easily by raising their head. The instructions given to the children were those of the BHK manual [15]. An example of a text written by a child from each group is shown in Fig. 2.

Procedure. The experiment started with an exploration phase (EXP) during which the text was revealed, and the instructions were given orally to the participant. The duration of this phase was not fixed, because the time necessary to fully understand the instructions may vary between participants. Then came the

Fig. 1. The three areas of interest of the eye-tracking analysis.

BHK copy phase (BHK) during which the child began to copy the text, after a signal from the examiner. Once the copy was finished, the recordings were stopped and the child was de-equipped.

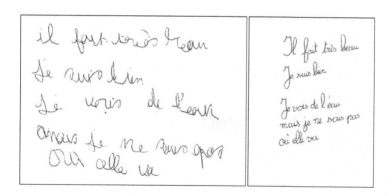

Fig. 2. Examples of the 5 first lines of a BHK written by two 3rd-grade children : one from the DCD group (left) and one from the CTL group (right).

Metrics Analyzed. Eye movements were analyzed using Tobii Pro Lab. For the BHK phase, we analyzed eye movements only during the copy of the 5 first lines of the BHK, to work on comparable materials between children. Three areas of interest were defined: the Writing Area (WA), the Text Area (TA) and the Surroundings Area (SA) (Fig. 1). The WA is a circle centered on the pen tip, the TA is a circle including the whole text copied (i.e. the 5 lines of the BHK), and the SA consists in the rest of the window. Different eye-tracking metrics were computed in each area. They focused on the analysis of fixations and of glances, which are the time intervals during which the gaze is in the same area. A glance starts when the gaze enters an area and ends when it leaves the area. Because of the definition of the SA, it means that the gaze is always in an area, so each glance is directly followed by a new one.

The absolute number of fixations can be misleading, because any difference between the groups may only be due to a different time spent to copy the 5 first lines, in particular in children with dysgraphia. To overcome this problem, we computed the percentage of total fixation for each area (normalization by the total number of fixations). The same reasoning was applied to the number of fixations per second in the area and the percentage of time doing fixations (both normalized by the total time spent in the area), the number of glances per second and the percentage of total time spent (both normalized by the total time of the phase - EXP or BHK). For each area, we thus ended up with 8 metrics: the percentage of total time in the area, the number of fixations per second in the area, the average duration of a fixation, the percentage of total fixations made in the area, the percentage of time in area doing fixations, the number of glances per second, the total duration of glances, and the average duration of a glance.

Statistical Analysis. Because of the reduced number of children in each group, comparisons between groups for the different metrics were performed with a Kruskall-Wallis test. Effect sizes were expressed using partial eta^2.

3   Results

3.1   Eye Movements During the Exploration Phase.

Results of eye movements' analysis during the EXP phase are shown in Table 2. The percentage of total time spent in each area attests that the main focus of attention during this phase was first on the text (44% of their time for the DCD group, 49.7% for CTL), then on the surroundings (where the examiner was), and last on the writing area. Although the difference is not significant (p = .076), the average duration of a fixation in the text area is smaller in the DCD group. The % of time doing fixation in the Writing Area is significantly lower for the DCD group ($p < 0.05$). There is no difference in the time spent reading the text or paying attention to the surroundings for this phase.

3.2   Eye Movements During the BHK Copying Phase

The results of eye movements' analysis of the BHK copying phase are shown in Table 3. Both groups spent the most time looking at the WA (68% for DCD,

Table 2. The eye-tracking metrics for each area are presented in the form of Mean (SD). The p-values and eta^2 are the result of a Kruskall-Wallis test. The average duration of a fixation and the average duration of a glance were not computed for the Surroundings Area. $+ = p < .1; * = p < .05$.

Area of interest	Surroundings			Text Area			Writing Area		
	DCD	CTL	p-value (eta^2)	DCD	CTL	p-value (eta^2)	DCD	CTL	p-value (eta^2)
% of total time	41.3 (14.1)	38.1 (15.2)	0.741 (0.01)	44.0 (14.1)	49.7 (17.4)	0.409 (0.036)	13.8 (12.6)	10.1 (5.6)	0.869 (0.001)
Number of Fixations per s	2.14 (0.69)	1.96 (0.49)	0.563 (0.02)	3.62 (0.64)	3.31 (0.79)	0.215 (0.081)	4.51 (1.96)	3.94 (1.30)	0.934 (0.0)
Average duration of a fixation (ms)	NA	NA	NA	174.88 (60.34)	223.91 (64.16)	0.076+ (0.166)	154.63 (77.19)	220.82 (101.43)	0.215 (0.081)
% of total Fixations	30.6 (13.3)	28.5 (13.7)	0.869 (0.001)	53.9 (11.5)	58.1 (16.6)	0.869 (0.001)	15.5 (11.7)	13.4 (6.7)	0.934 (0.0)
% of time on Fixations	31.8 (12.7)	40.1 (14.9)	0.186 (0.092)	60.9 (14.8)	71.5 (14.4)	0.160 (0.104)	59.0 (16.5)	75.7 (16.8)	0.039* (0.224)
Number of Glances per s	0.041 (0.011)	0.044 (0.015)	0.509 (0.023)	0.255 (0.098)	0.272 (0.101)	0.62 (0.013)	0.163 (0.125)	0.164 (0.092)	0.68 (0.009)
Total duration of Glances (s)	10.71 (3.29)	10.33 (5.03)	0.741 (0.006)	11.95 (5.88)	13.97 (6.86)	0.62 (0.013)	3.47 (3.46)	2.43 (1.32)	1.0 (0.0)
Average duration of a Glance (s)	NA	NA	NA	2.067 (1.099)	1.936 (0.713)	0.869 (0.001)	0.787 (0.478)	0.665 (0.269)	0.934 (0.0)

77.2% for CTL), but the difference between groups is not significant (p = .16). The DCD group tended to do more fixations (2.96 fixations per second in the area for the DCD group vs. 2.37 for the CTL group; p = 0.099), but shorter (206 ms mean duration of a fixation for the DCD group vs. 349 ms for the CTL group; p = 0.023), in this area. Moreover, they spent less overall time doing fixation during writing (59.3% of the time spent looking at the WA is spent doing fixations for the DCD group vs. 75.3% for the CTL group; p = 0.01). There is no significant difference between groups for the number of fixations per second, the average duration of fixations, and the percentage of the time spent on fixations in the TA. The number of glances in the TA, normalized by the total time of the task, is also not significantly different between groups. These results are in disagreement with our hypotheses.

4 Discussion

In this pilot study, eye movements during a copying handwriting task were explored in a group of children with DCD in comparison to a group of typically developing children. The Exploration phase was first analyzed, to ensure that the focus of the children on the examiner (present in the Surroundings) and the text did not differ between groups. The time taken looking at the text model was similar in the two groups, and there are no other attention point in the TA than the text itself, suggesting that both groups had a comparable reading time of the text beforehand. This finding is in disagreement with our initial hypotheses: children with DCD did not need to read the text for longer than CTL children

During the BHK copying phase, although spending a comparable time in the writing area, children with DCD tend to make more fixations in this area than the CTL group, but these fixations are shorter. Thus, the total fixation time during writing is shorter for children with DCD than for CTL. Their patterns of eye movements seem to differ from that of typical children: they do more fixations in the writing area but each fixation is shorter.

The number and duration of fixations is related to the focus in costly cognitive tasks. Our results in children with DCD may be due to the fact that they

Table 3. The eye-tracking metrics for each area are presented in the form of Mean (SD). The p-values and eta^2 are the result of a Kruskall-Wallis test. The average duration of a fixation and the average duration of a glance were not computed for the Surroundings Area. $+ = p < .1; * = p < .05$.

Area of interest	Surroundings			Text Area			Writing Area		
	DCD	CTL	p-value (eta^2)	DCD	CTL	p-value (eta^2)	DCD	CTL	p-value (eta^2)
% of total time	15.7 (9.9)	10.0 (4.5)	0.117 (0.13)	16.0 (12.3)	12.6 (8.0)	0.62 (0.013)	68.0 (14.5)	77.2 (7.5)	0.16 (0.104)
Number of Fixations per s	0.27 (0.36)	0.15 (0.20)	0.611 (0.014)	4.47 (0.83)	4.82 (1.25)	0.684 (0.009)	2.96 (0.63)	2.37 (0.61)	0.099+ (0.144)
Average duration of a fixation (ms)	NA	NA	NA	167.86 (47.80)	148.91 (44.28)	0.441 (0.033)	206.13 (68.36)	349.27 (132.81)	0.023* (0.272)
% of total Fixations	2.3 (3.3)	0.6 (0.7)	0.309 (0.054)	23.0 (14.3)	23.4 (13.7)	1.0 (0.0)	74.7 (13.0)	76.0 (13.6)	0.869 (0.001)
% of time on Fixations	10.3 (18.6)	4.9 (4.7)	0.934 (0.0)	71.3 (6.8)	68.5 (13.8)	0.821 (0.003)	59.3 (15.8)	75.3 (14.2)	0.01* (0.345)
Number of Glances per s	0.011 (0.003)	0.013 (0.004)	0.322 (0.052)	0.186 (0.091)	0.194 (0.088)	0.934 (0.0)	0.216 (0.075)	0.206 (0.078)	0.68 (0.009)
Total duration of Glances (s)	16.00 (10.68)	8.37 (4.20)	0.16 (0.104)	17.79 (14.61)	11.84 (8.85)	0.509 (0.023)	64.69 (13.87)	65.86 (17.38)	0.934 (0.0)
Average duration of a Glance (s)	NA	NA	NA	0.804 (0.448)	0.610 (0.291)	0.39 (0.041)	4.095 (3.051)	4.626 (2.555)	0.364 (0.043)

look more back-and-forth in order to check for potential mistakes in their writing. Alternatively, it may reflect a lower stability of the gaze, perhaps related to deficits in oculomotor control. Indeed, we did not discriminate the different subtypes of DCD among our participants, and some may have visuo-spatial deficits. These results are in line with previous findings showing that children with DCD had deficits in maintaining engagement and attention on a visual target [9].

During the copying phase, children from the DCD group did not spend more time looking at the model. This observation is again in disagreement with our hypotheses. However, although the difference between groups is not significant, children with DCD seem to look away from the writing area more often. This may be due to the presence of different strategies among the DCD group for the copy task. It may be difficult for some of them to maintain their gaze in the focus area, either because of a lower stability of the gaze or of a difficulty in maintaining their attention on the task [9]. This latter hypothesis is further supported by the fact that at least one third of our DCD children displayed or were suspected of comorbid ADHD. Indeed, ADHD affects eye movements [12]. In addition, the overrepresentation of boys in the DCD group may also affect our results, although recent findings contradict this assumption and support the Gender Similarities Hypothesis regarding cognitive functions [13]. However, for others it seems that they memorized the entire text during the EXP phase, and did not once look back at the model during the BHK phase. The diversity of strategies used by children with DCD could explain the difficulty to see a precise tendency in their pattern of visual exploration.

Although our study is exploratory, our results are in line with previous findings showing that children with DCD have abnormal eye-movements [2,7,9,11], and add new insights into eye movements and visual strategies used by children with DCD during handwriting copy tasks, a field that has never been investigated before. Further analyses of the position of fixations on the writing and text model areas would help to better understand the visual strategies used by DCD children during a copy task. Also, gathering more data, and separating children with DCD between groups based on their visual strategy could help to better understand the needs and particularity of each strategy. It would also be very informative to concomitantly analyze eye movements and handwriting kinematics to investigate the visuomotor relationship between the visual strategy used and the motor impairments in handwriting in these children. All these informations would lead to a better understanding of handwriting deficits in DCD children, and could eventually lead to new tools for the diagnosis and/or remediation of these deficits.

Acknowledgements. The authors are grateful to Nathalie Guyader for her help in the analysis of eye-tracking data, Vincent Brault for the precious feedback and the parents and the children for their contribution. This work was supported by a grant from the CDP IDEX NeuroCoG and the FR/SFR Pôle Grenoble Cognition from the University.

References

1. Alamargot, D., Chesnet, D., Dansac, C., Ros, C.: Eye and pen: a new device for studying reading during writing. Behav. Res. Meth. **38**, 278–299 (2006)
2. Arthur, T., et al.: Visuo-motor attention during object interaction in children with developmental coordination disorder. Cortex **138**, 318–328 (2021)
3. Barnett, A.L., Prunty, M.: Handwriting difficulties in developmental coordination disorder (DCD). Curr. Dev. Disord. Rep. **8**, 1–9 (2020)
4. Fancher, L.A., Priestley-Hopkins, D.A., Jeffries, L.M.: Handwriting acquisition and intervention: a systematic review. J. Occup. Ther Schools, Early Interv. **11**, 454–473 (2018)
5. Fears, N.E., Bailey, B.C., Youmans, B., Lockman, J.J.: An eye-tracking method for directly assessing children's visual-motor integration. Phys. Ther. **99**, 797–806 (2019)
6. Gomez, A., Sirigu, A.: Developmental coordination disorder: core sensori-motor deficits, neurobiology and etiology. Neuropsychologia **79**, 272–287 (2015)
7. Gomez, A., Huron, C.: Subitizing and counting impairments in children with developmental coordination disorder. Res. Dev. Disab. **104**, 103717 (2020)
8. Hacker, D.J., Keener, M.C., Kircher, J.C.: TRAKTEXT: investigating writing processes using eye-tracking technology. Method. Innov. **10**, 1–18 (2017)
9. Sumner, E., Hutton, S.B., Kuhn, G., Hill, E.L.: Oculomotor atypicalities in developmental coordination disorder. Dev. Sci. **21**, e12501 (2018)
10. Wechsler, D.: WISC-IV - Echelle d'intelligence de Wechsler pour enfants et adolescents-, 4ème ECPA, Paris (2005)
11. Wilmut, K., Wann, J.P., Brown, J.H.: Problems in the coupling of eye and hand in the sequential movements of children with developmental coordination disorder. child: care. Health Dev. **32**, 665–678 (2006)
12. Lev, A., Braw, Y., Elbaum, T., Wagner, M., Rassovsky, Y.: Eye tracking during a continuous performance test: utility for assessing ADHD patients. J. Atten. Disord. **26**(2), 245–255 (2022). https://doi.org/10.1177/1087054720972786
13. Hyde, J.S.: Sex and cognition: gender and cognitive functions. Current Opinion Neurobiolo. 38, 53–56 (2016). https://doi.org/10.1016/j.conb.2016.02.007. ISSN 0959–4388
14. American Psychiatric Association: Diagnostic and Statistical Manual of Mental Disorders (DSM-5®). American Psychiatric Pub, Washington, DC (2013)
15. Charles, E., Soppelsa, R., Albaret, J.-M.: BHK: échelle d'évaluation rapide de l'écriture. ECPA, Paris (2003)

16. Chung, P., Patel, D.R., Nizami, I.: Disorder of written expression and dysgraphia: definition, diagnosis, and management. Transl. Pediatr. **9**, S46–S54 (2020)
17. Lefavrais, P.: Test de l'Alouette, version révisée. ECPA, Paris (2005)
18. Soppelsa, R., Albaret, J.-M.: Manuel de la Batterie d'Evaluation du Mouvement chez l'Enfant. ECPA, Paris (2004)

Handwriting Analysis

On the Analysis of Saturated Pressure to Detect Fatigue

Marcos Faundez-Zanuy[1]([✉]) [iD], Josep Lopez-Xarbau[1] [iD], Moises Diaz[2] [iD],
and Manuel Garnacho-Castaño[3] [iD]

[1] Tecnocampus Universitat Pompeu Fabra, Avda. Ernest Lluch 32, 08302 Mataró, Spain
faundez@tecnocampus.cat
[2] iDeTIC, Universidad de Las Palmas de Gran Canaria, Juan de Quesada, 30, 35001 Las Palmas
de Gran Canaria, Spain
[3] DAFNiS Group. Sant Joan de Déu Sant Boi, Doctor Antoni Pujadas, 42, 08830 Sant Boi de
Llobregat, Spain

Abstract. This paper examines the saturation of pressure signals during various handwriting tasks, including drawings, cursive text, capital words text, and signature, under different levels of fatigue. Experimental results demonstrate a significant rise in the proportion of saturated samples following strenuous exercise in tasks performed without resting wrist. The analysis of saturation highlights significant differences when comparing the results to the baseline situation and strenuous fatigue.

Keywords: Pressure · Fatigue · Online handwriting

1 Introduction

Online handwriting acquisition using digitizing tablets, such as WACOM intuos, has a wide range of applications from e-security to e-health [2]. Depending on the specific application, certain tasks may be more suitable than the others, with greater variability in tasks when dealing with e-health applications [4]. In all the cases, the writer is required to perform a task such as his own signature, copying a drawing, performing a repetitive task, such as concentric circles, etc. While these tasks may not be specially challenging for healthy individuals, those with conditions like dementia may find them impossible to perform correctly. This inability is used as a biomarker, which is an indicator of pathology. The inability to perform the task is usually detected by incorrect or missing parts of the strokes, tremors, and other factors that mainly focus on the spatial x and y coordinates, with automated analysis replicating the visual inspection performed by health experts, such as in the pentagon drawing test of the Folstein's mini-mental [6]. This approach has been successfully applied to analyze prevalent pathologies such as Parkinson disease [1] and Alzheimer disease [8]. In the e-security applications, the challenge is to differentiate a genuine signature from an impostor one. This is a challenging task as impostors can replicate dynamic information, such as spatial coordinates, angles and pressure, from a genuine signature. Although the connection between fatigue and handwriting could be

A. Parziale et al. (Eds.): IGS 2023, LNCS 14285, pp. 47–57, 2023.
https://doi.org/10.1007/978-3-031-45461-5_4

under debate, a fatigued person has poor coordination of the movements and fine motor control skills. It can be manifested in the handwriting in diverse characteristics like the shape of the letters, speed, uneven spacing, and so on. In this paper, we propose a more in-depth analysis of pressure signals and their variation under different levels of fatigue, using an existing database known as Tecnocampus fatigue database [7].

1.1 State of the Art

The impact of fatigue on performance in sports and professional activities, including those utilizing brain-computer interfaces (BCI), has been extensively studied. In reference [20], researchers examined BCI systems and explored how fatigue levels change during BCI usage. They reported that fatigue had an effect on signal quality, drawing insights from an analysis of five hours of BCI usage data. In reference [13], the focus was on investigating the influence of three mental states: fatigue, frustration, and attention on BCI performance. The findings revealed that the relationships between these variables were complex and non-monotonic, potentially attributed to the presence of poorly induced fatigue, which was not assessed through other means. Lastly, in reference [19], a new signal-processing approach, inspired by BCI computing, was proposed to detect mental fatigue.

Several studies have focused on the effects of fatigue on handwriting, particularly through visual inspection by calligraphic experts. These studies primarily analyze offline handwriting, which refers to situations where a person performs a handwriting task and it is later examined. One book, referenced as [12], categorizes human stress into emotional and physical forms. While a fatigued writer can still produce signatures, such as when attending a physical fitness center or signing a receipt, it is less common in formal documents due to the unique circumstances surrounding the act. In formal cases, individuals are typically given enough time to recover from fatigue before writing, which explains the limited number of studies exploring the relationship between fatigue and handwriting.

Initial studies published in [9] and [10] identified fatigue as one of several factors that can affect handwriting. In [14], the author reported on changes in the writing of a subject who wrote an eighteen-word sentence after climbing four flights of stairs. The findings, summarized in [12], revealed changes similar to those caused by intoxication, particularly an increase in lateral expansion without a significant increase in height. Another study, presented in [18], examined 30 writers experiencing extreme and moderate states of fatigue, localized in their forearms. The study involved evaluating healthy young males who were asked to write a modified version of the London Letter under four different test conditions. The author observed an increase in vertical height in both lowercase and uppercase letters in over 90% of the cases analyzed, without significant changes in proportions or relative heights. Additionally, there was an increase in letter width or lateral expansion in 77% of the subjects. Regarding word spacing, the author found a combination of expansion and contraction in 50% of the subjects, with each tendency remaining consistent. Factors such as speed, slope, rhythm, and fluency habits were not significantly affected, although there was a minor deterioration in writing quality, leading to a less careful and somewhat scrawled appearance. Only one case exhibited increased pen pressure, and no evidence of tremor was found. Fatigue resulted in fewer patchings and over-writings while also enlarging minute movements, although fundamental changes in writing habits were not observed. Some propensity for spelling errors, abbreviations, and omissions of punctuation and diacritics ("i" dots) was noted. There was no apparent difference between the effects of general body fatigue and forearm fatigue, although the severity of fatigue did produce some variation. The data from Roulston's work, fully reported in his publication, confirmed the effects of fatigue. However, the statement made by Harrison [11] that "fatigue and a poor state of health can have a most deleterious effect upon handwriting" might be an exaggeration, considering the evidence.

Remillard's paper [17] studied 21 high school students to assess whether the impairment in their writing correlated with the pulse rate of their heart under different levels of exertion. The study aimed to identify the nature of the impairment and determine if stress-induced writing could be correctly identified. The author found that physical stress, resulting in abnormally high pulse rates, did affect the individual's writing performance. However, the reading of pulse rates could only serve as an indicator of the subject's stress level. The author could not conclusively attribute pulse rates as the sole cause of impairment, although they could contribute to it. The impairment in writing was characterized by deterioration in letter formation, excessive overwriting and corrections, increased lateral expansion (especially in letter spacing) and frequent misjudgment of word lengths at the ends of lines, a tendency to write larger, reduced writing speed with inconsistent pen pressure, failure to maintain good alignment and proper baseline, and an overall decline in writing quality accompanied by greater carelessness. In a remarkable outcome, 15 experienced writing examiners accurately identified the writing samples affected by different stress levels, despite the impairments observed. These findings aligned with those reported in [18]. The study's author made an interesting concluding remark, stating that the impairment caused by physical stress (after running various distances) was generally similar to, but not as pronounced as, the impairment resulting from alcohol ingestion. Extreme fatigue affected the control of the writing instrument, leading to increased expansion of the writing both vertically and horizontally. This expansion could be observed in the enlargement of the more minute movements of the writing process, indicating a tendency toward a scrawled appearance. The effects of fatigue were relatively short-lived, and writing returned to normal once the body had sufficient time to recover its energy.

These aforementioned studies, referenced in [12], primarily rely on visual inspection by calligraphic experts rather than computer analysis of documents. Consequently, they may be subject to the subjective interpretation of the human examiner.

Additional studies have explored the effects of fatigue in specific populations and contexts. For instance, [10] compared the impact of fatigue on individuals with movement disorders to that on control populations. The study involved analyzing online recordings and offline samples of handwriting under pre-fatigue and fatigue conditions. The findings showed differences attributed to fatigue, with certain movement disorder patients displaying more pronounced variations in aspects such as printing, letter size, tremor, and baseline compared to the control subjects, who exhibited primarily expansion. In terms of online analysis, the patients wrote at a slower pace and with more variability than the controls. Some patients showed increased speed and reduced relative pen down duration during the fatigue condition. Individual responses to fatigue play a crucial role in assessing the range of variation within individuals, as fatigue has a more significant impact on the variability of motor-disordered handwriting compared to healthy handwriting.

In [15], the authors concluded that both children with poor and good handwriting performance demonstrated poorer results after writing long texts. Although both groups were influenced by fatigue, the poor hand-writers consistently scored lower than the good hand-writers in both fatigue and non-fatigue conditions across most variables.

Lastly, [16] investigated the relevance of fatigue in forensic assessment. The study involved writers with good writing speed and above-average writing skills, as well as writers with lower speed and writing skills. Writers with good writing speed and skill completed the entire test without significant deviations from their normal handwriting characteristics. Conversely, writers with lower speed and skills rapidly deviated from their original characteristics as they attempted to improve their writing speed. This led to a quick deterioration in handwriting features, potentially compromising its forensic comparison. Notable handwriting changes induced by fatigue included departure from the writing line, absolute and relative size increase in writing, lengthening of lower and/or upper strokes, increased lateral spacing between letters and words, and a general increase in writing speed.

In summary, these studies highlight the influence of fatigue on handwriting, illustrating changes in various aspects such as size, spacing, speed, alignment, and overall writing quality. The effects of fatigue are of relatively short duration, and writing tends to return to normal once the body has sufficient time to recover its energy. Additionally, the subjective nature of visual inspection by calligraphic experts should be taken into account when interpreting the findings. Further research has explored the impact of fatigue in specific populations, such as individuals with movement disorders and children, as well as its relevance in forensic assessments.

2 Methodology

2.1 Database

In this study we used the Tecnocampus fatigue database [7], which comprises data from 21 healthy male subjects who completed nine different handwritten tasks:

- task 1: Folstein's pentagon copying
- task 2: house drawing copying
- task 3: Archimedes spiral drawing
- task 4: signature
- task 5: repeated concentric circles
- task 6: words in capital letters copying
- task 7: cursive sentence copying
- task 8: signature (same than task 4)
- task 9: spring drawing

These nine tasks are performed under different levels of induced fatigue, and acquired in five different sessions (S1, ..., S5). Fatigue was induced by means of a set of physical exercises in young sportive people.

The database was initially developed by the authors for the purpose of detecting fatigue and studying its impact on e-security biometric recognition using signatures and capitalized text [21]. The database is not publicly available due to regulations in the data protection law. Figure 1 shows the nine acquired tasks for one user and during one out five acquisition session.

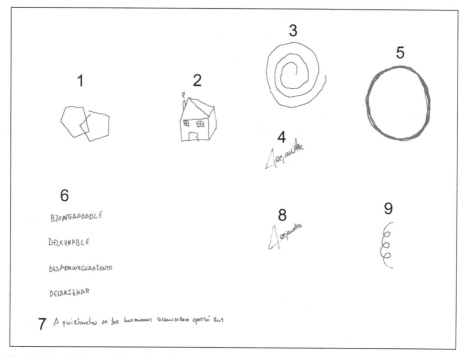

Fig. 1. Graphical example of the nine tasks executed by a control enrolled in the Tecnocampus-fatigue database during one out five sessions.

As we can see, the signature was acquired twice per session (tasks 4 and 8). Therefore, there were 8 different tasks in the database.

The sessions are summarized in Fig. 2. A complete explanation of the differences between sessions can be found in [7].

2.2 Feature Extraction

In this paper, we propose a novel feature for handwriting analysis: the percentage of saturated samples in a specific task. This feature can be defined by the Eq. (1).

$$saturated = \frac{1}{n}\sum_{i=1}^{n}\left[pressure\_signal_i \geq sat\_level\right] \qquad (1)$$

where: *saturated* contains the proportion of saturated values in a handwriting, *pressure_signal* is the input pressure signal vector, *sat_level* is the given saturation level (depends on tablet model) and *n* is the length of the input pressure signal vector.

Equation (1) is calculated using the MATLAB function shown in Fig. 3, where pressure_signal is the pressure vector of the handwritten task and sat_level is the maximum pressure level (i.e. saturation level). For the Wacom tablet used in Tecnocampus fatigue database, sat_level = 1023. This saturation level is equivalent to 45 N/mm^2 following our previous work [3].

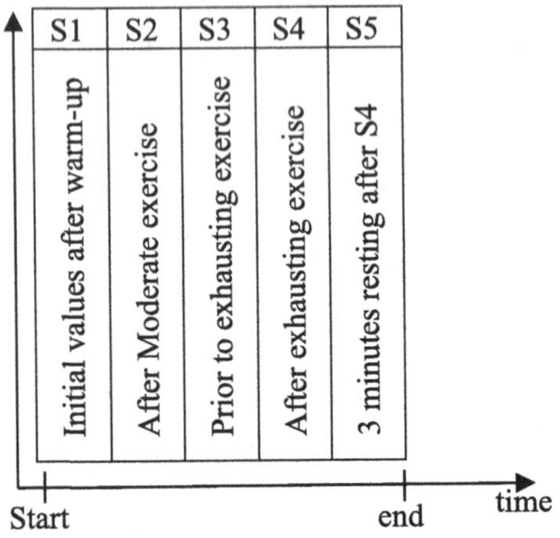

Fig. 2. Summary of the five acquisition sessions, where fatigue corresponds to session 4 and 5.

```
function [saturated]=saturation(pressure_signal,sat_level)
    [i]=find(pressure_signal>=sat_level);
    saturated=length(i)/length(pressure_signal);
end
```

Fig. 3. Script of MATLAB to count the percentage of saturated samples on the pressure signal of a specific task

3   Experimental Results

The dots in Fig. 4 shows the percentage of saturated samples for each session and task. We can observe two groups of tasks based on the variation between sessions:

a) High variation: There is a variation in the number of saturated samples between the fatigue and rest situation that can be up to five times higher for the pentagon and house, Archimedean spiral and concentric loop copy tasks. These four tasks are marked with bold solid lines in Fig. 4.
b) Low variation: There is almost no difference for the tasks of signature, capital letters, spring drawing, and cursive text.

Figure 5 represents the mean pressure for each task and session. From Fig. 5, it can be observed that:

- The mean pressure of loops and Archimedes spiral is larger than the mean pressure of the other tasks.
- Similar values of mean pressure are seen in different sessions.
- There is slightly higher pressure in session number 4 than in the other ones for the following tasks: concentric loops, Archimedes spiral, pentagon and house copying test.

Comparing Figs. 4 and 5, it can be observed that the percentage of saturated samples exhibits higher sensibility to fatigue than the mean pressure value. As such, the percentage of saturated samples can be considered a potential feature with sensibility to detect fatigue in some specific tasks.

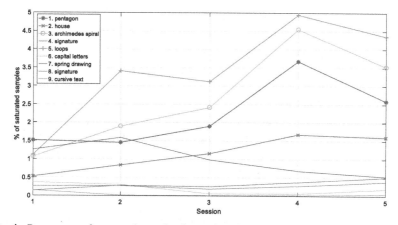

Fig. 4. Percentage of saturated samples for each task and session, averaging all the users.

Table 1 shows the standard deviation for the mean pressure values depicted in Fig. 5.

Table 1. Standard deviation (std) for mean pressure vales depicted in Fig. 5.

session	T1	T2	T3	T4	T5	T6	T7	T8	T9
1	242	136	147	128	171	106	209	124	126
2	211	154	153	152	189	107	212	145	121
3	240	164	175	174	190	107	206	135	120
4	239	178	181	169	200	97	221	137	124
5	237	187	168	150	192	112	216	145	131

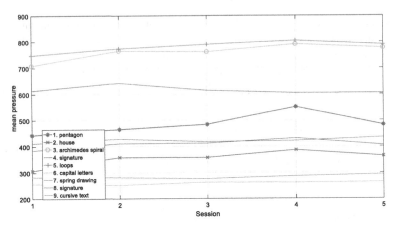

Fig. 5. Mean pressure for each task and session, averaging all the users.

In order to quantitatively analyze the differences under fatigue, we present a couple of figures. Figure 6 shows the y-coordinate and pressure of user number 12 for task 5 (concentric loops) in session 1 and 4. Figure 7 shows the speed in x and y coordinates for this same user, task and sessions. In this case we have computed the speed by means of Eq. 2, where f is the feature (x or y-coordinate) and i is the sample index.

$$\dot{f_i} = \frac{f_i(l+1) - f_i(l)}{1} = f_i(l+1) - f_i(l) \qquad (2)$$

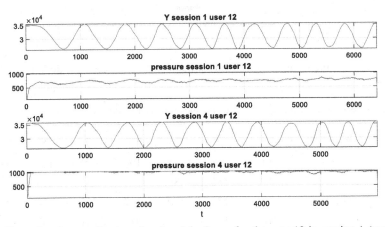

Fig. 6. Example of y-coordinate and p signal for loops for the user 12 in session 1 (top) and 4 (bottom).

Equation (2) represents an approximation for derivative of a discrete signal, obtained from classical derivative equation for a continuous signal (3).

$$\dot{f_i} = \lim_{h \to 0} \frac{f_i(l+h) - f_i(l)}{h} \qquad (3)$$

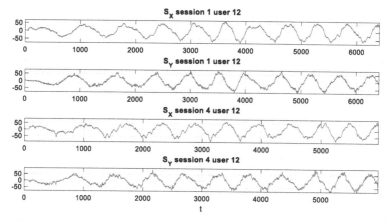

Fig. 7. Speed of x and y-coordinates for the user 12 in session 1 (top) and 4 (bottom).

Another approximation for first derivative is also possible, and has been studied in our recent paper [5].

Figure 6 reveals the saturation phenomenon in session 4 (saturation level is 1023). On the other hand, in Fig. 7 we observe that the dynamics of x and y-coordinate are mainly the same, without evident variations in instantaneous speed.

The tasks that are most affected by fatigue are concentric loops and Archimedes spiral. It is worth pointing out that these tasks require that the user does not rest the wrist on the tablet surface. This implies more difficult pressure control, which seems indeed affected by fatigue. For the pentagon and house drawing tests, although some parts can be performed with wrist resting, wrist up in the air is preferred to perform the task in a simple way. On the other hand, text and signature writing is usually executed by resting the wrist and forearm, so the saturation increasing phenomenon is not observed.

To determine whether these differences are significant or not, a Wilcoxon rank sum test for equal medians is performed. The test performs a two-sided rank sum test of the hypothesis that two independent samples, represented by the pressure in session x and pressure in session y (Sx-Sy, $x, y \in [1, 5]$), come from distributions with equal medians and returns the p-value from the test. The p-value represents the probability of observing the given result or one more extreme by chance if the null hypothesis ("medians are equal") is true. Small values of p cast doubt on the validity of the null hypothesis.

Table 2 shows the p-values obtained from pairwise comparisons between sessions. We conducted 10 comparisons for each task, considering the five sessions included in the database. As expected, we observed significant statistical differences when we compared extreme sessions (p-values < 0.05). Moreover, as we noted earlier, the concentric loops and Archimedes spiral tasks showed high statistical differences across sessions 1 and 4. In other words, this analysis has confirmed our observation that more attention should be paid to tasks where fatigue has a greater impact on pressure signal saturation.

Table 2. Represents the p value obtained by Wilcoxon rank sum test when comparing different tasks and sessions.

task	S1-S2	S1-S3	S1-S4	S1-S5	S2-S3	S2-S4	S2-S5	S3-S4	S3-S5	S4-S5
1	0.642	0.943	0.162	0.977	0.600	0.056	0.667	0.187	0.860	0.178
2	0.329	0.160	0.070	0.104	0.639	0.328	0.404	0.630	0.734	0.845
3	0.463	0.642	**0.025**	0.130	0.806	0.113	0.468	0.079	0.346	0.462
4	0.967	0.463	0.614	0.399	0.533	0.727	0.463	0.889	0.866	0.806
5	0.296	0.208	**0.041**	0.208	0.865	0.394	0.874	0.399	0.977	0.545
6	0.920	0.946	0.659	0.795	1.000	0.528	0.672	0.549	0.672	0.878
7	0.973	0.729	0.920	0.624	0.82	0.946	0.599	0.682	0.346	0.599
8	0.698	0.757	0.441	0.419	0.898	0.806	0.726	0.624	0.599	0.946
9	0.359	0.076	0.575	0.674	0.348	0.727	0.587	0.180	0.166	0.869

4 Conclusions

In summary, this paper has introduced a novel feature for handwriting analysis, namely the percentage of saturated samples in a handwriting task. Our experimental findings demonstrate that this feature has discriminatory power in detecting fatigue during tasks that do not involve wrist resting. We believe that this feature could be further explored in different contexts and applications for automatic classification purposes.

In summary, our research contributes to the advancement of improved and precise techniques for analyzing handwriting data. In forthcoming studies, we aim to explore this effect in various contexts and applications to facilitate automatic classification using diverse databases.

Acknowledgements. This work has been funded by a collaboration between the MINECO Spanish grants number PID2020-113242RB-I00 and PID2019-109099RB-C41.

References

1. Drotár, P., Mekyska, J., Rektorová, I., Masarová, L., Smékal, Z., Faundez-Zanuy, M.: Evaluation of handwriting kinematics and pressure for differential diagnosis of Parkinson's disease. Artif. Intell. Med. **67**, 39–46 (2016). https://doi.org/10.1016/j.artmed.2016.01.004. Epub 2016 Feb 4 PMID: 26874552
2. Faundez-Zanuy, M., Fierrez, J., Ferrer, M.A., et al.: Handwriting biometrics: applications and future trends in e-security and e-health. Cogn. Comput. **12**, 940–953 (2020). https://doi.org/10.1007/s12559-020-09755-z
3. Faundez-Zanuy, M., Brotons-Rufes, O., Paul-Recarens, C., Plamondon, R.: On handwriting pressure normalization for interoperability of different acquisition stylus. IEEE Access **9**, 18443–18453 (2021). https://doi.org/10.1109/ACCESS.2021.3053499

4. Faundez-Zanuy, M., Mekyska, J., Impedovo, D.: Online handwriting, signature and touch dynamics: tasks and potential applications in the field of security and health. Cogn. Comput. **13**, 1406–1421 (2021). https://doi.org/10.1007/s12559-021-09938-2

5. Faundez-Zanuy, M., Diaz, M.: On the use of first and second derivative approximations for biometric online signature recognition Accepted for publication in 17th International Work-Conference on Artificial Neural Networks IWANN'2023 , Ponta Delgada (Portugal), to be published in Springer-Verlag Lecture Notes in Computer Science (LNCS) series

6. Folstein, M.P., Folstein, S.E., McHugh, P.R.: Mini-Mental state: a practical method for grading the cognitive state of patient for the clinician. J. Psychiatr. Res. **12**, 189–198 (1975)

7. Garnacho-Castaño, M.-V., Faundez-Zanuy, M., Lopez-Xarbau, J.: On the handwriting tasks' analysis to detect fatigue. Appl. Sci. **10**, 7630 (2020). https://doi.org/10.3390/app10217630

8. Garre-Olmo, J., Faundez-Zanuy, M., López-de-Ipiña, K., Calvó-Perxas, L., Turró-Garriga, O.: Kinematic and pressure features of handwriting and drawing: preliminary results between patients with mild cognitive impairment, Alzheimer disease and healthy controls. Curr Alzheimer Res. **14**(9), 960–968 (2017). https://doi.org/10.2174/15672050146661703091 20708. PMID: 28290244; PMCID: PMC5735518

9. Hagan, W.E.: Disputed Handwriting; Banks & Brothers: Albany, NY, USA, 1894

10. Harralson, H.H., Teulings, H.L., Farley, B.G.: Handwriting variability in movement disorder patients and effects of fatigue. In: Proceedings of the Fourteenth Biennial Conference of the International Graphonomics Society (2009)

11. Harrison, W.R.: Suspect Documents; Frederick A Praeger: New York, NY, USA, p. 297 (1958)

12. Harralson, H.H., Miller, L.S.: Huber and Headrick's Handwriting Identification: Facts and Fundamentals, 2nd ed. CRC Press, Boca Raton (2017). ISBN 9781498751308

13. Myrden, A., Chau, T.: Effects of user mental state on EEG-BCI performance. Front. Hum. Neurosci. **9**, 308 (2015). https://doi.org/10.3389/fnhum.2015.00308

14. Nousianen, H.: Some observations on the factors causing changes in writing style. Nord. Krim. Tidsskr. (North. Crim. Tech. J.) 21, 8 (1951)

15. Parush, S., Pindak, V., Hahn-Markowitz, J., Mazor-Karsenty, T.: Does fatigue influence children's handwriting performance? Work **11**(3), 307–313 (1998). https://doi.org/10.3233/WOR-1998-11307. PMID: 24441601

16. Poulin, G.: The influence of writing fatigue on handwriting characteristics in a selected population part one: General considerations. Int. J. Forensic Document Examiners **5**, 193–220 (1999)

17. Remillard, J.L.G.: Abnormal cardiac rhythm and handwriting (Ottawa: an unpublished study conducted at the RCMP crime detection laboratories, May 1970). Can. Soc. Forensic Sci. J. **4**, 145–153 (1971)

18. Roulston, M.G.: The Fatigue Factor: An Essay Dealing with the Effects of Physical Fatigue on Handwriting Habits; (An Unpublished Report of a Study Conducted by the RCMP Crime Detection Laboratories, 1959); RCMP Crime Detection Laboratories: Vancouver, BC, Canada (1959)

19. Roy, R., Charbonnier, S., Bonnet, S.: Detection of mental fatigue using an active BCI inspired signal processing chain. IFAC Proc. **47**, 2963–2968 (2014). https://doi.org/10.3182/20140824-6-za-1003.00897

20. Seo, S.-P., Lee, M.-H., Williamson, J., Lee, S.-W.: Changes in fatigue and EEG amplitude during a longtime use of brain-computer interface. In: Proceedings of the 2019 7th International Winter Conference on Brain-Computer Interface (BCI), Gangwon, Korea, 18–20 February 2019 (2019). https://doi.org/10.1109/IWW-BCI.2019.8737306

21. Sesa-Nogueras, E., Faundez-Zanuy, M. Garnacho-Castaño, M.V.: The effect of fatigue on the performance of online writer recognition. Cogn. Comput. **13**, 1374–1388 (2021). https://doi.org/10.1007/s12559-021-09943-5

Handwriting for Education

IntuiSketch, a Pen-Based Tutoring System for Anatomy Sketch Learning

Islam Barchouch[1], Omar Krichen[1], Eric Anquetil[1], and Nathalie Girard[2]([⊠])

[1] Univ Rennes, INSA Rennes, CNRS, IRISA, Rennes, France
{islam.barchouch,omar.krichen,eric.anquetil}@irisa.fr
[2] Univ Rennes, CNRS, IRISA, Rennes, France
nathalie.girard@irisa.fr

Abstract. This paper presents the first works on IntuiSketch, a pen-based intelligent tutoring system for anatomy courses in higher education. Pen-based tablets offer the possibility to have pen and touch interaction, which mimics the traditional pen and paper setting. The objective here is to combine online recognition techniques, that enable to interpret the sketches drawn by the students, with tutoring techniques, that model the domain knowledge. IntuiSketch is able to analyze the student drawings relatively to a problem defined by the teacher, and generate corrective feedback. The online recognition is based on the bi-dimensional grammar CD-CMG (Context Driven Constraint Multiset Grammar) which models the document structure, coupled with a fuzzy incremental classifier, which is able to learn from few examples. The tutoring system is based on constraint modeling, which enables to define domain and problem knowledge, and to analyse the student production relatively to the constraints that have to be satisfied to solve the problem. In this paper, we present a new architecture for anatomy sketch targeted intelligent tutoring system that combines different techniques. We also present a qualitative study of the feedback that our first system version is able to generate on a case study.

Keywords: Online sketch recognition · Bi-dimensional grammar · Constraint-based tutors · Digital learning · Generative drawing

1 Introduction

This work is part of the SKETCH project, which aims to design an intelligent tutoring system for anatomy courses in higher education. Figure 1 illustrates an anatomy sketch used as source material in class. The pedagogical foundation of this work lies in the concept of generative drawing [6], which stipulates that learning by drawing can enhance student performance and understanding of the course material. We are therefore interested in problem solving by drawing anatomy sketches that satisfy the constraints defined in the instruction. Another pedagogical foundation of this work is the importance of generating

A. Parziale et al. (Eds.): IGS 2023, LNCS 14285, pp. 61–74, 2023.
https://doi.org/10.1007/978-3-031-45461-5_5

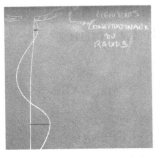  

(a) First drawing step of the spine   (b) Intermediate drawing step of the spine   (c) Last drawing step of the spine

Fig. 1. Example of the different steps of drawing a complete spine, created by a teacher in class.

prompt feedback adapted to the problem-solving process followed by each student. In education psychology, there are generally two types of feedback: delayed, and prompt feedback. According to [8], real-time feedback is more effective for student learning, since it enables him/her to quickly detect errors and correct them.

The objective of our work is to design a pen-based tutoring system based on these pedagogical principles. To ensure an intuitive user experience, our system has to allow free-hand sketching, *i.e.* there is no need to use drag-and-drop techniques to compose an anatomy sketch.

In this context of freehand drawing, our IntuiSketch system must be able to interpret these so-called semi-structured drawings. That is to say, the interpretation is not only in terms of their shape, but also in terms of their structure, *i.e.* spatial and geometric relations linking each element in the drawing. In this work, we use a combination of syntactic [3,9] and statistical [12,13] approaches for the online interpretation of student productions. Moreover, the interpretation is not only online, but also *eager*, *i.e.* strokes are interpreted in an incremental manner (stroke by stroke). This eager interpretation mode allows the generation of prompt feedback. The syntactic approach consists in using a bi-dimensional grammar CD-CMG (Context Driven Constraint Multiset Grammar) [10], which enables to model the document structure with composition rules. The statistical approach uses a fuzzy inference system named Evolve [2], which is able to learn from few examples. This capacity is important in our context, since our aim is to let the teacher define, by drawing them, new anatomy sketch exercises *via* an author mode. Therefore, new classes of anatomy objects are learned by the system each time the teacher introduces a new concept. This is one of the reasons we did not consider deep learning techniques in our work, even if these techniques have made great strides recently and are the state of the art in terms of graphics and handwriting recognition [4,11]. Another reason is, even though deep learning techniques are the best suited to recognize isolated and complex shapes, that are not able to model the document structure in a fine explainable way that could be translated, or used to generate, corrective and adaptive feedback to the students. This recognition part of the system is encapsulated in a *recognition engine*. This paper will focus on the tutoring aspect of the system and its interaction with the recognition engine. A tutoring system is, as defined in [1], a "computer program that uses AI techniques to provide intelligent tutors that know what they teach, whom they teach, and how to teach". There are two major approaches for knowledge modeling for tutoring systems: *cognitive tutors* and *constraint based tutors*. Cognitive tutors model the knowledge in terms of expert rules. The basic principle in place here is that each step of the student solution is compared to an ideal step modeled by a chain of expert rules. If a match is found, the step is valid, or else a corrective feedback is generated. These kind of systems are costly to build, especially for ill-defined domains like anatomy sketching, which are not characterized by a formal theory that can be defined beforehand (contrary to other domains such as geometry [7] or mechanics [3]). Constraint-based tutors take a simpler approach, that each problem, and each step, can be defined by a set of constraints that must be satisfied. The analysis of student's production step by step then consists in checking that no constraint defined for the current step is violated. If there is, a corrective feedback is generated in relation to the error made by the student. This kind of modeling is more suited to our field.

In this work, we propose a hybrid architecture for a sketching-based tutoring system to finely analyze student's productions and provide relevant feedback in the context of anatomy courses. This architecture is based on the one proposed in IntuiGeo [7], a pen-based tutor for learning geometry. Our IntuiSketch project focuses on the composition of anatomical structures, which presents a higher degree of freedom compared to the drawing of geometric figures. As a result, we are faced with more challenging tasks, both in terms of interpreting such semi-structured sketches, as well as the fine analysis of these production relatively to a defined problem constraints.

Indeed, if the geometric constraints are sufficient to model the knowledge of the domain in the context of IntuiGeo, for anatomy drawings this is not the case, we therefore propose here to combine different types of information: shape, structure, position, in addition to certain geometric constraints. This enables the system to tackle the more challenging task of analyzing semi-structured patterns.

This paper is organized as follows. Section 2 presents the interpretation approach based on CD-CMG grammar and Evolve classifier. The tutoring system architecture is presented in Sect. 3. The interaction between constraint based modeling and pattern recognition is detailed in Sect. 4. First (preliminary) qualitative experiments on a defined use case (*i.e.* anatomy problem) will show the feedback typology in Sect. 5. Conclusion and future works are given in Sect. 6.

2 Recognition Engine

The 2D recognition engine is at the core of the IntuiSketch intelligent tutoring system, and is based on the Context Driven Constraint Multiset Grammar (CD-CMG) [7] for the structural modeling of the document and the incremental classifier Evolve [2] for the statistical recognition of anatomical shapes.

2.1   CD-CMG Principles

The structural aspect of CD-CMG ensures that the recognition process takes into account the surrounding context of each element. This context can include the relative position of other elements, their semantic associations, and the overall structure of the sketch. The CD-CMG formalism is a set of production rules that describe the syntax and semantics of elements in the overall sketch. As illustrated in Fig. 2 (detailed thereafter), the production rules of this formalism define the process of replacing one multiset of elements by another, *i.e.* creating new elements by specifying the conditions under which this replacement can take place. By incorporating contextual constraints, the grammar ensures that the recognized elements respect the structures expected in the specific domain. It combines the concepts of contextual analysis, constraint satisfaction and multiset operations to capture the complexity and variability of sketches.

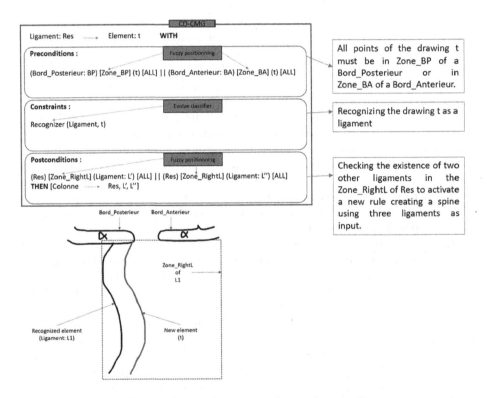

Fig. 2. One CD-CMG production rule representing an intermediate step to create a ligament (in red) in the spine example. (Color figure online)

By applying these rules iteratively, the recognition engine can analyze and recognize the various elements of the document.

In CD-CMG, preconditions, constraints and postconditions are an integral part of grammar rules. Figure 2 represents the intermediate step of the example mentioned in Fig. 1b, the CD-CMG production rule for the creation of a ligament takes as input an elementary stroke t. Firstly, the preconditions in the CD-CMG grammar rule define the requirements that must be satisfied before the rule can be applied, to check the rule applicability. Contextual consistency is confirmed by checking that the trace t belongs to defined zones of the document, using fuzzy positioning [5] which uses fuzzy logic to process uncertain spatial information. It represents spatial information using fuzzy inference systems to determine the degree of certainty of an element's position. This approach, according to [5], enables flexible and robust processing of imprecise or ambiguous spatial relationships. Next come the constraints used to enforce consistency, as well as structural or semantic coherence within the grammar. This enables to recognize the shape of the pattern and check the structural constraints that allow to recognize the pattern as a ligament, using the Evolve classifier. Finally, postconditions are used to define the changes or transformations that occur in the structure or attributes of elements after the rule has been applied. They define the transformation or replacement that takes place in the document structure so that new elements are predicted and the document is updated.

The CD-CMG mechanism allows domain-specific knowledge and problem constraints to be modeled. These constraints define the expected properties and relationships between sketch elements, ensuring that the elements recognized comply to the principles and rules of anatomy provided by the teacher in author mode. By checking these constraints, the recognition engine guarantees the validity and consistency of the sketches interpreted in student mode.

2.2 Incremental Classifier Evolve

To improve the recognition process, we use the Evolve classifier [2], which is capable of learning from a few examples. Indeed, some patterns cannot be modeled by the CD-CMG grammar like those shown in Fig. 3. Such patterns are characterized by a high degree of drawing liberty and require the integration of a classifier in order to recognize them. Evolve is well suited to the dynamic nature of sketch recognition, as it adapts and evolves according to the nature of the sketches encountered and the annotations associated with it, as defined in [2]. The Evolve classifier adapts its own internal parameters and updates its knowledge representation based on new examples and their associated labels.

The recognition engine is designed to analyze user's input in real time, taking into account what pen-based tablets have to offer in terms of interaction. As students draw their anatomical sketches, the recognition engine continuously analyzes the features and uses CD-CMG grammar to recognize and classify the different elements present in the document. Once the user's input is recognized, the tutoring aspect of the system takes place by analyzing the validity of the drawing relatively to the defined problem and the generation of feedback that is adapted to the student resolution state. We present in the next section the new tutoring architecture of IntuiSketch.

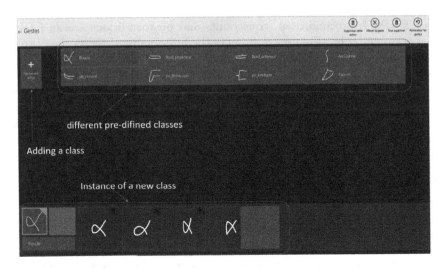

Fig. 3. Class set of drawings defined through examples drawn by the user in Evolve classifier.

3   IntuiSketch Architecture

3.1   Architecture Founding Principles

The IntuiSketch system is based on a new architecture (presented in Fig. 4), which builds on the IntuiGeo tutoring system [7]. It is composed of a *recognition engine* which interprets the sketches drawn by the user on the basis of structural and statistical knowledge. The *authoring module* enables teachers to create exercises by drawing a solution example. The *domain module* represents the domain declarative knowledge. Since it is inspired by the Constraint Based Model paradigm, our domain model encapsulates, in the form of a knowledge graph, the constraints that a correct student solution must satisfy, given the teacher reference sketch.

The learner module (known also as student model in the literature) uses the knowledge graph (K.G.) and the recognition engine to check each step of the student resolution. Each drawn stroke is either recognized as an element by the recognition engine or rejected (if it does not correspond to any of the defined classes). The result of the interpretation is then matched with the knowledge graph to check the satisfied and unsatisfied constraints. There are different types of constraints: geometric, spatial zoning, and shape. Geometric constraints are directly checked within the knowledge graph while spatial zoning and shape constraints require the learner module to interact with the recognition engine (namely Evolve and the zoning/positional algorithms of the CD-CMG grammar) to verify them. If one or more constraints are not satisfied, a corrective feedback is generated for the student.

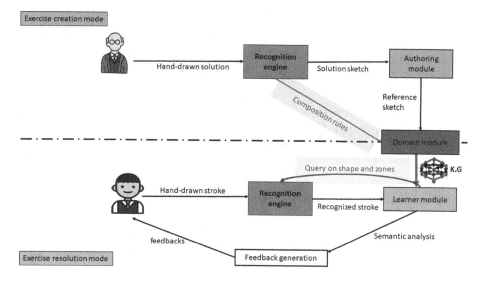

Fig. 4. IntuiSketch tutoring system architecture.

3.2   Adaptation of the Architecture for Complex Sketches

The novelty of this approach, compared to IntuiGeo, is the evolving nature of the recognition engine and the domain module. Since Geometry is a well-defined domain, the knowledge base of IntuiGeo was static, *i.e.* defined by 2D euclidean geometry theorems. By contrast, anatomy sketching is an ill-defined domain, which means that is impossible to code a priori the domain knowledge. Therefore, this new domain knowledge has to be *evolving*, *i.e.* be able to acquire new knowledge from each new exercise created by the teacher that introduces new anatomy concepts. By the same token, the recognition engine has to be evolving too, *i.e.* able to learn new anatomic shapes, as well as new composition rules, if the teacher introduces unseen elements in his/her drawing. Here the domain knowledge will be enriched directly from the evolving recognition engine, with new composition rules feeding the domain module each time a new concept is introduced by the teacher in his/her drawings (red arrow in Fig. 4).

Another important improvement in this new architecture is the interaction between tutoring and pattern recognition. In the geometry domain, the learner module just checks the geometric constraints validity, there is therefore no need for an interaction with the recognition engine. In this new domain, there are new types of constraints (shape and zoning) which mean the learner module and the recognition engine are in constant dialogue to check constraint satisfaction (gray arrow in Fig. 4).

In this paper, we present first works on this new architecture. We focus on a use case problem (a spine exercise), with a priori defined composition rules and shapes classes (*cf.* Sect. 2), as well as the knowledge base of the domain model. Automatizing these processes, by putting the teacher in the loop, will be the subject of future works. Details on the interaction between the tutoring aspect of our system and the recognition aspect are given in the following section.

4   Interaction Between Tutoring and Pattern Recognition

The interaction between tutoring and recognition takes place in the domain module which represents the domain declarative knowledge. This interaction takes also place in the learner module, which is responsible of analyzing the resolution state of the student.

4.1   Domain Module: Knowledge Graph Construction

Figure 5 illustrates part of a spine's drawing, including three constituting ligaments, the structure of the spine, and a cervical element. As shown in Sect. 2, all these elements are linked by spatial zoning relations (fuzzy positioning) and mathematical constraints (*e.g.* parallelism). An element is also defined by its shape, which can be described structurally (a spine is composed of three parallel ligaments) or described statistically with Evolve, classifying the stroke as one of the defined anatomy classes. These constraints are fed, in the domain module, to a knowledge graph which represents the objects present in the document and their relations, as illustrated in Fig. 6.

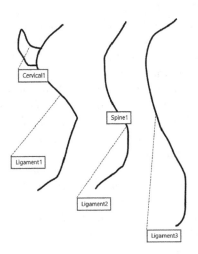

Fig. 5. Part of spine solution sketch.

The spine rule is *purely structural*, *i.e.* the spine depends only on three ligaments that are parallel and close together in space. Therefore, in the K.G., we consider the spine as a child of its three components. The geometric constraints (in red in Fig. 6) are propagated from the spine rule to the ligament nodes, thus creating links between these nodes (two directional arrows). Self directional arrows (light blue) represent the reflexive constraints, directly extracted from the CD-CMG production constraints block (see *e.g.* Fig. 7).

According to the cervical production rule presented in Fig. 8, the cervical composition depends on the presence of a spine, and its relative position with respect to the said spine, this position being defined in the preconditions of the grammatical rule. This creates a link from the cervical node to the spine node containing the zoning constraint, extracted from the production preconditions bloc (*cf.* Fig. 6).

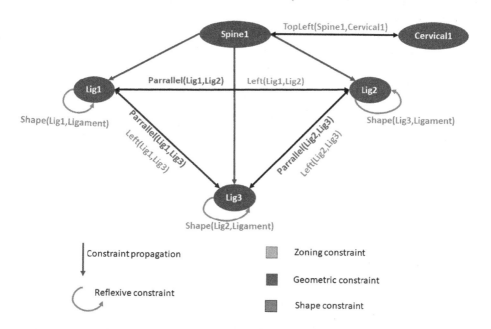

Fig. 6. Part of the knowledge graph for the spine example.

| Ligament l → Stroke s with:
Preconditions:
...
Constraints:
Recognizer(s, Ligament)
Postconditions:
... | Cervical c → Stroke s with:
Preconditions:
(Spine S1) [TopLeft] (s) [All]
Constraints:
Recognizer(s, Cervical)
Postconditions:
... |

Fig. 7. Ligament composition rule.   **Fig. 8.** Cervical composition rule.

From this example, we can see that the knowledge graph representation is a kind of *conversion from a grammatical representation of the document to a graphical representation of the document.* This knowledge representation enables constraint-based modeling of the student's resolution process, by matching his/her actions with the nodes of the graph, as well as verifying the validity of his/her solutions against the problem constraints.

4.2 Learner Module: Matching and Feedback Generation

In the exercise resolution mode, the problem and its constraints are represented by the knowledge graph. We can say that we are in the context of constraint-based modeling of the student's solution since we formulate the sketching exercise in terms of a set of anatomy objects (nodes) and the constraints that connect them (arrows), all of which must be satisfied for the problem to be solved.

Each student action, *i.e.* new stroke, is first analysed by the recognition engine (*cf.* Fig. 4). And, the resulting recognized element (or elements) is matched with one of the knowledge graph nodes. The matching principle is based on the minimization of a constraint score defined as follows.

Definition 1. (Constraint score).
The constraint score of a node n when matched with a new element E_{new} is:

$$Score(E_{\text{new}}, n) = \frac{CGeom(E_{new}, n) + CZones(E_{new}, n) + CShape(E_{new}, n)}{|CGeom(n)| + |CZones(n)| + |CShape(n)|}$$

with CGeom representing the geometric constraints of n, CZones the zoning constraints, and CShape the shape constraints.

These constraints differ in their evaluation, due to their different nature:

– Geometric constraints (such as parallelism) are strict, *i.e.* CGeom $\in \{0,1\}$;
– Zoning and shape constraints are fuzzy, *i.e.* CZones, CShape $\in [0, 1]$.

This is where the interaction between the learner module and the recognition engine lies. Although it is possible to verify the geometric constraints independently from the CD-CMG and Evolve duo (*e.g.* by defining the predicates directly in the domain module), the learner module has to query the recognition engine to check the satisfaction of the zoning (fuzzy positioning in CD-CMG) and shape (Evolve recognition score for a particular class) constraints.

Once a new element is matched with a knowledge graph node, the process of generating corrective feedback to the student is straightforward. The unsatisfied constraints of the node are translated into textual corrective feedback. Details on the typology of this feedback are developed in the next section.

5 Qualitative Evaluation

In this section, we provide an overview of the feedback typology that we have defined for the first version of IntuiSketch. Feedback plays a crucial role in guiding the student during the exercise resolution mode. We take the example of the

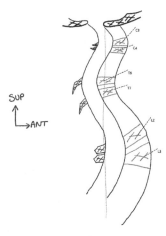

Fig. 9. Example of the spine exercise proposed by the teacher in author mode.

spine to give a more detailed demonstration of the steps involved in producing this anatomy sketch from the beginning to the end. Figure 9 shows the example provided by the teacher, which we intend to follow closely for this exercise.

Figure 10 illustrates steps in a construction problem we are currently working on. The segmented part of the sketch represents a specific element that the student needs to draw correctly. During this process, the system generates personalized feedback to help the student to improve their sketch (see captions for each sub-figure in Fig. 10).

As shown in the Fig. 10a, the IntuiSketch system interprets the student's drawings stroke by stroke. Once a stroke is recognized, the system displays the label of the recognized stroke.

Figure 10b illustrates an example of positive feedback provided to the student upon successful drawing of the left ligament. The feedback displayed includes relevant information about the exercise and textual feedback, recognizing the student's correct representation.

In contrast, Fig. 10c presents corrective feedback for a wrong drawing. Here, the student draws a stroke (strokeN), which the recognition system rejects because it doesn't match any CD-CMG production rule (the classification score is below a defined threshold). However, the shape of the stroke is similar to the shape of a ligament, leading the system to provide specific feedback on the shape and the geometric relationship between strokeN and ligament1 (i.e. they should be parallel). Figure 10d highlights another case where the student draws a stroke that matches the cervical node. However, the positioning of the stroke is incorrect, as it should be in the top-left zone of the spine. Consequently, the system generates corrective feedback targeting both the zoning and shape constraints.

Figure 10e represents the final step of the spine exercise. The system recognized and interpreted all sketches after having guided the student through all

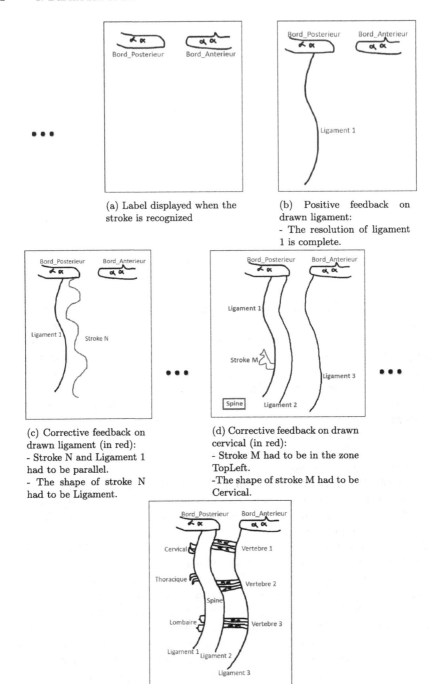

(a) Label displayed when the stroke is recognized

(b) Positive feedback on drawn ligament:
- The resolution of ligament 1 is complete.

(c) Corrective feedback on drawn ligament (in red):
- Stroke N and Ligament 1 had to be parallel.
- The shape of stroke N had to be Ligament.

(d) Corrective feedback on drawn cervical (in red):
- Stroke M had to be in the zone TopLeft.
-The shape of stroke M had to be Cervical.

(e) The complete example of the spine drawn step by step

Fig. 10. Personalized feedbacks generated to the student during his realization for the spine example.

the steps, providing different types of feedback by comparing what the student had done to the model drawn by the teacher in Fig. 9.

This example shows all the feedback we can generate to date, and, that work is ongoing.

6   Conclusion and Perspectives

In this paper, we introduced IntuiSketch, an intelligent tutoring system for anatomy courses. The system combines online recognition techniques with tutoring techniques to provide personalized feedback to students. Online recognition is based on the CD-CMG grammar combined with the Evolve incremental classifier and the fuzzy positioning, which enables sketches to be interpreted in real time. The tutoring aspect is based on constraint modeling, which enables the analysis of the student's production in relation to the problem constraints and the generation of feedback.

A new tutoring architecture has been introduced for the IntuiSketch system, with an emphasis on the interaction between the recognition and tutoring aspects, and the combination of different kind of information -shape, position, geometric constraints- to model the domain knowledge.

Future work will focus on improving and extending the capabilities of IntuiSketch. We aim to infer composition rules dynamically based on reference sketches created by the teacher in author mode, thus automatically enriching the domain module. The objective is to evolve the grammar incrementally, adding new production rules each time the teacher introduces new concepts by drawing reference sketches. Furthermore, we will carry out more in-depth evaluations of the IntuiSketch system in real-life educational settings. This will include larger-scale deployments and the gathering of feedback from both teachers and students to assess the system's ability to improve learning experience using pen-based tablets.

Acknowledgements. This work is funded by the ANR project number 21-CE38-0009. We would like to thank our collaborators from the LP3C laboratory (Psychology, Cognition, Behavior and Communication).

References

1. Alkhatlan, A., Kalita, J.: Intelligent tutoring systems: a comprehensive historical survey with recent developments. Int. J. Comput. Appl. **181**(43), 1–20 (2019). https://doi.org/10.5120/ijca2019918451. http://www.ijcaonline.org/archives/volume181/number43/30402-2019918451
2. Almaksour, A., Anquetil, E.: ILClass: error-driven antecedent learning for evolving Takagi-Sugeno classification systems. Appl. Soft Comput. **19**, 419–429 (2014). https://doi.org/10.1016/j.asoc.2013.10.007. https://www.sciencedirect.com/science/article/pii/S1568494613003414

3. Atilola, O., et al.: Mechanix: a natural sketch interface tool for teaching truss analysis and free-body diagrams. AI EDAM **28**(2), 169–192 (2014). https://doi.org/10.1017/S0890060414000079

4. Carbune, V., et al.: Fast multi-language LSTM-based online handwriting recognition. Int. J. Doc. Anal. Recogn. (IJDAR), 89–102 (2020). https://doi.org/10.1007/s10032-020-00350-4

5. Delaye, A., Anquetil, E., Macé, S.: Explicit fuzzy modeling of shapes and positioning for handwritten Chinese character recognition. In: 2009 10th International Conference on Document Analysis and Recognition, pp. 1121–1125 (2009). https://doi.org/10.1109/ICDAR.2009.141

6. Fiorella, L., Mayer, R.E.: Learning as a Generative Activity: Eight Learning Strategies that Promote Understanding. Cambridge University Press (2015). https://doi.org/10.1017/CBO9781107707085

7. Krichen, O., Anquetil, E., Girard, N.: IntuiGeo: interactive tutor for online geometry problems resolution on pen-based tablets. In: European Conference on Artificial Intelligence (ECAI) 2020, pp. 1842–1849. Santiago de compostela, Spain, August 2020. https://hal.science/hal-02544384

8. Kulik, J.A., Kulik, C.L.C.: Timing of feedback and verbal learning. Rev. Educ. Res. **58**(1), 79–97 (1988). https://doi.org/10.3102/00346543058001079

9. Álvaro, F., Sánchez, J.A., Benedí, J.M.: An integrated grammar-based approach for mathematical expression recognition. Pattern Recogn. **51**, 135–147 (2016). https://doi.org/10.1016/j.patcog.2015.09.013. https://www.sciencedirect.com/science/article/pii/S0031320315003441

10. Macé, S., Anquetil, E.: Eager interpretation of on-line hand-drawn structured documents: the Dali methodology. Pattern Recogn. **42**(12), 3202–3214 (2009). https://doi.org/10.1016/j.patcog.2008.10.018. https://www.sciencedirect.com/science/article/pii/S0031320308004482. New Frontiers in Handwriting Recognition

11. Sarvadevabhatla, R.K., Kundu, J.: Enabling my robot to play pictionary: recurrent neural networks for sketch recognition. In: Proceedings of the 24th ACM International Conference on Multimedia, MM 2016, pp. 247–251. Association for Computing Machinery, New York, NY, USA (2016). https://doi.org/10.1145/2964284.2967220

12. Wang, X., Chen, X., Zha, Z.: SketchPointNet: a compact network for robust sketch recognition. In: 2018 25th IEEE International Conference on Image Processing (ICIP), pp. 2994–2998 (2018). https://doi.org/10.1109/ICIP.2018.8451288

13. Zhang, X., Huang, Y., Zou, Q., Pei, Y., Zhang, R., Wang, S.: A hybrid convolutional neural network for sketch recognition. Pattern Recogn. Lett. **130**, 73–82 (2020). https://doi.org/10.1016/j.patrec.2019.01.006. https://www.sciencedirect.com/science/article/pii/S0167865519300078. image/Video Understanding and Analysis (IUVA)

Towards Visuo-Structural Handwriting Evaluation Based on Graph Matching

Anna Scius-Bertrand[1,2], Céline Rémi[3(✉)], Emmanuel Biabiany[3],
Jimmy Nagau[3], and Andreas Fischer[1,2]

[1] University of Applied Sciences and Arts Western Switzerland, Fribourg, Switzerland
{anna.scius-bertrand,andreas.fischer}@hefr.ch
[2] University of Fribourg, Fribourg, Switzerland
[3] Université des Antilles, B.P. 592, 97157 Pointe à Pitre Cedex, France
{celine.remi,emmanuel.biabiany,jimmy.nagau}@univ-antilles.fr

Abstract. Judging the quality of handwriting based on visuo-structural criteria is fundamental for teachers when accompanying children who are learning to write. Automatic methods for quality assessment can support teachers when dealing with a large number of handwritings, in order to identify children who are having difficulties. In this paper, we investigate the potential of graph-based handwriting representation and graph matching to capture visuo-structural features and determine the legibility of cursive handwriting. On a comprehensive dataset of words written by children aged from 3 to 11 years, we compare the judgment of human experts with a graph-based analysis, both with respect to classification and clustering. The results are promising and highlight the potential of graph-based methods for handwriting evaluation.

Keywords: scholar handwriting · legibility · children · graph-matching · similarity metrics · clustering

1 Introduction

Handwriting remains a skill and a crucial mode of communication in our societies. As a result, the characterization of the quality of handwritten traces is a problem shared by multiple communities of researchers and experts who must manipulate and process such offline and online productions [13]. The literature reports numerous works on evaluation of the quality of written productions [23]. Then the specialists of reeducation of non-proficient handwriting, as well as researchers interested in the acquisition of handwriting, have various batteries of tests for the analytical evaluation of the quality of children [8,12,14,19] as well as adolescents [15,28] handwriting. Whether the methods for such qualitative evaluation are global or analytical, they are based on visuo-structural criteria. Those criteria are estimated on specific sequences of patterns of handwriting, like word, sentence, paragraph or text, thanks to psychometric exercises. These criteria have usually to reflect both: the sharpness and fidelity of the form of

A. Parziale et al. (Eds.): IGS 2023, LNCS 14285, pp. 75–88, 2023.
https://doi.org/10.1007/978-3-031-45461-5_6

each of the symbols or trajectories constituting the handwritten word produced in relation to some reference models taught at school; the spatial organization of their traces and their proportions within the plot space considering the writing conventions taught; or their spatial organization and proportions in relation to each other.

So, considering those visuo-structural criteria seems fundamental for human experts when analyzing the quality of children's handwriting. It is also an important issue for the processes of comprehension [22] and accompaniment [11,30] of learning to write. This, whether these processes take place in schools and whether they involve the use of digital applications or not. Whatever the education system, official school curricula clearly stipulate the importance for the pupil of acquiring and then maintaining the criterion of legibility alongside fluidity [1]. This, throughout the school curriculum that will see him go from the status of novice apprentice scripter to that of adolescent learner mastering the gestures and principles of written expression. Also, in the case of the school context, the evaluation of the visuo-structural quality carried out by the expert teacher consists in a visual global judgement of the legibility of the written productions of the pupils. However, more often, the global criterion of legibility turns out to be partly subjective since teachers have neither common training in evaluation of this criterion, nor shared principles or tools for evaluating it so that it is otherwise [2]. Some previous works have been realized to deal with such problem and to develop new tools for class teachers like the Handwriting Legibility Scale (HLS) [3] for a more objective global scoring of legibility at school. However, we assume that computerized methods would be of great help to provide a uniform basis for evaluation of legibility and to deal with large quantities of handwriting samples, such that children with difficulties can be identified and accompanied by the teacher.

This observation and many others, led the University of the West Indies and the Regional Academy of Guadeloupe to initiate together a project, propelled by the application Copilotr@ce [20]. This project focuses for the moment on the French language that prevails in the teachings provided in their territories of establishment. It aims to make local teaching teams of the first and second degree collaborate with researchers for the development of collaborative digital tools of assistance: individualized and continuous support of learning from kindergarten to entry into college, help in identifying and remediating identified difficulties. In the case of learning to write, one of the challenges is the design of objective and automated solutions for the assessment of readability. These solutions must behave in terms of judgment that are as consistent and faithful as possible to that of a pool of expert teachers confronted with the same set of plots.

Among the possible solutions to this end, this article proposes to explore the use of Graph-based methods from structural pattern recognition [6]. We have chosen to firstly explore these methods because they are promising ways to capture and analyze the global structure of the handwriting based on images, as it has been put in evidence by studies on handwriting recognition [9], handwritten keyword spotting [21,27,29], and signature verification [18], to name just a few.

In the present paper, we investigate the potential of graph-based methods for the automatic qualitative evaluation of isolated cursive words handwritten by students. Our study has two main objectives, which we will refer to as O1 and O2.

O1- First, it is necessary to establish whether usual measure of similarity of graphs constructed from visuo-structural data extracted from offline images of handwritten words can allow decision-making analogous to those of human experts concerning:

– the similarity of the visuo-structural quality of students' handwritten productions?
– the legibility of handwritten productions of words?

O2- Next, we need to assess whether a scoring based on such measures of similarity could contribute to the identification of relevant handwritten words groupings, i.e., models meaning from a school point of view.

To test and to compare the results of our graph-based method, we needed some criteria and ground truth annotations. So, the first challenge for qualitative evaluation consists in choosing criteria that match with usual human scholar features used for qualitative evaluations. We have chosen to retain the overall legibility of the handwritten words. Therefore, results provided by our automated graph-based approach for objectives O1-a and O2 will be confronted with the qualitative criterion of legibility for both the O1 and O2 objectives. This article will be structured as follows. First, the next section will develop the context and the methodology used to produce the dataset and its ground truth. Next, the structural graph-based method we have chosen will be introduced and described. Subsequently, the experimental results will be presented and discussed. Finally, we draw some conclusions.

2   Dataset Used for This Study

2.1   Tool Used for Online Acquisition and Human Evaluation of Images

Trace acquisition and evaluation were carried out using the Copilotr@ce [20] application. Copilotr@ce is a web application for capturing handwritten gestures, available on all types of screen-based hardware.

Copilotr@ce works with or without an Internet connection, in online or offline mode. It offers the possibility of directly displaying or replaying traces made on its platform during acquisition campaigns.

The handwritten gesture capture session can be contextualized by activities requiring the use of graphomotor gestures.

Copilotr@ce captures and records over time sequences of points produced by the movement of a writing tool on the work surface at a frequency of 100 Hz. Depending on the hardware, these sequences can be produced using a finger, a writing tool such as a stylus for touch-screen hardware, or a mouse for computers with traditional screens.

Depending on the configuration chosen for an experiment, it is possible to start recording a sequence of points at the start of an activity, or from the first contact between the writing tool and the work surface.

In addition to the raw trace data recorded in real time (dating, coordinates, pressure, etc.), Copilotr@ce provides a set of indicators derived from the trace during and at the end of the experiment. These data can be used in models to provide evaluation and positioning indicators.

Copilotr@ce enables the collection of contextualized traces as part of action research. These collections are programmed on cohorts of anonymized scribblers.

Copilotr@ce enables the evaluation of traces contained in its information database, depending on the study context, by cohorts of evaluators or experts. The information databases contained in Copilotr@ce are represented by: activity contexts, writers' traces, as well as human or automatic evaluations. All this data is used to conduct studies with the aim of evaluating and building automatic analysis models, which can then be fed back into its knowledge base for validation in the field.

2.2   Nature and Context of the Image Acquisition

The partnership project powered by the Copilotr@ce platform, has already allowed to collect a substantial mass of handwritten traces of great diversity produced by pupils from 3 up to 14 years old. Among those handwritten traces we have chosen to consider 814 images of handwritten isolated words collected for this study. They were handwritten by 321 all-comers aged 3 to 11 years old from kindergarten to middle school. All these traces were made by these pupils with a stylus on touch tablets during a task of copying cursive models of each of the words: "lundi" (Monday), "lunes" (moons), and "plumes" (feathers) (see Figs. 1 and 2). We have chosen these three words because when we began this present study, they were those that were more represented in the dataset created thanks to Copilotr@ce. Indeed, they had been the most frequently and spontaneously handwritten among all those that were presented to the participants in the scholar action-researches driven from the first grade of kindergarten up to the first one of the middle school.

Fig. 1. Cursive patterns of the words "lundi" and "lunes" presented during the copy task.

This copy task was proposed by the Copilotr@ce application to pupils during school time according to the same modalities. As the successive presentations of the isolated words on the screen, the students copied them into a reserved area with their finger or stylus on the surface of the touch tablet. This area could present a baseline as shown by Fig. 2 for the word "plumes". Figure 3 shows three examples of productions for pupils who participated in this activity.

Fig. 2. The model of the word "plumes" and baseline presented by Copilotr@ce during the copy task.

Fig. 3. Examples of copies of the words "lunes", "lundi" and "plumes" made by 3 students.

2.3   Description of the Ground Truth

The ground truth was built by mobilizing three of the co-authors of this contribution who are also teachers. The latter took no part in the @MaGma project either as teachers in one of the participating classes or as accompanists of cohorts of pupils that had handwritten the words which are considered in this study.

We provide two levels of ground truth for each handwritten word: one with two classes "legible" and "illegible" and one with three classes "legible", "not very legible", and "illegible". First, the two-class annotation is performed and then, in a second step, for some of the samples the third class "not very legible" is attributed. This third class represents uncertainty of the human experts and concerns both samples previously labeled as legible and illegible. The human experts did not agree among themselves on all samples. We use majority voting to assign a final label to each handwritten word.

3   Methods

To classify the children's handwriting, we use graph matching. Once the similarity between each graph has been calculated, we compare two methods to assign the closest class: classification with KNN and clustering with K-Medoids and Agglomerative Hierarchical Clustering.

3.1 Graph-Based Approach Principle

A graph is a mathematical representation of the components of an object and the relationships between them, such as molecules with linked atoms, proteins with linked amino acids – or handwriting with linked strokes. It is called a structural representation because it captures the global structure of the object. Representing handwriting by graphs enables us, among other things, to compare the similarity between two words. We assume that when comparing a set of handwritten words, words categorized as legible should be the most similar to each other; and the same for not very legible and illegible words. This would enable us to identify students in need of remediation.

Graph Definition. A graph g is defined by four components:

$$g = (V, E, \mu, \nu) \tag{1}$$

where V is a finite set of nodes, E a set of edges with $E \subseteq V \times V$, $\mu : V \to L$ corresponds to the labels of the nodes and $\nu : E \to L$ corresponds to the labels of the edges.

A graph may or may not have labels and may or may not be directed. Graphs whose edges have no direction are undirected graphs. Conversely, graphs whose edges have a direction are called directed graphs. Nodes and/or edges can have labels. Labels can be part of any domain, they can be numerical (L = 1, 2, ..., n) or vectorial (L = $\mathbb{R}^n$) or symbolic (L = $\{\alpha, \beta, ..., n\}$) or even a set of colors (L = {violet, yellow, green, ...}).

Graph Extraction. The first step in comparing two graphs is to extract graphs from each of the word images to be matched. We have chosen keypoint graphs [9] as our graph representation, as they allow us to represent the trace of a word as closely as possible. Furthermore, they have shown very good results in handwriting analysis [18,27,29].

Formally, keypoint graphs use coordinates $(x, y) \in \mathbb{R}^2$ as node labels and edges are unlabelled. Note that a relatively large number of nodes replaces the need for more complex edge labels. Adding edge labels, such as distances or angles, have not led to improved performance for handwriting analysis in preliminary experiments.

To extract keypoint graphs, first, a difference of Gaussians filter (DoG) is applied to enhance the edges. Next, a binarization is performed with a global threshold. Then a skeleton is extracted by reducing the thickness of each line to one pixel. Three types of points are then detected: stroke ends, intersections and a random point on circular structures. We then add additional points on the skeleton at distance D. Each point becomes a node, and the strokes between each point become edges. A visual representation of a word sample is provided Fig. 4.

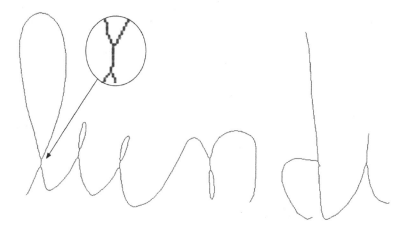

Fig. 4. Graph representation of a Monday's sample. Nodes are in red and edge are in blue. A closer look is made for the intersection strokes of the l. (Color figure online)

Graph Matching. Once we have obtained a set of graphs, Graph Edit Distance (GED) allows us to calculate a minimal transformation cost between two graphs. The cost takes into account to node deletion ($u \rightarrow \epsilon$), node insertion ($\epsilon \rightarrow v$), node label substitution ($u \rightarrow v$), edge deletion ($s \rightarrow \epsilon$), and edge insertion ($\epsilon \rightarrow t$). However, GED is NP-complete, which makes the computation infeasible when a graph has more than a few dozen nodes. This is why we use the Hausdorff Edit Distance (HED) [10] to compute a lower bound approximation in quadratic time:

$$HED_c(g_1, g_2) = \sum_{u \in V_1} \min_{v \in V_2 \cup \{\epsilon\}} f_c(u, v) + \sum_{v \in V_2} \min_{u \in V_1 \cup \{\epsilon\}} f_c(u, v) \qquad (2)$$

where c is the cost function for the edit operations and $f_c(u, v)$ the cost for assigning node u to node v, taking into account its adjacent edges as well.

The Euclidean cost function is used, i.e. constant costs c_V and c_E

$$\begin{aligned} c(u \rightarrow \epsilon) &= c(\epsilon \rightarrow v) = c_V \\ c(s \rightarrow \epsilon) &= c(\epsilon \rightarrow t) = c_E \end{aligned} \qquad (3)$$

for node and edge deletion and insertion, and the Euclidean distance

$$c(u \rightarrow v) = ||(x_u, y_u) - (x_v, y_v)|| \qquad (4)$$

for node label substitution.

3.2   Classification of Graphs Using Similarity Measures

The first objective of our study (O1) is concerned with comparing automatic classification with human judgment. For this prupose, we use a standard classifier

that operates directly on the pairwise dissimilarity obtained by HED, namely
k-nearest neighbors (KNN) classification. It compares a test graph with a set of
training graph and selects the k most similar training samples with respect to
the dissimilarity measure, HED in our case. Afterwards the class that is most
frequent among the k nearest neighbors is chosen as the class of the test graph.
In the case of a tie, the class of the nearest neighbor is chosen.

We are using a simple accuracy measure (see Eq. 5) to evaluate the performance regarding the classification of the samples. We count for the whole test
set the amount of correctly classified samples and divide it by the size of the
test set.

$$Accuracy = \frac{\#correct}{\#total} \tag{5}$$

The results of this classification approach are presented and discussed in a
Subsect. 4.2.

3.3   Clustering of Graphs Using Similarity Measures

The second objective of our study (O2) is concerned with assessing the graph-
based similarity measure with respect to its ability to group handwritten words
that share visuo-structural features. For this purpose, we consider clustering
algorithms.

We first determine the dissimilarities between all graphs using HED, thereby
producing a distance matrix. Secondly, this matrix is used by clustering algorithms as custom metric in order to identify groups of homogeneous graphs
(with the same characteristics according to the similarity measure). The use of
a metric adjusted to the specific data and constraints of a study makes it possible to obtain relevant results in the field of climate informatics [4,5], and this
experiment aims to verify this principle on another field of research.

K-Medoïds (KMED) and Agglomerative Hierarchical Clustering (AHC) algorithms are used with different settings in order to compare their results [16,17,
25,26]. The number of clusters (k), the choice of algorithm and the quality of
the grouping will be determined using the Silhouette index [7,24]. This index
varies between -1 and 1, with negative values indicating the absence of data
patterning, a value of 0 indicating the presence of a single group and values
above 0.2 indicating the presence of data patterning. Therefore, the higher the
index, the more relevant the clustering.

The results of this clustering approach are presented and discussed in a Subsect. 4.3.

4   Experimental Evaluation

To evaluate our method for classifying the legibility of handwritten words by
children, we conducted a series of experiments. First, we optimized the parameters of the graphs on the words at our disposal. Then we calculated the distance
between words. Next, we interpreted these distances from the perspective of
classification and clustering, respectively.

In the following, we first describe our experimental setup, then the results with classification and clustering.

4.1   Parameter Optimisation

In order to benefit from as much data as possible to optimize parameters and test our method, we have divided our dataset into two parts: validation set (30%) and testset (70%). Tables 1 and 2 list the number of words in the test set for the three and two classes, respectively.

Table 1. Test set of handwritten words with three classes.

	Lundi	Lunes	Plumes
Legible	141	183	15
Not very legible	12	54	49
Illegible	21	63	35
Total	174	300	99

Table 2. Test set of handwritten words with two classes.

	Lundi	Lunes	Plumes
Legible	141	230	63
Illegible	33	70	36
Total	174	300	99

The parameter optimisation is performed with respect to KNN-based classification on the validation set using a leave-one-out strategy, i.e. each sample of the validation set is classified with respect to all others. The setup is as follows. Node labels have been normalized to a zero mean and a unit variance (z-score), since word positions vary significantly from one example to another (top left, center, bottom...). For the optimization, we evaluated several parameters:

- **For graph extraction**, we tested different node distance values: $D \in \{3, 5, 10, 15\}$.
- **For graph matching parameters**, we tested the following values for node costs c_V and edge costs c_E: $c_V, c_E \in \{0.5, 1.0, 1.5\}$.
- **For classification**, we tested the following values of k for KNN-based classification: $k \in \{1, 3, 5, 7, 9\}$.

The optimization result for each word is shown in Table 3. The first parameter set P1, which has been optimized for the word "lundi", favors graphs with a high resolution (small node distance D = 5 on the skeleton) and has relatively low costs for node insertion/deletion (0.5 standard deviations). P2 and P3 have a lower resolution and higher node/edge costs.

Table 3. Meta-parameters after optimization.

Parameters	P1 (lundi)	P2 (lunes)	P3 (plumes)
D	5	10	10
Node cost c_V	0.5	1.0	1.5
Edge cost c_E	1.0	1.0	1.5
k	1	5	5

4.2   Results with Classification

To evaluate the automatic evaluation of handwriting, we perform a KNN-based classification on the test set. Tables 4 and 5 show the accuracy results obtained for three and two classes, respectively.

For three classes (legible, not very legible, illegible), we achieve a promising accuracy between 68.7–82.2%. For two classes (legible, illegible) the accuracy is even better, between 78.8–85.0% depending on the word. The improved accuracy for two classes is as expected, because the classification task is simplified, focusing only on the two extreme cases.

In all cases, the parameter set P2 is the best, which was optimized for the word "lunes" during validation. A possible explanation is that this word had the largest number of samples in the validation set, which leads to a more stable estimation of the optimal parameters. Overall, the results lie close together for all parameter sets, which means that there was not too much overfitting to a particular word during validation.

However, it is interesting to observe that the performance of handwriting evaluation is different for the three words. This motivates further studies to determine what kind of words, or characters, are best suited to automatically assess the learning progress of children with respect to legibility.

Table 4. Classification accuracy on the test set with three classes.

Parameters	Lundi	Lunes	Plumes
P1	0.753	0.693	0.667
P2	**0.822**	**0.730**	**0.687**
P3	0.810	0.720	0.657

Table 5. Classification accuracy on the test set with two classes.

Parameters	Lundi	Lunes	Plumes
P1	0.776	0.847	0.758
P2	**0.822**	**0.850**	**0.788**
P3	0.816	0.843	0.747

With respect to the first objective of our study (O1), we can summarize that the automatic evaluation of legibility corresponds well to human judgement but it leaves room for improvements regarding the classification accuracy.

4.3   Results with Clustering

To evaluate if the graph-based approach leads to meaningful groupings of the handwritten words, we focus on one of the words, "lundi", and use the same set of optimized meta-parameters that was established for the task of classification.

The Silhouette index [7,24] to assess the quality of the clustering produced. It is therefore possible to compare the results of clustering methods and algorithms, and also to determine the number of clusters to retain [4,5]. Figure 5 shows the evolution of the silhouette index as a function of the number of clusters k and the value of the index is higher for $k = 2$.

The next step is to analyse the content of the clusters produced using the classes assigned by the experts. Table 6 shows the frequency of ground truth labels in the clusters with $k = 2$ for all clustering methods. In order to simplify understanding of the table, the clustering algorithms producing the same distribution statistics have been grouped together (from A1 to A4).

A1 produces two clusters, gathering 75% of the words marked legible in C2 and up to 75% of the not very legible and illegible in C2. Algorithms A2 to A4 do not produce significant results, yet their silhouette index values are higher overall than those of A1.

With respect to the second objective of our study (O2), we can summarize that the graph-based dissimilarity leads to a generally good clustering quality. However, the legibility alone cannot explain the groupings that result from graph-based matching.

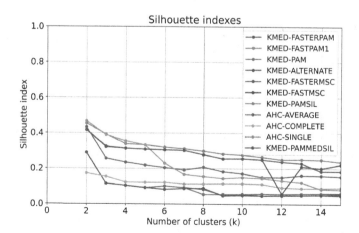

Fig. 5. Evolution of the silhouette index as a function of the number of clusters k from 2 to 15 for "lundi"; KMED and AHC algorithms were used with different configurations (PAM, FASTERPAM, AVERAGE, COMPLETE, etc.).

Table 6. Frequency of expert classes per cluster for each group of clustering algorithms for $k = 2$ (with A1: AHC-COMPLETE; A2: KMED-FATERPAM, KMED-FASTPAM1, KMED-PAM, KMED-ALTERNATE; A3: KMED-FASTERMSC, KMED-FASTMSC, KMED-PAMMEDSIL; A4: AHC-AVERAGE, AHC-SINGLE, KMED-PAMSIL).

Algorithm	Cluster	Expert classes (EC)		
		Legible	Not very legible	Illegible
A1	C1	0.255	**0.75**	**0.667**
	C2	**0.745**	0.25	0.333
A2	C1	0.34	0.333	0.333
	C2	0.659	0.667	0.667
A3	C1	0.021	0.083	0.048
	C2	0.979	0.917	0.952
A4	C1	0.007	0.0	0.0
	C2	0.993	1.0	1.0

5 Conclusion

In this paper, we have investigated graph-based representation of handwriting and graph matching for performing a visuo-structural evaluation of handwriting with respect to legibility.

The experimental evaluation demonstrates that the automatic method is well related to the judgment of human experts. For the two-class problem between legible and illegible, we report a classification accuracy between 79–85% depending on the word. For the three-class problem between legible, not very legible, and illegible, the performance drops but we still achieve an accuracy between 69–82%. Our clustering experiments have demonstrated that the graph-based similarity leads to clear groups of words but legibility on its own cannot explain these groupings.

It is noteworthy that the ground truth itself is ambiguous in the sense that also human experts tend to disagree on the legibility. In future work we aim to further improve the quality of the ground truth by including a larger number of experts. Such challenge can be supported by the crowdsourcing function of Copilotr@ce that has already been used by two of the three experts for this present study. Furthermore, we would like to include more diverse words in our study, as the accuracy varies among different words. It would also be interesting to perform the analysis at the level of patterns like characters rather than words, and to investigate what kind of words and characters are best suited to assess the handwriting quality. Finally, we would like to highlight that we have focused our investigation on one particular type of graph, keypoint graphs, and one particular type of graph matching, the Hausdorff edit distance. Thus, these non-language-dependent choices imply that our method is a priori suitable for any spelling and linguistic system and not only those of the French language. A promising line of research would be to investigate and compare other representation and matching paradigms in more detail for other languages such as, for example, Creole, English, Spanish which are those of the many allophone students schooled in Guadeloupe.

References

1. Bara, F., Gentaz, É., Colé, P.: Comment les enfants apprennent-ils à écrire et comment les y aider. Apprentissages et enseignement. Sciences cognitives et éducation, 9–24 (2006)
2. Bara, F., Morin, M.-F., Montésinos-Gelet, I., Lavoie, N.: Conceptions et pratiques en graphomotricité chez des enseignants de primaire en france et au québec. Revue française de pédagogie. Recherches en éducation (176), 41–56 (2011)
3. Barnett, L., Anna, M.P., Rosenblum, S.: Development of the handwriting legibility scale (HLS): a preliminary examination of reliability and validity. Res. Dev. Disabil. **72**, 240–247 (2018)
4. Biabiany, E., Bernard, D.C., Page, V., Paugam-Moisy, H.: Design of an expert distance metric for climate clustering: the case of rainfall in the lesser Antilles. Comput. Geosci. **145**, 104612 (2020)
5. Biabiany, E., Page, V., Bernard, D.C., Paugam-Moisy, H.: Using an expert deviation carrying the knowledge of climate data in usual clustering algorithms. In: CAP and RFAIP Joint Conferences, Vannes, May 2020
6. Conte, D., Foggia, P., Sansone, C., Vento, M.: Thirty years of graph matching in pattern recognition. Int. J. Pattern Recogn. Artif. Intell. **18**(3), 265–298 (2004)
7. Amorim, R.C.D., Hennig, C.: Recovering the number of clusters in data sets with noise features using feature rescaling factors. Inf. Sci. **324**, 126–145 (2015)
8. Erez, N., Parush, S.: The Hebrew handwriting evaluation. School of Occupational Therapy. Faculty of Medicine. Hebrew University of Jerusalem, Israel (1999)
9. Fischer, A., Riesen, K., Bunke, H.: Graph similarity features for HMM-based handwriting recognition in historical documents. In: Proceedings International Conference on Frontiers in Handwriting Recognition, pp. 253–258 (2010)
10. Fischer, A., Suen, C.Y., Frinken, V., Riesen, K., Bunke, H.: Approximation of graph edit distance based on Hausdorff matching. Pattern Recogn. **48**(2), 331–343 (2015)
11. Florence, B., Nathalie, B.-B.: Handwriting isolated cursive letters in young children: effect of the visual trace deletion. Learn. Instr. **74**, 101439 (2021)
12. Fogel, Y., Rosenblum, S., Barnett, A.L.: Handwriting legibility across different writing tasks in school-aged children. Hong Kong J. Occup. Ther. **35**(1), 44–51 (2022)
13. Hamdi, Y., Akouaydi, H., Boubaker, H., Alimi, A.M.: Handwriting quality analysis using online-offline models. Multimedia Tools Appl. **81**(30), 43411–43439 (2022)
14. Hamstra-Bletz, L., DeBie, J., Den Brinker, B.P.L.M., et al.: Concise evaluation scale for children's handwriting. Lisse Swets **1**, 623–662 (1987)
15. Larsen, S.C., Hammill, D.D.: Test of legible handwriting (Pro-Ed, Austin, TX) (1989)
16. Lenssen, L., Schubert, E.: Clustering by direct optimization of the medoid silhouette. In: Skopal, T., Falchi, F., Lokoč, J., Sapino, M.L., Bartolini, I., Patella, M. (eds.) Similarity Search and Applications, pp. 190–204. Springer, Cham (2022). https://doi.org/10.1007/978-3-031-17849-8_15

17. Li, T., Rezaeipanah, A., El Din, E.M.T.: An ensemble agglomerative hierarchical clustering algorithm based on clusters clustering technique and the novel similarity measurement. J. King Saud Univ. Comput. Inf. Sci. **34**(6, Part B), 3828–3842 (2022)

18. Maergner, P., et al.: Combining graph edit distance and triplet networks for offline signature verification. Pattern Recogn. Lett. **125**, 527–533 (2019)

19. Phelps, J., Stempel, L.: Handwriting: evolution and evaluation. Ann. Dyslexia **37**, 228–239 (1987)

20. Rémi, C., Nagau, J.: Copilotrace: a platform to process graphomotor tasks for education and graphonomics research. In: Carmona-Duarte, C., Díaz, M., Ferrer, M.A., Morales, A. (eds.) Intertwining Graphonomics with Human Movements - 20th International Conference of the International Graphonomics Society, IGS 2021, Las Palmas de Gran Canaria, Spain, 7–9 June 2022, Proceedings. LNCS, vol. 13424, pp. 129–143. Springer, Cham (2022). https://doi.org/10.1007/978-3-031-19745-1_10

21. Riba, P., Lladós, J., Fornés, A.: Handwritten word spotting by inexact matching of grapheme graphs. In: Proceedings 13th International Conference on Document Analysis and Recognition, pp. 781–785 (2015)

22. Rosenblum, S., Parush, S., Weiss, P.L.: Computerized temporal handwriting characteristics of proficient and non-proficient handwriters. Am. J. Occup. Ther. **57**(2), 129–138 (2003)

23. Rosenblum, S., Weiss, P.L., Parush, S.: Product and process evaluation of handwriting difficulties. Educ. Psychol. Rev. **15**, 41–81 (2003)

24. Rousseeuw, P.J.: Silhouettes: a graphical aid to the interpretation and validation of cluster analysis. Comput. Appl. Math. **20**, 53–65 (1987)

25. Schubert, E., Lenssen, L.: Fast K-medoids clustering in rust and Python. J. Open Source Softw. **7**(75), 4183 (2022)

26. Schubert, E., Rousseeuw, P.J.: Fast and eager K-medoids clustering: O(k) runtime improvement of the PAM, CLARA, and CLARANS algorithms. Inf. Syst. **101**, 101804 (2021)

27. Scius-Bertrand, A., Studer, L., Fischer, A., Bui, M.: Annotation-free keyword spotting in historical Vietnamese manuscripts using graph matching. In: Proceedings International Workshop on Structural and Syntactic Pattern Recognition (SSPR) (2022)

28. Soppelsa, R., Albaret, J.-M.: Evaluation de l'écriture chez l'adolescent. le bhk ado. Entretiens de Psychomotricité, 66–76 (2012)

29. Stauffer, M., Fischer, A., Riesen, K.: Graph-Based Keyword Spotting. World Scientific (2019)

30. Vinter, A., Chartrel, E.: Effects of different types of learning on handwriting movements in young children. Learn. Instr. **20**(6), 476–486 (2010)

Copilotr@ce Put to the Crowdsourcing Test

Keïla Gaëte, Céline Rémi[(⊠)], and Jimmy Nagau

Université des Antilles, B.P. 592, 97157 Pointe à Pitre Cedex, France
keila.gaete@etu.univ-antilles.fr, {celine.remi,
jimmy.nagau}@univ-antilles.fr

Abstract. Scientific research increasingly uses modern information-gathering methods such as crowdsourcing. There are several platforms that use the contribution of many individuals to perform specific tasks such as object identification in images. It is an interesting process to set up because it facilitates problem solving, analysis and data collection and knowledge sharing. Copilotr@ce is a platform set up for the analysis of graphomotor gestures. We show through an experiment still in progress the contributions of this tool for the implementation of crowdsourcing to meet the needs of annotation or evaluation of documents and graphomotor productions online.

Keywords: crowdsourcing · annotation · labeling · graphomotor gesture · online and offline images

1 Introduction

Crowdsourcing, defined by Howe J. [1], means the outsourcing of activities to the crowd, made up of different actors outside a project or company. It provides the possibility, with the participation of a large public, to conduct tasks that are not yet achievable by automated systems. Crowdsourcing makes it possible to collect a wide variety of data and to better represent or codify information on it. This practice is used to decipher historical documents that serve the conservation of cultural heritage [2]. It is also used to annotate histological plans or other medical images for the recognition of tumor foci [3]. In science, crowdsourcing can be defined as an online collaborative process, whereby scientists involve a group of self-selected individuals with varied knowledge and skills, via an open call on the internet or online platforms, to undertake specific research tasks [4].

There are several platforms where this practice is implemented, such as the Zooniverse platform [5], which offers a citizen science approach. This approach is exploited in a wide range of scientific research projects, requiring human input such as image classification or animal identification. There is also the Transcrire platform [6] which allows the collaborative transcription of historical documents.

The objective of this article is to provide answers to the following questions: Can Copilotr@ce be used for crowdsourcing purposes? If so, what would be the benefits of the use of Copilotr@ce? To answer these questions first, we will present this tool and its

A. Parziale et al. (Eds.): IGS 2023, LNCS 14285, pp. 89–100, 2023.
https://doi.org/10.1007/978-3-031-45461-5_7

initial uses. Then, we will see through an experiment how it can be exploited as part of a process exploiting the graphomotor gesture for the annotation or labeling of documents or images acquired online. We will then specify two concrete cases of use of the result of this experiment. Finally, the contributions and limitations of the use of Copilotr@ce will be discussed before concluding.

2 Presentation of Copilotr@ce and Its First Uses

Copilotr@ce is a web application for capturing handwritten gesture available on any type of screen material (smartphone, tablet, computer, etc.). It is presented as a digital notebook that makes it possible to acquire online, organize, preserve, and evaluate traces of activities mobilizing graphomotor gestures [7]. Copilotr@ce is designed as a "Progressive Web Application" available through the following path: https://copilotrace.univ-ant illes.fr. Initially, the Copilotr@ce platform was developed for use in graphomotricity research, but also in the education system for learning. A teacher or a pool of teachers, as accompanists, administer and manage groups of students, the scripters, after the creation of their accounts. The scripters can then conduct activities with precise instructions, chosen by the accompanying persons, on the different devices with different tools (fingers, pen, etc.). This leads to the creation of graphomotor productions whose traces are subject to automatic or human analysis. In the case of use for research as in that of use for human learning, these analyses can deal with different topics depending on the nature of the activity and the educational objectives pursued. They may relate to procedural skills related, for example, to the management of pen lifts [8] or qualitative aspects of traces or implementation procedures [9]. Their subject may also concern the fluidity and regularity of graphomotor gestures [10] or biomechanical behavior by focusing on the control of the pressure or orientation of the scripting tool if the equipment allows it. Tablet browsers can provide high-precision data. This is possible thanks to hardware acceleration that offers processing speeds close to those of software implemented in a native language to operating systems. The use case diagram for the most recent version of Copilotr@ce, in Fig. 1, shows two new usage profiles that complement the accompanist and writer profiles. The first profile, that of experimenter, is useful in situations of design and experimentation for pedagogical purposes or research activities of evaluation of aspects not directly perceptible by Copilotr@ce during a pedagogical activity. This is the case, for example, of the enthusiasm or physical pain felt by the student during pedagogical activities he has completed. The second profile, that of evaluator, is for example useful in situations of manual annotation of offline or online images of traces of a graphomotor activity produced by each learner during phases of acquisition or reinforcement of skills.

This profile, depending on whether it is endorsed by the student or the teacher, can make it possible to create and manage in the Copilotr@ce ecosystem pedagogical situations of self-evaluation, peer evaluation or evaluation by the teacher of graphomotor gestures and their results.

In the case of a use for the implementation of a crowdsourcing approach of a task of labeling graphomotor acts captured in the form of online images, it is also these two profiles of experimenter and evaluator that can be used. The application section below illustrates the principle in a concrete case before detailing two examples of use of the dataset then built.

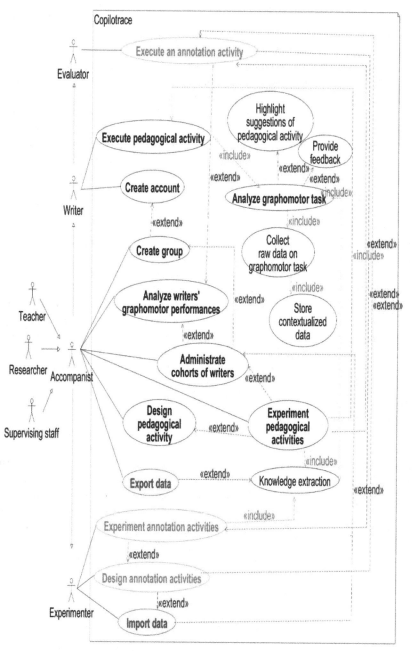

Fig. 1. Copilotr@ce use case diagram with scripter, accompanist, experimenter, and evaluator profiles

3 Application

3.1 First Crowdsourcing Experience Initiated with Copilotr@ce

To demonstrate the possibilities of propelling crowdsourcing actions of Copilotr@ce, an experiment aimed at the participatory labeling of offline images was initiated. These images were generated by Copilotr@ce from the online signals acquired along pupils' execution of pedagogical activities. Those signals represent the traces of children's graphomotor behaviors when they have copied isolated cursive words [7]. To initiate this experiment, a call for voluntary participation was launched to a population of students enrolled in a bachelor's degree at the University of the West Indies via the educational network of this institution. This experience has since been opened to both student and teacher members from other educational communities. The common point between these various populations is that they regularly mobilize or examine graphic traces resulting from the production of graphomotor writing gestures.

Under the procedure shown in Fig. 2, two tasks are assigned to the crowd of volunteer participants. Each of these tasks can be performed anonymously, directly in the Chrome, Edge, Firefox, or Safari browser, from a visual examination of the images of drawn words, without any other knowledge of the context in which they are produced.

Task (1) shown in Fig. 2 consists of delimiting the letters in each visualized plot by means of vertical handwritten lines. Task (2) consists of filling in all or part of a set of criteria relating to the visual quality of the observed traces. These criteria relate to legibility, respect for proportions, alignment, linking, presence, and order of letters within the handwritten path produced as well as its conformity to the model.

For compliance checking, the template proposed to the writer when performing the write task is displayed on the screen for the evaluator. Figure 3 illustrates this display for each of the four words: "lundi" (Monday), "mardi" (Tuesday), "lunes" (moons) and "plumes" (feathers).

Each evaluator contributes anonymously to the crowd of volunteers involved in this crowdsourcing operation dedicated to the qualitative labeling and annotation of graphomotor productions. The evaluator freely chooses the tasks he performs, he can annotate, label each of the words he chooses to evaluate or do both.

It should be noted that any word that will be evaluated by an evaluator during a session will no longer be presented during this same session. This choice associated with a substantial number of participants can maximize the chances that the opinions issued for the same word will not all be issued by a single member of the crowd of reviewers.

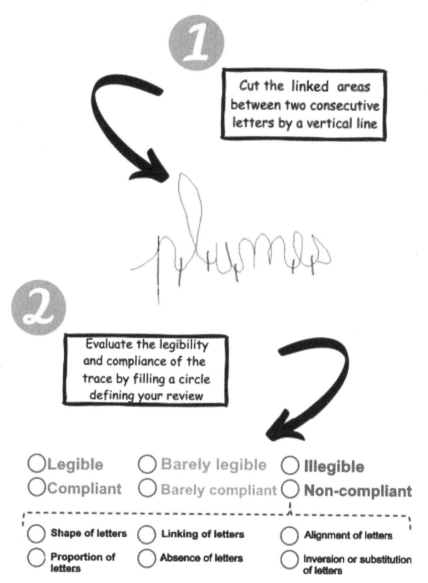

Fig. 2. Word Path Labeling Procedure

94   K. Gaëte et al.

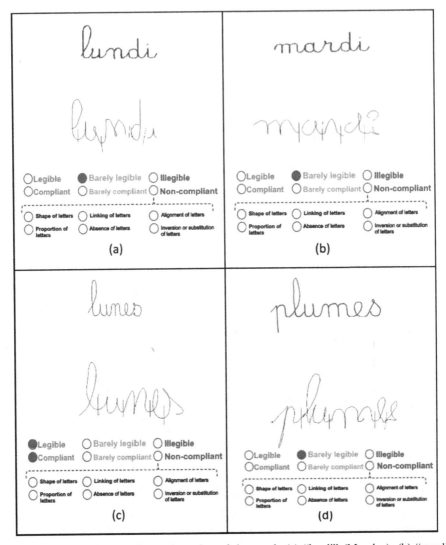

Fig. 3. Examples of annotation and tagging of the words (a) "lundi" (Monday), (b) "mardi" (Tuesday), (c) "lunes" (moons) and (d) "plumes" (feathers).

During each evaluation, the evaluator mobilizes a specific type of graphomotor gesture that he can perform with his finger or stylus for each type of task. This is the graphomotor gesture of pointing in the case of labeling, consisting in assigning a value to each of the eight qualitative criteria. The annotation mobilizes the graphomotor gesture of handwritten stroke for the segmentation of the letters identified by the evaluator within the word trace. The result of each of these labeling and annotation tasks is saved as an online image for each trace. It is thus possible to replay each evaluation process implemented by an evaluator via Copilotr@ce. It is also possible to exploit an online annotation either to guide automatic processing such as the letter-based segmentation of words acquired online or to evaluate the performance of such processing by comparing them with human perceptual data generated by the crowd of evaluators. Labels are saved in a structured way. Thus, they can be used to ground truths. When evaluating a trace, in addition to saving the trace and annotations in an offline state, the sequence of traces made by the evaluator as part of his or her evaluation process is also preserved through parameters such as the spatial position of the point of contact between the writing tool and the tactile surface, pressure, dating, etc. This information helps to define the evaluator's intention or complete the evaluation data.

3.2 Provisional Assessment of this Copilotr@ce Crowdsourcing Experiment

We have established a provisional assessment of this initiated experiment which is still underway at the beginning of May 2023. As participation is anonymous, without user authentication, we were able to estimate the number of participants at least 110 students. Table 1 provides data describing the provisional result of this in progress experiment. Table 2 provides the rates for diverse types of devices and browsers used by the evaluators.

Table 1. Data describing the provisional result of this crowdsourcing experiment.

Template	lunes	mardi	lundi	plumes	Total
Total number of annotation-labelling sessions performed	953	530	987	877	3347
Number of tracks labeled by at least one evaluator	168	88	309	63	628

Table 2. Rates (%) of each type of device and browser used during the sessions of evaluation.

Type of devices	Firefox	Opera	Chrome	Total
Computer	95,1	89,7	80,5	82,9
Tablet	0,0	1,6	0,1	0,5
Smartphone	4,9	8,8	19,3	16,6
All types	0,6	24,9	74,6	100,0

Tables 3, 4, 5, 6, 7, 8, 9, 10 provide the overall labeling rates achieved by word model with each of the values of the criteria: compliance, readability, presence, order alignment, ligature, proportions, and shape of letters.

At this stage of the evaluation process by the crowd of evaluators, Tables 3, 4 and 5 show that "lundi" (Monday) is the model for which handwritten words were most frequently deemed illegible and non-compliant. Moreover, the rate of the criterion absence of letters into handwritten words was twice greater for this model that had to be reproduced. Last, whatever the model, weak compliance like uncompliance were not factors that annihilated de facto readability of handwritten words by evaluators.

Table 3. Evaluation rates per word for values of the criterion compliance to the model.

Value of annotation	lundi	mardi	lunes	plumes	Total
Compliant	18,54%	14,15%	19,10%	20,87%	18,61%
Not very compliant	32,42%	42,26%	39,14%	36,72%	37,02%
Non-compliant	**42,96%**	36,79%	33,37%	34,78%	37,11%
No opinion	6,08%	6,79%	8,39%	7,64%	7,26%

Table 4. Evaluation rates per word for values of the criterion readability.

Value of annotation	lundi	mardi	lunes	plumes	Total
Readable	43,26%	43,40%	46,38%	55,07%	47,27%
Not very readable	25,84%	30,75%	29,38%	24,06%	27,16%
Unreadable	**23,30%**	19,43%	17,00%	16,42%	19,09%
No opinion	7,60%	6,42%	7,24%	4,45%	6,48%

Tables 6, 7, 8, 9, 10 show that the template "plumes" is the word for which defects in ligature, proportion, alignment, and shape of the letters were most often reported. The shape of letters criterion is in the case of model "lunes" the criterion for which there are equivalent rates of opinions on both sides. In the case of the models "mardi" and "plumes" the rates of incorrect shapes of letters are more than eleven points greater than the rate of correct shapes.

Table 5. Evaluation rates per word for values of the criterion presence of letters.

Value of annotation	lundi	mardi	lunes	plumes	Total
Absence of letters	**26,55%**	11,89%	17,00%	6,61%	16,28%
Letters expected present	73,45%	88,11%	83,00%	93,39%	83,72%

Table 6. Evaluation rates per word for values of the criterion order of letters.

Value of annotation	lundi	mardi	lunes	plumes	Total
Incorrect order of letters	3,24%	2,45%	1,78%	**6,39%**	3,53%
Correct order of letters	96,76%	97,55%	98,22%	93,61%	96,47%

Table 7. Evaluation rates per word for values of the criterion alignment of letters.

Value of annotation	lundi	mardi	lunes	plumes	Total
Incorrect letter alignment	20,67%	22,83%	21,83%	**33,87%**	24,80%
Correct letter alignment	79,33%	77,17%	78,17%	66,13%	75,20%

Table 8. Evaluation rates per word for values of the criterion ligature of letters.

Value of annotation	lundi	mardi	lunes	plumes	Total
Incorrect ligature	23,61%	31,70%	23,40%	**36,60%**	28,23%
Correct ligature	76,39%	68,30%	76,60%	63,40%	71,77%

Table 9. Evaluation rates per word for values of the criterion proportion of letters.

Value of annotation	lundi	mardi	lunes	plumes	Total
Incorrect proportions	26,95%	33,40%	34,42%	**38,88%**	33,22%
Correct proportions	73,05%	66,60%	65,58%	61,12%	66,78%

Table 10. Evaluation rates per word for values of the criterion shape of letters.

Value of annotation	lundi	mardi	lunes	plumes	Total
Incorrect letter shapes	42,05%	55,28%	51,84%	**56,78%**	50,79%
Correct letter shapes	57,95%	44,72%	48,16%	43,22%	49,21%

3.3 Potential Application of Dataset Built from this Crowdsourcing Experiment

The dataset produced thanks to this first still-in-progress crowdsourcing experiment could be considered by studies concerned by automated qualitative evaluation of children's handwriting behaviors. The first we should initiate concerns the automated evaluation of readability. The second one should concern the potential impacts of the procedure for performing pen lifts while writing, in the case of the Latin cursive script on the visual qualities of pupils' productions. In such study it would be necessary to consider all the eight criteria that are evaluated, while they are related to qualitative expectations on visual and orthographic students' productions [11–13].

4 Discussion

We have shown through the experiment presented that Copilotr@ce can allow the massive collection of information on visual supports by third-party evaluators through the implementation of the principle of crowdsourcing. The media then submitted for evaluation can take the form of offline images representing text, photographs, sketches, tables, or formulas or even composite documents structured of any kind from an informational point of view. Media can also take the form of online images or offline image sequences representing dynamic content. As part of the propelled collection operations, Copilotr@ce offers the possibility of affixing contexts that enrich the content to be evaluated. Thus, Copilotr@ce allows two types of information collection on the data carriers made available to participants: labeling and annotation.

- Labeling is the simplest case where a form with a checkbox will appear superimposed on the medium to be evaluated,
- In the case of annotation, the graphomotor gesture capture functions of Copilotr@ce are invoked. Handwritten annotation traces (write, bind, strike, circle, etc.) are performed by the overlay evaluator on the display surface of the data carried to be evaluated. The collection of the evaluator's opinion for archiving is enabled by automatic approaches for image processing and analysis.

The originality in these two types of collection conducted using the Copilotr@ce application lies in the conservation of the sequences of points captured during the evaluation. These points describe the sequences of the evaluator's actions. The context of the acquisition of an evaluator's opinions is therefore preserved. It will allow the extraction of properties that could describe the commitment of the evaluator during the experiment such as the time taken to perform an action, the ordering of the actions performed as well as the modifications of choices made that can for example reflect hesitation, doubt, etc. These data can be useful to evaluate a posteriori of a campaign, the confidence to be given to certain opinions compared to others or to exclude certain media from a database to be exploited.

5 Conclusion

This article presents how Copilotr@ce can contribute to the implementation of participatory activities called crowdsourcing, where individuals can label or annotate graphomotor productions. Reviewers may be anonymous users or individuals with access to hyperlinks to perform these reviews. These evaluators will make handwritten remarks on the productions, on the different devices and the tools at their disposal. The assessments and acquired data are then retained and can be used. Copilotr@ce also offers new possibilities to import documents and images compatible with the application. Users also have the choice to create their own canvas for annotation and tagging activities. These activities can be deployed and shared so that the crowd of mobilized evaluators complements them. To become a member of the crowd of volunteers involved in a crowdsourcing experience powered by Copilotr@ce, it is enough to be a human being who can read, write and be able:

- To perceive the visuospatial organization of the constituent elements of the presented traces,
- To issue opinions by choosing among the proposed criteria values,
- To mobilize the types of simple graphomotor gestures necessary to conduct each of the planned labeling and annotation tasks.

We have shown that the modalities of implementation via Copilotr@ce of crowdsourcing experiments allow the production of datasets and field truths. These can be useful for reflective practices of studying the effects of pedagogical practices based on image analysis (online or offline) of graphomotor productions of cohorts of students. They can also be useful for learning or evaluating the performance of object, word, or other static or dynamic pattern recognition models, such as procedures from online or offline images. The principle of implementing crowdsourcing can therefore be implemented via the Copilotr@ce platform to involve a large audience of contributors for the collection and enrichment of information. This represents a significant real time saving for each of these two contexts of exploration, use and processing of the products of graphomotor gestures.

The first crowdsourcing experiment is still active. Others can be deployed on an experimental basis according to the needs of actors in the educational or research communities, as the pattern recognition one.

Copilotr@ce can easily position itself, within the framework of a crowdsourcing project, between the data to be analyzed, evaluated, and collected, and the extraction of knowledge from this data with the aim of moving towards automation. Crowdsourcing begins within the framework of a project where the objective is to collect information to compensate for a lack of data. The data gathered through crowdsourcing then gives rise to analysis, processing, and knowledge extraction, leading in the best case to automatic decisions based on the wealth of knowledge available to the public. In this context, a time-consuming process can be put in place, initially to define the steps involved in implementing the data organization, collection, and evaluation methodology. At the end of this first process comes the implementation of the IT mechanisms to achieve this. Copilotr@ce, with its focus on capturing and analyzing handwritten gestures, can facilitate the implementation of these points by offering a collection platform that can be tailored to the objectives defined within an application.

Acknowledgment. We would like to extend our heartfelt appreciation to the students, teachers and participants who have contributed to the evaluation campaigns.

References

1. Howe, J.: The Rise of Crowdsourcing. Wired Mag. **14**(6), 134–145 (2006)
2. Granell Romero, E., Martínez Hinarejos, C.D.: Multimodal crowdsourcing for transcribing handwritten documents. IEEE/ACM Trans. Audio Speech Lang. Process. **25**(2), 409–419 (2017). https://doi.org/10.1109/TASLP.2016.2634123
3. Irshad, H., et al.: Crowdsourcing image annotation for nucleus detection and segmentation in computational pathology: evaluating experts, automated methods, and the crowd. In: Pacific Symposium on Biocomputing, pp. 294–305 (2014). https://doi.org/10.13140/2.1.4067.0721

4. Lenart-Gansiniec, R., Czakon, W., Sułkowski, Ł, Pocek, J.: Understanding crowdsourcing in science. RMS (2022). https://doi.org/10.1007/s11846-022-00602-z

5. Zooniverse Homepage. https://www.zooniverse.org/. Accessed 5 June 2023

6. Transcrire Homepage. https://transcrire.huma-num.fr/. Accessed 15 June 2023

7. Rémi, C., Nagau, J.: Copilotrace: a platform to process graphomotor tasks for education and graphonomics research. In: Carmona-Duarte, C., Diaz, M., Angel Ferrer, M., Morales, A. (eds.) 20th International Conference of the International Graphonomics Society 2022, LNCS, vol. 13424, pp. 129–143. Springer, Heidelberg (2022). https://doi.org/10.1007/978-3-031-19745-1_10

8. Rémi, C., Nagau, J., Vaillant, J., Plamondon, R.: Could sigma-lognormal modeling help teachers to characterize the kinematic efficiency of Pupils' cursive procedures of handwriting? In: Plamondon, R., Marcelli, A., Ferrer, M.A. (eds.) The Lognormality Principle and its Applications in e-Security, e-Learning, and e-Health, pp. 87–116. World Scientific Publishing Company (2020). https://doi.org/10.1142/9789811226830_0004

9. Renau-Ferrer, N., Rémi, C.: Procedural analysis of a sketching activity: principles and applications. In: 2012 International Conference on Frontiers in Handwriting Recognition, pp. 461–466. Institute of Electrical and Electronics Engineers (IEEE), Bari, Italy (2012). https://doi.org/10.1109/ICFHR.2012.255

10. Duval, T., Remi, C., Prevost, L., Dorville, A., Plamondon, R.: Etude de la faisabilité de l'évaluation de l'efficacité des mouvements de tracé du jeune apprenti-scripteur. Feasibility study of evaluating the effectiveness of tracing movements in young apprentice writers. In: 26th French-speaking Conference on Human-Computer Interaction, Lille, France, pp. 29–37 (2014)

11. Guinet, E., Kandel, S.: Ductus: a software package for the study of handwriting production. Behav. Res. Methods 42(1), 326–332 (2010). https://doi.org/10.3758/BRM.42.1.326

12. Chartrel, E., Vinter, A.: The impact of spatio-temporal constraints on cursive letter handwriting in children. Learn. Instr. 18(6), 537–547 (2008). https://doi.org/10.1016/j.learninstruc.2007.11.003

13. Bara, F., Morin, M.F.: Does the handwriting style learnt in first grade determine the style learned in fourth and fifth grade and influence handwriting speed and quality? A comparison between French and Quebecker children. Psychol. Sch. 50(6), 601–617 (2013). https://doi.org/10.1002/pits.21691

Handwriting for Neurodegenerative Disorders

A Machine Learning Approach to Analyze the Effects of Alzheimer's Disease on Handwriting Through Lognormal Features

Tiziana D'Alessandro[2]([✉]), Cristina Carmona-Duarte[1], Claudio De Stefano[2], Moises Diaz[1], Miguel Angel Ferrer[1], and Francesco Fontanella[2]

[1] IDeTIC: Instituto para el Desarrollo Tecnológico y la Innovación en Comunicaciones, Universidad de Las Palmas de Gran Canaria, Las Palmas de Gran Canaria, Spain
[2] Department of Electrical and Information Engineering (DIEI), University of Cassino and Southern Lazio, Via G. Di Biasio 43, 03043 Cassino, FR, Italy
tiziana.dalessandro@unicas.it

Abstract. Alzheimer's disease is one of the most incisive illnesses among the neurodegenerative ones, and it causes a progressive decline in cognitive abilities that, in the worst cases, becomes severe enough to interfere with daily life. Currently, there is no cure, so an early diagnosis is strongly needed to try and slow its progression through medical treatments. Handwriting analysis is considered a potential tool for detecting and understanding certain neurological conditions, including Alzheimer's disease. While handwriting analysis alone cannot provide a definitive diagnosis of Alzheimer's, it may offer some insights and be used for a comprehensive assessment. The Sigma-lognormal model is conceived for movement analysis and can also be applied to handwriting. This model returns a set of lognormal parameters as output, which forms the basis for the computation of novel and significant features. This paper presents a machine learning approach applied to handwriting features extracted through the sigma-lognormal model. The aim is to develop a support system to help doctors in the diagnosis and study of Alzheimer, evaluate the effectiveness of the extracted features and finally study the relation among them.

1 Introduction

Neurodegenerative diseases are characterized by the progressive degeneration of neurons in the brain; they are irreversible and can affect cognitive and physical abilities. Due to the life-lengthening, they are becoming increasingly common, but one of them has a higher incidence: Alzheimer's disease (AD). AD provokes a progressive decline in mental functions, affecting several skills, such as memory, thought, judgment and learning. Currently, there is no resolution cure, but medical treatments can help manage the symptoms and slow the progression

A. Parziale et al. (Eds.): IGS 2023, LNCS 14285, pp. 103–121, 2023.
https://doi.org/10.1007/978-3-031-45461-5_8

of AD, improving the quality of life of patients and their family. The effectiveness of those medications is not the same for every person, and it is potentially correlated to the time AD is first detected. This means that the time when the diagnosis is made is crucial; the earliest, the better. These reasons led researchers to continuously investigate new techniques and methods to take care of as early as possible. Handwriting is known to be one of the first skills to suffer impairment because of AD, as it is the result of both cognitive and movement skills, and it also requires spatial organization and good coordination. Therefore, the study of handwriting can provide a cheap and completely non-invasive way to evaluate the AD insurgence or progression [1–3]. Machine learning (ML) is a subcategory of artificial intelligence that focuses on developing algorithms and models that allow computers to learn from data and make predictions without being explicitly programmed. In recent years, the application of this technology has seen widespread adoption across various fields, including handwriting analysis, motor function rehabilitation, and advancements in the field of medicine [4,5]. The wide spread of technologies aimed to record movements and their kinematics, such as tablets or watches, led researchers to support the diagnosis and the treatment of AD [6–10]. In this research, we analysed the handwriting through the Kinematic Theory of rapid movements by applying the Sigma-Lognormal model, for which every complex movement can be decomposed into a vector summation of simple time-overlapped movements [11–13]. This theory can be applied in many fields for movement modelling, such as speech [14], but also handwriting [15–17] and neuromuscular disorders [18–21].

This research aims to develop a classification system for AD diagnosis based on handwriting features extracted by applying the sigma-lognormal model, extending the set computed in [22]. We study the effectiveness of those features through a set of ML experiments detailed in the following sections and discuss the obtained results.

The paper is organized as follows: Sect. 2 describes the Sigma-lognormal model, in Sect. 3.1, we present the tasks used to collect handwriting data and the features extracted using the Sigma-lognormal model. Section 4 details the experimental workflow, its results and features findings. Section 5 outlines concluding remarks and possible future investigations.

2   The Sigma-Lognormal Model

The Sigma-Lognormal model allows the decomposition of rapid movements into a vector summation of simple time-overlapped movements and focuses on the Kinematic Theory of rapid movements [11–13]. This assumption led to the development of several algorithms, and in this work, we adopted the IDeLog algorithm [23].

The Sigma-Lognormal model characterizes the resulting velocity of each individual fast movement primitive by utilizing a lognormal function, which represents the velocity peaks situated between two minimum speeds, effectively modelling the velocity profile:

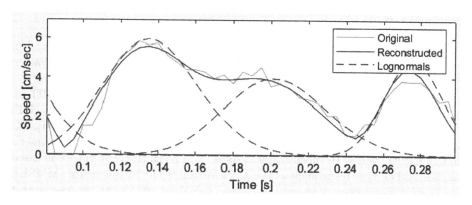

Fig. 1. Comparison between the original (green) and the reconstructed (blue) velocity profile. Dotted blue lines show the lognormal functions that generated the reconstructed profile. (Color figure online)

$$v_j(t; t_{0_j}, \mu_j, \sigma_j^2) = D_j \Lambda(t; t_{0_j}, \mu_j, \sigma_j^2) = \frac{D_j}{\sigma_j \sqrt{2\pi}(t - t_{0_j})} exp\{\frac{[-ln(t - t_{0_j}) - \mu_j]^2}{2\sigma_j^2}\}$$

(1)

where t is the time basis, D_j the amplitude, t_{0_j} the time of occurrence, μ_j the log-time delay and σ_j the response log-time. The lognormal parameters, t_{0_j}, μ_j and σ_j^2 are calculated and adjusted by iterative interactions between the original trajectory profile and the reconstructed one to minimize the error between the reconstructed lognormal and the original velocity profile.

Figure 1, illustrates a case of a rapid movement, and as it is the succession of M simple movements, its velocity profile is obtained from the time superposition of M lognormals:

$$v_n(t) = \sum_{j=1}^{M} v_j(t; t_{0_j}, \mu_j, \sigma_j^2) = \sum_{j=1}^{M} D_j \begin{bmatrix} \cos(\Phi_j(t)) \\ \sin(\Phi_j(t)) \end{bmatrix} \Lambda(t; t_{0_j}, \mu_j, \sigma_j^2)$$

(2)

where $\Phi_j(t)$ is the angular position given by:

$$\Phi_j(t) = \Theta_{s_j} + \frac{(\Theta_{e_j} - \Theta_{s_j})}{2}[1 + erf(\frac{ln(t - t_{0_j}) - \mu_j}{\sigma_j \sqrt{2}})]$$

(3)

being Θ_{s_j} and Θ_{e_j} are the starting and the end angular direction of the jth simple movement.

3   Description

This Section details the handwriting tasks considered, how they were acquired and the features extracted through the sigma-lognormal model.

3.1   Data Collection

The data collection comes from the execution of a protocol [24] composed of different kinds of handwriting tasks. They were performed with the Wacom Bamboo Folio tablet. Such a tool allows recording the handwriting in terms of $x-y$ spatial coordinates and pressure p, for each point at a sampling rate of 200 Hz. A total of 174 people were involved in the acquisition phase, 89 patients (PT) suffering from AD and a healthy control group (HC) of 85 people. Participants were selected with the support of the geriatrics department and Alzheimer's unit of the "Federico II" hospital in Naples. The recruiting criteria were based on standard clinical tests, such as the Mini-Mental State Examination (MMSE), the Frontal Assessment Battery (FAB) and the Montreal Cognitive Assessment (MoCA).

3.2   Tasks

This research aims to check which task performs best with our system and understand if the sigma-lognormal model and the extracted features are adequate for our problem. This reasoning led us to consider the data collected from each task execution to test our experimental setting. In [24] is detailed the protocol used and the 25 tasks that made it. The choice of tasks was based on literature to analyze different aspects of handwriting and the deterioration of the skills required to perform them. Every task requires different abilities that AD may compromise, like cognitive, kinesthetic and perceptive-motor functions [25], such as language comprehension, muscle control, spatial organization and coordination. Four different groups of tasks can be distinguished in the protocol, taking into account their objectives:

- Graphic tasks to test the patient's ability in writing elementary traits, joining some points and drawing figures (simple or complex and scaled in various dimensions).
- Copy and Reverse Copy tasks, to test the patient's abilities in repeating complex graphic gestures with a semantic meaning, such as letters, words and numbers (of different lengths and with different spatial organizations).
- Memory tasks, to test the variation of the graphic section, keep a word, a letter, a graphic gesture or a motor planning in memory.
- Dictation, to investigate how the writing in the task varies (with phrases or numbers) in which the use of the working memory is necessary.

There is a rationale behind the choice of every subgroup of tasks that comes from the study of the symptoms of Alzheimer's [24]. It's known that this disease's effects can change from person to person. Some people show more impairment on the mental side, others on the muscular side, and many people can also find compensation for them, mostly for the physical ones. With its 25 tasks, this protocol means to study if the handwriting is altered by Alzheimer's, taking into account its symptoms.

3.3 Feature Engineering

The feature engineering process was done taking into account the outcomes from [16,17], but also several studies about the normative range of variations in the lognormal parameters, which give a notion of how an ideal movement could be [26], based on lognormal movement decomposition. In this way, it was possible to extract a wide set of features that could be exhaustive to characterize one person's handwriting and, in particular, to enhance an eventual difference between the execution of a person affected by Alzheimer's and healthy control. The first step of this process is applying the Sigma-Lognormal model, defined in Sect. 2, to the data acquired as mentioned in Sect. 3.1. As a result, every task was decomposed into a vector summation of simple time-overlapped movements, for each one is associated with a lognormal function and a set of Sigma-Lognormal parameters was obtained $P_j = [D_j, t_{0_j}, \mu_j, \sigma_j, \theta_{s_j}, \theta_{e_j}]$, where j refers to the jth lognormal. From each task execution, we only processed points from the first time the pen touched the paper to the last time (first and last pen-down), as the tool also record movements when the person is approaching for the first time to the paper or is leaving it for the last time. This step was necessary to clean the data from those movements that don't belong to the execution of the task but precede or follow the real handwriting gesture we meant to analyze. Once obtained the sigma-lognormal parameters three groups of features were computed, related to different aspects and measures of the handwriting execution:

1. Time: features that represent temporal aspects of the execution, such as total time to execute a task, contact time, that is, the portion of total time in which the movements were performed without losing contact with the tablet, it means that the pen was at a maximum distance of 3 cm from the tablet surface. The remaining portion of the total time is the losing time. Some of these features are also related to the number of lognormals counted in the reconstructed velocity profile. This information is usually proportionally related to the task and the time of execution;
2. Signal-to-noise ratio (SNR): this measure, and features related to it, give the information of the goodness of the reconstructed trace (SNRt) and velocity profile (SNRv) from the sigma-lognormal model;
3. Geometric shapes of the reconstructed speed profile: they are useful to understand the movements' velocity, stability and fluency. Some features are computed starting from the lognormal parameters D and σ; others are from geometrical shapes (area, height and width) of lognormals in the reconstructed velocity profile. In detail, with the term area, we refer to the overlapping area between two consecutive lognormal, while height is the maximum and width is the base of a lognormal function [17].

Tables 1 and 2 show the computed features, whose name is written in the form of fxx next to their explanation. This step aims to understand if AD can be estimated using the features extracted from handwriting movements through the sigma-lognormal model. Besides the aforementioned features group, we also used personal features in the experiments: age, gender, education and type of profession. Alzheimer's effects lead to the choice of every group of features. Temporal features are interesting because a person who is impaired should take more time to execute a task and, according to the illness progression level, also more losing time. The latter is the amount of time the person lifted the pen too far from the tablet to be detected, maybe because of fatigue or distraction. Among the time features, there is also the number of lognormal generated from the velocity profile and the number of segments, where each segment refers to an entire trace acquired without losing contact. We expect all the temporal features to be higher for people affected by AD. The signal-to-noise ratio measures the reconstruction quality and, when divided by the number of lognormals is useful to describe how fluent a movement is [16]. Geometrical features are computed starting from three sequences: overlapping areas, heights and widths of the lognormal functions. They give us information about the fluency of the handwriting: the greater the overlapping area, the more fluent the handwriting, without strong deceleration or pauses. The height is proportional to the speed, while a larger width denotes a slower movement. Among the geometrical features, some related to the lognormal parameters D and sigma give information about the lognormal distance covered in the kinematic space and the lognormal response time. Understanding how those measures change during a handwriting task or relating them to the temporal feature can provide valuable information.

Table 1. Time and SNR related features.

Features			
TIME		SNR	
f1	number of lognormals	f15	mean(SNRt)
f2	number of segments	f16	std(SNRt)
f3	task total time	f17	mean(SNRv)
f4	contact time	f18	std(SNRv)
f5	losing time	f19	sum(SNRt)/f1
f6	standard deviation of seg. time	f20	f15/f1
f7	f3/f2	f21	f16/f1
f8	f3/f1	f22	sum(SNRv)/f1
f9	f4/f2	f23	f17/f1
f10	f4/f1	f24	f18/f1
f11	f5/f2		
f12	f5/f1		
f13	mean(number of log.s per seg.)		
f14	std(number of log.s per seg.)		

Table 2. Geometrical features.

Features					
GEOMETRICAL					
f25	std(areas)	f39	mean(areas)/f25	f53	dif(widths)/1
f26	std(heights)	f40	mean(heights)*exp(f26)	f54	dev(widths)/1
f27	std(widths)	f41	mean(heights)*ln(f26)	f55	'seg_difA_div_nlog'
f28	sum(areas)/f3	f42	mean(heights)/f26	f56	'std_seg_difA_div_nlog'
f29	sum(areas)/f4	f43	mean(widths)*exp(f27)	f57	dif(sigma)/f1
f30	sum(areas)/f1	f44	mean(widths)*ln(f27)	f58	std(sigma)/f1
f31	sum(heights)/f3	f45	mean(widths)/f27	f59	dif(sigma)/f4
f32	sum(heights)/f4	f46	f25/f4	f60	std(sigma)/f4
f33	sum(heights)/f1	f47	f26/f4	f61	dif(D)/f1
f34	sum(widths)/f3	f48	f27/f4	f62	std(D)/f1
f35	sum(widths)/f4	f49	dif(areas)/f1	f63	dif(D)/f4
f36	sum(widths)/f1	f50	std(areas)/f1	f64	std(D)/f4
f37	mean(areas)*exp(f25)	f51	dif(heights)/f1		
f38	mean(areas)*ln(f25)	f52	std(heights)/f1		

4 Experimental Phase

This section describes the experimental phase of the research and the results achieved. The experiments were carried out relying on classical machine learning techniques and algorithms. The following subsection illustrates the adopted workflow.

4.1 Workflow

The previous feature extraction step, discussed in Sect. 3.3, generated a set of several features for every task, so every task has its dataset. The workflow adopted can be better discussed considering a three-step approach, discussed in the following and shown in Fig. 2.

First Step: ML Classification. For the first step, we chose seven well-known classification algorithms to perform a classification for every task dataset: XGBoost (XGB), Random Forest (RF), Decision Tree (DT), Support Vector Machine (SVM), Multilayer Perceptron (MLP), K-Nearest Neighbors (KNN), Logistic Regression (LR). Before proceeding with the training, we applied three ML techniques to increase the discriminative power of our system:

- Feature scaling;
- Grid search;
- Feature Selection: RFECV/SelectKBest.

The grid search procedure was carried out with 50% of data randomly selected from the whole dataset. Once the best set of hyperparameters and features for every algorithm was obtained, the training started one task at a time. In detail, we randomly divided the dataset into train and test sets, assigning to each set 50% of the total samples, keeping the balance between the two classes of the problem: Healthy Controls (HC) and Patients (PT). Thirty random runs were performed to obtain more reliable and robust performance estimates for the classifier, and the final results were averaged over the thirty runs.

Second Step: Stacking. The second step of our classification approach is a stacking technique [27]. It is an ML approach, a stacked generalization or ensemble stacking. It combines the predictions of multiple models or base learners to create a more powerful and accurate final prediction. It involves training multiple diverse models on the same dataset and then using a "meta-learner" to learn from the predictions of these base models. We considered this technique to increase the predictive power and robustness of our system. By combining multiple models, in fact, you can leverage their complementary strengths and reduce their individual weaknesses, potentially capturing complex relationships and patterns in the data. Given these assumptions, we used the output prediction provided by the classifiers of the first step. In particular, we merged the responses obtained for all the tasks so that the new feature vector for each sample (person) comprises the predictions that a classifier has attributed to that sample for each task. As the process is iterated over all the runs, the final score is the average of the stacking results obtained over the 30 runs. After a testing phase, we selected XGB as the estimator of the stacking technique, as it is the classifier which allowed us to reach the highest performance.

Third Step: Ranking and Majority Vote. The third step of the experimental approach was inputting the outcome from the first step detailed above (Sect. 4.1). First, for each classifier, we performed a ranking technique, an algorithm that orders a set of items, in our case, the tasks, based on their relevance, the accuracy metric. We chose accuracy because it measures the classifier's effectiveness, so we achieved a list of tasks sorted in ascendent order concerning this metric. This process is followed by a combination rule: the majority vote. This rule is applied for problems with multiple classifiers or models to make predictions, and the majority opinion determines the final prediction. Each classifier's prediction is considered a vote, and the class with the most votes is chosen as the final prediction. We applied it by combining every classifier prediction for a different set of tasks, run by run, and finally, we averaged the accuracy over the thirty runs. We considered the list of tasks given as output by the ranking process to select significant subsets of tasks to apply the majority vote.

4.2   Results

The results obtained with the experimental setting, reported in Sect. 4.1, are shown and discussed in the following.

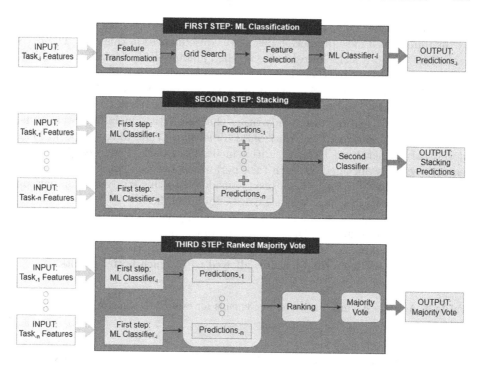

Fig. 2. Workflow Representation.

First Step Results. The results obtained from the first experimental step are shown in Table 3, as the average accuracy (percentage value) for each task and classifier over 30 runs. Note that for every task, the performance of the best classifier is in bold. The average accuracies range from the minimum value of 58.31%, achieved from KNN on the 1st task, to the maximum of 78.41% obtained from RF on the 23rd task. In particular, RF outperformed the other classifiers on seven tasks out of 25, while KNN never reached the highest result. Independently from the type of classifier, the table shows that the 1st task obtained the worst performances, while the 23rd was the best. The 1st task required a person to perform their signature; instead, the 23rd required writing a telephone number under dictation. As the 23rd task reached the best accuracy, we decided to investigate more aspects of this experiment by computing more evaluation metrics [28]: precision (PRE), sensitivity (SEN), specificity (SPE), False Negative Rate (FNR), F1 score (F1S) and Area Under the Curve (AUC) [29]. Table 4 contains the classifier used on the 23rd task in the first column, while the other columns report the metric's value in the header, averaging over 30 runs. All the metrics are expressed as percentage values except for the AUC, which varies from 0 to 1. We enhanced in bold the best metric value in every column. This table shows that the best classifier for this task was RF, according to the accuracy and the other metrics, except for the precision and the specificity. These last two indicate that RF wasn't the best classifier to classify healthy controls correctly,

112   T. D'Alessandro et al.

but in the medical field, the most important thing is to identify those affected by the illness, as a false prediction has more consequences in this case. The FNR is at 22.07%, and it's the lowest value reached among all the classifiers, meaning that RF was the best to recognize patients. Table 5 shows a comparison between the results obtained on every task using a set of dynamic features, with those obtained with the lognormal features extracted for this study.

The dynamic features are handwriting characteristics, including Start time, Duration, Vertical dimension, Horizontal dimension, Vertical speed peak, Peak of vertical acceleration, Relative initial inclination, Jerk, Pen pressure etc. A feature vector is obtained for each task performed by each subject. It is worth noticing that those features have been considered in this study for comparison purposes only. An in-depth analysis can be found in [30].

In detail, the table contains accuracy percentage values computed by averaging this metric over 30 runs. Only the results of the best classifier are shown, and the best performance for each task is in bold. Most of the time, the classification with our proposed lognormal features allowed us to reach better results.

Table 3. Average Accuracy achieved on 30 runs for every ML algorithm on lognormal features.

T	XGB	RF	DT	SVM	MLP	KNN	LR	T	XGB	RF	DT	SVM	MLP	KNN	LR
	Accuracy								**Accuracy**						
1	**67.6**	66.3	60.3	62.7	60.1	58.3	65.0	14	**68.3**	67.4	61.6	66.2	64.9	65.0	66.7
2	65.3	66.3	60.0	**68.6**	65.5	61.7	65.1	15	71.0	72.5	67.6	73.2	73.0	69.3	**73.3**
3	66.9	68.1	64.8	**68.5**	63.8	62.0	67.6	16	65.8	64.2	59.2	**67.4**	63.0	61.4	67.4
4	65.0	66.3	58.4	66.4	66.6	62.6	**67.7**	17	74.6	**75.7**	71.3	71.8	70.9	65.6	75.0
5	67.2	69.0	62.0	66.8	65.0	61.5	**69.9**	18	64.5	**68.4**	62.2	67.2	64.9	62.9	67.7
6	70.6	75.0	67.4	**75.6**	61.8	64.1	75.0	19	65.0	**66.4**	61.9	66.2	59.4	66.0	65.1
7	70.5	68.61	68.6	**73.7**	69.8	66.3	71.4	20	66.2	66.8	64.7	67.6	66.1	66.5	**69.9**
8	68.3	68.6	65.2	**69.1**	68.2	64.5	65.6	21	66.3	**67.2**	58.7	63.8	59.0	61.8	67.0
9	76.5	**77.3**	70.0	74.6	67.1	74.4	76.0	22	**72.9**	72.3	68.3	71.6	68.6	66.7	68.8
10	**71.2**	69.5	62.8	68.9	63.5	65.0	70.2	23	77.4	**78.4**	70.7	78.3	66.7	75.0	78.0
11	69.0	69.3	63.3	65.5	68.0	64.7	**70.1**	24	**76.4**	73.9	65.9	65.3	68.0	62.3	67.5
12	68.3	68.6	62.4	66.1	64.9	60.5	**70.6**	25	72.8	**74.6**	63.2	73.1	68.8	68.1	71.3
13	**67.3**	62.6	58.7	63.7	67.1	62.8	66.7								

Second Step Results. As mentioned above, stacking is a very popular technique in ML when dealing with multiple classifiers because it can potentially improve the overall predictive performance compared to using individual models separately. The meta-model can learn to leverage the strengths of different base models and compensate for their weaknesses. Table 6 displays the evaluation for every classifier according to different metrics: accuracy (ACC), precision (PRE), sensitivity (SEN), specificity (SPE), False Negative Rate (FNR), F1 score (F1S) and Area Under the Curve (AUC). Those parameters allowed us to analyze a

Table 4. Average results achieved on 30 runs for every ML algorithm on lognormal features, extracted from the execution of task 23, i.e. the one that reached the best performance according to Table 3.

CLS	ACC	PRE	SEN	SPE	FNR	F1S	AUC
XGB	77.43	77.67	77.03	77.88	22.97	77.18	0.83
RF	**78.41**	78.72	**77.93**	78.89	**22.07**	**78.14**	**0.85**
DT	70.78	78.77	58.16	83.25	41.84	65.21	0.70
SVM	78.39	81.53	73.51	83.23	26.49	77.06	0.84
MLP	66.72	**90.23**	36.38	**96.73**	63.62	49.67	0.81
KNN	75.06	77.04	71.57	78.54	28.43	74.01	0.80
LR	78.02	79.88	75.37	80.69	24.63	77.24	0.84

Table 5. Comparison between average Accuracy achieved on 30 runs for every task with the best-performing ML algorithm for Dynamic and Lognormal features.

T	DYN. FEAT. CLS	ACC	LOG. FEAT. CLS	ACC	T	DYN. FEAT. CLS	ACC	LOG. FEAT. CLS	ACC
1	XGB	64.5	XGB	**67.6**	14	XGB	64.1	XGB	**68.3**
2	XGB	63.0	SVM	**68.6**	15	XGB	64.3	LR	**73.3**
3	XGB	57.3	SVM	**68.5**	16	XGB	67.0	SVM	**67.4**
4	XGB	59.2	LR	**67.7**	17	XGB	69.3	RF	**75.7**
5	DT	69.0	LR	**69.9**	18	XGB	**68.9**	RF	68.4
6	XGB	57.4	SVM	**75.6**	19	XGB	**68.3**	RF	66.4
7	DT	58.4	SVM	**73.7**	20	XGB	66.1	LR	**69.9**
8	DT	61.7	SVM	**69.1**	21	DT	55.1	RF	**67.2**
9	XGB	64.5	RF	**77.3**	22	RF	70.0	XGB	**72.9**
10	XGB	61.6	XGB	**71.2**	23	XGB	72.3	RF	**78.4**
11	XGB	66.4	LR	**70.1**	24	XGB	56.0	XGB	**76.4**
12	XGB	67.2	LR	**70.6**	25	DT	59.8	RF	**74.6**
13	XGB	**68.3**	XGB	67.3					

classifier's performance better. Regarding the accuracy, for each classifier, the stacking reached a value higher than the average accuracy over all tasks from the first step of classification. Considering all the parameters, the best result is given by applying the stacking on the outcome from XGB as the first classifier, and the final stacking accuracy is 76.29%.

Table 6. Stacking results averaged over thirty runs with XGB classifiers, with the output of first-step classifiers.

1st CLS	ACC	PRE	SEN	SPE	FNR	F1S	AUC
XGB	**76.29**	77.99	**76.09**	76.52	**23.91**	**76.32**	**0.84**
RF	75.15	76.78	74.55	75.75	25.45	75.31	0.83
DT	70.98	73.89	68.85	73.39	31.15	70.2	0.78
SVM	75.38	**78.45**	72.24	**78.7**	27.76	74.91	0.83
MLP	69.41	70.78	69.86	69.00	30.14	69.63	0.76
KNN	71.75	74.79	69.1	74.58	30.9	71.16	0.77
LR	75.68	76.78	76.02	75.3	23.98	75.81	0.83

Third Step Results. The third step of our experimental phase, as described in Sect. 4.1, regards the application of two popular techniques in ML: ranking and Majority vote. Table 7 shows the ranked lists of tasks based on their accuracy for each classifier. Looking at the table is easy to notice the multiple occurrences of some tasks in the first positions, independently from the algorithm. In detail, task number 23 occurs at the first position five times out of seven algorithms; task 9 is between the first three positions for six algorithms, and task 17 is in the first four positions for five algorithms. Other tasks that also seem to show relevance are 6, 7, 15, 22 and 24. The 23rd required the writing of a phone number under dictation, the 9th the writing of the bigram 'le' four times continuously, and for the 17th the person had to write 6 words in defined boxes; every word had a different level of complexity. Regarding the other relevant tasks, the 6th involves the writing of 'l, m, p'; the 7th 'n, l, o, g' in apposite spaces; the 15th is a reverse copy of 'bottiglia'; the 22nd the direct copy of a phone number; while the 24 is the clock drawing test. Table 8 shows the performance of the majority vote for different sets of tasks taking the first n tasks from the ranking lists. The first column, denoted as "T_set", represents the number of tasks considered for each set of tasks, ranging from a minimum of three to a maximum of 25, which means all the tasks. After the fifth set, 11 tasks, the majority vote accuracy decreases. The best majority vote accuracy is 82.5% achieved by combining the predictions obtained by XGB from the first three tasks of the ranked list.

Table 7. Tasks ranking for each ML Classifier.

XGB	RF	DT	SVM	MLP	KNN	LR
T23	T23	T17	T23	T15	T23	T23
T09	T09	T23	T06	T17	T09	T09
T24	T17	T09	T09	T07	T15	T06
T17	T06	T07	T07	T25	T25	T17
T22	T25	T22	T15	T22	T22	T15
T25	T24	T15	T25	T08	T20	T07
T10	T15	T06	T17	T24	T07	T25
T15	T22	T24	T22	T11	T19	T12
T06	T10	T08	T08	T13	T17	T10
T07	T11	T03	T10	T09	T14	T11
T11	T05	T20	T02	T23	T10	T20
T12	T12	T11	T03	T04	T11	T05
T08	T08	T25	T20	T20	T08	T22
T14	T07	T10	T16	T02	T06	T18
T01	T18	T12	T18	T05	T18	T04
T13	T03	T18	T05	T14	T13	T03
T05	T14	T05	T04	T18	T04	T24
T03	T21	T19	T19	T12	T24	T16
T21	T20	T14	T14	T03	T03	T21
T20	T19	T01	T12	T10	T21	T13
T16	T02	T02	T11	T16	T02	T14
T02	T01	T16	T24	T06	T05	T08
T19	T04	T13	T21	T01	T16	T19
T04	T16	T21	T13	T19	T12	T02
T18	T13	T04	T01	T21	T01	T01

Table 8. Majority vote to a different set of ranked tasks.

T_set	XGB	RF	DT	SVM	MLP	KNN	LR
3	**82.5**	79.23	76.16	81.22	**76.32**	**77.40**	79.35
5	79.81	80.35	76.10	**81.88**	75.37	75.21	**79.95**
7	79.46	**81.17**	77.30	80.26	74.53	75.06	79.72
9	79.67	80.10	**77.75**	79.99	74.37	74.99	78.10
11	78.82	79.70	77.58	80.32	75.54	74.84	78.02
13	77.94	78.35	77.14	78.64	75.06	74.33	77.67
15	77.86	78.08	76.80	77.76	73.60	72.66	76.42
17	77.60	77.24	76.92	77.20	72.43	72.71	76.69
19	77.19	77.75	76.37	76.83	72.23	72.37	76.36
21	76.74	77.34	75.42	77.24	72.51	72.58	75.56
23	76.54	77.07	75.53	77.49	71.73	72.04	74.58
ALL	76.39	76.64	75.19	76.99	71.93	71.76	74.04

4.3   Feature Findings

This Section is conceived for the discussion of findings related to the feature selection output and the relation between the computed features and a person's age and educational level.

Feature Selection Discussion. We applied a feature selection procedure after the grid search in the first step of the experiment phase. This allowed the classifier to concentrate on the most important features by deleting redundant or uninteresting ones. The chosen algorithm was Recursive Feature Elimination (RFECV) for most classifiers, except for MLP and KNN, for which we used SelectKBest. Different sets of features were selected for every classifier and task, but looking at them, it was possible to notice some common patterns and make some considerations. Some personal features were always selected for almost every task: age, profession and education. Regarding temporal features the most selected were f1, f4, f3, f7 and f9; while, among the geometrical ones the most selected were f62, f47, f26, f28, f61, f60, f49, f64; finally for SNR features f19 f20 f22 f23 were selected the most. All these features have been selected on at least ten tasks out of 25 from the classifier that achieved the best result, XGB. The features selected from the temporal set denote that our assumptions had foundations: impaired people take more time to execute a handwriting task, generating more lognormal functions in the velocity profile and segments in the trace acquisition. Among features related to SNR and geometric shapes, the most important are those that describe the variation of a measure sequence. In particular, relating SNR or geometrical features to the temporal ones can help to make more robust features enlarging the difference between the two classes we mean to distinguish.

To better understand the relevance of each feature for the examined problem, a parametric statistical test, the $t - test$, was used to evaluate whether the difference between the means of the two groups was statistically significant. This test returns a probability measure called the $p - value$ for every characteristic that indicates the strength of evidence against the null hypothesis. A significance level of 0.05 is the predetermined threshold below which the null hypothesis is rejected, so if the $p - value$ is smaller than this threshold, there is evidence that the feature is significant in distinguishing between the two classes. All the aforementioned features reported a $p - value$ smaller than the threshold in our case.

Relations Between Features, Educational Level and Age. The above discussion suggests valuable features among the extracted ones. However, the results obtained from the first step procedure still require improvement for a classification system, especially in the medical field. To try and explain this behaviour, we analyzed our features deeply. First, we checked how the people in our dataset are distributed concerning personal features. Note that, from this point on, we refer to education level as the number of years of school attended by a person. This analysis was necessary as the dataset comprises people aged between 44 and 88 years old and with an education level which ranges from 2 to 21 years of school. We investigate whether these personal features could strictly influence handwriting tasks. Table 9 shows how people in our dataset are distributed according to age and education (school years). Both for age and education, we distinguished two ranges.

Box plots in Fig. 3 show how the contact time feature changes according to age, years of school and, obviously, the presence or not of Alzheimer's. These plots refer to the 23rd task, which outperformed all the others according to Table 7. These representations are useful for comparing the distribution of a feature between the two education ranges considered for a particular group of people. In detail, the x-axis shows the education range, the y-axis the contact time feature expressed in seconds, and every plot refers to a particular group of people (All, HC, PT) for a particular age range, where the first is [44, 66] and the second is [67, 88].

This figure highlights some evident trends:

- Younger people are faster; if they have fewer years of school, they take more time and the deviation increases (Fig. 3(a) and (b));
- There's no variation between healthy people belonging to the first age range, independently from education (Fig. 3(c));
- Older healthy controls take more time than younger healthy controls, especially if they have a lower education level. It seems that education years are information that counts for elderly people (Fig. 3(c) and (d))
- The feature doesn't change so much for impaired people if they belong to the first age range, independently from the years of school (Fig. 3(e));
- Elderly patients show significantly different behaviour that depends on their education. Impaired elderly people take more time to complete handwriting tasks if they have fewer years of school (Fig. 3(f)).

Those findings hold for other features, too, mostly for the geometrical ones and those related to contact time and the number of lognormals. The relation between extracted features and personal information is extremely interesting. This study allowed us to understand that a younger patient of AD could perform a task similarly or even better than an older healthy person with a fewer education level. Those findings can explain the performance obtained from the first step because there is an evident difference between young, healthy controls (c) and old patients (f). Furthermore, it decreases a lot between older healthy controls (d) and younger patients (e) or older ones but belonging to a major

Table 9. Distribution of people according to Education level and Age.

Education level Distribution				Age Distribution			
School years	Total	HC	PT	Age intervals	Total	HC	PT
[2, 11]	70	22	48	[44, 66]	69	50	19
[12, 21]	104	63	41	[67, 88]	105	35	70

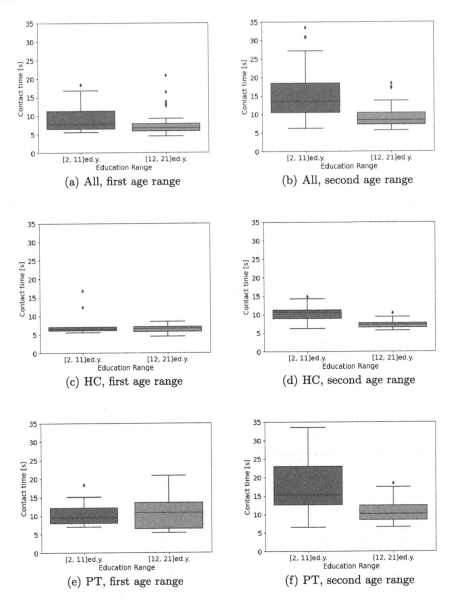

Fig. 3. Box plots showing how the contact time feature is related to age and education. The first age range is from 44 to 66 years old, while the second is from 67 to 88 years old.

education range (f). There could be multiple reasons why healthy old people are not distinguished from younger patients. Older people, even if they don't suffer from AD, can have other impairments that affect their skills, and however, is known that a person's abilities deteriorate while getting older. Regarding younger patients, their execution depends on the stage of the illness, and they are probably more able to compensate for its effect concerning older people who lose control. It would be very interesting to know the stage of the disease of younger patients and to understand if they developed a compensation mechanism which makes them very similar to old healthy controls.

5   Conclusions and Future Work

Alzheimer's disease is a progressive impairment which also affects handwriting, and it has no cure, so it is necessary to have an early diagnosis. In this research, we used a classification system based on ML, Ensemble and combining rules to distinguish between patients and healthy control through features extracted by applying the sigma-lognormal model to several handwriting tasks. The findings are interesting, though the results are still insufficient for a diagnostic aid system in the medical field. The best result from ML algorithms was achieved with an accuracy of 78.41% on the 23rd task from RF. Regarding the stacking ensemble, the best performer was XGB, with an accuracy of 76.29%. The majority vote combining rule obtains an 82.5% of accuracy, combining the predictions from the first three tasks of a list where tasks are ranked according to their predictive ability. We discovered that the extracted lognormal features are useful in studying handwriting, particularly its dynamic and fluency. The results obtained are not enough for a medical problem, so we tried to find an explanation:

- In our dataset we noticed that in some cases people belonging to the control group took a lot of time to execute some tasks, which is not expected. In other cases, people performing a task didn't follow strictly the requirements. Given this, we noticed that the velocity profile given by the sigma-lognormal model wasn't able to enhance the difference between HC and PT enough;
- Handwriting and the features are related to age and education. While it's easy to find differences between young HC and old PT, this difference strongly decreases when comparing old HC and young PT.

This research has room to be improved, also, we mean to investigate more on our findings. We want to understand how to distinguish between older HC and younger PT, why they are so similar, and which technique or acquiring system we should consider. An interesting path that we mean to follow is to find a way to combine signal processing features with personal ones and understand if it is possible to measure or study how a person tries to cope with AD symptoms while writing and how he compensates. Future work will also focus on applying our system to different disease datasets and understanding if we obtain the same conclusions regarding results and discovered relations.

Acknowledgements. This work has been supported by the Spanish project PID2021-122687OA-I00/AEI/10.13039/501100011033/FEDER, UE.

The research leading to these results has received funding from Project "Ecosistema dell'innovazione - Rome Technopole" financed by EU in NextGenerationEU plan through MUR Decree n. 1051 23.06.2022 - CUP H33C22000420001.

References

1. Impedovo, D., Pirlo, G., Vessio, G.: Dynamic handwriting analysis for supporting earlier Parkinson's disease diagnosis. Information **9**(10), 247 (2018)
2. Singh, P., Yadav, H.: Influence of neurodegenerative diseases on handwriting. Forensic Res. Criminol. Int. J. **9**(3), 110–114 (2021)
3. Werner, P., Rosenblum, S., Bar-On, G., Heinik, J., Korczyn, A.: Handwriting process variables discriminating mild Alzheimer's disease and mild cognitive impairment. J. Gerontol. Ser. B **61**(4), P228–P236 (2006)
4. Myszczynska, M.A., et al.: Applications of machine learning to diagnosis and treatment of neurodegenerative diseases. Nat. Rev. Neurol. **16**, 440–456 (2020)
5. Albu, A., Precup, R.E., Teban, T.A.: Results and challenges of artificial neural networks used for decision making and control in medical applications. Facta Universitatis Ser. Mech. Eng. **17**(3), 285–308 (2019)
6. Tanveer, M., et al.: Machine learning techniques for the diagnosis of Alzheimer's disease: a review. ACM Trans. Multimedia Comput. Commun. Appl. **16**(1s), 1–35 (2020)
7. Vessio, G.: Dynamic handwriting analysis for neurodegenerative disease assessment: a literary review. Appl. Sci. **9**(21), 4666 (2019)
8. Impedovo, D., Pirlo, G.: Dynamic handwriting analysis for the assessment of neurodegenerative diseases: a pattern recognition perspective. IEEE Rev. Biomed. Eng. **12**, 209–220 (2018)
9. Qi, H., et al.: A study of auxiliary screening for Alzheimer's disease based on handwriting characteristics. Front. Aging Neurosci. **15**, 1117250 (2023)
10. Kobayashi, M., Yamada, Y., Shinkawa, K., Nemoto, M., Nemoto, K., Arai, T.: Automated early detection of Alzheimer's disease by capturing impairments in multiple cognitive domains with multiple drawing tasks. J. Alzheimers Dis. **88**(3), 1075–1089 (2022)
11. Plamondon, R.: A kinematic theory of rapid human movements: Part I. Movement representation and generation. Biol. Cybern. **72**(4), 295–307 (1995)
12. Plamondon, R.: A kinematic theory of rapid human movements - Part II. Movement time and control. Biol. Cybern. **72**(4), 309–320 (1995)
13. Plamondon, R.: A kinematic theory of rapid human movements: Part III. Kinetic outcomes. Biol. Cybern. **78**(2), 133–145 (1998)
14. Carmona-Duarte, C., Ferrer, M.A., Plamondon, R., Gómez-Rodellar, A., Gómez-Vilda, P.: Sigma-lognormal modeling of speech. Cogn. Comput. **13**(2), 488–503 (2021)
15. O'Reilly, C., Plamondon, R.: Development of a sigma-lognormal representation for on-line signatures. Pattern Recognit. **42**(12), 3324–3337 (2009)
16. Zhang, Z., O'Reilly, C., Plamondon, R.: Comparing symbolic and connectionist algorithms for correlating the age of healthy children with sigma-lognormal neuromuscular parameters. In: 2022 26th International Conference on Pattern Recognition (ICPR), pp. 4385–4391 (2022)
17. Díaz, M., Ferrer, M.A., Guest, R.M., Pal, U.: Graphomotor evolution in the handwriting of Bengali children through sigma-lognormal based-parameters: a preliminary study (2019)
18. O'Reilly, C., Plamondon, R.: Design of a neuromuscular disorders diagnostic system using human movement analysis. In: 2012 11th International Conference on Information Science, Signal Processing and their Applications, ISSPA 2012, pp. 787–792 (2012)

19. Plamondon, R., Pirlo, G., Anquetil, É., Rémi, C., Teulings, H.-L., Nakagawa, M.: Personal digital bodyguards for e-security, e-learning and e-health: a prospective survey. Pattern Recogn. **81**, 633–659 (2018)
20. Impedovo, D.: Velocity-based signal features for the assessment of parkinsonian handwriting. IEEE Signal Process. Lett. **26**(4), 632–636 (2019)
21. Impedovo, D., Pirlo, G., Balducci, F., Dentamaro, V., Sarcinella, L., Vessio, G.: Investigating the sigma-lognormal model for disease classification by handwriting. In: The Lognormality Principle And its Applications in E-Security, E-Learning and E-Health, pp. 195–209. World Scientific (2021)
22. Cilia, N.D., et al.: Lognormal features for early diagnosis of Alzheimer's disease through handwriting analysis. In: Carmona-Duarte, C., Diaz, M., Ferrer, M.A., Morales, A. (eds.) IGS 2022. LNCS, vol. 13424, pp. 322–335. Springer, Cham (2022). https://doi.org/10.1007/978-3-031-19745-1_24
23. Ferrer, M.A., Diaz, M., Carmona-Duarte, C., Plamondon, R.: IDeLog: iterative dual spatial and kinematic extraction of sigma-lognormal parameters. IEEE Trans. Pattern Anal. Mach. Intell. **42**(1), 114–125 (2020)
24. Cilia, N.D., De Stefano, C., Fontanella, F., Di Freca, A.S.: An experimental protocol to support cognitive impairment diagnosis by using handwriting analysis. Procedia Comput. Sci. **141**, 466–471 (2018)
25. Tseng, M.H., Cermak, S.A.: The influence of ergonomic factors and perceptual-motor abilities on handwriting performance. Am. J. Occup. Ther. **47**(10), 919–926 (1993)
26. Plamondon, R., O'Reilly, C., Rémi, C., Duval, T.: The lognormal handwriter: learning, performing, and declining. Front. Psychol. **4**, 945 (2013)
27. Wolpert, D.H.: Stacked generalization. Neural Netw. **5**(2), 241–259 (1992)
28. Müller, A.C., Guido, S.: Introduction to Machine Learning with Python: A Guide for Data Scientists. O'Reilly Media, Sebastopol (2016)
29. Hanley, J.A., McNeil, B.J.: The meaning and use of the area under a receiver operating characteristic (ROC) curve. Radiology **143**(1), 29–36 (1982)
30. Cilia, N.D., De Stefano, C., Fontanella, F., Di Freca, A.S.: Feature selection as a tool to support the diagnosis of cognitive impairments through handwriting analysis. IEEE Access **9**, 78226–78240 (2021)

Feature Evaluation in Handwriting Analysis for Alzheimer's Disease Using Bayesian Network

Tiziana D'Alessandro, Claudio De Stefano⬤, Francesco Fontanella⬤,
Emanuele Nardone⬤, and Alessandra Scotto di Freca$^{(\boxtimes)}$⬤

Department of Electrical and Information Engineering, University of Cassino and
Southern Lazio, 03043 Cassino, Italy
{tiziana.dalessandro,destefano,fontanella,emanuele.nardone}@unicas.it,
a.scotto@uncias.it

Abstract. Alzheimer's disease, recognized as the most widespread neurodegenerative disorder worldwide, is intricately linked to cognitive impairments. The cognitive impairments, range from mild to severe and are a risk factor for Alzheimer's disease. They have profound implications for individuals, even as they maintain some level of daily functionality. In previous studies, it was proposed a protocol involving handwriting tasks as a potential diagnostic tool, and a comparative analysis of well-known and widely-used feature selection approach to determine the most effective features for predicting the symptoms related to cognitive impairments via handwriting analysis. In the presented study, we use a Bayesian Network to conduct further analysis of the most effective features extracted from handwriting. Our objective is to exploit the structural learning of Bayesian Networks to discover correlations among the most effective features for predicting impairment symptoms through handwriting analysis and deepen our understanding of the underlying cognitive functions affected. The results showed that the Bayesian Network chooses features conditionally dependent on the determination of the disease, and several features are selected more times than others, underlining their importance in the diagnosis. Moreover, comparing the results with those achieved by well-known and widely-used feature selection and classification approaches, the Bayesian networks exhibit the best performance by using a reduced set of features.

Keywords: Medical expert systems · cognitive impairments · Bayesian Networks · feature selection

1 Introduction

The World Health Organization recognizes that dementia is significantly underdiagnosed globally and emphasizes that even when a diagnosis is made, it often occurs at a relatively advanced stage. Delaying the onset of Alzheimer's disease

A. Parziale et al. (Eds.): IGS 2023, LNCS 14285, pp. 122–135, 2023.
https://doi.org/10.1007/978-3-031-45461-5_9

(AD) can have substantial benefits, including reduced care costs and increased lifespan for individuals. Therefore, early diagnosis of AD is crucial to enhance awareness and provide timely interventions. Mild cognitive impairment (MCI) is an early stage in the progression towards Alzheimer's disease (AD); its accurate diagnosis is essential for initiating timely treatment to delay the onset of AD. Individuals experiencing MCI may start noticing alterations in their cognitive abilities, yet they are still capable of performing their daily tasks. However, severe levels of impairment can significantly impact the comprehension of events and the significance of information conveyed through speech and writing, ultimately leading to the loss of independent living. Currently, AD diagnosis relies on various methods such as imaging, blood tests, and lumbar punctures (spinal sampling), among others. Recent research has demonstrated that individuals with AD exhibit disrupted spatial organization and impaired motor control. Therefore, the assessment of motor activities, including the analysis of handwriting, which encompasses a complex interplay of cognitive, kinesthetic, and perceptual motor skills, holds significant potential in diagnosing AD. An illustrative example is the occurrence of dysgraphia in both the early and progressive stages of AD [8, 24]. Within this context, numerous studies in medicine and psychology have investigated the relationship between the disease and various handwriting features, utilizing conventional statistical methods [16, 19, 21]. However, these studies often neglect the intricate interactions that can arise among multiple features, failing to capture the complexity inherent in the analysis. In many instances, individual features that exhibit weak correlations with the target class could significantly enhance classification accuracy when combined with complementary features. Conversely, features that are individually relevant may become redundant when utilized alongside other features. In a previous study [4], the authors assessed the efficacy of the extracted features and their relationship with the diseases they potentially contribute to prediction. The techniques employed a search strategy to identify optimal solutions, i.e., the best feature subsets, based on a predefined evaluation function. The approaches used to define the best features are typically categorized into three main classes: filter, wrapper, and embedded methods. Filter methods primarily rely on statistical properties of the feature subset space. Wrapper methods, on the other hand, assess the performance of a specific classifier when utilizing a particular feature subset. Embedded methods incorporate feature selection as an integral part of the training process. In this previous work, the analysis of features extracted from the handwriting of individuals with neurodegenerative diseases and cognitive impairment is done using wrapper methods. In this paper, we present a novel approach based on Bayesian Networks to further investigate the complex interactions that may emerge among multiple features. A Bayesian Network (BN) is a probabilistic graphical model that encodes the joint probability of a set of variables that, in our case, can be the features and the disease identification. The feature selection problem has seen the extensive application of Bayesian networks [2, 18]. Once the BN has been learned from instances in a dataset, it allows the identification of a reduced set of features conditionally dependent on the disease identification. Such a reduced set is also known as Markov Blanket (MB). Existing approaches involve learning a Bayesian network from the given dataset and subsequently utilizing the Markov Blanket of the target feature as the criterion for selecting relevant features. Thus, in this paper, we want to primarily explore the relationship between these diseases and individual features and then study the complex interactions that may emerge among multiple features. In this way, we can fill the gap in the literature regarding the comprehensive understanding of the interplay among various handwriting features in relation to AD and cognitive impairments (CI) [6]. The remainder of the paper is organized as follows. In Sect. 2 we describe the protocol we used to acquire the handwriting data, and the used features. Section 3 introduces the BNs and describes how they can be applied for selecting features. Finally, Sect. 4 reports the experimental results.

2   Acquisition Protocol and Features

We have developed a comprehensive protocol to collect data on handwriting movements from patients with CI and a control group of healthy individuals. The protocol, described in [4], consists of twenty-five tasks categorized as follows: graphic tasks, copy and reverse copy tasks, memory tasks, and dictation tasks. Graphic tasks assess the ability to write basic strokes, connect dots, and draw geometric shapes of varying complexity. Copy and reverse copy tasks evaluate the proficiency in reproducing complex gestures with semantic meaning, such as letters, words, and numbers. Memory tasks examine changes in the writing process for previously memorized words or words associated with depicted objects. Dictation tasks aim to investigate how handwriting performance is influenced by working memory usage.

It is important to note that each task was designed to assess either functional or parametric aspects. For example, in task number 17, participants were asked to write six different words that were analyzed in two different ways: the former, by averaging feature values across the entire word set, and the latter, by averaging feature values for each individual word. This led to the subdivision of the 17th task into six additional sub-tasks from 26th to 31th. A similar approach was applied to task number 14, which involved memorizing and rewriting the Italian words "telefono", "cane", and "negozio" added the sub-tasks 32, 33, and 34. The reasoning for this approach is to measure the impact of tiredness, i.e., if writing performance deteriorates more rapidly in participants suffering from neurodegenerative disorders when they are required to write multiple words consecutively. To summarize, we have a collection of thirty-four tasks that characterize each patient. The recruitment for the study uses standard clinical tests, including the Mini-Mental State Examination (MMSE) [11], Frontal Assessment Battery (FAB) [14], and Montreal Cognitive Assessment (MoCA) [17]. These tests assessed cognitive abilities across various domains, such as orientation, recall, and registration. To ensure unbiased results, the control group was carefully matched with the patient group regarding age, education level, gender, and type of work (manual or intellectual), as shown in Table 1. Participants using psychotropic medication or any other drugs that could influence cognitive abilities were excluded. Moreover, we excluded patients with severely compromised cognitive abilities.

Table 1. Average demographic data of participants. Standard deviations are shown in parentheses.

	Age	Education	#Women	#Men
Patients	71.5(9.5)	10.8(5.1)	46	44
Control group	68.9(12)	12.9(4.4)	51	39

For data acquisition, we utilized a Wacom Bamboo Folio smart pad paired with a pen that allowed participants to write naturally on A4 white paper sheets placed on it. The smart pad recorded the x-y coordinates of pen movements (at a frequency of 200 Hz) on the paper's surface. We also captured the pressure applied when the pen tip touched the sheet and the pen's movements when lifted in the air within a maximum distance of 3 cm. The smart pad was positioned approximately seventy centimeters away from the participants during the data collection process. Importantly, all participants underwent the acquisition under identical conditions.

The features extracted from the raw data available, i.e., (x, y) coordinates, pressure, and timestamps, were calculated on the strokes making up the handwritten traits and then averaged over the entire task. Our goal is to describe, for each task, the behavior of a subject, taking into account a fixed number of features that are described in Table 2.

Considering the significant variation in the number of strokes across different subjects and tasks, we have adopted an averaging approach to consolidate the values extracted from individual strokes. Specifically, the feature denoted as f_{22} represents the total number of strokes. For each of the features from f_1 to f_{21}, we have calculated the average and standard deviation, symbolized by f and $\hat{f}$, respectively. Consequently, the first 21 features are duplicated for each patient, encompassing static and dynamic handwriting characteristics. Additionally, features ranging from f_{23} to f_{26} consider variations associated with factors such as sex, age, work, and education.

As many studies in the literature show significant differences in patients' motor performance between in-air and on-paper traits, each feature was calculated separately for the in-air or on-paper traits. In particular, we extracted four groups of features:

– **On-paper:** The features extracted from the written traits (i.e., during pendown and the successive pen-up). Note that in this case, forty-seven features represented each sample.

Table 2. Feature list description.

f_{ID}	Name	Description
f_1	Duration	Time interval between the first and the last points in a stroke
f_2	Start Vertical Position	Vertical start position relative to the lower edge of the active digitizer area
f_3	Vertical Size	Difference between the highest and lowest y coordinates of the stroke
f_4	Peak vertical velocity	Maximum value of vertical velocity among the points of the stroke
f_5	Peak vertical acceleration	Maximum value of vertical acceleration among the points of the stroke
f_6	Start horizontal position	Horizontal start position relative to the lower edge of the active tablet area
f_7	Horizontal size	Difference between the highest (rightmost) and lowest (leftmost) I coordinates of the stroke
f_8	Straightness error	It is calculated by estimating the length of the straight line, fitting the straight line, estimating the (perpendicular) distances of each point to the fitted line, estimating the standard deviation of the distances, and dividing it by the length of the line between beginning and end
f_9	Slant	Direction from the beginning point to endpoint of the stroke, in radiant
f_{10}	Loop Surface	Area of the loop enclosed by the previous and the present stroke
f_{11}	Relative initial slant	Departure of the direction during the first 80 ms to the slant of the entire stroke
f_{12}	Relative time to peak vertical velocity	Ratio of the time duration at which the maximum peak velocity occurs (from the start time) to the total duration
f_{13}	Absolute size	Calculated from the vertical and horizontal sizes
f_{14}	Average absolute velocity	Average absolute velocity computed across all the samples of the stroke
f_{15}	Road length	Length of a stroke from beginning to end, dimensionless
f_{16}	Absolute y jerk	The root mean square (RMS) value of the absolute jerk along the vertical direction, across all points of the stroke
f_{17}	Normalized y jerk	Dimensionless as it is normalized for stroke duration and size
f_{18}	Absolute jerk	The Root Mean Square (RMS) value of the absolute jerk across all points of the stroke
f_{19}	Normalized jerk	Dimensionless as it is normalized for stroke duration and size
f_{20}	Number of peak acceleration points	Number of acceleration peaks both up-going and down-going in the stroke
f_{21}	Pen pressure	Average pen pressure computed over the points of the stroke
f_{22}	number of strokes	Total number of strokes of the task
f_{23}	Sex	Subject's gender
f_{24}	Age	Subject's age
f_{25}	Work	Type of work of the subject (intellectual or manual)
f_{26}	Education	Subject's education level expressed in years

- **In-air:** The features extracted from the in-air traits. These movements characterize the planning activity for positioning the pen tip between two successive written traits. Note that in this case, we extracted forty-five features because pressure (feature f_{21}) is always zero.
- **All:** In this scenario, each feature vector includes in-air (af_i) and on-paper (pf_i) attributes (where the subscript i indicates the feature number), thus reporting the values of both On-paper and In-air feature vectors. The aim was twofold: facilitating a direct in-air versus on-paper feature comparison and delving into the intricate interplay between the two. It is worth noting that eighty-eight distinct features were considered, excluding repeated personal features and pressure variables regarding the in-air part.
- **In-air-On-paper:** The computation of these features disregards the differentiation between in-air and on-paper characteristics. In practice, the value of each feature is obtained by averaging the values derived from both in-air

and on-paper traits. The only exception is for the pressure, whose values are obviously obtained considering on-paper traits. This approach represents an alternative method of supplying global information to the classification system, considering as equivalent the motor planning for both handwritten and in-air strokes.

Summarizing, we considered four categories of features: we have forty-five features for In-air category, forty-seven features for both On-paper and In-air-On-paper categories, and eighty-eight for the category All.

3   Bayesian Network for Feature Evaluation

The problem of feature evaluation can be handled by estimating the joint probability of each feature and the class label. A Bayesian Network (BN) may effectively solve this problem. A BN is a probabilistic graphical model that allows the representation of a joint probability distribution of a set of random variables through a Direct Acyclic Graph (DAG) [20]. The graph nodes represent the variables, while the arcs encode the statistical dependencies among the variables. An arrow from a node f_i to a node f_j encodes the conditional dependence between the node f_j and node f_i, and we can define f_i as a *parent* of f_j. In a BN, the i–th node f_i is associated with a conditional probability function $p(f_i|pa_{f_i})$, where pa_{f_i} indicates the set of nodes which are parents of f_i. Such a function quantifies the effect that the parents have on that node. The process of learning a BN entails acquiring knowledge from a training set of examples. This learning phase involves capturing both the network structure, which defines the statistical dependencies among variables, and the parameters of the probability distributions associated with those variables. Among structural learning methods, there are constraint-based methods like PC [22], IAMB [23] that exploit conditional independence relationships in the data to uncover the network structure; there are also score-based methods that evaluate different network structures based on a scoring metric to find the structure with the highest score or the lowest complexity. Among score-based methods, there are K2 [5], TAN [12] etc. The third category of structural learning methods, the hybrid ones combine the strengths of constraint-based and score-based approaches. These methods balance computational efficiency and the ability to handle complex network structures. Among them, there are methods also based on evolutionary algorithm [7]. On the other hand, parameter learning generally uses the Maximum Likelihood Estimation that estimates the parameters of a BN by maximizing the likelihood of the observed data. Once the statistical dependencies among variables have been learned, the DAG structure encodes them, and the joint probability of the set of variables $F = \{f_1, \ldots, f_L\}$ can be described as:

$$p(f_1 \ldots, f_L) = \prod_{f_i \in F} p(f_i|pa_{f_i}) \qquad (1)$$

In the feature evaluation framework, this property can be used to infer the true class c of an unknown sample only by a subset of features. In fact, suppose to have L features, then the class label c and the L features can be modeled as a set of $(L+1)$ variables $\{c, f_1, \ldots, f_L\}$, and the Eq. (1) allows the description of their joint probability as:

$$p(c, f_1, \ldots, f_L) = p(c \mid pa_c) \prod_{f_i \in F} p(f_i \mid pa_{f_i}) \qquad (2)$$

The node c may be the parent of one or more of the nodes of the DAG. For example, if we consider the BN depicted in Fig. 1, we have that c is the parent of nodes f_6 and f_5. While the nodes f_2 and f_3 are the parents of c. Therefore, it may be useful to divide the set of DAG nodes that are not parents of c into two groups: the first, denoted F_c, contains the nodes having the node c among their parents, and the second, denoted $F_{\bar{c}}$, the remaining ones. Note that among F_c nodes there also are nodes, like, f_7 that are not parents of c, but are modeled in the conditional probability that also contains the node c. With this assumption, Eq. (2) can be rewritten as:

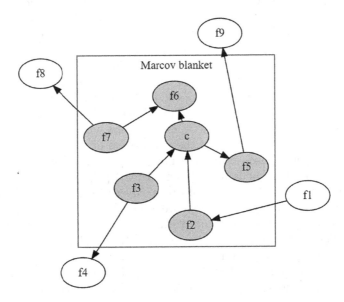

Fig. 1. An example of Bayesian Network and the Markov Blanket in case of 9 features available.

$$p(c, f_1, \ldots, f_L) = p(c \mid pa_c) \prod_{f_i \in F_c} p(f_i \mid pa_{f_i}) \prod_{f_i \in F_{\bar{c}}} p(f_i \mid pa_{f_i}) \qquad (3)$$

This property allows a BN to recognize a given sample only considering the responses provided by the feature represented by the nodes that are directly linked to the class node. The group F_c and pa_c is also known as Markov Blanket (MB) of node c and in $F_{\bar{c}}$ group are all nodes d-separated from c, that is, it contains features conditionally independent from class label c. Therefore, the MB of node c consists of its parents, children, and spouses, and the c is independent of all other nodes given its MB.

This behavior encoded by the BN is particularly useful in the testing phase when, from the feature vector of all features, the class label is inferred. In fact, given the set of responses concerning a sample, we can use the conditional probability $p(c|f_1, \ldots, f_L)$ estimated by the BN for assigning the most probable class $\widehat{c}$ to the unknown sample, as follows:

$$\widehat{c} = \arg\max_{c \in C} p\left(c|f_1, ..., f_L\right) \tag{4}$$

where C is the set of classes. Considering the definition of conditional probability, and omitting the terms not depending on the variable c, the above equation can be rewritten as follows:

$$\widehat{c} = \arg\max_{c \in C} \frac{p\left(c, f_1, ..., f_L\right)}{p\left(f_1, ..., f_L\right)} = \arg\max_{c \in C} p\left(c, f_1, ..., f_L\right) \tag{5}$$

which involves only the joint probabilities $p\left(c, f_1, ..., f_L\right)$. According to Eq. (3), and discarding the term conditionally independent on c, Eq. (5) assumes the form:

$$\widehat{c} = \arg\max_{c \in C} p\left(c|pa_c\right) \prod_{f_i \in F_c} p\left(f_i|pa_{f_i}\right) \tag{6}$$

An example of the application of this rule is shown in Fig. 1, where only 9 features have been considered for the sake of clearness. In this case, the above equation becomes $\widehat{c} = \arg\max_{c \in C} p(f_6|c, f_7)p(f_5|c)p(c|f_3, f_2)$. Then in the case of the learned BN of Fig. 1 we have to know only features f_2, f_3, f_5, f_6 and f_7 to infer c. In fact, during the learning procedure, the set of experts $F_{\overline{c}}$, which does not add information to the choice of $\widehat{c}$, is individuated and it is discarded in the testing phase. In our example, in fact, the contribution of features f_1, f_4, f_8 are considered not necessary, and they can be discarded in the testing phase. Thus, the BN-based feature selection approach uses only the features in the MB of node c.

4   Experimental Findings

In this section, we will describe the experimental setup and procedures implemented to assess the performance of our system. The data were acquired according to the protocol described in Sect. 2 and refer to 18 subjects, including 90 patients and 90 healthy people. The purpose of the experimentation was twofold: to show that our approach allows us to accurately classify patients and healthy subject using the features extracted fro their handwriting, and to underline which features are more relevant to provide the diagnosis. In order to achieve our aim, we learned the BN DAG structure and the conditional probabilities among features and the class label, using the available data. Given the DAG structure, we extracted the MB, which highlights the features conditionally dependent on the class node. We performed the aforementioned procedure by running the K2 algorithm 30 times, setting to 3 the maximum number of parents for each node. The value selected for the maximum number of parents represent a compromise between algorithm efficiency and computational cost, while the number of runs of the algorithm k2 was chosen to average the effects of the initial ordering of the input variables. Its efficiency, in fact, is strongly dependent on this ordering and therefore a different initial order of the variables were considered in each run. We used the WEKA software for feature selection and classification, whereas we used the KNIME software for data pre-processing (managing missing values, filtering null columns, and encoding categorical variables). Although real-world data often includes a combination of discrete and continuous variables, BN structure learning algorithms generally assume that all random variables are discrete. As a consequence, continuous variables are typically discretized to comply with this assumption. In our implementation, we applied the sample quantile technique to discretize continuous variables into five binning intervals. These pre-processing steps were crucial in preparing the data for the subsequent classification analysis.

In order to investigate the importance of the used features, we plotted the histogram of the features selected more than 10% of the times in the MB among the 30 runs (see Fig. 2) for each category, namely In-air, On-paper, In-air-On-paper and All. Even if the results relative to the feature category All indicate that the features derived from on-paper traits are selected more frequently than those related to on air traits, the importance of on air traits is confirmed by our results reported in Table 3 as well as by the results reported in [9]. From the figure, we can see that the age, feature f_{24} (see Table 2), is the most selected in the four categories, with a minimum value of 0.47 (On-Paper). This confirms that age significantly affects the handwriting process of people with Alzheimer's disease, due to the changes in brain structure, such as the decrease in the size of the brain's memory center (hippocampus). Even if these changes typically worsen with age [10], they are more relevant in subjects with mild cognitive impairment and even more dramatic in people with Alzheimer's disease. Another feature selected with high frequency in 3 of the 4 categories is the education, feature f_{26}, with a minimum value of 0.43. Comparing these results with the ones obtained in [4], where the education was selected few times, we can say that BNs seem more effective in estimating the correlation among variables, and thus the joint contribution of groups of features in distinguishing patients from healthy people. Other two significant features selected with high frequency are f_2 and f_3, measuring the start vertical position and the vertical size, respectively. The joint selection of these features confirms the importance of evaluating the spatial coordination of subjects, and indicates that their variability differs between healthy people and AD patients. As regards the evaluation of the dynamic parameters of the handwriting process, separate evaluations can be made for data On-Paper and In-Air data. The peak vertical acceleration f_5 appears with its mean value and its mean and standard deviation in On-Paper group, underlining the importance of the variability of this feature. In In-Air group, the presence of f_5 together with the standard deviation of the number of peak acceleration points $\hat{f}_{20}$ and the standard deviation of the normalized y jerk $\hat{f}_{17}$, suggests that the variability of in-air movements may highlight anomalies in the handwriting of AD patients. On the other hand, also the movements performed with the pen tip touching the paper are characterized by different dynamics in AD patients and healthy people. In fact, in the On-Paper category, the mean value of jerk f_{18}, the absolute y jerk f_{16}, the average absolute velocity f_{14} and the standard deviation of peak vertical acceleration $\hat{f}_4$, are the most selected features, underlining the importance of hesitations in the handwriting process. In the On-Paper category, features like f_3, f_{13}, f_1, f_6, and f_9 that measure the space occupation, are also very important. In case of In-Air-On-Paper group, the features are obtained by averaging the values from both in-air and on-paper attributes for each task, thus assuming that the generation of the handwritten strokes is obtained by concatenating in air and on paper movements. Apart from the already mentioned features, the most important features are the absolute jerk f_{18}, peak vertical velocity f_4, the road length f_{15}, but also the duration f_1, the average absolute velocity f_{14}, the start horizontal f_6 and vertical position, f_2, with their mean and standard deviation. These results confirm that globally handwriting dynamic and spatial coordination are very important. When we apply the BNs to the category All, the effect is to produce a ranking of the features computed on both In-Air and On-Paper traits. In particular, we have the predominance of On-Paper features, where the most selected features are pen pressure f_{21}, the pen absolute velocity f_{14}, the absolute y jerk f_{16}, the start vertical position f_2, loop surface f_{10}, the road length f_{15}, duration f_1. The only feature computed on in-air traits present in the histogram is the feature the vertical size f_3. It is interesting to note that the features f_{10} emerge only in this group, meaning that they probably assume importance only in correlation with other features of both In-Air and On-Paper category. Finally, note that the feature road length f_{15} is present in all the histograms except for the one relating to the in-air category.

We used the Recursive Feature Elimination with Cross-Validation (RFE) [13] to select the most relevant features for comparison purposes. This technique recursively eliminates features and evaluates their impact on the performance of basic classifiers. We used a 10-fold cross-validation setup and evaluated the performance using the XGBoost [3], Decision Tree [15], and Random Forest [1] classifiers. We performed 30 classification runs, each time using the relevant features selected by each method. Table 3 shows the results obtained in all the aforementioned experiments; the first column shows the algorithm used for the feature selection, whereas the second column shows the algorithm used for the classification step. For each method, we reported the accuracy mean and the standard deviation along the 30 runs, with the average mean number of features selected (NF). From the table, we can observe that the best results are obtained every time with BN selection and classification. It is also worth noticing that when we apply another classification method to the feature selected by BNs it never achieved the result obtained by using BN as a classifier. This behavior proves that both structural and parametric learning of the BN is very effective

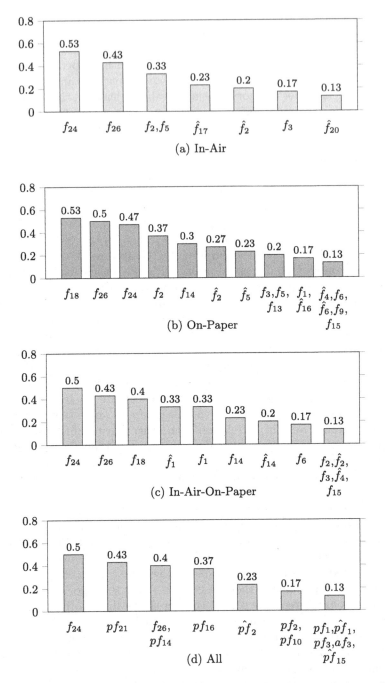

Fig. 2. Feature percentage greater than 10% selected by the proposed approach. Each bar of the histogram shows the fraction of time the corresponding feature(s) was selected among the 30 runs.

in selecting features and classifying healthy subjects and AD patients. Moreover, among the four categories, the best performing is All and then, in the order, In-air-On-paper, On-paper and In-air, and This result shows that BN optimally exploits the information coming from the two groups when this information is not averaged. Furthermore, as also shown in Fig. 2(d), the best features are those derived by the On-Paper category, where the In-Air ones are exploited as complementary information to obtain the best recognition performance.

Table 3. Classification results using BN, RF, XGBoost, and DT in term of average accuracy (Acc) and its standard deviation (in brackets), and average number of selected features (NF).

Feature Selection	Classifier	All		In-Air		In-air-On-paper		On-Paper	
		Acc	NF	Acc	NF	Acc	NF	Acc	NF
BN	BN	74.99 (5.74)	48.13	71.22 (4.03)	25.27	73.26 (4.47)	24.77	73.11 (4.11)	23.73
	RF	61.34 (4.76)	48.13	61.53 (4.72)	25.27	61.15 (4.24)	24.77	59.57 (3.68)	23.73
	XGB	57.20 (4.88)	48.13	58.73 (5.64)	25.27	58.69 (4.45)	24.77	56.91 (5.31)	23.73
	DT	64.31 (6.66)	48.13	58.12 (6.53)	25.27	63.52 (7.24)	24.77	63.32 (6.89)	23.73
RFE	RF	61.90 (4.26)	17.03	62.15 (3.93)	19.09	61.93 (4.81)	22.41	61.56 (5.36)	14.38
	XGB	61.02 (5.69)	11.90	60.28 (4.47)	10.60	59.94 (6.16)	11.20	59.86 (5.41)	10.40
	DT	63.39 (6.38)	10.25	62.56 (5.39)	11.38	64.63 (4.44)	10.25	64.28 (4.69)	10.19

5 Conclusions

In this study, we presented a novel approach based on Bayesian networks to evaluate the statistical dependencies among different features extracted from handwriting samples, in order to maximize the performance of a system for early AD diagnosis. The data were obtained by administering handwriting tests according to a protocol including 35 tasks, to a group of 180 subjects including 90 healthy controls and 90 AD patients. From these data, four datasets were obtained including feature relative to on paper and on air traits: this choice allowed us to estimate the distinctive power of the different considered feature categories and to study the complex interactions among groups of features.

The results seem very encouraging and demonstrate the effectiveness of the proposed approach: in particular, the Bayesian network allowed the selection of about half of the whole set of available features, significantly improving the performance with respect to other state of the art feature selection methods. As future works, we plan to increase the number of parents in the BN structural learning algorithm and to evaluate the sensitivity of the proposed system to variations of this parameter. The number of parents, in fact, has a very strong impact on the computational cost of the BN learning algorithms. We also plan to apply hybrid structural learning techniques to Bayesian networks [7].

Acknowledgements. The research leading to these results has received funding from Project "Ecosistema dell'innovazione - Rome Technopole" financed by EU in NextGenerationEU plan through MUR Decree n. 1051 23.06.2022 - CUP H33C22000420001.

References

1. Breiman, L.: Random forests. Mach. Learn. **45**(1), 5–32 (2001)
2. Castro, P.A.D., Von Zuben, F.J.: Learning Bayesian networks to perform feature selection. In: 2009 International Joint Conference on Neural Networks, pp. 467–473 (2009)
3. Chen, T., Guestrin, C.: XGBoost: a scalable tree boosting system. In: Proceedings of the 22nd ACM SIGKDD International Conference on Knowledge Discovery and Data Mining, KDD 2016, pp. 785–794. ACM, New York (2016)
4. Cilia, N.D., De Stefano, C., Fontanella, F., Scotto di Freca, A.: Feature selection as a tool to support the diagnosis of cognitive impairments through handwriting analysis. IEEE Access **9**, 78226–78240 (2021)
5. Cooper, G.F., Herskovits, E.: A Bayesian method for the induction of probabilistic networks from data. Mach. Learn. **9**(4), 309–347 (1992)
6. De Stefano, C., Fontanella, F., Impedovo, D., Pirlo, G., Scotto di Freca, A.: Handwriting analysis to support neurodegenerative diseases diagnosis: a review. Pattern Recognit. Lett. **121**, 37–45 (2019)
7. De Stefano, C., Fontanella, F., Marrocco, C., di Freca, A.S.: A hybrid evolutionary algorithm for Bayesian networks learning: an application to classifier combination. In: Di Chio, C., et al. (eds.) EvoApplications 2010. LNCS, vol. 6024, pp. 221–230. Springer, Heidelberg (2010). https://doi.org/10.1007/978-3-642-12239-2_23
8. Di Mauro, G., Bevilacqua, V., Colizzi, L., Di Pierro, D.: Testgraphia, a software system for the early diagnosis of dysgraphia. IEEE Access **8**, 19564–19575 (2020)
9. Drotár, P., Mekyska, J., Rektorová, I., Masarová, L., Smékal, Z., Faundez-Zanuy, M.: A new modality for quantitative evaluation of parkinson's disease: in-air movement. In: 13th IEEE International Conference on BioInformatics and BioEngineering, pp. 1–4 (2013). https://doi.org/10.1109/BIBE.2013.6701692
10. El-Yacoubi, M.A., Garcia-Salicetti, S., Kahindo, C., Rigaud, A.S., Cristancho-Lacroix, V.: From aging to early-stage Alzheimer's: uncovering handwriting multimodal behaviors by semi-supervised learning and sequential representation learning. Pattern Recognit. **86**, 112–133 (2019). https://doi.org/10.1016/j.patcog.2018.07.029. https://www.sciencedirect.com/science/article/pii/S0031320318302693
11. Folstein, M.F., Folstein, S.E., McHugh, P.R.: 'Mini-mental state': a practical method for grading the cognitive state of patients for the clinician. J. Psychiatric Res. **12**(3), 189–198 (1975)
12. Friedman, N., Geiger, D., Goldszmidt, M.: Bayesian network classifiers. Mach. Learn. **29**(2–3), 131–163 (1997)
13. Guyon, I., Weston, J., Barnhill, S., Vapnik, V.: Gene selection for cancer classification using support vector machines. Mach. Learn. **46**(1–3), 389–422 (2002)
14. Iavarone, A., Ronga, B., Pellegrino, L., Loré, E., Vitaliano, S., Galeone, F., Carlomagno, S.: The frontal assessment battery (FAB): normative data from an Italian sample and performances of patients with Alzheimer's disease and frontotemporal dementia. Funct. Neurol. **19**, 191–195 (2004)
15. L. Breiman, J. Friedman, R.O., Stone, C.: Classification and regression trees. Wadsworth (1984)
16. Müller, S., Preische, O., Heymann, P., Elbing, U., Laske, C.: Diagnostic value of a tablet-based drawing task for discrimination of patients in the early course of Alzheimer's disease from healthy individuals. J. Alzheimers Dis. **55**(4), 1463–1469 (2017)

17. Nasreddine, Z.S., et al.: The Montreal cognitive assessment, MoCA: a brief screening tool for mild cognitive impairment. J. Am. Geriatr. Soc. **53**(4), 695–699 (2005)
18. Njah, H., Jamoussi, S., Mahdi, W.: Interpretable Bayesian network abstraction for dimension reduction. Neural Comput. Appl. **35**(14), 10031–10049 (2023)
19. Onofri, E., Mercuri, M., Salesi, M., Ricciardi, M., Archer, T.: Dysgraphia in relation to cognitive performance in patients with Alzheimer's disease. J. Intellect. Disabil. Diagn. Treat. **1**, 113–124 (2013)
20. Pearl, J.: Probabilistic Reasoning in Intelligent Systems: Networks of Plausible Inference. Morgan Kaufmann, Burlington (1988)
21. Small, J., Sandhu, N.: Episodic and semantic memory influences on picture naming in Alzheimer's disease. Brain Lang. **104**(1), 1–9 (2008)
22. Spirtes, P., Glymour, C., Scheines, R.: Causation, Prediction, and Search. MIT Press, Cambridge (2000)
23. Tsamardinos, I., Aliferis, C.F., Statnikov, A.R., Statnikov, E.: Algorithms for large scale Markov blanket discovery. In: FLAIRS Conference, St. Augustine, FL, vol. 2, pp. 376–380 (2003)
24. Yan, J.H., Rountree, S., Massman, P., Doody, R.S., Li, H.: Alzheimer's disease and mild cognitive impairment deteriorate fine movement control. J. Psychiatr. Res. **42**(14), 1203–1212 (2008)

I Can't Believe It's Not Better: In-air Movement for Alzheimer Handwriting Synthetic Generation

Asma Bensalah[1,2]($\boxtimes$) , Antonio Parziale[3,4] , Giuseppe De Gregorio[3,4] ,
Angelo Marcelli[3,4] , Alicia Fornés[1,2] , and Josep Lladós[1,2]

[1] Computer Vision Center, Universitat Autònoma de Barcelona, Bellaterra, Spain
{afornes,josep,abensalah}@cvc.uab.es
[2] Computer Science Department, Universitat Autònoma de Barcelona,
Bellaterra, Spain
[3] DIEM, University of Salerno, Via Giovanni Paolo II 132, 84084 Fisciano, SA, Italy
{anparziale,gdegregorio,amarcelli}@unisa.it
[4] AI3S Unit, CINI National Laboratory of Artificial Intelligence and Intelligent
Systems, University of Salerno, Fisciano, SA, Italy

Abstract. During recent years, there here has been a boom in terms
of deep learning use for handwriting analysis and recognition. One main
application for handwriting analysis is early detection and diagnosis in
the health field. Unfortunately, most real case problems still suffer a
scarcity of data, which makes difficult the use of deep learning-based
models. To alleviate this problem, some works resort to synthetic data
generation. Lately, more works are directed towards guided data synthetic generation, a generation that uses the domain and data knowledge
to generate realistic data that can be useful to train deep learning models.
In this work, we combine the domain knowledge about the Alzheimer's
disease for handwriting and use it for a more guided data generation.
Concretely, we have explored the use of in-air movements for synthetic
data generation.

Keywords: In-air Movements · Online handwriting recognition ·
Synthetic Data Generation · Alzheimer disease · Recurrent Neural
Networks · Convolutional Neural Networks

1 Introduction

Deep learning models are data hungry. Hence, in many application scenarios,
additionally to collecting more data specific to the relevant task, generating
samples synthetically has been widely adopted as an alternative to alleviate the
few data issue [1]. It is well known that when it comes to tasks related to the
medical field, data scarcity is more severe since collecting data in clinical setups
is tough and there exist privacy preservation concerns [2].

© The Author(s), under exclusive license to Springer Nature Switzerland AG 2023
A. Parziale et al. (Eds.): IGS 2023, LNCS 14285, pp. 136–148, 2023.
https://doi.org/10.1007/978-3-031-45461-5_10

Alzheimer's disease (AD) can be defined as a slowly progressive irreversible degenerative disease with well-defined pathophysiological mechanisms [3]. AD is marked by a decrease in cognitive skills and the individual's independence levels when performing daily life activities [4]; besides being the most common reason behind dementia.

Early AD detection is essential for screening purposes and later AD patients' disease management. Moreover, it serves to help the patients and their caregivers to plan for the future thus help the patient to maintain a desired quality of life as long as possible. Very often, AD diagnosis in clinical practice can be complicated due to time constraints and due to the fact that AD symptoms can be considered as normal aging symptoms. Furthermore, AD early diagnosis can lessen the financial cost related to AD patients' and their caregivers' support [5,6]. In this scenario, handwriting analysis remains an affordable and efficient alternative for AD early diagnosis and detection contrary to other AD early diagnosis and detection approaches such as invasive and non-invasive biomarkers methods. The latter are generally expensive and limited in terms of availability in clinical practice. In addition, there is a need for special expertise when dealing with technologies that perform invasive biomarkers examinations [7].

Furthermore, it is well known that handwriting problems arise among neurodegenerative patients and AD patients in particular [8]. For instance, small handwriting size referred to as micrographia is linked to Parkinson's disease (PD), meanwhile dysgraphia, defined as the neurological condition that cripples writing abilities [9], is observed among AD patients [10–13]. Hence, handwriting could be deemed an important biomarker to diagnose AD [14,15]. It is assumed that smoother velocity profiles mean more efficient neuromotor systems. Indeed, upon this assumption was built the poor handwriting theory [16]. The theory claims that once a motor system fails to limit the noise behind the accelerate and decelerative forces, it is not kinetically optimal and unpredictable spatially.

Werner et al. [17] examined kinematically the handwriting process amid mild cognitive impairment (MCI), mild AD, and healthy populations. In addition, they assessed the relative significance of handwriting's kinematic features across the three populations. The authors found out that, apart from velocity, all kinematic measures consistently differentiate between healthy and AD individuals.

One interesting finding shown in [17] was the increase in in-air time within AD and MCI groups compared to the control group (healthy). In-air time was defined as the time when the pen is not on whatever writing support used (e.g. paper, tablet, etc.). Several reasons were cited to interpret this outcome: the first one was related to the writing characteristics of the language used for the experiments (concretely, Hebrew) which already requires more pen lifts than Latin-based languages due to the specific language writing characteristics. The second one was related to the theoretical model of Van Galen and Teulings [18], in which the model discerns three phases in the writing response: motor programming (patterns retrieval), parameter setting, and motor initiations (impulse generation for particular muscles). On the ground of these three steps, it could be deduced that the increase in in-air time is due to the deficit in motor programming

138   A. Bensalah et al.

a)   b)

Fig. 1. On-paper (black) and in-air movements (gray) for the word "Mamma" written above a line. a) Healthy individual 1; b) AD patient 2.

amid AD patients who take relatively a longer time to start a movement [19,20]. Finally, the authors suggested that visuospatial deficit among AD patients could be a possible reason [21,22].

Therefore, we are impelled by this work on the relevant discrimination power of in-air movements in AD patients' handwriting and our observations across many datasets for neurodegenerative diseases (see Figs. 2 and 1) into the bargain, coupled with synthetic generation to face the data scarcity for neurodegenerative diseases. In essence, we explore in this work the use of in-air movements for synthetic handwriting generation. Our initial hypothesis is that in-air movement information could lead to generating good-quality synthetic samples and therefore, models trained with this data can reach better classification accuracies.

To our best knowledge, handwriting synthetic generation for AD detection and diagnosis, in particular, is not a prosperous research area, which requires more research efforts from the scientific community.

The rest of the article is organized as follows: Sect. 2 reviews relevant related works. Next, Sect. 3 describes the generator/discriminator duality in our implementation. Afterwards, experiment details are given in Sect. 5 for reproducibility purposes. Then, Sect. 6 presents the different results, which are discussed later in Sect. 7. Finally, we draw conclusions in Sect. 8.

2   Related Work

Many works covered online handwriting analysis for neurodegenerative patients as it offers more information about the individual's kinematics and fine motor skills than offline analysis. Most of those works take into account kinematic features to automatically discriminate between a control group of healthy individuals and a patient group [10,23]. All those works fall into the line of Computer Aided Diagnosis (CAD) systems which help clinicians and doctors by providing biomarker computations and analysis. CAD systems could be integrated in already existing clinical workflows in order to maximize early diagnosis and detection chances [24].

a)   b)

Fig. 2. On-paper (black) and in-air movements (gray) for the word "bottiglia" written in reverse. a) Healthy individual 1; b) AD patient 2.

The analyzed tasks can be classified into the following categories:

- Drawing tasks: individuals are asked to draw different forms: spirals [25], meanders, lines [26], etc.
- Writing tasks: individuals are asked to write a letter or a sequence of letters, words, sentences [27], etc.
- Complex tasks: individuals are asked to perform the writing/drawing task in addition to another motor/cognitive task with the purpose of increasing the task load, thus revealing more motor/cognitive issues [28].

Traditionally, statistical tests (for instance, ANOVA) are used to analyze online handwriting [29]. In the past years, the handwriting analysis area has benefited from the machine/deep learning boom, in particular handwriting analysis for CAD systems: neurodegenerative diseases and others [30,31].

Some works have tackled synthetic sample handwriting generation for neurodegenerative diseases [32,33].

Nevertheless, there is still a gap in data generation for Alzheimer's disease, in particular, and a lack of works that focus on the domain knowledge for guided data generation.

3   Methodology

As explained in the introduction, we aim to evaluate the impact of in-air movements in the generation of synthetic samples and in the classification tasks.

We have used the architecture presented in [33] to generate and select the synthetic samples used for training the classifier that discriminates between the handwriting sample drawn by AD patients or healthy subjects. The architecture consists of a Generator (RNN), trained to generate new samples, and a Discriminator (CNN network), which classifies the generated images into fake or real samples. Once the discriminator can be fooled, the generation is supposed to generate good-quality data that can be used with real data to train the final classifier.

Contrary to conventional GANs architectures, the GAN loss does not backpropagate through the generator to update each layer's weights. Instead, the

Generator and Discriminator in this architecture are parallel. Thus the generator does not learn from the discriminator's feedback (code compatibility reasons).

The two modules are further described in the next subsections.

3.1 Generator

First, the real data is organised into 5 folds, and used later for training and testing. Then, synthetic images are generated. The generator is inspired by Alex Graves's work [34], where recurrent neural networks (RNNs) were used to generate realistic handwriting sequences. Rather than having the RNNs model predict exactly what the future point will be, Graves's work discusses predicting a probability distribution of the future given the prior information.

The generator is fed with two channels of the input time series: acceleration through x (a_x) and y (a_y) axis. A two-layer stacked basic LSTM has been used, with 256 nodes in each layer. The generator output is a sequence of SL points, where SL is chosen so that the distribution of synthetic samples per number of points was similar to the distribution of real samples per number of points.

3.2 Discriminator

The discriminator validates the data outputted by the generator. A synthetic image is hold when the discriminator assigns to it the correct class, otherwise is discarded.

The discriminator is an ensemble of 5 Convolutional Neural Networks (CNNs) and it classifies samples by a majority vote rule. The dataset of real samples is shuffled 5 times and each time one of the CNN belonging to the ensemble is trained with 35% of the data.

Each CNN of the ensemble is made-up of 5 convolutional layers and its architecture is equal to the CIFAR-10 neural network presented in [35]. Figure 3 shows the neural network and the hyper-parameters related to each layer. Table 2 reports the hyper-parameter values chosen for training the 5 CNNs.

The adopted discriminator elaborates 2D images so, both the real and generated time series are converted into 2D grayscale images, as described in [33]. In particular, the time series of each real or synthetic handwriting sample are rearranged into a squared matrix that is then resized in a 64 × 64 image using the Lanczos re-sampling method.

4 Dataset

The DARWIN dataset was introduced in [27] as the largest publicly available dataset [36] in terms of participants' numbers. The dataset includes handwriting samples from 174 individuals: 89 AD patients and 85 healthy individuals. To ensure maximum pattern matching between the two groups, participants from both groups have the same age distribution, educational background, and work profession type (intellectual/manual).

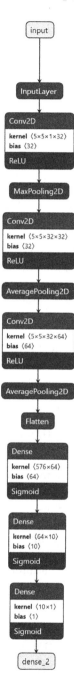

Fig. 3. One of the 5 CNN that make up the Discriminator architecture.

The dataset was obtained by writing with a pen on an A4 sheet of white paper placed over a Wacom's Bamboo tablet. The recorded information is:

1. timestamp;
2. x coordinate;
3. y coordinate;
4. binary pen-down property;
5. the pressure applied by the pen on the paper.

Individuals were asked to perform 25 tasks, for instance:

- Joining two points with a horizontal line, continuously four times;
- Retracing a circle (6 cm in diameter) continuously four times;
- Copying the word "foglio";
- Copying the letters 'l', 'm', and 'p';
- Copying the letters on the adjacent rows;
- Writing cursively a sequence of four lowercase letters 'l', in a single smooth movement;
- Writing cursively a sequence of four lowercase cursive bigram 'le', in a single smooth movement;
- Copying in reverse the word "casa";
- Drawing a clock with all hours and putting hands at 11:05 (Clock Drawing Test);
- Copying a paragraph;

For our work, we are interested in particular by two of these tasks:

- Task 13: Copy the word 'mamma' (the Italian word for mom) above a line;
- Task 16: Copy in reverse the word 'bottiglia' (the Italian word for bottle);

Task 13 has been chosen over many works dealing with neurodegenerative diseases handwriting analysis [37] because of its significant presence in someone's language since early childhood, besides the fact that it is a word commonly repeated by AD patients in advanced disease stages.

On the other hand Task 16 is an interesting task because it is a complex one since it consists of a word reverse copying which implies a cognitive effort (inspired from the Mini Mental State Examination).

5   Experiments

We define two experimentation scenarios for each Task:

- In-air movements: using only movements performed with the pen when it is not on writing support;
- In-air + On-paper: using both movements recorded when the pen is and is not on the writing support;

Initially, authors in [33] have found that feeding the generator with more than two channels from the input time series has weak effects on the method's performance. For the same reason and for optimal memory and computation time, we have chosen the a_x and a_y channels. For reproducibility uses, Table 1 describes the generator's hyperparameters.

It's worth nothing that for each scenario and for each task we trained 2 different RNNs: the first synthesized samples drawn by healthy subjects, the second synthesized samples drawn by AD patients.

Moreover, for each scenario and for each task, a CNN that discriminates between samples drawn by a healthy subject or AD patient was trained with the hyperparameters reported in Table 2 and using both real and synthetic samples. The number of generated synthetic samples has been either 500 (500 AD and 500 healthy) or 1000 (1000 AD and 1000 healthy), for each task. The performance was measured by averaging on 5 training of the CNN. At each training, the real dataset was shuffled and 50% of subjects were kept apart as test set.

Table 1. Generator's hyperparameters.

Parameter	Chosen Value
RNN hidden state	256
Number of layers	2
Cell Type	LSTM
SL	150
Number of epochs	301
Learning rate	0.01
Number of Mixture M	20
Dropout keep probability	0.8
Training/validation set	(70%,30%)
Loss Function	Log likelihood loss

6   Results

Table 3 provides the average classification accuracies for both Task 13 (mamma) and Task 16 (bottiglia) when generating 500 synthetic samples, while Table 4 compares the average accuracies when generating 1000 synthetic samples. In both cases, we compare the performance of there scenarios using: in-air movements, on-paper movements and in-air movements together with on-paper movements.

Table 2. Experimental setup to classify 2D images with the CNN.

Parameter	Value
Kernel Initializer	Glorot Normal
Bias Initializer	0
Pseudorandom number generators	Fixed Seeds
Training/Validation	35%/15%
k-fold cross validation	5-fold
Batch size	5
Optimization algorithm	SGD
Learning Rate	2×10^{-5}
Momentum	0.9
Nesterov Momentum	True
Loss	Binary Cross Entropy
Early stopping	Min Validation Loss
Epochs	10000

Table 3. Average accuracies for Task 13 and Task 16 using 500 synthetic samples.

	500 synthetic samples		
	In-air	on-paper	In-air+on-paper
Task13 (mamma)	35,71%	43,77%	45,15%
Task16 (bottiglia)	45,15%	54,66%	51,46%

Although we observe that there's a significant decrease in terms of average accuracy for Task 13 when using in-air movements only to generate synthetic samples, Table 4 shows that accuracies remain almost the same when using in-air and in-air+ on-paper movements for sample generation with a tiny difference of 0,43%. We observe that using in-air movements, the average classification accuracy is higher for Task 16 compared to Task 13 (Table 3).

It is interesting to notice that while for task 13 using in-air and on-paper movements together leads to better accuracies (45,15%) compared to when they are used separately (35,71%, 43,77%) to generate synthetic data, it is not the case for task 16. This pattern is similar for the case of task 16, when more synthetic samples are generated (see Table 4), the best accuracy is still achieved with on-paper movements solely.

Table 4. Average accuracies for Task 16 using 1000 synthetic samples.

	1000 synthetic samples		
	In-air	On-paper	In-air+On-paper
Task16 (bottiglia)	51,59%	54,14%	52,02%

For comparison purposes, Table 5 provides the average accuracies when using in-air movements per fold when no synthetic samples are generated. It can be observed that the average accuracy reaches 56,78% for Task 13 while it is higher by 0,34% for Task 16.

Table 5. Average accuracies using in-air movements per Fold with no synthetic data.

In-air (No synthetic samples)						
Accuracy	Fold 1	Fold 2	Fold 3	Fold 4	Fold 5	Average
Task 13 (mamma)	62,50%	57,14%	50%	50%	64,28%	**56,78%**
Task 16 (bottiglia)	50%	71,42%	52,94	68,42%	42,85	**57,12%**

7   Discussion

Our initial hypothesis was that in-air movements represent discriminative patterns for the Alzheimer's Disease patient population. Overall, the results show that there is a gap between classification accuracies when using only in-air movements versus the use of in-air plus on-paper movements and this gap depends on the task complexity and the number of synthetic samples.

First of all, contrary to what we expected, the model performed better without synthetic data at all. This surprising result could be explained by the extreme variability of in-air movements, which could not be modeled in the right way by the network used to generate synthetic data. The absence of visual feedback during in-air movements results in the patients' inability to control their movements and the generation of complex, almost random, in-air trajectories. Hence, predicting the probability distribution of the next in-air point is challenging. This is clear even visually, in Task 16, where the cognitive deficit resulted in very different forms of in-air movements (as many patients had difficulties in terms of motor programming when asked to write in reverse, see Fig. 4).

Next, the results show that the performance gap varies depending on the task. Task 16 involves a greater cognitive effort (writing backwards) than Task 13 and that results in the generation of longer and more complex in-air movements. On one hand, the greater cognitive effort of Task 16 makes the handwriting of AD patients more easily recognisable than the healthy controls' handwriting when compared to the other task. On the other hand, the complexity of in-air movements has the drawback that a greater number of synthetic samples is required before they become beneficial with respect to the on-paper movements.

a)   b)

Fig. 4. On-paper (black) and in-air movements (gray) for the word "bottiglia" written in reverse by two different patients. a) AD patient 1; b) AD patient 2.

8   Conclusion

In this work, we have explored the use of in-air movements for synthetic sample generation, particularly for a neurodegenerative disease like Alzheimer's disease. In accordance with the work in [17], which states that in-air movements hold discriminative patterns, we have observed that indeed in-air movements have an impact in terms of model performance.

We have observed that in-air movement quality and quantity depend on the nature of the task and the subject's motor and cognitive abilities, thus a subject/task-centered approach could lead to interesting results. Finally, further synthetic sample experiments could be done in the future to assess the model's performance with and without synthetic data. In addition, as future work, we plan to explore other methods for data generation, which may be more suitable for this particular task.

In summary, this work highlights the importance of exploring domain and data knowledge for improving data generation for health applications.

Acknowledgment. This work has been partially supported by the Spanish project PID2021-126808OB-I00 (GRAIL) and the FI fellowship AGAUR 2020 FI-SDUR 00497 (with the support of the Secretaria d'Universitats i Recerca of the Generalitat de Catalunya and the Fons Social Europeu). The authors acknowledge the support of the Generalitat de Catalunya CERCA Program to CVC's general activities.

References

1. Gal, M., Lynskey, O.: Synthetic data: legal implications of the data-generation revolution. 2023 109 (2023)
2. Bansal, M.A., Sharma, D.R., Kathuria, D.M.: A systematic review on data scarcity problem in deep learning: solution and applications. ACM Comput. Surv. 54(10s), 1–29 (2022)
3. De Paula, V.J., Radanovic, M., Diniz, B., Forlenza, O.: Alzheimer's disease. Sub-Cell. Biochem. 65, 352 (2012)

4. Breijyeh, Z., Karaman, R.: Comprehensive review on Alzheimer's disease: causes and treatment. Molecules **25**, 5789 (2020)
5. Porsteinsson, A.P., Isaacson, R., Knox, S.A., Sabbagh, M.N., Rubino, I.: Diagnosis of early Alzheimer's disease: clinical practice in 2021. J. Prev. Alzheimer's Dis. **8**, 371–386 (2021)
6. Wells, C., Horton, J.: An overview of new and emerging technologies for early diagnosis of Alzheimer disease. Can. J. Health Technol. **2**(5) (2022)
7. Bature, F., Pappas, Y., Pang, D., Guinn, B.: Can non-invasive biomarkers lead to an earlier diagnosis of Alzheimer's disease? Curr. Alzheimer Res. **18**, 12 (2021)
8. Margarete, D., Zamarian, L., Djamshidian, A.: Handwriting in Alzheimer's disease. J. Alzheimer's Dis. **82**, 1–9 (2021)
9. Devi, A., Kavya, G.: Dysgraphia disorder forecasting and classification technique using intelligent deep learning approaches. Prog. Neuropsychopharmacol. Biol. Psychiatry **120**, 110647 (2023)
10. Impedovo, D., Pirlo, G.: Dynamic handwriting analysis for the assessment of neurodegenerative diseases: a pattern recognition perspective. IEEE Rev. Biomed. Eng. **12**, 209–220 (2019)
11. Fairhurst, M., Hoque, S., Razian, M.A.: Improved screening of developmental dyspraxia using on-line image analysis. In: Proceedings of the 8th World Multi-Conference on Systemics, Cybernetics and Informatics (SCI2004), vol. 1, pp. 160–165. International Institute of Informatics and Systemics (2004)
12. Glenat, S., Heutte, L., Paquet, T., Mellier, D.: Computer-based diagnosis of dyspraxia: the MEDDRAW project. In: 12th Conference of the International Graphonomics Society, IGS (2005)
13. Onofri, E., et al.: Dysgraphia in relation to cognitive performance in patients with Alzheimer's disease (2013)
14. De Stefano, C., Fontanella, F., Impedovo, D., Pirlo, G., di Freca, A.S.: Handwriting analysis to support neurodegenerative diseases diagnosis: a review. Pattern Recognit. Lett. **121**, 37–45 (2019)
15. Ishikawa, T., et al.: Handwriting features of multiple drawing tests for early detection of Alzheimer's disease: a preliminary result. In: MedInfo, pp. 168–172 (2019)
16. van Galen, G.P., Portier, S.J., Smits-Engelsman, B.C.M., Schomaker, L.R.B.: Neuromotor noise and poor handwriting in children. Acta Physiol. (Oxf) **82**(1), 161–178 (1993)
17. Werner, P., Rosenblum, S., Bar-On, G., Heinik, J., Korczyn, A.: Handwriting process variables discriminating mild Alzheimer's disease and mild cognitive impairment. J. Gerontol. Ser. B **61**(4), P228–P236 (2006)
18. van Galen, G.P., Teulings, H.-L.: The independent monitoring of form and scale factors in handwriting. Acta Physiol. **54**(1), 9–22 (1983)
19. Bellgrove, M.A., Phillips, J.G., Bradshaw, J.L., Hall, K.A., Presnell, I., Hecht, H.: Response programming in dementia of the Alzheimer type: a kinematic analysis. Neuropsychologia **35**(3), 229–240 (1997)
20. Gordon, B., Carson, K.: The basis for choice reaction time slowing in Alzheimer's disease. Brain Cogn. **13**(2), 148–166 (1990)
21. Johnson, D., Morris, J., Galvin, J.: Verbal and visuospatial deficits in dementia with lewy bodies. Neurology **65**, 1232–1238 (2005)
22. Weintraub, S., Wicklund, A.H., Salmon, D.P.: The neuropsychological profile of Alzheimer disease. Cold Spring Harbor Perspect. Med. **2**(4), a006171 (2012)
23. Thomas, M., Lenka, A., Kumar Pal, P.: Handwriting analysis in Parkinson's disease: current status and future directions. Mov. Disord. Clin. Pract. **4**(6), 806–818 (2017)

24. Pérez Pelegrí, M.: Applications of Deep Leaning on Cardiac MRI: Design Approaches for a Computer Aided Diagnosis – riunet.upv.es. https://riunet.upv.es/handle/10251/192988. Accessed 21 June 2023

25. Legrand, A.P., et al.: New insight in spiral drawing analysis methods - application to action tremor quantification. Clin. Neurophysiol. **128**(10), 1823–1834 (2017)

26. Müller, T., Kuhn, W.: Complex motion series performance differs between previously untreated patients with Parkinson's disease and controls. J. Neural Transm. **129**, 595–600 (2022)

27. Cilia, N.D., De Gregorio, G., De Stefano, C., Fontanella, F., Marcelli, A., Parziale, A.: Diagnosing Alzheimer's disease from on-line handwriting: a novel dataset and performance benchmarking. Eng. Appl. Artif. Intell. **111**, 104822 (2022)

28. Broeder, S., Nackaerts, E., Nieuwboer, A., Smits-Engelsman, B., Swinnen, S., Heremans, E.: The effects of dual tasking on handwriting in patients with Parkinson's disease. Neuroscience **263**, 193–202 (2014)

29. Garre-Olmo, J., Faúndez-Zanuy, M., López-de Ipiña, K., Calvó-Perxas, L., Turró-Garriga, O.: Kinematic and pressure features of handwriting and drawing: preliminary results between patients with mild cognitive impairment, Alzheimer disease and healthy controls. Curr. Alzheimer Res. **14**(9), 960–968 (2017)

30. Fröhlich, H., et al.: Leveraging the potential of digital technology for better individualized treatment of Parkinson's disease. Front. Neurol. **13**, 788427 (2022)

31. Dao, Q., El-Yacoubi, M.A., Rigaud, A.-S.: Detection of Alzheimer disease on online handwriting using 1d convolutional neural network. IEEE Access **11**, 2148–2155 (2023)

32. Dzotsenidze, E., Valla, E., Nõmm, S., Medijainen, K., Taba, P., Toomela, A.: Generative adversarial networks as a data augmentation tool for CNN-based Parkinson's disease diagnostics. IFAC-PapersOnLine **55**(29), 108–113 (2022)

33. Gemito, G., Marcelli, A., Parziale, A.: Generation of synthetic drawing samples to diagnose Parkinson's disease. In: Carmona-Duarte, C., Diaz, M., Ferrer, M.A., Morales, A. (eds.) IGS 2022. LNCS, vol. 13424, pp. 269–284. Springer, Cham (2022). https://doi.org/10.1007/978-3-031-19745-1_20

34. Graves, A.: Generating sequences with recurrent neural networks. CoRR, abs/1308.0850 (2013)

35. Pereira, C.R., et al.: A new computer vision-based approach to aid the diagnosis of Parkinson's disease. Comput. Methods Programs Biomed. **136**, 79–88 (2016)

36. Fontanella, F.: DARWIN. UCI Machine Learning Repository (2022). https://doi.org/10.24432/C55D0K

37. Impedovo, D., Pirlo, G., Barbuzzi, D., Balestrucci, A., Impedovo, S.: Handwritten processing for pre diagnosis of Alzheimer disease. In: Proceedings of the International Conference on Biomedical Electronics and Devices - Volume 1: BIODEVICES, (BIOSTEC 2014), pp. 193–199. INSTICC, SciTePress (2014)

Handwritten Historical Documents

The Neglected Role of GUI in Performance Evaluation of AI-Based Transcription Tools for Handwritten Documents

Giuseppe De Gregorio$^{(\boxtimes)}$ (ID) and Angelo Marcelli (ID)

DIEM, University of Salerno, Via Giovanni Paolo II 132, 84084 Fisciano, SA, Italy
{gdegregorio,amarcelli}@unisa.it

Abstract. This paper aims to inspect the often neglected role of Graphical User Interfaces (GUI) in AI-based tools designed to assist in the transcription of handwritten documents. While the precision and recall of the handwritten word recognition have traditionally been the primary focus, we argue that the time parameter associated with the GUI, specifically in terms of validation and correction, plays an equally crucial role. By investigating the influence of GUI design on the validation and correction aspects of transcription we want to highlight how the time that the user must take to interact with the interface must be taken into account to evaluate the performance of the transcription process. Through comprehensive analysis and experimentation, we illustrate the profound impact that GUI design can have on the overall efficiency of transcription tools. We demonstrate how the time saved through the utilization of an assistant tool is heavily dependent on the operations performed within the interface and the diverse features it offers. By recognizing GUI design as an essential component of transcription tools, we can unlock their full potential and significantly improve their effectiveness.

Keywords: Handwritten · Document Transcription · Document Analysis · Historical Document Processing

1 Introduction

In an increasingly digital world, the task of converting handwritten documents into a digital format can be time-consuming and challenging. The rapid advancements in artificial intelligence (AI) have paved the way for innovative solutions in various fields, including transcription [9]. AI tools that focus on transcribing handwritten text offer immense potential for increased efficiency and accuracy, potentially revolutionizing how we manage handwritten documents.

The utilization of AI tools for transcription purposes involves leveraging sophisticated algorithms, neural networks, and machine learning techniques to interpret and convert handwritten text into digital form. These tools learn from

A. Parziale et al. (Eds.): IGS 2023, LNCS 14285, pp. 151–164, 2023.
https://doi.org/10.1007/978-3-031-45461-5_11

vast amounts of data, acquiring the ability to recognize patterns, characters, and words, enabling them to accurately transcribe handwritten documents with increasing precision.

This technology has the potential to significantly streamline workflows, improve accessibility, and facilitate data analysis. Indeed, one of the primary benefits of using AI tools for transcribing handwritten documents is the potential for significant time savings [5]. What used to take hours or even days to manually transcribe can now be accomplished in a fraction of the time. This increased efficiency not only enhances productivity for individuals and organizations but also allows for expedited access to critical information contained within handwritten documents.

However, it is essential to consider the limitations and challenges associated with using AI tools for transcription. Handwriting can vary significantly between individuals, making it difficult for AI systems to accurately interpret unique styles and idiosyncrasies. Complex or degraded handwriting, smudges, or unclear markings can further compound the challenge. Additionally, certain languages or scripts pose additional difficulties, as AI tools may be primarily trained on specific languages or character sets. An important example is given by handwritten documents of historical interest [7]. Working with handwritten historical documents poses unique challenges. The passage of time, exposure to the elements, and ageing of materials can cause deterioration, making the texts difficult to read or comprehend. The use of archaic language, abbreviations, and unique writing conventions prevalent in different time periods can also pose challenges for contemporary readers and researchers.

The use of AI tools for transcribing can facilitate the digitization and transcription process. These tools can assist in deciphering handwriting, enhancing legibility, and converting the content into searchable digital formats, making the documents more accessible to researchers and the general public [3,18]. However, the process of assisted transcription raises questions and considerations regarding the accuracy and the role of human involvement. While AI models have made significant progress, errors can still occur, especially when confronted with ambiguous or illegible handwriting. It is crucial to approach AI-transcribed documents with caution and consider essential the need for human intervention or verification to ensure accuracy and reliability.

Traditionally, the primary emphasis in transcription systems has been on achieving high accuracy rates in recognizing handwritten words. While this is undoubtedly important, it is equally essential to recognize the equally critical role played by the Graphical User Interfaces (GUI), particularly in terms of validation and correction processes. The time parameter associated with these GUI interactions can significantly impact the overall efficiency of transcription tools.

Given the need for user intervention to ensure an accurate and error-free document transcript, regardless of the AI technology employed, human-machine interaction plays a significant role. Consequently, the time saved by using this system does not simply depend on the performance of the AI model used and its ability to recognize handwritten text after proper training; it is equally important to consider how quickly users can interact with the system interface.

The user must verify that the AI tool has accurately associated transcriptions with the images of words present in the documents to be transcribed. All transcriptions correctly linked should be validated. Furthermore, any mistakes made by the text recognition system must be corrected by replacing wrong transcriptions with accurate ones. Lastly, if the AI system was unable to recognize any words, a transcript must be provided manually for them.

All of these operations take time, and the amount of time is contingent on the design choices of the interface, what basic operations were chosen to interact with it, and how many and which features are available to the user. Intuitively, it makes sense that these operations should require less time than manually transcribing a word since using the entire system can lead to faster total transcription. It is more difficult to grasp what impact each element has on obtaining an overall reduction in the time gain. In this work, we focus our attention on trying to determine how much time can be dedicated to validating and correcting output from text recognition systems while sustaining the decrease in transcription time.

The paper is then organized as follows: in Sect. 2, we provide a detailed overview of the transcription process when it is assisted by a Keyword Spotting (KWS) system, emphasizing the time course of the typical interaction between the user and the validation/correction interface; in Sect. 3, we present the experimental results obtained from three datasets containing handwritten documents from the 13th to 18th centuries; while, in Sect. 4, we discuss the experimental findings; lastly, in Sect. 5, we draw some preliminary conclusions and outline future investigations.

2   The Transcription Process

In the process of transcribing a set of handwritten documents, a Keyword Spotting system can be utilized to reduce the user workload. A KWS system is a machine learning tool that has the charge of locating words it knows how to represent within images of handwritten pages. The preparatory phase requires creating a training set, hereinafter referred to as TS, containing the representation of each word image (in terms of a suitable set of features) and its correct transcription. For the sake of performance, it is usual that a smaller portion of the total collection is used, and it is crucial that an accurate and complete transcription of TS is available; when it does not exist, it is up to the user to manually transcribe selected documents for use in TS. In such a case the user must spend the time t_{man} to read a word of the document and type-in the transcript. Thus, t_{man} depends mostly on the proficiency of the user in reading and providing the transcript.

For the transcription of the rest of the collection, hereinafter referred to as the data set and denoted by DS, the Keyword Spotting system can be utilized to retrieve words that are most similar in representation to those of the keyword list. As such, it is possible to recover transcripts for keywords within DS without the system having to explicitly recognize the text present in the images. This allows KWS systems to be robust when dealing with manuscript collections consisting of a small number of documents [1].

Ultimately, the goal of the system is to accurately transcribe the list of word images present in DS, so that manual transcription is no longer necessary, thus saving user time and effort. High values of the KWS system Precision p and Recall r would further optimize the transcription process, as a greater number of correctly identified words yield more savings in terms of time required for transcribing a collection. Consequently, it is important that KWS systems strive for an optimal performance output so as to achieve maximum efficiency in obtaining an accurate transcription.

The performance of a KWS system, is given in terms of its p and recall r, and since they are both smaller than 1, the KWS is liable for mistakes in spotting the word image corresponding to the keyword of the query, thus providing the wrong transcript, as well as for missing some words, thus being unable to transcribe all of the words of DS. Additionally, KWS systems can struggle with the problem of out-of-vocabulary (OOV) words, i.e. words present in DS but not included in TS, resulting in either no spotting at all or a significant drop in performance. Consequently, it is necessary to incorporate a validation stage to guarantee that all the words in the documents are accurately transcribed. This includes verifying the output of the KWS system, confirming correct transcriptions, correcting errors, and manually transcribing any missed word.

This user-system interaction necessitates a Graphical User Interface that enables the user to view the image of the word to transcribe in addition to the list of transcription options generated by the KWS system from which to choose the correct one, thus spending the time t_{val} to achieve the transcription of the word. Thus, t_{val} is contingent on how the GUI was constructed and which operation is dedicated to validate the correct transcript. As an example, one could envision validating the output by clicking on the right transcription with a mouse, or using the arrow keys on the keyboard to pick out the correct entry from the list, or interacting directly with the interface through a touchscreen device. Moreover, if the list is ranked according to the likelihood of a word to be the right transcription and the default option is that the top-ranking element is the correct interpretation, whenever this happens to be true the correct transcription can be obtained by clicking a mouse button, or by pressing/touching a dedicated key. The time t_{val} depends also on how many transcription options are available to the users via the GUI; a quick scrolling is possible when there are few elements in the list, but having few alternatives decreases the likelihood of the correct transcription to be in the list. Figure 1 illustrates an example of an interface for assisting the user during the validation of system output. In the figure, the interface proceeds line by line, showing the current line of text on top of the screen, with the word to transcribe highlighted in the text line and displayed at the centre of the interface while on its right side is the list of possible transcriptions proposed by the system from which the user must choose the correct one.

When the system is unable to provide the right option in the transcription options list, or when it cannot produce any (which may occur when the word is an OOV word), the correct transcription must be provided manually. The

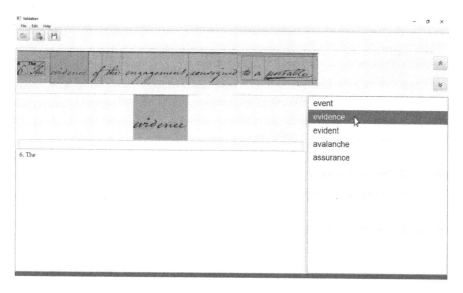

Fig. 1. An example of an interface during the validation process. The transcript of the current word *"evidence"* is present in the list of options and the user must simply validate it by selecting the correct transcript from the list.

time t_{cor} to perform this operation also depends on the features of the system interface. For instance, the interface can be fitted with an auto-complete mode that can expedite and accelerate the typing of the transcriptions. After typing in the initial letters of the correct transcription, the system can search for relevant keywords compatible with those same letters. At this point, the GUI could potentially offer up the correct transcription that can be selected without writing out all of it (Fig. 2). Similarly to the previous case, the use of the system is profitable when $t_{cor} \leq t_{man}$.

The parameters that define the interaction with the interface, thus, are t_{val} and t_{cor}. In short, the former represents the time taken for a user to view a handwritten word and determine if the correct transcription is among those presented by the system. The latter indicates how much time is required to enter a transcription manually when it has been determined that no valid alternative was supplied. Paying attention to these parameters when designing a validation/correction graphical interface can be of utmost importance. An interface that requires too much time for interactions may effectively cancel out the gain in time that the use of a KWS system provides. Additionally, interaction operations necessary for interface effectiveness, even when designed well, are not instantaneous. It is therefore important to consider how the time gain is influenced by the elementary operations required by a particular interface given the performance of the KWS system used. For these reasons, it is important to estimate the time gain G obtainable by the system depending on *both* the performance indexes of the KWS system r and p and on the time parameters of the interface t_{val} and t_{cor}:

$$G(p, r, t_{val}, t_{cor}) \tag{1}$$

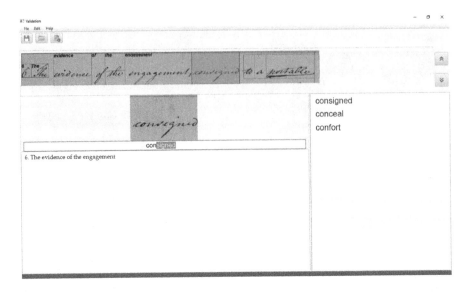

Fig. 2. The word *"consigned"* was not recognized by the system, so the user is forced to enter the transcript manually. The autocomplete system allows the identification of the correct transcription after the user has entered just three letters.

It is worth noting that when both t_{val} and t_{cor} are equal to t_{man} there is no gain, and that it increases as t_{val} and t_{cor} becomes smaller and smaller with respect to t_{man}.

3   Experimental Results

In this section, we experimentally assess the impact of the GUI temporal parameters t_{val} and t_{cor} on the temporal gains obtainable using a KWS to assist the transcription of an entire collection of handwritten documents. We first assess the performance of KWS in terms of the size of the training set TS. Once the size of TS has been established and the performance indices p and r determined, we then investigate how varying the time parameters t_{val} and t_{cor} impacts the resulting time gain G.

3.1   Datasets

For experimentation, three collections of historical handwritten documents commonly used as benchmarks for KWS systems [2,11,13,14,16,17] were taken into consideration, namely the George Washington dataset, [10], the Bentham dataset [12], and the Parzival dataset [6]. For the purpose of the experiments, only 20 pages extracted from the Bentham dataset were used, while the entire dataset was used in the remaining cases. The George Washington and the Bentham datasets both originate from the 18th century and are written in English by a single writer, while the pages of the Parzival dataset are written in Middle High German and were produced by three authors in the 13th century.

Each dataset has been divided into the training set TS, composed of some pages of the collection, and the DS set made up of the remaining pages to be transcribed. Table 1 shows the details of the different datasets highlighting the number of pages and the number of words contained in each of them.

Table 1. Composition of datasets in terms of number of pages and number of words.

Dataset	Num Pages	Num Words
Washington	20	4819
Bentham	20	3478
Parzival	47	23412

3.2 KWS System

The Keyword Spotting System (KWS) we used is based on PHOCNet [15] and it was set up for segmentation-based Query-by-Example search (QbS). The images and transcriptions of the terms in the training set TS were used to train the PHOCnet. During query time, all distinct transcriptions from TS were taken and their corresponding PHOC representation was used as the keyword list. Bray-Curtis dissimilarity [4] was utilized to measure the similarity between images in the keyword list and the images of the words to be transcribed in the set DS. The KWS is able to return an ordered list of possible transcriptions for a query word image, and the order of the entries in the list is defined by the distance measured between the query word and the keywords.

3.3 KWS Performance

In the first experimental phase, the KWS system's performance in terms of Precision and Recall were assessed for each DS reported in Table 1. Figure 3 illustrates how varying the number of pages in TS affects Precision and Recall for each dataset. The experiments were executed three times for each dataset, randomly selecting the order of pages in TS each time, and the results are reported in terms of the average values.

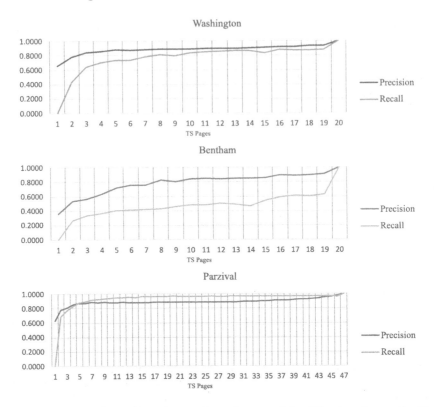

Fig. 3. Precision and Recall as the number of pages of the TS set varies on the three datasets.

3.4   How GUI Times Affects the Time Gain

As illustrated by the graphs in Fig. 3, the precision and recall value is contingent upon the number of pages in the training set TS and tends to remain steady for TS comprised of 5 to 10 pages. To analyze how the temporal gain of the transcription varies based on temporal-dependent user interface parameters, we use the values obtained from $TS = 5$ pages and $TS = 10$ pages.

The time parameters of the interface t_{val} and t_{cor}, along with the performance indices p and r of the KWS system, affect the time required to achieve a complete and accurate transcription of a collection of handwritten documents. Marcelli et al [8] derive this dependency by proposing a model that can estimate the time gain achievable utilizing a KWS system to support the transcription process; it is notable that the parameters for a lexicon-based KWS are similar to those considered in this study. We then employ the model introduced in [8] to compute the time gain and assess how different timescale values of the t_{val} and t_{cor} influence performance in terms of time gain. It is essential to note that the model predicts using precision and recall indices p_i and r_i computed for each keyword in the list. In this work, we assumed the same average precision and recall values p and r for each keyword, as is commonly done in the literature. Similarly, we use for t_{man} the average instead of a different t_{man_i} for each word, and lastly, following the observation reported at the end of Sect. 2, express t_{val} and t_{cor} with respect to t_{man} rather than independently. By doing so, it will be possible to estimate the gain given the *implementation* of the interface by using their values measured in the preliminary phase, but also to set the time constraints for the *design* of the interface to achieve the desired estimated gain. We then adjust the two GUI time parameters t_{val} and t_{cor} from 0.1% to 100% of t_{man} and estimate the gain.

Figure 4, Fig. 5, and Fig. 6 illustrate the results of the Washington, Bentham, and Parzival datasets. The left panel of the figures displays the case in which TS is made of 5 pages, while the right panel shows the results obtained when TS is made of 10 pages. The graphs at the top of the figure illustrate how the values of t_{cor} and t_{val} vary when the temporal gain of the transcript is set to zero. The Zero Gain Line delineates which time parameters reset the gain, dividing the plane into two semi-planes. The area below the line is the positive gain area, that is the area in which a positive gain and therefore a reduction in transcription time is obtained, while above the line there is the negative gain area, which represents the area in which the transcription time is greater than the time necessary for a completely manual transcription. Moving downward further away from the Zero Gain Line the absolute value of temporal gain increases. This behaviour can be observed more clearly in the lower part of the figures, which highlights bands that link to gain range, which we will refer to as Time Gain Bands; only below the Zero Gain Line are bands with positive gains, and travelling further down from it increases the value of the temporal gain.

Observing the figures, it can be noted that with a TS of 10 pages, the area of positive gain increases, while the number of gain bands decreases. This implies that larger time gains are achievable when the TS consists of 5 pages, but stricter constraints for the interplay between validation and correction times must be enforced since the area for positive gain is reduced.

4 Discussion

Upon analyzing Figs. 4, 5, and 6, it becomes evident that regardless of the case, the positive gain area is more significant when using a training set TS composed of 10 pages compared to 5 pages. This observation suggests that achieving a positive gain becomes easier when working with a larger training set. This behaviour aligns with the trends exhibited by the performance indices of the Keyword Spotting system, as illustrated in Fig. 3. The larger the training set, the higher the potential for improving the KWS system's performance. Additionally, with a larger training set, the keyword list expands, while the number of pages requiring transcription decreases.

However, it is intriguing to note that when examining the Time Gain Band graphs, it is apparent that higher time gains can be achieved with a training set consisting of only 5 pages. Furthermore, for the case of $TS = 5$, once a

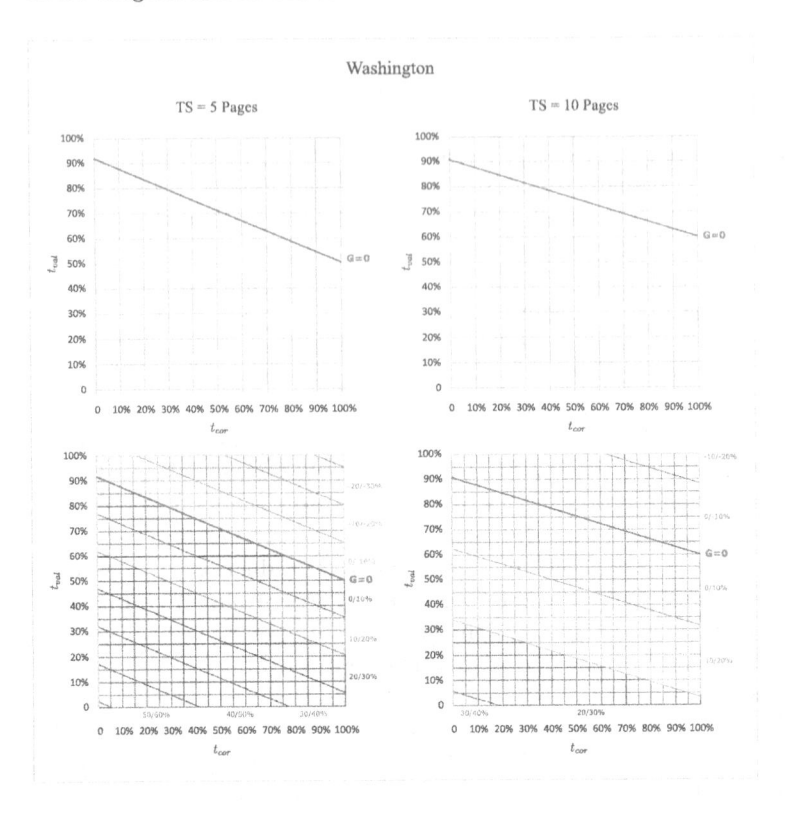

Fig. 4. The graphs above illustrate the Zero Gain Line in the t_{cor}/t_{val} plane, whereas the graphs below depict the varied Time Gain Bands for the Washington dataset. The axes values are expressed in percentage with respect to the manual transcription time of a word t_{man}.

desired time gain has been established, it is observed that a wider range of time parameters can lead to achieving this time gain. To clarify this behaviour, Table 2 presents the constraints that the validation time t_{val} must meet to achieve at least 10% and 20% of the time gain when the correction time t_{cor} is set at half the duration of manual transcription t_{man}. Notably, when the training set size TS is smaller, there is more flexibility in terms of the validation time allowed for achieving the target gain.

These findings indicate that while a larger training set generally leads to more favourable outcomes in improving the KWS system performance and obtaining a larger positive gain area, utilizing a smaller training set can result in higher time gains. The Time Gain Band analysis highlights the range of validation times that can be considered while achieving a desired time gain, especially when working with a smaller training set. This information underscores the importance of carefully selecting the appropriate training set size and considering the associated validation and correction times to optimize time gains in the transcription process.

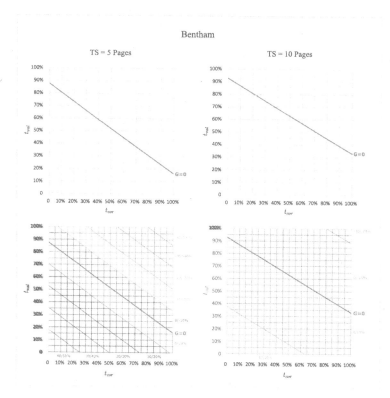

Fig. 5. The graphs above illustrate the Zero Gain Line in the t_{cor}/t_{val} plane, whereas the graphs below depict the varied Time Gain Bands for the Bentham dataset. The axes values are expressed in percentage with respect to the manual transcription time of a word t_{man}.

Table 2. Constrain on the validation time t_{val} when the t_{cor} is set at the half of ms and a time gain of at least 10% and at least 20% is desired.

Gain	Dataset	t_{val} (%t_{man})	
		$TS = 5$	$TS = 10$
10%	Wasingthon	<65%	<50%
	Benham	<35%	<10%
	Parzival	<60%	<50%
20%	Wasinghton	<55%	<20%
	Bentham	<15%	N/A
	Parzival	<50%	<25%

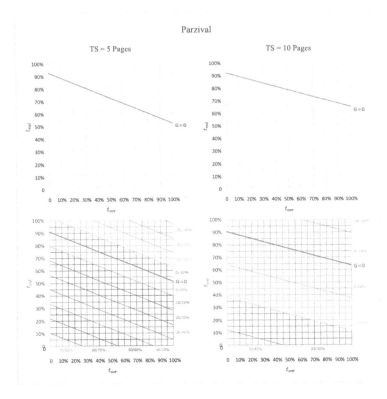

Fig. 6. The graphs above illustrate the Zero Gain Line in the t_{cor}/t_{val} plane, whereas the graphs below depict the varied Time Gain Bands for the Parzival dataset. The axes values are expressed in percentage with respect to the manual transcription time of a word t_{man}.

5   Conclusions

In conclusion, the study conducted sheds light on the impact of temporal parameters within the user interface of an assisted transcription system for handwritten documents. The findings demonstrate the crucial role these parameters play in determining the time saved through the utilization of such a system. By conducting various experiments and analyzing the results, the study establishes a clear link between the temporal parameters of the interface and the achievable time gain. It becomes evident that not only does the performance of the AI-based supporting machine learning tool contribute to reducing transcription time, but the design and functionality of the user interface also significantly influence the overall efficiency.

Moreover, the study implies that in situations where handwriting recognition systems fail to meet desired performance levels, it becomes essential to implement strategies aimed at minimizing interface interaction time in order to maintain a positive time gain. One possible strategy could involve limiting the number of options presented during the validation phase, thereby expediting the process. This observation suggests a potential correlation between the performance indices of the keyword spotting system and the time parameters within the interface, especially when aiming to achieve a desired time gain. To gain further insights, future investigations should focus on clarifying this relationship, ultimately aiming to provide valuable observations and recommendations for the design and development of graphical interfaces used in assistance systems for handwritten document transcription.

By conducting more research in this domain, it will be possible to refine the design and functionality of the validation and correction interfaces. These improvements can lead to enhanced usability and efficiency, ultimately benefiting users of transcription assistance systems for handwritten documents. The study's findings offer valuable insights into the intricate interplay in human-computer interaction, hopefully paving the way for future advancements in this field.

References

1. Ahmed, R., Al-Khatib, W.G., Mahmoud, S.: A survey on handwritten documents word spotting. Int. J. Multimed. Inf. Retr. **6**, 31–47 (2017)
2. Aldavert, D., Rusiñol, M., Toledo, R., Lladós, J.: A study of bag-of-visual-words representations for handwritten keyword spotting. Int. J. Doc. Anal. Recognit. (IJDAR) **18**, 223–234 (2015)
3. Aqab, S., Tariq, M.U.: Handwriting recognition using artificial intelligence neural network and image processing. Int. J. Adv. Comput. Sci. Appl. **11**(7) (2020)
4. Bray, J.R., Curtis, J.: An ordination of the upland forest communities of southern wisconsin. Ecol. Monogr. **27**, 325–349 (1957)
5. Cordell, R.: Machine learning and libraries: a report on the state of the field. Library of Congress (2020)
6. Fischer, A., et al.: Automatic transcription of handwritten medieval documents. In: 2009 15th International Conference on Virtual Systems and Multimedia, pp. 137–142. IEEE (2009)
7. Lombardi, F., Marinai, S.: Deep learning for historical document analysis and recognition-a survey. J. Imaging **6**(10), 110 (2020)
8. Marcelli, A., De Gregorio, G., Santoro, A.: A model for evaluating the performance of a multiple keywords spotting system for the transcription of historical handwritten documents. J. Imaging **6**(11), 117 (2020)
9. Memon, J., Sami, M., Khan, R.A., Uddin, M.: Handwritten optical character recognition (OCR): a comprehensive systematic literature review (SLR). IEEE Access **8**, 142642–142668 (2020)
10. Rath, T.M., Manmatha, R.: Word spotting for historical documents. Int. J. Doc. Anal. Recogn. **9**(2–4), 139 (2007)
11. Retsinas, G., Louloudis, G., Stamatopoulos, N., Gatos, B.: Keyword spotting in handwritten documents using projections of oriented gradients. In: 2016 12th IAPR Workshop on Document Analysis Systems (DAS), pp. 411–416. IEEE (2016)
12. Sánchez, J.A., Romero, V., Toselli, A.H., Vidal, E.: ICFHR 2014 competition on handwritten text recognition on transcriptorium datasets (HTRTS). In: 2014 14th International Conference on Frontiers in Handwriting Recognition, pp. 785–790. IEEE (2014)

13. Serdouk, Y., Eglin, V., Bres, S., Pardoen, M.: Keyword spotting using siamese triplet deep neural networks. In: 2019 International Conference on Document Analysis and Recognition (ICDAR), pp. 1157–1162. IEEE (2019)
14. Sfikas, G., Gatos, B., Nikou, C.: Semicca: a new semi-supervised probabilistic CCA model for keyword spotting. In: 2017 IEEE International Conference on Image Processing (ICIP), pp. 1107–1111. IEEE (2017)
15. Sudholt, S., Fink, G.A.: Phocnet: a deep convolutional neural network for word spotting in handwritten documents. In: 2016 15th International Conference on Frontiers in Handwriting Recognition (ICFHR), pp. 277–282. IEEE (2016)
16. Toselli, A.H., Vidal, E., Romero, V., Frinken, V.: Hmm word graph based keyword spotting in handwritten document images. Inf. Sci. **370**, 497–518 (2016)
17. Wicht, B., Fischer, A., Hennebert, J.: Deep learning features for handwritten keyword spotting. In: 2016 23rd International Conference on Pattern Recognition (ICPR), pp. 3434–3439. IEEE (2016)
18. Yadav, P., Yadav, N.: Handwriting recognition system-a review. Int. J. Comput. Appl. **114**(19), 36–40 (2015)

Estimating the Optimal Training Set Size of Keyword Spotting for Historical Handwritten Document Transcription

Giuseppe De Gregorio[(✉)] and Angelo Marcelli

DIEM, University of Salerno, Via Giovanni Paolo II 132, 84084 Fisciano, SA, Italy
{gdegregorio,amarcelli}@unisa.it

Abstract. We address the problem of estimating the tradeoff between the size of the training set and the performance of a KWS when used to assist the transcription of small collections of historical handwritten documents. As this application domain is characterized by a lack of data, and techniques such as transfer learning and data augmentation require more resources than those that are commonly available in the organizations holding the collections, we address the problem of getting the best out of the available data. For this purpose, we reformulate the problem as that of finding the size of the training set leading to a KWS whose performance, when used to support the transcription, allows to obtain the largest reduction of the human efforts to achieve the complete transcription of the collection. The results of a large set of experiments on three publicly available datasets largely adopted as a benchmark for performance evaluation show that a training set made of 5 to 8 pages is enough for achieving the largest reduction, independently of the actual pages included in the training set and the corresponding keyword lists. They also show that the actual time reduction depends much more on the keyword list than on the KWS performance.

Keywords: Historical document processing · Keyword spotting · Performance evaluation

1 Introduction

The quick advances that the field of Artificial Intelligence (AI) and particularly Machine Learning (ML) has made in recent years are leading to the development and use of a wide variety of tools that enable people to rethink the way they approach problems in different domains. This new approach enables more efficient interaction with information, deeper and faster data analysis, and leads to improvements in decision-making and workflows that are undergoing effective transformation [2,5].

ML algorithms learn from training data to define a model capable of transforming the input information with the goal of generating an output capable of solving a given problem. The learned models, thus, strictly depend on training data and the success of a model depends on the ability to train with large amounts of data [19]. However, in some application domains, it is hardly possible to have large amounts of training data and this can be a strong obstacle to the profitable use of ML techniques. Techniques such as transfer learning [25], data augmentation and synthetic data generation [19] try to propose a solution to the lack of training data by attempting to integrate the original training set with other datasets that are, in some way, related to the referring domains. However, the application of these techniques is sometimes not easy to make. In fact, it is required for a skilled user to be able to adapt and choose the pre-trained models for the desired application use. In other words, the user who wants to utilise the system must have the technical skills to integrate transfer learning or data augmentation solutions to his own process, and he must also be able to choose the pre-training data domain that most suit the desired solution, provided that this domain exists and is available.

In this paper, we would like to propose a different view, that in our opinion fit with the overall context sketched above. We assume that the profitability of the KWS in supporting the transcription can be evaluated by the ratio between the amount of human effort required to achieve the complete and error-free transcription of the collection with and without the support of the system, and then asked ourselves whether it is better to spend the human efforts mostly for producing the training set leading to the best performance of the KWS, or rather to train the KWS on a smaller (than in the previous case) dataset and spending most of the human efforts required to validate the outputs of the KWS on a larger (than in the previous case) number of pages. As a case study, we considered the transcription process of collections of handwritten documents of historical interest using a KeyWord Spotting system (KWS) as an ML tool to help the transcription [1]. This application area is of particular interest because the lack of data is a distinctive feature of this domain; some collections of historical interest are inherently made up of smallish data, and the stylistic and graphical features may be specific to the collection and therefore unique. Consequently, documents drawn up at different times or in different geographical areas can have extremely different characteristics, even when the content is expressed in the same language. This implies that the data sets built on particular collections are poorly able to adapt to the characteristics of collections produced at different times and locations. Therefore, and particularly for collections of limited size, the only way left to have data available to build the training set for the KWS is to manually transcribe part of the collection itself. Also, small collections are often held at small organizations, such as small museums, local archives or libraries. While the hardware and human resources required to use modern ML techniques may not be a problem for large organizations, this may not be the case for small organizations and archives. Small organizations' hardware resources are often limited, and processing large amounts of data can be difficult. Furthermore, modern image processing techniques based on artificial intelligence or deep learning technologies sometimes require not only particular and specific hardware, but also adequate technical skills, and therefore the presence of highly qualified and trained personnel to fully exploit the potential of the technologies used. Therefore, solutions that are simple to apply to small data collections and that limit their use to only the information available from the collection itself can be useful, which however allows to simplify and reduce the human efforts required for achieving the transcription of the entire collection.

The process of transcribing such collections usually involves the manual transcription part of the collection by the user to be used to train the KWS system. Once such a system is trained, it can be used to support the transcription of the remaining pages of the collection. In this perspective, and considering that the output of the KWS must be validated for an error-free transcription, the performance of the supporting ML system takes a back seat. While it is easy to imagine that the larger the training set, the better the KWS system performs, building a large training set comes at a cost, which in our case is represented by the time the user has to spend transcribing the pages (of the training set) without a support system. Moreover, expanding the training set, i.e. transcribing a greater portion of the collection, leaves fewer documents to be transcribed with the help of the KWS to complete the entire collection, and the fewer the pages left to be transcribed, the lower the benefits introduced by the KWS on the time required for the complete transcription.

The results of a large set of experiments, performed on three public historical documents datasets largely used as benchmarks for performance evaluation and aimed at evaluating how long it takes to get a correct transcription of the whole collection as the size of the training set for the KWS system increases, show that training sets made up of 8 to 10 pages allow achieving the greatest gain in terms of human efforts, in all the cases and independently of the actual pages composing the training set. They also show that higher recall rates of the KWS lead to higher gains in the transcription time, mostly independently of the precision rate.

The remaining of the paper is organized as follows: in Sect. 2 we review the work proposing either TL or DA to deal with data scarcity in the case of historical documents, to highlight the reason why they might not be viable in the case of small collections of documents, while in Sect. 3 we describe the implementation of the transcription process that has been used for the experiments. The experimental setting is described in Sect. 4, and the results of the experiments we have designed and performed are reported in Sect. 5. Eventually, in Sect. 6, we discuss the experimental findings, draw some preliminary conclusions and outline future investigations.

2   Releated Works

When it comes to machine learning, one common issue is the lack of available data to train models. However, there are two potential solutions - transfer learning (TL) and data augmentation (DA). The approach of TL involves first training a model on a more general task that contains a vast amount of data. This initial model can then serve as a starting point for training a second model that aims to solve a different task [24]. On the other hand, the DA technique allows for generating new training data by manipulating the original data through transformations. The goal of DA is to expand and enhance a small set of training data [19].

These techniques have also been explored in the field of Historical Document Analysis, which is a difficult domain since historical documents are collections with specific and particular characteristics and generally can be of small size [12].

Transfer learning is commonly employed in computer vision to take advantage of the availability of public image datasets. However, applying this approach to historical records can be challenging due to the distinct nature of such data. Studer et al. [20] demonstrate that leveraging pre-trained ImageNet networks can enhance the accuracy of certain historical data analysis tasks. Nevertheless, this technique might lower the performance of other tasks, such as semantic segmentation. Despite the diversity of domains, this technique can generally improve performance [8,9,22] but the need to add a small amount of target data in learning to obtain a minimum rate of performance is always evident.

One common strategy for augmenting training data involves applying various transformations to the original images, such as flipping, rotation, or scaling. Noise can also be added or data can be purposefully degraded. [6,11,14] Recently, more advanced techniques have emerged, such as generative methods that generate entirely new training elements or combine different components (e.g., backgrounds, text, and images) to produce new documents [4,10,16]. Lately, some generative networks of the GAN type have been used to generate documents of a historical type with the aim of obtaining documents reporting a reference style [13,23].

Both methods have the ability to enhance the efficiency of pre-existing models, but they require labelled starting datasets to work, even if they are not extensive. Additionally, the efficiency of transfer learning is affected not only by the starting pre-training dataset but also by the specific task it is attempting to address. For example, layout analysis displays more significant performance enhancements when compared to the gains achievable with handwritten text recognition. In regards to data augmentation, it is essential to use this technique with caution since going overboard can lead to the introduction of unwanted noise and artefacts during training, resulting in a decline in model performance. This is especially important to keep in mind when the initial dataset size is small because the small dimension can also limit the effectiveness of augmentation techniques.

However, both techniques require a minimum amount of labelled real data; DA needs real instances to apply transformations to or as reference instances for generation, while TL needs a fine-tuning phase on real data. When, as in the case of transcription of small handwritten collections using a KWS system, these data are not available the methods do not avoid the need to prepare such datasets manually.

3   The Transcription Process

The human efforts required by the transcription process of a small collection of handwritten documents of cultural and historical interest can be reduced by adopting ML tools and technologies, and among them, Keyword Spotting system (KWS) has shown better performance than handwritten text recognition to deal with the writing style variations occurring in documents produced at different times and places. A KWS has the task of finding instances of words of which it knows a representation, in the pages of the collection to be transcribed. In the preparation phase (*training*) of the KWS system, the knowledge base of the system is built up, which consists of *keywords*, i.e. words of whom the system knows both the representation and the correct transcription. The running system thus aims to retrieve the words whose representations are most similar to those of the keywords in the entire collection and link the transcription of the keywords to them. In this way, the system attempts to retrieve words without having to explicitly recognise the text contained in an image, and this property allows such systems to adapt to situations with limited data [1].

A user who wishes to use a KWS for transcription intents must create a list of keywords to be used to support the process. For this purpose, in the absence of preliminary data, the user must transcribe a part of the collection, which we call TS (Training Set), and use this as training information to prepare the KWS system. Once the KWS has been trained, the system can be used to support the transcription of the remaining part of the collection, which we will call DS (Data Set). The system's task is to recover the transcription of the words in the keyword list that are present in the DS so that the user no longer has to enter the transcription of these words manually.

Since the aim of the process is to obtain an error-free transcription, a validation phase of the output of the KWS system on the DS set is required. In other words, the user must check the system's output, validate the words correctly recognised by the KWS, correct the errors made by the system and, finally, produce a transcription for the words outside the vocabulary (OOV - Out Of Vocabulary), i.e. for the words that appear only in DS and for which the KWS system cannot provide a transcription. The validation process of a correct KWS output must be done by an extremely simple and fast procedure, e.g. a simple click of the mouse while scrolling through the list of options provided by the system. It is important that this procedure is faster than the time needed to transcribe a word manually because in this way the KWS can bring an effective improvement of the time needed to transcribe the whole collection. Once all the correct responses have been validated, the user has to provide the correct transcription for the words that the system did not recognize and for the words that the system is unable to recognize, i.e. the OOV words. The transcription of these words must be provided manually.

The process then expects the user to spend a time T_{TS} to transcribe the words in TS and create the keyword list, and then a time T_{DS} to validate and correct the system's output on DS. The use of the KWS system is beneficial for the transcription process if the sum of the times T_{TS} and T_{TD} is less than the time T_m needed for the same user to transcribe the whole collection manually without the help of a KWS:

$$T_{TS} + T_{DS} < T_m \tag{1}$$

At this point, it becomes clear how important the size of the training set TS is. The larger it is, the more training data is available to prepare the KWS system. Moreover, by increasing TS the number of OOV words in the DS set decreases, simply because the cardinality of the keyword list increases. This leads to the assumption that large TS sets enable the KWS system to perform better and thus reduce the time T_{DS}. On the other hand, to get a large training set, the user has to manually transcribe more words, which increases the time T_{TS}. Since it is the sum of the two times that determines the usefulness of the system, the size of the set TS turns out to be a parameter with crucial importance.

4   Experimentation Details

4.1   Datasets

Two small datasets composed of handwritten cursive script dating back to the 18th century were considered for the experimentation, namely the George Washington dataset [17] and the Bentham Collection [18]. Both datasets collect 20 pages of handwritten documents written by a single writer. A third dataset is considered, the Parzival dataset [7] which is a record consisting of 47 pages by three writers. These pages were taken from a 13th-century medieval German manuscript containing the epic poem Parzival by Wolfram von Eschenbach. The Fig. 1 shows three excerpts from the various datasets and highlights the differences in the visual characteristics and writing style of the three collections. Table 1 reports the size of the three datasets in terms of words contained. The table shows both the total number of words contained in the collections and the number of unique words, i.e. the number of different words present. Looking at the relationship between the number of words in the collection and the number of pages, we find that the pages of the Bentham collection contain a smaller number of words, while the Parzival collection is the one with the most words per page, having almost three times as many words per page as the Bentham collection.

Table 1. Dataset details.

Dataset	Num Pages	Num Words	Num Unique Words
Washington	20	4819	1187
Bentham	20	3478	1091
Parzival	47	23412	4616

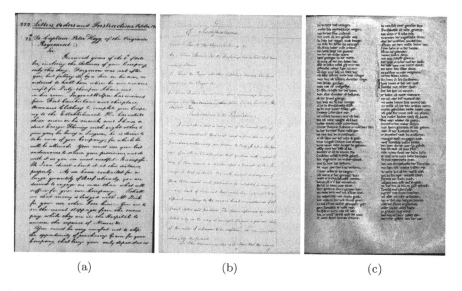

(a)   (b)   (c)

Fig. 1. Examples of documents from the three collections analysed: (a) Washington; (b) Bentham; (c) Parzival.

4.2 KWS System

The KWS used during the experiments is based on the PHOCNet [21], which has been configured to be used in a segmentation-based QbS scenario. First, the words contained in TS are transcribed manually and the labelled data is used to train the PHOCnet. During the query time, we extract all unique transcriptions in TS and use their PHOC representation as a query list. Then, the similarity between the images from DS and the words in the keyword list is calculated using the Bray-Curtis dissimilarity [3]. As a performance measure, recall and precision are calculated on DS by varying the distance acceptance threshold.

4.3 Temporal Gain

Having established the performance indices for the accuracy and recall of the KWS system, it is possible, given the size in words of the sets TS and DS, to estimate the time saving that can be achieved in transcribing the entire collection by using the performance estimation model presented in [15]. The model provides the percentage time gain G obtainable by using a KWS to transcribe documents after the validation and correction process that the user has to go through in order to obtain an error-proof transcription of the entire collection. The temporal gain can be calculated as:

$$G = 1 - T_u/T_m \tag{2}$$

where T_m is the manual transcription time, while T_u is the time taken to complete the transcription using the assistance system. While the time T_m depends only on the capabilities of the user who is transcribing, T_u also depends on the performance of the KWS system and therefore on the size of the keyword list.

In order to assess how the size of TS affects the time needed for transcription, we calculated the time gain obtainable by letting the number of pages used to build TS vary. This was done by starting with a single page TS and adding a new page to it until the entire collection was used as the training set. To generalise the results obtained, three randomly defined page orders were considered for each dataset and the results for each of the trials were recorded. Finally, the results are given by averaging the results of each trial.

5   Results

It is interesting to see how the number of OOV words and in-vocabulary words varies in the different collections as the pages of TS vary. Figure 2 shows how the distribution of words changes as the number of training pages increases. It is interesting to note that the trend of the curves is similar in all cases and that the number of OOV words tends to be relatively low for a TS which consists of a page count between 5 and 10. A difference can be seen in the Bentham dataset, as in this case, the ratio between OOV and in-vocabulary words tends to decrease less slowly than in the other two datasets. This could mean that the transcription of the Bentham dataset is more complex due to the larger number of OOV words.

Figure 3 shows the Precision/Recall curves of the KWS system recorded on DS when the pages used to define the TS of the different datasets vary. Looking at the curve plot, it is immediately noticeable that the KWS system, as easily expected, shows increasingly better performance as the training set dimension is increased. In fact, the KWS system continues to learn over the entire collection. However, it should be noted that in all cases, the performance of the network with very few training pages (less than 5) is always unsatisfactory. However, when the training set consists of more than 5 pages, the KWS performance seems to improve as the size of TS increases, but the performance gain is limited. A slightly different case is that of the Bentham dataset, where the network has more difficulty learning and more pages are needed in TS to achieve satisfactory performance. As can be seen from the Table 1, the Bentham is the dataset where the pages have the least written words, and therefore with the least useful information per page. It is therefore not surprising that it turns out to be the dataset on which the KWS has the most difficulty learning.

Finally, Fig. 4 shows the gain in transcription time obtained by varying the pages of the TS set. Interestingly, all systems achieve the maximum gain with a TS set consisting of 5 to 8 pages, regardless of the total size of the collection. It is also interesting that the maximum gain is related to the performance of the KWS system. The highest gain among the three cases is obtained with the Parzival dataset, the same dataset where the KWS system could achieve the best performance. In contrast, the lowest gain was obtained in the Bentham dataset, where the KWS system performed the worst.

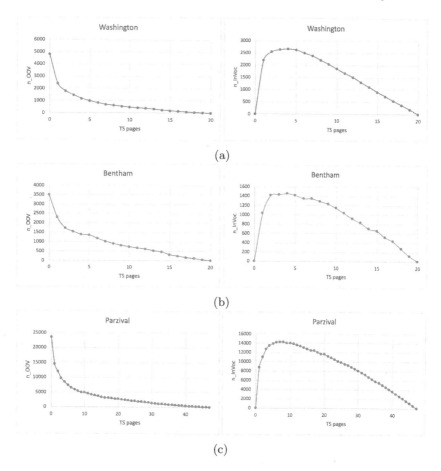

Fig. 2. Trend of OOV words (on the left) and in-vocabulary words (on the right) as the number of TS pages vary for the different datasets: (a) Washington; (b) Bentham; (c) Parzival.

6   Discussion and Conclusion

With this work, we have investigated how the time required to obtain a complete and error-free transcription of a small collection of handwritten documents using a KWS system to support the process varies depending on the size of the training set provided to the KWS.

Taking into account the distinctive features of the collections we are interested in and the cultural institutions that hold them, we assume that only information obtained from the collection itself can be used for training the KWS. In the absence of data from other datasets, then, training the KWS system requires manually transcribing a portion of the collection to create the training set. This process must be done manually by a user and takes some time. Once the training set is built and the KWS is trained, the user must validate and correct the

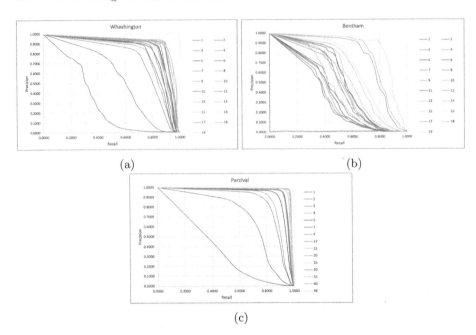

(a)   (b)

(c)

Fig. 3. Precision/Recall curve of the KWS system as TS pages vary for the different datasets: (a) Washington; (b) Bentham; (c) Parzival.

solutions proposed by the system to obtain an error-free transcription of the entire collection. It follows that the use of the KWS system becomes profitable when the sum of these times is less than the time required for the same user to transcribe the same collection, as described in Eq. 1. So the question arises on whether spending most of the human efforts to provide the KWS with the largest affordable training set so as to achieve top performance is the best strategy to achieve the largest reduction of the human efforts required for the complete transcription.

The experiments performed on the three datasets of different sizes showed that focusing on the performance of the KWS and trying to maximize it does not allow the user to achieve the best reduction of the time required for transcription. From the curves in Fig. 3, it can be seen that the KWS continues to improve its performance as the amount of training set TS increases. On the other hand, observing Fig. 4, it can be seen that a TS made up of a few pages is already enough to obtain the largest user time gain. It is interesting to note that the maximum time gain was achieved with a TS consisting of a number of pages between 5 and 8 in all three datasets, regardless of actual pages, the list of keywords of the training set, the distribution between in-vocabulary and OOV words, and size of the collection.

It is also clear from the curves of Fig. 4 that the nature of the data set plays an important role in the achievable gain. The lowest gain was recorded for the Bentham dataset, which is the smallest collection in terms of the number of

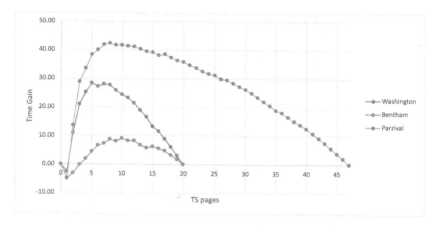

Fig. 4. The curves show the trend of the time gain obtainable by varying the pages in TS for the three different datasets considered.

words and has the largest ratio of OOV words to in-vocabulary words. This collection is the one that would take the least time of the three in the case of manual transcription, but it is also the collection that requires the user to consume the most resources in the validation and correction phase of the DS set due to the low power of the KWS and the high OOV word rate. The other extreme is the behaviour of the Parzival collection. This, in contrast, is the largest collection with a low ratio of OOV to in-vocabulary. However, it is interesting to point out that in both cases the best temporal gain was recorded with a TS consisting of 8 pages. We can therefore conclude that, although the ability to train a well-performing KWS is important, it is the nature of the dataset, its size, the length of the keyword list, and the distribution of the OOV words that affect performance in terms of transcription time gain. Eventually, the precision-recall curves in Fig. 3 indicate that the recall rate of the KWS plays a much relevant role than precision on the actual gain, and therefore KWS is capable of spotting OOV words may allow for a big leap in performance when used to assist the transcription of small collections of handwritten historical documents.

References

1. Ahmed, R., Al-Khatib, W.G., Mahmoud, S.: A survey on handwritten documents word spotting. Int. J. Multimed. Inf. Retr. **6**, 31–47 (2017)
2. Ashok, M., Madan, R., Joha, A., Sivarajah, U.: Ethical framework for artificial intelligence and digital technologies. Int. J. Inf. Manage. **62**, 102433 (2022)
3. Bray, J.R., Curtis, J.: An ordination of the upland forest communities of southern wisconsin. Ecol. Monogr. **27**, 325–349 (1957)
4. Capobianco, S., Marinai, S.: Docemul: a toolkit to generate structured historical documents. In: 2017 14th IAPR International Conference on Document Analysis and Recognition (ICDAR), vol. 1, pp. 1186–1191. IEEE (2017)

5. Cockburn, I.M., Henderson, R., Stern, S.: The impact of artificial intelligence on innovation: an exploratory analysis. In: The Economics of Artificial Intelligence: An Agenda, pp. 115–146. University of Chicago Press (2018)

6. Fischer, A., Visani, M., Kieu, V.C., Suen, C.Y.: Generation of learning samples for historical handwriting recognition using image degradation. In: Proceedings of the 2nd International Workshop on Historical Document Imaging and Processing, pp. 73–79 (2013)

7. Fischer, A., et al.: Automatic transcription of handwritten medieval documents. In: 2009 15th International Conference on Virtual Systems and Multimedia, pp. 137–142. IEEE (2009)

8. Granet, A., Morin, E., Mouchère, H., Quiniou, S., Viard-Gaudin, C.: Transfer learning for a letter-ngrams to word decoder in the context of historical handwriting recognition with scarce resources. In: 27th International Conference on Computational Linguistics (COLING), pp. 1474–1484 (2018)

9. Granet, A., Morin, E., Mouchère, H., Quiniou, S., Viard-Gaudin, C.: Transfer learning for handwriting recognition on historical documents. In: 7th International Conference on Pattern Recognition Applications and Methods (ICPRAM) (2018)

10. Journet, N., Visani, M., Mansencal, B., Van-Cuong, K., Billy, A.: Doccreator: a new software for creating synthetic ground-truthed document images. J. Imaging 3(4), 62 (2017)

11. Kieu, V., Visani, M., Journet, N., Domenger, J.P., Mullot, R.: A character degradation model for grayscale ancient document images. In: Proceedings of the 21st International Conference on Pattern Recognition (ICPR 2012), pp. 685–688. IEEE (2012)

12. Lombardi, F., Marinai, S.: Deep learning for historical document analysis and recognition-a survey. J. Imaging 6(10), 110 (2020)

13. Madi, B., Alaasam, R., Droby, A., El-Sana, J.: HST-GAN: historical style transfer GAN for generating historical text images. In: Uchida, S., Barney, E., Eglin, V. (eds.) DAS 2022. LNCS, vol. 13237, pp. 523–537. Springer, Cham (2022). https://doi.org/10.1007/978-3-031-06555-2_35

14. Maini, S., Groleau, A., Chee, K.W., Larson, S., Boarman, J.: Augraphy: a data augmentation library for document images. arXiv preprint arXiv:2208.14558 (2022)

15. Marcelli, A., De Gregorio, G., Santoro, A.: A model for evaluating the performance of a multiple keywords spotting system for the transcription of historical handwritten documents. J. Imaging 6(11) (2020). https://doi.org/10.3390/jimaging6110117. https://www.mdpi.com/2313-433X/6/11/117

16. Monnier, T., Aubry, M.: Docextractor: an off-the-shelf historical document element extraction. In: 2020 17th International Conference on Frontiers in Handwriting Recognition (ICFHR), pp. 91–96. IEEE (2020)

17. Rath, T.M., Manmatha, R.: Word spotting for historical documents. Int. J. Doc. Anal. Recogn. 9(2–4), 139 (2007)

18. Sánchez, J.A., Romero, V., Toselli, A.H., Vidal, E.: ICFHR 2014 competition on handwritten text recognition on transcriptorium datasets (HTRTS). In: 2014 14th International Conference on Frontiers in Handwriting Recognition, pp. 785–790. IEEE (2014)

19. Shorten, C., Khoshgoftaar, T.M.: A survey on image data augmentation for deep learning. J. Big Data 6(1), 1–48 (2019)

20. Studer, L., et al.: A comprehensive study of imagenet pre-training for historical document image analysis. In: 2019 International Conference on Document Analysis and Recognition (ICDAR), pp. 720–725. IEEE (2019)

21. Sudholt, S., Fink, G.A.: Phocnet: a deep convolutional neural network for word spotting in handwritten documents. In: 2016 15th International Conference on Frontiers in Handwriting Recognition (ICFHR), pp. 277–282. IEEE (2016)
22. Todorov, K., Colavizza, G., et al.: Transfer learning for historical corpora: an assessment on post-OCR correction and named entity recognition. In: CHR, pp. 310–339 (2020)
23. Vögtlin, L., Drazyk, M., Pondenkandath, V., Alberti, M., Ingold, R.: Generating synthetic handwritten historical documents with OCR constrained GANs. In: Lladós, J., Lopresti, D., Uchida, S. (eds.) ICDAR 2021. LNCS, vol. 12823, pp. 610–625. Springer, Cham (2021). https://doi.org/10.1007/978-3-030-86334-0_40
24. Weiss, K., Khoshgoftaar, T.M., Wang, D.: A survey of transfer learning. J. Big Data 3(1), 1–40 (2016)
25. Zhuang, F., et al.: A comprehensive survey on transfer learning. Proc. IEEE 109(1), 43–76 (2020)

A Digital Analysis of Mozart's F-Clefs

Anthony H. Jarvis[✉] [iD]

Charles Darwin University, Darwin, NT 0810, Australia
ajarv010@gmail.com

Abstract. Using image analysis tools and statistical tests, this article compares f-clefs taken from Mozart's Thematic Catalogue with clefs taken from two of his autograph manuscripts. Based on the assumption that the natural variation of a single composer's f-clefs would be distributed normally around a mean, it was found that, by assigning each clef a numerical value and grouping them by document, the Thematic Catalogue's f-clefs were distributed around a different mean than the clefs from the autographs. It was then concluded that the most likely explanation for this difference was that the f-clefs in the Thematic Catalogue were written by a different hand.

Keywords: clef analysis · W. A. Mozart · image analysis · feature extraction

1 Introduction

W. A. Mozart's Thematic Catalogue is a historic document that was said to be used by Mozart to keep a record of his musical compositions from 1784 until his death in 1791. Each entry contains a date, the instrumentation, and a short incipit of his compositions. In recent years, however, the veracity of the catalogue has been called into question.

Due to several inconsistencies in the catalogue including, but not limited to, the signature on the cover, the dates attributed to certain compositions, as well as deviations in handwriting, scholars have begun questioning its veracity. For example, in September 2022, Professor Martin Jarvis and Affiliate Professor Heidi Harralson argued that the document was most likely not genuine [1].

In addition to signature analysis, one of the central focuses of Jarvis and Harralson's analysis was the style of f-clefs written in the catalogue, which they argued differed from other examples of Mozart's f-clefs, such as those found in his Masonic Cantata (KV 623).

Using Jarvis and Harralson's research as a starting point, this article makes use of image analysis tools and statistical tests to conduct a data-driven comparison of Mozart's f-clefs. Specifically, it compares f-clefs taken from the Thematic Catalogue with f-clefs from two autograph manuscripts attributed to Mozart.

In addition to the Thematic Catalogue, the documents examined in this article were the Masonic Cantata (KV 623) and Mozart's Masonic Funeral Music (KV 477). The Thematic Catalogue is held at the British Library [8], KV 623 is held at the Gesellschaft der Musikfreunde in Vienna [6], and KV 477 is held by Staatsbibliothek zu Berlin - PK [7].

As a way of ensuring that this research remained objective, the method of analysis used below did not compare individual examples of f-clefs, nor did it focus on small differences in style. Instead, each clef was assigned a numerical value that represented its size and shape. The clefs were then grouped by year and source document. Statistical tests were then used to compare the distribution of the clef values in each document.

The null hypothesis of this analysis was that all documents examined were written in Mozart's hand. Only if a statistically significant difference between the Thematic Catalogue and the other documents was found was it possible for this hypothesis to be rejected.

It was assumed that, whilst a certain amount of variation in clef size and shape was to be expected, the variation of Mozart's f-clefs would be distributed normally around a mean. Therefore, when comparing different documents, if a statistically significant difference between each document's f-clef distribution was found, then this would be a strong indication that the documents were written by different hands.

Therefore, when a difference between the Thematic Catalogue and the chosen autograph manuscripts was found, the relationship between the documents was brought into question. It was concluded that the most likely explanation for this difference was that the Thematic Catalogue was not written in the same hand as the other manuscripts.

There were, however, several limitations to this approach. The most significant of which was sample size. Indeed, the sample size of each f-clef group was small, i.e., n < 30. The smallest group was KV 623, where there were only 6 f-clefs in total. When working with small sample sizes, statistical tests can suffer from an increased margin of error. That being said, the test used to compare the documents – the two-sample t-test – is effective at comparing small samples. Therefore, it is unlikely that the sample size of the groups adversely affected the results of the tests in any serious way.

Next, by assuming that all the documents were written by a single scribe, the possibility that one or more of the documents had been written by multiple contributors was precluded from consideration. Therefore, during the research design phase, a method was developed to exclusively use documents as the main unit of analysis. As such, this approach was only able to investigate the relationship between the different manuscripts and was not able to explore the possibility of multiple scribes per document.

Nevertheless, despite these limitations, it was still possible to derive several important insights into the relationship between the Thematic Catalogue and Mozart's autograph manuscripts. The following section outlines in more detail the process that was followed.

2   Methodology

Clef analysis is a long-established approach for music manuscript examination. For example, Musicologists such as Wolfgang Plath incorporated clef analysis as part of his attempt to identify different scribes in Nannerl Mozart's Notebook [3]. In the digital age, scholars such as Niitsuma and Tomita utilized image processing and machine learning techniques to analyze clefs for the purposes of categorizing manuscripts [2].

One of the biggest challenges for clef analysis is the variation of clef size and shape, due to both natural and time-based variation. Indeed, when comparing Wolfgang and Leopold Mozart's f-clefs in Nannerl's Notebook, Plath wrote that the significant in-person variation made some types of comparisons pointless [3]. As expected, the clefs in the Thematic Catalogue varied quite noticeably, especially in the later years. As such, it was a challenge to determine what variation should be considered an anomaly and what variation should be considered normal.

To account for time-based variation, all the clefs in the Thematic Catalogue were grouped by year and were treated as different documents. Therefore, when comparing KV 623 and KV 477 with the Thematic Catalogue, the autographs could be compared with clefs from the Thematic Catalogue written in the same year as the original score.

The next issue was natural variation. To control for this type of variation, all examples examined were assigned a numerical value based on the size and shape of the clef and then grouped by source document. The act of comparing the clefs as groups, instead of as individual examples, resulted in the natural variation being captured by the distribution of clef values in each document.

Whilst Jarvis and Harralson primarily used f-clefs extracted from KV 623 in their own comparison, this article chose to expand its scope to also include KV 477. The reason for this expansion was that despite KV 477 being dedicated to two of Mozart's associates that passed away in November 1785, the composition's incipit in the catalogue was dated July that same year [17]. This inconsistency was compounded by the fact that the next incipit was also dated incorrectly. By comparing the similarity between f-clefs taken from KV 477 and those from the Thematic Catalogue dated 1785, it was thought a new perspective could be given as to whether the incorrect date in the catalogue was indeed evidence of fraud or an innocent mistake.

In short, the method used in this research to compare Mozart's f-clefs was as follows:

1. Pre-process clef images.
2. Extract features using the OpenCV package [9] in Python [10].
3. Use features to generate a unique numerical value for each clef so that similar clefs were assigned similar numerical values.
4. Group clef values by year and by document.
5. Use statistical tests [11, 12] to compare the similarity of the groups.
6. Analyze the results.

2.1 Preprocessing

Before any analysis could take place, a certain amount of image preprocessing was required. This section outlines how each clef was prepared for analysis.

1. Extract the clefs from each manuscript. During the extraction process, care was taken to ensure that the comparative size of each clef was maintained by using the staves as a guide for cutting the clef from the image. The upper and lower bounds of the canvas were set 7.5% above and below the staff, resulting in a 15% margin. This was done so that any clefs that may have extended beyond the boundaries of the stave lines were not partially cut-off.
2. Remove all irrelevant content, leaving just the clef on a blank background.

3. Convert to greyscale.
4. Binarize images by setting all pixel values below a set threshold to 0 and above to 255, leaving only black and white pixels.
5. Import images into Python.
6. Resize each image to a height of 100 pixels, retaining the aspect ratio.
7. Reverse the pixel values.
8. Crop blank space from each image.
9. Centre clefs onto a canvas of 100 × 100 pixels.

Fig. 1. Examples of preprocessed f-clefs from the Thematic Catalogue from 1785 year-group.

This involved more manual work than originally anticipated. Whilst it is possible to automate the removal of stave lines from 17th century manuscripts, as demonstrated in [13–15], due to the frequent occurrence of symbol overlap, such as with braces, bar lines, and other notation (see Fig. 2), initial attempts to automate the extraction indicated that manual intervention would still have been necessary to remove residual information from the image. It was therefore decided that manual extraction would be the most efficient option due to the relatively small sample size.

Fig. 2. Examples of the same f-clefs from Fig. 1, both of which had overlap.

Additionally, during the process of extraction, a handful of f-clefs were deemed too poor quality for use. The main two reasons for exclusion were fading, and incompleteness. Thankfully, the total number of exclusions was limited to a handful of examples, therefore these exclusions would not have had much influence on the results.

2.2 Feature Extraction

The next challenge was to find a reproducible method of quantifying the clefs in a way that resulted in similar clefs being assigned similar numerical values.

Because the computational analysis of musical clefs is a relatively niche topic of research, a limited amount of literature was available for reference. This meant that, after considering the approaches used by other researchers, there was still significant room for experimentation.

Senoner et al. (2000) used a Fourier transform to analyze g-clefs for the purposes of identifying the origin of an unknown manuscript suspected to be the work of Arnold Schoenberg [4]. Using a reference set made up of Schoenberg's g-clefs and a false set made up of g-clefs written by his pupils, the authors identified a threshold of correlation that could be used to determine whether a questioned g-clef was likely genuine or not. The way the authors dealt with the inter-group variation in the reference set was by comparing each questioned clef with all the examples in the reference set and if the maximum correlation value was above the threshold, then it was considered genuine. Because most clefs surpassed this threshold, the authors concluded that the document was likely by Schoenberg.

Schmucker and Yan (2003) were interested in the effectiveness of embedding watermarking information into clefs [5]. To retrieve the watermarking information, the authors used a variety of feature extraction methods. They used moments for clef rotation, the outer contour to measure size, and vertical and horizontal summation for segmentation purposes.

Fornés and Lladós (2010) used a symbol-dependent method to identify different writers of music scores dated from the 17th to 19th century [15]. This involved analyzing the shape of clefs and notation. To extract the features for classification, the authors used a Blurred Symbol Model (BSM) descriptor, which captures the probabilistic pixel density of different regions in the image [16]. The manuscripts were then identified using a k nearest neighbor (k-NN) classifier which compared each clef from each questioned document with a training set. A process of voting then followed, and a classification was given based on which writer received the greatest number of votes.

Niitsuma and Tomita (2011) attempted to sort a selection of Bach's c-clefs into different time periods using machine learning models [2]. To do this, the authors extracted 15 features including area, aspect ratio, total number of pixels occupied by the clef, compactness, moments, topmost and bottommost pixels, as well as volume.

The types of features used by these authors provided excellent guidance as to what sorts of digital clef analysis had been conducted previously. For the analysis at hand, it needed to be possible to produce a single feature value for each clef so that the clefs could be grouped by document and compared as groups rather than as individual examples.

The feature selection process was therefore determined by how accurately the final feature value represented each clef. This was judged by seeing how well each feature sorted the clefs by size and shape (see Fig. 3).

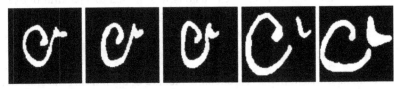

Fig. 3. Examples of f-clefs roughly ordered by size and shape. The first three examples were taken from the Thematic Catalogue 1785 year-group and the latter two were found in KV 477.

The approach used in [4] could not be repurposed to compare Mozart's f-clefs because the feature output was an autocorrelation value reached by comparing only two clefs at a time. Fourier transform could, therefore, not be used to compare groups. Similarly, whilst many different image analysis techniques were used by the authors in [5], the purpose of their article was to identify watermarking in clefs, not compare clefs from different documents, which rendered most of their methods ineffective for the present task. Whilst the BSM descriptor used in [15] proved to be an effective way of representing clef shape, the output of a BSM descriptor is a vector histogram, which is better suited for individual example comparisons rather than group comparisons. On the other hand, several of the features used in [2] did have potential to be used to compare Mozart's manuscripts.

Different combinations of features were trialed to generate a single feature value that met the criteria outlined earlier in this section. However, the process of distilling multiple features into a single number proved to be difficult. Multiple approaches were used, including using Principal Component Analysis to reduce dimensionality, however these attempts did not manage to produce a value that could effectively sort the f-clefs by size and shape.

As such, the process of feature selection moved on from combining features to using individual features related to size and shape. Features tested included aspect ratio, clef body height, clef body width, bounding box area, and convex hull area. In the end, it was found that the most effective way of ordering the f-clefs by size and shape was to use the square root of the convex hull area. A convex hull, in laymen's terms, is the smallest possible boundary that can be used to completely enclose a shape or set of points. As such, the convex hull area is simply the area of this boundary. The square root was used to help stabilize the variation.

Fig. 4. Example of f-clefs with convex hull area outline. The first two were once again taken from the Thematic Catalogue 1785 year-group and the latter two from KV 477.

Figure 4 shows 4 examples of f-clefs with the convex hull drawn around them. The first two clefs had a feature value of 41.40 and 41.90 respectively, whilst the latter two had feature values of 59.45 and 60.62. This shows that similarly sized and shaped clefs could be assigned similar feature values.

The reason this feature was chosen over other viable options was twofold. First, convex hull area is easy to reproduce. This meant that similar experiments in the future could replicate this approach without any major problems. Second, despite the feature's simplicity, the convex hull area consistently proved to be one of the most effective measures for ordering clefs by size and shape.

There was concern that by using a single value to represent the clefs a degree of overfitting or bias towards a certain result would occur. However, because the selection criteria limited the possible features that could be used to those related to size and shape, one could reasonably substitute the convex hull area with body height or width, or even other measures of area such as minimum bounding box area, and still reach a similar result.

The only way a feature substitution would drastically change the final result would be if the selection criteria was modified and clef size was no longer included as an influencing factor, for example by substituting it with aspect ratio, thus focusing specifically on shape. It is argued here, however, that clef size is an important feature that should not be excluded from consideration.

Of course, it is entirely possible for f-clefs written by different scribes in different styles to have a similar convex hull area, just as clefs written by the same scribe could vary in size and shape and thus have different convex hull areas. Therefore, this feature value should not be seen as a unique identifier. This was not a major concern because the primary reason for using this approach was to identify patterns that could only be observed when the feature values were examined as groups.

2.3   Method of Analysis

Unlike in [4, 15], the task at hand was not a typical classification problem but rather a comparison of similarity. For both articles, a threshold was able to be set for classification that could be pre-determined during a training stage. The documents were then given a class based on a majority vote from individual comparisons. Instead of comparing individual examples and using a voting system to determine overall similarity, a new method is proposed here. Namely, determining the similarity of the documents by comparing the distribution of clef feature values in each document. Assuming the manuscripts were all written by the same scribe, i.e., Wolfgang Amadeus Mozart, the expectation was that the variation of Mozart's f-clefs from a single year would be distributed normally around a single population mean. In this sense, if it was found the documents did not share a mean, this was taken as an indication that they were not written by the same hand.

To achieve this, a series of statistical tests were used. First, the clef groups were tested for normality. Because in all cases, the groups were normally distributed, a two-sample t-test could be used to compare two documents at a time.

The two-sample t-test is a method for estimating whether the population mean of two samples is equal. It has a null hypothesis that the population means are the same. If the resulting p-value output by the test falls below the critical value of 0.05, the null hypothesis is rejected and a statistically significant difference between the two input samples is reported.

Just as it was necessary to make clear above that the feature value is not a unique identifier of a single writer, it should be made clear here that it is possible for clefs written by different scribes to distribute around similar means. On the other hand, it is proposed here that it is unlikely for a single scribe to write clefs that are distributed around more than one mean. Therefore, because a p-value below 0.05 would be an indication that the input samples do not share the same mean, such a result should be interpreted as an indication that the documents do not have the same scribe.

This method of analysis is just one way of examining the relationship between documents and it would not be effective in all cases. For example, if the two documents had f-clefs that were stylistically different but had a similar size, this test would likely output a false positive. In such a case, a method that compares individual examples using a Blurred Symbol Model descriptor and voting system might yield better results. However, for the purposes of comparing Mozart's Thematic Catalogue with KV 623 and KV 477, the approach described proved to be effective.

3 Analysis

Using the methodology described above, two comparisons were made. The first was between KV 623 and the Thematic Catalogue's 1791 year-group, and the other was between KV 477 and the Thematic Catalogue's 1785 year-group. This section presents and discusses the results of these comparisons.

Before proceeding, however, as a way of verifying that a true positive would result when two groups known to be written by the same composer were input, two adjacent year-groups from the Thematic Catalogue were compared. Specifically, 1784 (n = 11) and 1785 (n = 21). After testing for normality, the two groups were input into the two-sample t-test, resulting in a p-value of 0.7755. Because it was known that both groups were written by a single hand, this confirmed that a true positive was possible.

Next, the Thematic Catalogue's 1791 year-group (n = 24) was compared with KV 623 (n = 6) using the same approach. Both groups were tested for normality before being compared using the two-sample t-test, which output a p-value of 0.00396, which was below the threshold of 0.05. Because of this, the null hypothesis was rejected and a statistically significant difference between the groups could be reported.

Looking at Fig. 5 below, the difference between the two clef groups becomes very apparent. Indeed, despite the small sample size of KV 623, the difference in means was estimated to be 16.13 (±9.11) with 95% confidence.

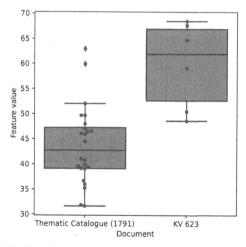

Fig. 5. Box plot of f-clef distributions for Thematic Catalogue year-group 1791 and KV 623

Moving onto the comparison of the Thematic Catalogue's 1785 year-group (n = 21) and KV 477 (n = 17), after confirming normality, the groups were input into the two-sample t-test and a p-value of <0.00001 was output. This meant that there was little to no similarity between the two groups. The difference in means was estimated to be 13.33 (±3.88) with 95% confidence. Once again, this difference can be visually confirmed by looking at Fig. 6 below.

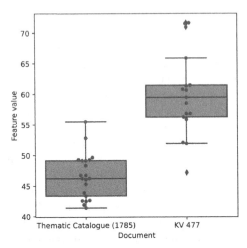

Fig. 6. Box plot of f-clef distributions for Thematic Catalogue year-group 1785 and KV 477

In both cases, it was found that the f-clefs from the Thematic Catalogue were distributed differently to the autograph manuscripts. If one accepts the assumption that the natural variation of a single composer's f-clefs would be distributed around a mean, then the most likely explanation for these differences would be that the catalogue and the autographs were not written by the same hand.

4   Conclusion

In conclusion, this research applied image analysis techniques and statistical tests to compare examples of f-clefs taken from Mozart's Thematic Catalogue with those from Mozart's Masonic Cantata (KV 623) and Mozart's Masonic Funeral Music (KV 477).

Rather than compare specific examples of f-clefs, this research grouped the f-clefs by document and compared the distribution of each document's feature values. To do this, each clef was first assigned a numerical value that reflected its underlying characteristics and then grouped by source. To control for time-based variation, each year of the Thematic Catalogue was treated as a separate document, which allowed for KV 623 and KV 477 to be compared with f-clefs from the catalogue written during a similar time. By grouping the f-clefs by document, the influence of natural variation was able to be factored into the analysis.

Whilst there were limitations to taking such an approach, such as small sample size, it was still possible to gain an insight into how the f-clefs were distributed in the different documents, as well as the relationship between these distributions.

In total, two comparisons were made. The first was between the Thematic Catalogue's 1791 year-group and KV 623, and the other was between the Thematic Catalogue's 1785 year-group and KV 477. A statistically significant difference was identified during both comparisons. Based on the assumption that the natural variation of a single composer's f-clefs would distribute around a single mean, it was suggested that the most likely explanation for these differences was that the f-clefs in the Thematic Catalogue were not written in the same hand as the ones found in both KV 623 and KV 477.

It is important to remember that forensic analysis of manuscripts usually makes use of multiple approaches including analysis of handwriting and notational style, as well as manuscript watermarking [2]. Therefore, whilst it is tempting to make broader claims about the authenticity of the Thematic Catalogue, only by combining the results of this analysis with the results of other approaches would it be possible to make wider claims.

It would also be worthwhile to explore the prospect of each document having multiple contributors. Indeed, one explanation for the high level of variation in the manuscripts that was not unpacked in this article was that more than one composer could have contributed to each manuscript. It would be worth considering this as a possibility in any future research into the topic. For example, future research could utilize a BSM descriptor in conjunction with an unsupervised learning algorithm to estimate the number of unique clef styles that were in the documents.

References

1. Jarvis, M., Harralson, H.: Why Wolfgang Amadeus Mozart, did not write The Thematic Catalogue [Conference presentation]. In: ANZFSS 25th International Symposium, Brisbane (2022)
2. Niitsuma, M., Tomita, Y.: Classifying Bach's handwritten C-clefs. In: 12th International Society for Music Information Retrieval Conference, ISMIR 2011, pp. 417–421 (2011)
3. Wolfgang, P.: Beiträge zur Mozart-Autographie I: Die Handschrift Leopold Mozarts, in: Mozart-Jahrbuch ... des Zentralinstitutes für Mozartforschung der Internationalen Stiftung Mozarteum Salzburg, vol. 1960/61 (1961)
4. Senoner, M., Krueger, S., Wernicke, G., Demoli, N., Gruber, H.: Investigations of handwritten manuscripts by means of optical correlation methods. In: Fotakis, C., Papazoglou, T.G., Kalpouzos, C. (eds) Optics and Lasers in Biomedicine and Culture. Series of the International Society on Optics Within Life Sciences, vol. 5. Springer, Heidelberg (2000). https://doi.org/10.1007/978-3-642-56965-4_23
5. Schmucker, M., Yan, H.: Music score watermarking by clef modifications. In: Security and Watermarking of Multimedia Contents V, vol. 5020, pp. 403–412. SPIE, June 2003
6. Mozart, W.A.: Freimaurerkantate, KV 623 autograph score, Gesellschaft der Musikfreunde in Wien (1791)
7. Mozart, W.A.: Maurerische Trauermusik; orch; c-Moll; KV 479a; KV 477, 1785, Staatsbibliothek zu Berlin – PK. http://resolver.staatsbibliothek-berlin.de/SBB000157BD00000000. Accessed 17 June 2023
8. Mozart, W.A.: Thematic Catalogue, Verzeichnüss/aller meiner Werke/vom Monath febrario 1784 bis Monath [November] 1[791]. Autograph. British Library. https://www.bl.uk/manuscripts/FullDisplay.aspx?ref=Zweig_MS_63. Accessed 17 June 2023
9. Bradski, G.: The OpenCV library. Dr Dobb's J. Softw. Tools (2000)
10. Van Rossum, G., Drake, F.L.: Python 3 Reference Manual. Scotts Valley, CA: CreateSpace (2009)

11. Virtanen, P.: SciPy 1.0: fundamental algorithms for scientific computing in Python. Nat. Methods **17**(3), 261–272 (2020)
12. Vallat, R.: Pingouin: statistics in Python. J. Open Source Softw. **3**(31), 1026 (2018). https://doi.org/10.21105/joss.01026
13. Fornés, A., Lladós, J., Sánchez, G.: Primitive segmentation in old handwritten music scores. In: Liu, W., Lladós, J. (eds.) GREC 2005. LNCS, vol. 3926, pp. 279–290. Springer, Heidelberg (2006). https://doi.org/10.1007/11767978_25
14. Fornés, A., Lladós, J., Sánchez, G., Bunke, H.: Writer identification in old handwritten music scores. In: 2008 The Eighth IAPR International Workshop on Document Analysis Systems, Nara, Japan, 2008, pp. 347–353 (2008). https://doi.org/10.1109/DAS.2008.29
15. Fornés, A., Lladós, J.: A symbol-dependent writer identification approach in old handwritten music scores. In: 2010 12th International Conference on Frontiers in Handwriting Recognition, Kolkata, India, 2010, pp. 634–639 (2010). https://doi.org/10.1109/ICFHR.2010.104
16. Fornés, A., Escalera, S., Lladós, J., Sánchez, G., Mas, J.: Hand drawn symbol recognition by blurred shape model descriptor and a multiclass classifier. In: Liu, W., Lladós, J., Ogier, J.-M. (eds.) GREC 2007. LNCS, vol. 5046, pp. 29–39. Springer, Heidelberg (2008). https://doi.org/10.1007/978-3-540-88188-9_4
17. Mozart, W.A.: K477 Masonic Mourning Music. http://mmc.kdl.kcl.ac.uk/entities/musical-work/masonic-mourning-music-k477. Accessed 17 June 2023

Special Session on Movement Variability

Methods for Analyzing Movement Variability

Orlando Fernandes[✉]

Évora University, Évora, Portugal
orlandj@uevora.pt

Abstract. Variability is a fact of life. Variability is variations that occur in Human performance after multiple repetitions. The central concept of behavioral flexibility in motor control was presented by Bernstein when he stated that movements are a "repetition without repetition" to describe how, well-learned movements, show variation when achieving the task outcome. Handwriting is an example of a complex task that results from a sequence of movements. It has a specific variability structure, and temporal organization, that inform the regularity with which children write as well as their adaptability to the task, e.g., a fractal dynamics behavior. Movement analysis using nonlinear dynamical systems theory for human behavior provides a better understanding of the execution of pathologies, psychomotor problems, or problems in motor control. Dynamic Systems theory suggests that biological systems self-organize according to the environment, and biomechanical and morphological constraints to find the most stable solution for producing a given movement. The concepts of variability and chaotic variation in human movement, along with advanced tools used to measure human movement variability open new perspectives to guide practice and a fundamental complementary means of diagnosis.

Keywords: Variability · Nonlinear · Handwriting

1 Introduction

1.1 Definition

Human Movement Variability can be described as the normal variations that occur in the motor performance of a task over multiple repetitions. Variability is a fact of life [1].

These variations can be observed in various aspects of movement, such as spatial, temporal, or kinematic parameters, over multiple repetitions of the same task. The central concept of behavioral flexibility in motor control was presented by Bernstein [2, 3] when he stated that movements are a "repetition without repetition" to describe how, well-learned movements, show variation when achieving the task outcome, each repetition involves unique but non-repetitive neural and motor patterns. According to Bernstein, human movement is characterized by a high degree of flexibility and adaptability. Despite the apparent repeatability of certain movements, such as walking or reaching for an object, each instance of the movement is unique due to various factors,

A. Parziale et al. (Eds.): IGS 2023, LNCS 14285, pp. 191–202, 2023.
https://doi.org/10.1007/978-3-031-45461-5_14

such as changes in the environment, internal physiological conditions, and the individual's intent. In other words, even though we perform similar actions repeatedly, no two executions of the same movement are entirely identical. There are always slight variations and adjustments in the movement pattern, which allow us to adapt to different situations and demands. They highlight the complexity and sophistication of human motor skills, showing that movements are not rigidly pre-programmed but rather dynamically adjusted based on the context and the continuous interaction between the nervous system, the body, and the environment. A given movement of the human body can be accomplished through various combinations of muscle activations, joint torques, and forces [4, 5]. In other words, multiple different muscle activation patterns can produce the same desired movement. To analyze those movements and given a specific set of muscle activations and joint torques, the goal is to predict the resulting movement of the body or segment [6, 7]. This problem is relatively straightforward, as it involves solving the equations of motion to determine the resulting motion based on the input forces and torques, is a forward dynamics solution. In contrast, the inverse dynamics problem is more complex. Here, the goal is to find the muscle activations and joint torques needed to achieve a desired movement. The challenge is that there are countless combinations of muscle activations and joint torques that can produce the same movement. Therefore, determining the specific muscle activation pattern that corresponds to a given movement becomes a challenging and sometimes underdetermined task. The inverse dynamics problem is essential in various applications, such as understanding human motor control, designing exoskeletons or prosthetics, and optimizing rehabilitation protocols [8, 9]. Solving this problem can provide insights into the strategies and coordination patterns that the nervous system employs to achieve specific movements. Mathematical models of the human musculoskeletal system can be used to simulate movements and estimate the muscle activations and joint torques required to achieve specific motions. These models help researchers understand the underlying biomechanics of human movements. Controlled experiments with human subjects can provide data on muscle activations, joint torques, and movement kinematics during various tasks [10]. By analyzing this data, researchers can gain insights into the motor control strategies employed by the nervous system. Optimization algorithms can be used to search for muscle activation patterns that minimize certain criteria (e.g., energy consumption or muscle effort) while achieving the desired movement [9, 11]. These approaches attempt to find optimal or near-optimal solutions to the inverse dynamics problem.

1.2 Human Movement Variability

Humans are biological systems with inherent variability. Two muscle activations or joint movements are not precisely identical due to natural biological fluctuations, such as differences in muscle properties, neural firing rates, and other physiological factors. During movement execution, humans continuously receive sensory feedback from proprioceptors (sensors in muscles and joints), vision, and other sensory modalities. This feedback helps in monitoring and adjusting ongoing movements. Variability in sensory feedback can influence motor control [1, 12, 13].

The environment in which movements occur is often unpredictable and dynamic. External factors, such as surface conditions, gravity, and external forces, can introduce perturbations that affect the motor control system and lead to variability. Cognitive processes, attention, and task demands can also influence motor variability. Different cognitive strategies or intentions can result in variations in how movements are planned and executed [14, 15].

Regarding chaoticity in human movements, the term "chaotic" refers to a type of deterministic yet unpredictable behavior observed in certain nonlinear systems. Chaotic systems are highly sensitive to initial conditions, which means that small differences in the starting conditions can lead to significantly divergent outcomes over time. Chaos is often associated with complex systems, and it has been a subject of interest in various scientific disciplines [3, 12]. While human movements do exhibit variability and sensitivity to initial conditions, it's important to note that not all human movements are chaotic in the technical sense. Human motor behavior is a blend of deterministic and stochastic (random) processes, and some movements may show chaotic-like behavior under specific conditions, but not all movements are chaotic. Instead, human movements are typically considered to have a mix of deterministic control (e.g., planned movements) and stochastic processes (e.g., noise or random fluctuations)[16–18]. This combination allows for the flexibility and adaptability required to deal with ever-changing environments and task demands. Overall, the study of motor variability and the potential chaotic-like behavior in human movements is a fascinating area of research that involves concepts from motor control, dynamical systems theory, and nonlinear dynamics [10, 19]. Understanding these complexities is essential for gaining insights into how humans plan, execute, and adapt their movements in a constantly changing world. Variability is not random but rather organized and serves as a means to adapt to changing conditions, optimize performance, and cope with uncertainties.

1.3 Dynamical Systems Theory

The Dynamical Systems Theory (DST) proposes that biological systems self-organize according to the environment, biomechanical and morphological constraints to find the most stable solution for producing a given movement. According to DST, human movement is not solely controlled by rigid, pre-programmed mechanisms. Instead, it is seen as the result of complex interactions between multiple factors, including the individual, the environment, and the task demands [20–22]. The DST suggests that when variability increases and reaches a specific critical point in certain dynamical systems and under certain conditions, the system becomes highly unstable and shifts to a new, more stable pattern of motion (with less variability) [20, 23].

The concepts of variability and chaotic variations in human movement and the advanced tools used to measure HMV open new perspectives for the study of Human Movement. The concepts of variability and chaotic variations in human movement are closely related to the principles of DST. Variability allows for adaptability and flexibility in movement, while chaos refers to a deterministic yet unpredictable behavior that arises from complex interactions. Advanced tools used to measure variability, such as motion capture systems and wearable sensors, can open new perspectives to guide practice. By analyzing movement patterns and variability, practitioners can optimize training methods, tailor rehabilitation programs, and enhance overall motor performance.

2 Non-linear Methods

Concepts and methods utilized for non-linear dynamics offer innovations in exploring variability and the potential for a better understanding of Human Movement and significant application possibilities for the study of Movement, to guide the practice, thus becoming another complementary means of diagnosis. Increased variability in a movement pattern usually indicates loss of stability, while decreased variability usually indicates highly stable behavior. Nonlinear analysis methods, such as fractal analysis, entropy measures, and recurrence quantification analysis, can provide valuable insights into human movement variability [1, 12, 16]. These techniques can reveal underlying patterns, attractor states, and dynamic properties that are not evident through traditional linear methods. By applying nonlinear analysis to movement data, researchers and clinicians can gain a better understanding of the execution of pathologies, psychomotor problems, and motor control issues, leading to improved diagnostics and targeted interventions.

2.1 Fractal Dimension

Fractal dynamics are sensitive to various individual constraints (e.g., age, neurological disease) and task constraints (e.g., speed, joint range of motion). Biomechanical and morphological constraints refer to the physical limitations and anatomical structures of an individual. These constraints play a crucial role in shaping movement variability and can influence the ability to find the most stable solution for producing a given movement. For example, if certain joints or muscles are restricted in their range of motion, it may limit the available movement options and increase variability as the system searches for alternative strategies to achieve the task [24–26].

Fractal analysis can reveal the inherent complexity and self-similarity in movement patterns. Fractals are geometric shapes characterized by their self-repeating patterns at different scales. In the context of movement, fractal analysis can help identify the presence of self-similar patterns in various aspects of motion, such as stride length, joint angles, or force profiles. The level of self-similarity can provide information about the coordination and control of movement. Fractal analysis can provide information about the underlying control processes involved in movement. Healthy and well-controlled movements often exhibit fractal patterns, indicating a certain level of adaptability and flexibility in motor control [24, 27, 28]. On the other hand, pathologies or motor control problems may lead to less complex and more regular movement patterns, signifying reduced adaptability. Fractal analysis can be applied to study movement variability over different time scales. It allows researchers to explore how movement variability changes with different task conditions, environmental constraints, or because of interventions. Understanding movement variability through fractal analysis can provide insights into motor learning, performance optimization, and injury risk assessment. Fractal analysis can serve as a sensitive tool to detect early signs of motor impairments or pathologies. Changes in the fractal properties of movement patterns may indicate alterations in neuromuscular control or coordination before they become clinically evident through traditional assessment methods. This early detection can enable timely intervention and treatment. Fractal analysis provides an objective and quantitative means to track progress during the rehabilitation process.

Another nonlinear parameter to measure the fractal dimension is the correlation dimension. Correlation dimension is a specific method used to estimate the fractal dimension of a set of points in a phase space. It is based on the concept of how the number of pairs of points within a certain distance of each other changes as the distance is varied [12, 16]. The correlation dimension is computed using the correlation integral, which quantifies the correlation between points in the system at different distances. The correlation dimension is often applied to study the complexity and self-similarity of chaotic and complex systems. Fractal dimension, on the other hand, is a more general concept used to describe the geometric properties of fractals and other complex structures. It is a measure of how the complexity of an object changes with scale. Fractal dimension can be calculated using various techniques, including box-counting, Hausdorff dimension, or information dimension. The fractal dimension provides information about the space-filling properties and self-similarity of a fractal or complex set. While correlation dimension is a specific method used to estimate the fractal dimension of a particular dataset, fractal dimension is a broader concept that applies to a wide range of self-similar and complex structures. The correlation dimension technique is particularly relevant in the context of analyzing chaotic and dynamical systems, while fractal dimension measurements have broader applications in various fields, including mathematics, physics, biology, and image analysis [12, 29].

2.2 Sample Entropy

Sample entropy is a measure of the complexity and regularity of time-series data. It quantifies the unpredictability of patterns in the data, which can be particularly relevant for assessing the coordination of human movement. Sample entropy can be used to assess the regularity or predictability of movement patterns during a motor task. Lower sample entropy values indicate more regular and repetitive movements, while higher values suggest greater variability and less predictability [30].

Sample entropy is a measure of the complexity and irregularity of a time series. In postural control analysis, sample entropy can provide information about the regularity and variability of sway patterns. Higher sample entropy values may indicate increased variability in postural control, while lower values may suggest more consistent and stable postural behavior.

Stability is the dynamic ability to compensate for an external disturbance, and variability reflects the motor system's ability to perform a variety of different solutions reliably under any environment or constraints and so are not directly associated. Thus, variability and stability represent different properties within the motor control process. In this way, the analysis of movement using the theory of non-linear dynamical systems for human behavior provides a better understanding of Human Movement Variability. It may relate to pathology, psychomotor problems, or problems in motor control [16, 18, 31].

Another possibility to increase behavioral flexibility is to increase the repertoire of movements/exercises during training or learning. This would effectively increase the degeneration of the system to more flexible behaviors and possibly increase the adaptive capacity in this case the children. In clinical contexts, sample entropy can help identify motor coordination abnormalities [3, 32]. For example, in conditions where motor control is impaired, such as Parkinson's disease or cerebral palsy, the sample entropy of movement data may be altered, reflecting disruptions in coordination [33–36].

2.3 Lyapunov Exponent

The Lyapunov exponent can help determine the stability of a motor task by quantifying how sensitive the movement system is to initial conditions. A low Lyapunov exponent indicates a stable and predictable movement pattern, while a high Lyapunov exponent suggests a more chaotic and less stable coordination [12, 16, 37]. A low Lyapunov exponent indicates a stable and predictable movement pattern, while a high Lyapunov exponent suggests a more chaotic and less stable coordination. Analyzing changes in the Lyapunov exponent over time can provide insights into motor learning processes. As individuals acquire new motor skills or refine their coordination, the Lyapunov exponent may decrease, indicating a more stable and efficient movement pattern [38–40].

2.4 Recurrence Quantification Analysis

Recurrence Quantification Analysis (RQA) is a method used to analyze the recurrence of a system to itself over time. In the context of postural control, RQA can help quantify the degree of stability and predictability in the postural sway pattern. It allows the detection of complex patterns, such as recurrent states and transitions between different postural configurations [41–43].

2.5 Handwriting and Nonlinear analysis

Handwriting is an example of a complex task that results from a sequence of movements. It has a specific variability structure, and temporal organization, that inform the regularity with which children write as well as their adaptability to the task, I would call this a, fractal dynamics behavior [44, 45]. Handwriting is a unique and complex motor skill that involves the coordination of various cognitive, perceptual, and motor processes.

As an example, if we draw an eight (8) and repeat it several times, always trying to keep the "pencil" on the first eight, it is possible to perceive several different forms of representation of the "eights". Through non-linear methods it is then possible to study the stability of this performance, more chaotic or less chaotic, to perceive the level of regularity, that is greater or lesser adaptability, and to study the similarities associated with the way the trace was performed, that is, to determine the fractal dimension contained in the performance of the task. The complex organization of variability in movement theoretically represents the adaptive capacity of the locomotor apparatus or, once more the fractal dynamics [46, 47].

When we write, we externalize our internal control processes onto paper, creating a tangible representation of the underlying cognitive and motor mechanisms. Handwriting is a unique and complex motor skill that involves the coordination of various cognitive, perceptual, and motor processes.

Handwriting analysis, also known as graphology, has been used as a tool to study and understand various aspects of the writer's psychology, emotions, personality traits, and even potential pathologies. While graphology is not considered a scientifically validated method for personality assessment, it has been a subject of interest for researchers and practitioners in fields like psychology, forensic science, psychomotricity, and occupational therapy. The act of handwriting involves the coordination of fine motor skills, muscle control, and proprioception. Variations in handwriting can provide insights into the writer's motor control and execution capabilities [47–49].

Emotional states and psychological factors can influence handwriting characteristics. For example, stress, anxiety, or other emotional states might manifest in the form of irregularities, pressure changes, or other features in the handwriting. Graphologists have attempted to link specific handwriting features with various personality traits. However, the scientific validity of these associations is a subject of debate, and no consensus exists within the scientific community regarding the accuracy of graphology for personality assessment. Certain neurological or pathological conditions may affect handwriting. Disorders like Parkinson's disease, essential tremor, or dysgraphia can lead to distinct handwriting patterns that clinicians might use for diagnostic purposes.

Handwriting can also be influenced by cultural and contextual factors. Different cultures and educational backgrounds can lead to variations in handwriting styles. While handwriting analysis may provide some insights into a person's motor control, emotions, and potential pathological conditions, it is essential to interpret such analyses with caution [50, 51].

Graphomotor problems refer to difficulties related to handwriting or fine motor skills involved in drawing and writing. These issues can manifest in children with developmental coordination disorder or other motor control disorders. Handwriting can be defined as acyclic movements refer to movements that do not repeat in a cyclical or repetitive manner. These movements involve a series of unique and non-repetitive actions. Even though acyclic movements do not exhibit exact repetitions, they can still involve the execution of associated motor control patterns. These motor control patterns are sequences of coordinated muscle activations and joint movements that are characteristic of a particular movement or task [51]. Authors who have discussed the concept of associated motor control patterns in the context of acyclic movements include researchers in the fields of motor control, neuroscience, and biomechanics.

Nonlinear analysis can help explore the following aspects of graphomotor problems. Nonlinear analysis methods, such as fractal dimension and Lyapunov exponent, can assess the complexity of handwriting and drawing movements. Higher fractal dimension values may indicate more intricate and adaptive movement patterns, whereas Lyapunov exponent can indicate the stability or chaotic nature of the movements. Analyzing movement variability through methods like Recurrence Quantification Analysis and sample entropy can provide insights into the consistency and coordination of graphomotor tasks [42, 52].

Increased variability in handwriting can be indicative of challenges in maintaining stable and precise movements. Analyzing movement variability through methods like Recurrence Quantification Analysis and sample entropy can provide insights into the consistency and coordination of graphomotor tasks. Increased variability in handwriting can be indicative of challenges in maintaining stable and precise movements. Nonlinear analysis can help understand motor learning processes in graphomotor tasks. By examining changes in nonlinear measures over time, researchers can track improvements in motor control and the acquisition of fine motor skills. Nonlinear analysis methods can be used to distinguish between typically developing individuals and those with graphomotor problems [3, 40]. The presence of distinct patterns in nonlinear measures can aid in the diagnosis and assessment of motor control deficits. Evaluating changes in nonlinear measures before and after interventions, such as handwriting training programs, can help assess the effectiveness of interventions in addressing graphomotor difficulties.

2.6 Virtual Reality and Movement

The relationship between postural control and cognitive (attentional) processes is a challenge in child developmental neurology [53]. An adequate acquisition and mastery of fundamental motor skills at the end of preschool age have been considered crucial in developing specialized and more complex motor skills. Postural stability is the basic condition for improving children's specific motor skills [54]. The posture-control system regulates the body's position in space for orientation and balance. It is based on the central integration of vestibular, visual, proprioceptive, and tactile information and an internal representation of the body's orientation in space. Postural control and fine motor skills are highly correlated attributes [44] and it is established that quiet standing requires cognitive resources [55].

Virtual reality provides a controlled and immersive environment where researchers can systematically manipulate sensory inputs and perturbations to study postural responses. Non-linear analysis techniques, such as Recurrence Quantification Analysis or Lyapunov exponent, can be applied to analyze postural sway patterns and detect subtle changes or differences in postural control across conditions. VR allows for the creation of real-life scenarios, providing a more ecologically valid representation of postural challenges compared to traditional laboratory settings. This enhanced realism allows researchers to examine postural control under more natural conditions, leading to a better understanding of real-world postural responses [56, 57].

VR systems can tailor the difficulty of postural challenges to each individual's abilities, allowing for personalized assessments and training. Non-linear methods can help identify individual differences in postural control strategies and determine the most effective training approaches for each person. In neurorehabilitation settings, VR combined with non-linear analysis can be utilized to study the recovery of postural. These findings regarding behavioral flexibility, suggest that the relationship between movement variability and motor dexterity is complex and mediated by many factors, changing with practice, and becoming especially relevant during learning while performing the task, in training or daily life or in rehabilitation. Many examples of behavioral flexibility are only feasible due to the characteristics of the athlete/practitioner/client - such as strength, speed, and joint range of motion control after neurological injuries, such as strokes or traumatic brain injuries. These methods offer insights into the plasticity of the nervous system and the effectiveness of rehabilitation programs.

Overall, the combination of virtual reality and non-linear analysis provides a powerful framework to study postural control in more dynamic and ecologically valid settings.

This approach has the potential to enhance our understanding of postural behavior, advance rehabilitation practices, and contribute to fall prevention strategies in various populations. As technology continues to advance, VR-based postural control assessments and interventions are expected to become even more valuable tools in research and clinical applications. Overall, solving the problem of understanding human movement with numerous degrees of freedom requires a multidisciplinary approach that integrates theoretical, experimental, and computational methods. The combination of these approaches can help researchers unravel the complexities of the human musculoskeletal system and advance our knowledge of motor control and movement planning [39, 56, 57].

3 Final Considerations

Human Movement variability can be described as the normal variations that occur in the motor performance of a task. Movement variability is a normal and inherent characteristic of human motor behavior, the study of movement variability through various methods and theories, such as Dynamical Systems theory and nonlinear analysis, offers valuable insights into human motor behavior. Dynamic Systems theory suggests that biological systems self-organize according to the environment, and biomechanical and morphological constraints to find the most stable solution for producing a given movement.

Movement analysis using nonlinear dynamical systems theory for human behavior provides a better understanding of the execution of pathologies, psychomotor problems, or problems in motor control. The concepts of variability and chaotic variation in human movement, along with advanced tools used to measure human movement variability open new perspectives to guide practice and a fundamental complementary means of diagnosis. Combining Lyapunov exponent and sample entropy analyses with traditional methods of coordination analysis allows researchers and practitioners to gain a more comprehensive understanding of human movement coordination. By leveraging these nonlinear analysis techniques, researchers can explore the complexity, stability, and adaptability of coordination patterns, leading to insights that may enhance performance, diagnose movement disorders, and design targeted interventions for motor rehabilitation.

Embracing the concepts of variability and chaotic variations, along with advanced measurement tools, can lead to new perspectives in guiding practice and providing complementary means of diagnosis in different domains. It's essential to note that while fractal analysis offers valuable insights into movement, it is just one tool in a comprehensive movement analysis toolkit. Combining fractal analysis with other methods, such as biomechanical assessments, kinematic analysis, and dynamic systems approaches, can provide a more comprehensive understanding of human motor behavior and its applications in various fields. It's essential to note that nonlinear analysis complements traditional linear methods in understanding motor behavior, and a combination of both approaches can provide a more comprehensive view of graphomotor problems. Additionally, the application of nonlinear analysis to graphomotor tasks is an active area of research, and further studies may reveal additional insights into the nature and mechanisms of graphomotor difficulties.

Handwriting is influenced by multiple factors, and the link between specific handwriting features and underlying psychological or neurological traits is not firmly established in scientific research.

Despite ongoing research efforts, the inverse dynamics problem remains a challenging and complex issue. The human body's redundancy and the vast number of possible muscle activation patterns make it difficult to uniquely determine the precise control strategy employed by the nervous system for a given movement. Nevertheless, progress in biomechanics, motor control, and computational methods continues to shed light on this fascinating area of study.

Movement variability analysis can be a fundamental complementary means of diagnosis in various fields, such as graphomotor problems, clinical medicine, rehabilitation, and sports science.

Monitoring and assessing an individual's movement patterns and variability can provide valuable information about their motor control, potential injury risks, and overall motor function. Moreover, identifying abnormal movement patterns through variability analysis can guide targeted interventions and personalized treatment plans.

References

1. Stergiou, N., Harbourne, R.T., Cavanaugh, J.T.: Optimal movement variability: a new theoretical perspective for neurologic physical therapy. J. Neurol. Phys. Ther. **30**, 120–129 (2006)
2. Profeta, V.L.S., Turvey, M.T.: Bernstein's levels of movement construction: a contemporary perspective. Hum. Mov. Sci. **57**, 111–133 (2018)
3. Harrison, S.J., Stergiou, N., Harrison, S.J.: Complex adaptive behavior and dexterous action, vol. 46 (2016)
4. Hamill, J., Palmer, C., Van Emmerik, R.E.A.: Coordinative variability and overuse injury. BMC Sports Sci. Med. Rehabil. **4**, 45 (2012)
5. Scafetta, N., Marchi, D., West, B.J.: Understanding the complexity of human gait dynamics. Chaos **19**, 026108 (2009). https://doi.org/10.1063/1.3143035
6. Aagaard, P., Simonsen, E.B., Andersen, J.L., Magnusson, P., Dyhre-Poulsen, P.: Increased rate of force development and neural drive of human skeletal muscle following resistance training. J. Appl. Physiol. **93**, 1318–1326 (2002)
7. Bonacci, J., Fox, A., Hall, M., Fuller, J.T., Vicenzino, B.: Effect of gait retraining on segment coordination and joint variability in individuals with patellofemoral pain. Clin. Biomech. **80**, 105179 (2020)
8. Stroppa, F., Soylemez, A., Yuksel, H.T., Akbas, B., Sarac, M.: Optimizing exoskeleton design with evolutionary computation: an intensive survey. Robotics **12**, 106 (2023)
9. Silva, M.P.T., Ambrósio, J.A.C.: Kinematic data consistency in the inverse dynamic analysis of biomechanical systems. Multibody Syst. Dyn. **8**, 219–239 (2002)
10. Amarantini, D., Rao, G., Martin, L., Berton, É.: EMG-based estimation of muscular efforts exerted during human movements. Mov. Sport Sci. **75**, 27 (2012)
11. Winter, D.A.: Biomechanics and Motor Control of Human Movement. Wiley, Hoboken (2009)
12. Harbourne, R.T., Stergiou, N.: Movement variability and the use of nonlinear tools: principles to guide physical therapist practice. Phys. Ther. **89**, 267–282 (2009)
13. Raffalt, P.C., Stergiou, N., Sommerfeld, J.H., Likens, A.D.: The temporal pattern and the probability distribution of visual cueing can alter the structure of stride-to-stride variability. Neurosci. Lett. **763**, 136193 (2021)

14. Saraiva, M., Marouvo, J., Fernandes, O., Castro, M.A., Vilas-Boas, J.P.: Postural control and sleep quality in cognitive dual tasking in healthy young adults. J. **4**, 257–265 (2021)
15. Saraiva, M., Vilas-Boas, J.P., Fernandes, O.J., Castro, M.A.: Effects of motor task difficulty on postural control complexity during dual tasks in young adults: a nonlinear approach. Sensors **23**, 628 (2023)
16. Deffeyes, J.E., Harbourne, R.T., Kyvelidou, A., Stuberg, W.A., Stergiou, N.: Nonlinear analysis of sitting postural sway indicates developmental delay in infants (2009)
17. Cavanaugh, J.T., Guskiewicz, K.M., Stergiou, N.: A nonlinear dynamic approach for evaluating postural control: new directions for the management of sport-related cerebral concussion. Sports Med. **35**, 935–950 (2005)
18. Kaipust, J.P., McGrath, D., Mukherjee, M., Stergiou, N.: Gait variability is altered in older adults when listening to auditory stimuli with differing temporal structures. Ann. Biomed. Eng. **41**, 1595–1603 (2013)
19. Taga, G.: Nonlinear dynamics of the human motor control (2000)
20. Favela, L.H.: Dynamical systems theory in cognitive science and neuroscience. Phil. Compass. **15**, 12695 (2020)
21. Duarte, R., et al.: Capturing complex human behaviors in representative sports contexts with a single camera. Medicina **46**, 408 (2010)
22. Araújo, D., et al.: Ecological dynamics of continuous and categorical decision-making: the regatta start in sailing. Eur. J. Sport Sci. **15**, 195–202 (2015)
23. Kugler, P.N., Scott Kelso, J.A., Turvey, M.T.: 1 on the concept of coordinative structures as dissipative structures: I. theoretical lines of convergence. In: Advances in Psychology, pp. 3–47. Elsevier (1980)
24. Rhea, C.K., et al.: Fractal gait patterns are retained after entrainment to a fractal stimulus. PLoS ONE **9**, e106755 (2014)
25. Delignières, D.: Synchronization with fractal rhythms, vol. 198 (2009)
26. Cavanaugh, J.T., Kelty-Stephen, D.G., Stergiou, N.: Multifractality, interactivity, and the adaptive capacity of the human movement system: a perspective for advancing the conceptual basis of neurologic physical therapy. J. Neurol. Phys. Ther. **41**, 245–251 (2017)
27. Marmelat, V.: 'Human paced' walking: followers adopt stride time dynamics of leaders. Neurosci. Lett. **5**, 67–71 (2014)
28. Marmelat, V., Torre, K., Beek, P.J., Daffertshofer, A.: Persistent fluctuations in stride intervals under fractal auditory stimulation. PLoS ONE **9**, e91949 (2014)
29. Yeh, R.-G.: Detrended fluctuation analyses of short-term heart rate variability in surgical intensive care units. Biomed. Eng. **18**, 6 (2006)
30. Yentes, J.M., Hunt, N., Schmid, K.K., Kaipust, J.P., McGrath, D., Stergiou, N.: The appropriate use of approximate entropy and sample entropy with short data sets. Ann. Biomed. Eng. **41**, 349–365 (2013)
31. Busa, M.A., van Emmerik, R.E.A.: Multiscale entropy: a tool for understanding the complexity of postural control. J. Sport Health Sci. **5**, 44–51 (2016)
32. Richman, J.S., Moorman, J.R.: Physiological time-series analysis using approximate entropy and sample entropy. Am. J. Physiol.-Heart Circul. Physiol. **278**, H2039–H2049 (2000)
33. Chen, P.-H., Wang, R.-L., Liou, D.-J., Shaw, J.-S.: Gait disorders in Parkinson's disease: assessment and management. Int. J. Gerontol. **7**, 189–193 (2013)
34. Harrison, E.C., McNeely, M.E., Earhart, G.M.: The feasibility of singing to improve gait in Parkinson disease. Gait Post. **53**, 224–229 (2017)
35. Huisinga, J.M., Yentes, J.M., Filipi, M.L., Stergiou, N.: Postural control strategy during standing is altered in patients with multiple sclerosis. Neurosci. Lett. **524**, 124–128 (2012)
36. Stergiou, N., Decker, L.M.: Human movement variability, nonlinear dynamics, and pathology: Is there a connection? Hum. Mov. Sci. **30**, 869–888 (2011)

37. Mehdizadeh, S.: The largest Lyapunov exponent of gait in young and elderly individuals: a systematic review. Gait Post. **60**, 241–250 (2018)
38. Wolf, A., Swift, J.B., Swinney, H.L., Vastano, J.A.: Determining Lyapunov exponents from a time series. Physica D **16**, 285–317 (1985)
39. Stergiou, N.: Biomechanics and Gait Analysis. Elsevier, Waltham (2020)
40. Stergiou, N. (ed.): Nonlinear analysis for human movement variability. Taylor & Francis, Taylor & Francis, a CRC title, part of the Taylor & Francis imprint, a member of the Taylor & Francis Group, the academic division of T&F Informa plc, Boca Raton (2016)
41. Smith, T.J.: Variability in human performance (2014)
42. Błażkiewicz, M., Hadamus, A., Borkowski, R.: Recurrence quantification analysis as a form of postural control assessment: a systematic review. Appl. Sci. **13**, 5587 (2023)
43. Prabhu, P., Pradhan, N.: Recurrence quantification analysis of human gait in neurological movement disorders. Int. J. Eng. Res. **5**(03), 1–6 (2016)
44. Flatters, I., Mushtaq, F., Hill, L.J.B., Holt, R.J., Wilkie, R.M., Mon-Williams, M.: The relationship between a child's postural stability and manual dexterity. Exp. Brain Res. **232**, 2907–2917 (2014)
45. Prattichizzo, D., Meli, L., Malvezzi, M.: Digital handwriting with a finger or a stylus: a biomechanical comparison. IEEE Trans. Haptics **8**, 356–370 (2015)
46. Longstaff, M.G., Heath, R.A.: The influence of motor system degradation on the control of handwriting movements: a dynamical systems analysis. Hum. Mov. Sci. **22**, 91–110 (2003)
47. Tseng, M.H., Chow, S.M.K.: Perceptual-motor function of school-age children with slow handwriting speed. Am. J. Occup. Ther. **54**, 83–88 (2000)
48. Scordella, A., et al.: The role of general dynamic coordination in the handwriting skills of children. Front. Psychol. **06**, 580 (2015)
49. Kushki, A., Schwellnus, H., Ilyas, F., Chau, T.: Changes in kinetics and kinematics of handwriting during a prolonged writing task in children with and without dysgraphia. Res. Dev. Disabil. **32**, 1058–1064 (2011)
50. Fernandes, D.N., Chau, T.: Fractal dimensions of pacing and grip force in drawing and handwriting production. J. Biomech. **41**, 40–46 (2008)
51. Garnacho-Castaño, M.-V., Faundez-Zanuy, M., Lopez-Xarbau, J.: On the handwriting tasks' analysis to detect fatigue. Appl. Sci. **10**, 7630 (2020)
52. Falk, T.H., Tam, C., Schellnus, H., Chau, T.: On the development of a computer-based handwriting assessment tool to objectively quantify handwriting proficiency in children. Comput. Methods Prog. Biomed. **104**, e102–e111 (2011)
53. Schmid, M., Conforto, S., Lopez, L., D'Alessio, T.: Cognitive load affects postural control in children. Exp. Brain Res. **179**, 375–385 (2007)
54. Plandowska, M., Lichota, M., Górniak, K.: Postural stability of 5-year-old girls and boys with different body heights. PLoS ONE **14**, e0227119 (2019)
55. Lacour, M., Bernard-Demanze, L., Dumitrescu, M.: Posture control, aging, and attention resources: models and posture-analysis methods. Neurophysiologie Clinique/Clin. Neurophysiol. **38**, 411–421 (2008)
56. Levac, D., Pierrynowski, M.R., Canestraro, M., Gurr, L., Leonard, L., Neeley, C.: Exploring children's movement characteristics during virtual reality video game play. Hum. Mov. Sci. **29**, 1023–1038 (2010)
57. Nelson, M., Koilias, A., Gubbi, S., Mousas, C.: Within a virtual crowd: exploring human movement behavior during immersive virtual crowd interaction. In: Proceedings of the 17th International Conference on Virtual-Reality Continuum and its Applications in Industry, pp. 1–10. ACM, Brisbane (2019)

Special Session on Lognormality

Lognormality: An Open Window
on Neuromotor Control

Réjean Plamondon[1]([✉]), Asma Bensalah[2], Karina Lebel[3], Romeo Salameh[4],
Guillaume Séguin de Broin[1], Christian O'Reilly[5], Mickael Begon[11],
Olivier Desbiens[1,6], Youssef Beloufa[1,6], Aymeric Guy[6], Daniel Berio[7],
Frederic Fol Leymarie[7], Simon-Pierre Boyoguéno-Bidias[1], Andreas Fischer[8],
Zigeng Zhang[1], Marie-France Morin[12], Denis Alamargot[13], Céline Rémi[9],
Nadir Faci[1], Raphaëlle Fortin[14], Marie-Noëlle Simard[15], and Caroline Bazinet[10]

[1] Laboratoire Scribens, Département de Génie Électrique, Polytechnique Montréal, Montréal,
Canada
{rejean.plamondon,guillaume.seguin-de-broin,olivier.desbiens,
youssef.beloufa,simon-pierre.boyogueno-bidias,zigeng.zhang,
nadir.faci}@polymtl.ca
[2] Computer Vision Center, Computer Science Department, Universitat Autònoma de Barcelona,
Bellaterra, Spain
abensalah@cvc.uab.es
[3] Département de Génie Électrique et Informatique, Université de Sherbrooke, Sherbrooke,
Canada
karina.lebel@usherbrooke.ca
[4] Faculté de Médecine, Université de Montréal, Montréal, Canada
romeo.salameh@umontreal.ca
[5] Department of Computer Science and Engineering, University of South Carolina, Columbia,
USA
christian.oreilly@sc.edu
[6] LifeEngine Technologies Inc., Montréal, Canada
aymeric.guy@lifeengine.ca
[7] Computing Department, Goldsmiths, University of London, London, UK
ffl@gold.ac.uk
[8] University of Applied Sciences and Arts, Fribourg, Switzerland
andreas.fischer@hefr.ch
[9] LAMIA, Université Des Antilles, Guadeloupe, France
celine.remi@univ-antilles.fr
[10] AleoVR Inc., Montréal, Canada
caroline.bazinet@aleovr.com
[11] Faculté de Médecine, École de Kinésiologie, Université de Montréal, Montréal, Canada
mickael.begon@umontreal.ca
[12] Laboratoire GRISE - Groupe de Recherche et d'Intervention sur les Adaptations Sociales de
l'Enfance, Université de Sherbrooke, Sherbrooke, Canada
marie-france.morin@usherbrooke.ca
[13] Laboratoire CeRCA-CNRS - Centre de Recherche sur la Cognition et l'Apprentissage ,
Université de Poitiers, Poitiers, France
Denis.Alamargot@univ-poitiers.fr

A. Parziale et al. (Eds.): IGS 2023, LNCS 14285, pp. 205–258, 2023.
https://doi.org/10.1007/978-3-031-45461-5_15

[14] Département de Psychologie, Université de Montréal, Montréal, Canada
`raphaelle.fortin.1@umontreal.ca`
[15] Faculté de Médecine, École de Réhabilitation, Université de Montréal, Montréal, Canada
`marie-noelle.simard@umontreal.ca`

Abstract. This invited special session of IGS 2023 presents the works carried out at *Laboratoire Scribens* and some of its collaborating laboratories. It summarises the 17 talks presented in the colloquium #611 entitled *« La lognormalité: une fenêtre ouverte sur le contrôle neuromoteur»* (Lognormality: a window opened on neuromotor control), at the 2023 conference of the *Association Francophone pour le Savoir* (ACFAS) on May 10, 2023. These talks covered a wide range of subjects related to the Kinematic Theory, including key elements of the theory, some gesture analysis algorithms that have emerged from it, and its application to various fields, particularly in biomedical engineering and human-machine interaction.

Keywords: Kinematic Theory · Lognormality Principle · Typical Applications

1   Introduction

The Kinematic Theory of rapid human movements describes, using a fundamental equation called the "lognormal function", the speed of an end effector. Various software packages have been developed to reverse-engineer movements by reconstructing them with lognormals. This reconstruction provides central parameters that represent the state of the brain, and peripheral parameters that describe the properties of the neuromuscular systems that produced the movement. Over the years, the theory has been tested and validated in numerous experiments, and successfully used to describe the essential properties of the velocity profiles of the fingers, wrist, trunk, head and eyes, etc. This led to postulate the Lognormality Principle, which states that the lognormal impulse response of a neuromuscular system emerges from a convergent process driven by the central limit theorem. This optimal global pattern reflects the behaviour of individuals who have perfect control over their movements. The production of complex movements is achieved by the temporal superposition and summation of lognormal velocity vectors, with the aim of minimising their number in a given task, to produce efficient and fluid gestures, optimising the energy required to generate them. As a corollary, motor control learning in children can be interpreted as a migration towards lognormality. Then, for most of their lives, normal adults take advantage of their lognormality to control their movements. Finally, as ageing and potential health problems increase, there is a progressive deviation from lognormality.

This manuscript presents the works carried out at the Scribens laboratory and some of its collaborating laboratories. It summarises the 17 selected talks presented in French in the colloquium #611 entitled « La lognormalité: une fenêtre ouverte sur le contrôle neuromoteur» (Lognormality: a window opened on neuromotor control), at the 2023 conference of the Association Francophone pour le Savoir (ACFAS) on May 10, 2023 https://www.acfas.ca/evenements/congres/programme/90/600/611/c. The ACFAS is a Canadian non-profit organization, based in Québec. Its community (4500 active members from 32 countries) promotes scientific activity, stimulates research and disseminates knowledge in French. Our workshop program focused on the key elements of the theory, some gesture analysis algorithms that have emerged from it, and provided an overview of various applications, particularly in the fields of biomedical engineering and human-machine interaction. Throughout this paper, we look back on these studies, as well as forward, and therefore cover past, current and future works. In addition to specialists in signal processing, neuropsychology, neuroscience, education, kinesiology, occupational therapy, pediatrics, students who have completed internships or studies at the Scribens laboratory and student entrepreneurs who plan to use lognormality as a metric in their products, have participated to this colloquium.

More specifically, this paper is an overview of the special session held and presented at the IGS 2023 conference by the first author.

2 The Lognormality Principle: Theory and Overview of Some Applications

2.1 Context

The asymmetric bell-shaped velocity profiles of rapid aimed movements and their invariant properties have been a subject of investigations for many decades in the last century. Among the various models that have been developed to explain these phe-nomena, the Kinematic Theory [118–120, 124] proposed an emergent ecological approach based on the central limit theorem to predict that these asymmetric bell-shaped velocity profiles can be optimally described with lognormal functions. Indeed, assuming that the invariant properties of these simple movements reflect the asymptotic behaviour of complex systems, composed of a large number of time coupled neuromuscular networks, such a neuromuscular system will have a lognormal impulse response that reflects its ideal behaviour, as long as such a neuromuscular system is made up of a large number of coupled subsystems and that the coupling is driven by a proportionality relationship between the subsystem cumulative time delays. This emergence towards lognormality is achieved from asymptotic convergence established over the years, from the exploratory oscillations of the baby's arm to the learning of precise gestures, as in handwriting exercises and sports.

2.2 The Lognormality in practice

Over the last 25 years, the Kinematic Theory has been very useful in terms of signal processing, as a reverse engineering methodology to reconstruct any movements and extract central and peripheral lognormal parameters:

t_0: Represents the time at which the motor command is emitted by the central nervous system. In psychomotor tests, this corresponds to the moment when the nervous system initiates a response after receiving a start signal, such as a sound or visual stimulus. The parameter t_0 makes the Kinematic Theory a causal theory, distinguishing it from all the other models in use nowadays [107].

D: Denotes the amplitude of a lognormal stroke. It corresponds to the total distance covered by the trajectory associated with the specific movement primitive.

μ: Reflects the logarithmic time delay. Exp(μ) defines the time required to reach the median of the motion distance. This parameter provides insight into the overall speed of the reaction.

σ: Represents the logarithmic response time, characterizing the duration of the motion.

θ_{start} and θ_{end}: Indicate the start and end angles of the motion, respectively, measured in radians.

SNR: The signal-to-noise ratio compares the quality of the reconstructed velocity profile to the recorded velocity. A higher SNR value signifies a more accurate reconstruction.

nbLog: This parameter represents the number of lognormal functions used to reconstruct a velocity profile. It serves as an index of motion smoothness, with lower values indicating smoother motion.

SNR/nbLog: This ratio reflects the fluidity of the movement and is calculated by dividing the SNR value by the nbLog.

Figure 1 (adapted from Faci et al. 2021) highlights the effect of these neuromotor parameters on a lognormal impulse response:

$$\Lambda\left(t;t_0,\mu,\sigma^2\right)=\begin{cases} \dfrac{1}{\sigma\sqrt{2\pi}\left(t-t_0\right)}\exp\left\{-\dfrac{1}{2\sigma^2}\left[\ln\left(t-t_0\right)-\mu\right]^2\right\} & \text{for } t>t_0 \\ 0 & \text{elsewhere} \end{cases}$$

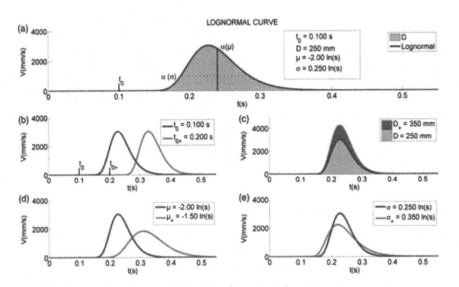

Fig. 1. Effect of the main parameter on a lognormal impulse response

Two major families of algorithms have been developed over the years, the Delta-Lognormal extractors used to reconstruct simple straight pointing movement with two lognormals, one agonist and the other one antagonist [67, 126, 41, 108, 19] and the Sigma-Lognormal extractors used to reconstruct any 2D [54, 105], and 3D [56, 59] complex movements. As it has been shown time and again, reconstructing various gestures with lognormal patterns provides a powerful representation of the underlying neuromotor processes involved in different gestures. So far, the Kinematic Theory has been extensively tested by more than 20 research teams from 8 countries with around 300 000 samples, 11 000 participants, 18 tablet models, 10 other motion capture devices with sampling frequency ranging from 15 to 240 Hz.

In summary, the Kinematic Theory offers researchers a strong realistic theoretical paradigm, a general equation and a set of physiologically meaningful parameters and a set of robust parameter extraction algorithms. [115, 116, 121, 158].

2.3 Workshop Program

The following sections present typical applications of this methodological approach. This can be seen as the tip of an iceberg. There are more projects going on all over the world. Those that were selected for the colloquium were those that could be presented by a French speaker.

The whole workshop has been divided into four themes.

Section 3 presents three papers on AGING: a proof of concept regarding the use of lognormality to monitor brain stroke rehabilitation, the development of a kinematic signature for people with Parkinson's and psoriatic arthritis and a search for Parkinson's disease kinematic biomarkers.

Section 4 deals with PERFORMANCE. The first paper deals with the modelling of electrocardiogram using lognormals, a novel set signals where lognormality can be exploited. The second report two recent studies, one characterizing muscular fatigue and the second interpreting lognormality in terms of optimal control. The third aims at providing tolls for an objective analysis of surgical performance, a brand-new field of potential applications. The fourth summarizes previous studies dealing with the kinematic reconstruction of static calligraphic traces to infer a physiologically plausible motion from an input trace image.

Section 5 deals with TECHNIQUES. The first paper presents a globally optimal delta lognormal parameter extractor based on a branch and bound search method combined with the interval arithmetic. The second describes the first 3D Sigma-Lognormal extractor that has been recently developed and tested. The third compares symbolic and connectionist algorithms to correlate the age of healthy children with Sigma-Lognormal neuromotor parameters.

Section 6 deals with CHILDHOOD. The first two deals with handwriting learning, one with the assessment of graphomotor skills in kindergarten and first grade students in France and Québec and the second with the characterization and analysis of graphomotor behaviours involving young learners in a school context, both studies based on the Kinematic Theory and its lognormal models. The next three papers deal with neurodevelopmental problems and investigate the usefulness of the pencil strokes test: a pilot study dealing with strokes produced by children with mild traumatic brain injury, another one with strokes produced by children with ADHD. The third one, a work in progress, dealing with the characterization of children born prematurely to evaluate the risk of developmental difficulties at preschool age. Finally, the last paper is a brand-new research proposal that aims at exploring the benefits of combining virtual reality and lognormality for prescreening ADHD in children.

3 AGING

3.1 Remote Monitoring of Stroke Patients via 3D Kinematics and Artificial Intelligence

Context. Being one of the top leading reasons for motor and cognitive impairment [30], stroke patient early detection and post-stroke monitoring has become major human concerns and research focus. Namely, post-stroke patient monitoring during the first weeks can optimise the rehabilitation process and lessen the human and financial burden on both the patients and caregivers. We propose a whole movement spotting and analysis pipeline, that have been validated in a clinical institution.

Experimentation Protocol. Our experimentation protocol has been influenced by the Fugl-Meyer clinical assessment, in an effort to make it as realistic as possible. It consists of four key target movements:M1: shoulder extension/flexion, M2: shoulder abduction/abduction, M3: external/internal shoulder rotation, M4: elbow flexion/extension.

We have designed two experimental scenarios:

- Scenario L1: the individual alternates between the four key movements, many times.
- Scenario L2: the individual performs a sequence of key target movements and non-target movement drawn from daily activities [12].

To record data individuals have had to wear an Apple Watch Series 4, in each wrist. A smartwatch application has been developed to extract the watch's signals and synchronize both watches.

Movement Spotting. Before analysing the movements, we needed to spot and recognise them. Therefore, we have implemented an architecture inspired from the work of [82]. The architecture starts with a convolution size set to be half the sampling rate, followed by two other wise separable convolutions. As well as, using SVM as a baseline classification.

Since it is difficult to perform the action spotting in scenario L2, given that there are many movement classes, we have opted for clustering the movements that are similar. Concretely, we have clustered all movements into two classes (C0, C4): C4: being all movements similar to M4; C0: the rest of movements.

Kinematic Analysis. In order to analyse movements and estimate the patients' progress, we have used a 3D algorithm [59] based on the Kinematic Theory of rapid human Movements [118–120, 124].

Results. *Spotting.* SVMs (accuracy $= 84\%$) have outperformed CNNs(accuracy $= 65\%$) for both healthy subjects, for scenario L1. The same pattern has been observed within patients. This is due to the lack of sufficient data for training, in the case of CNNs. For scenario L2, accuracy decreases to 61% for SVMs and 59% for CNNs for healthy samples and lower than that for the patients. For the patients, the task was even harder because of their motricity lack.

Kinematic Analysis. The SNR/nbLog (Signal-to-noise-ratio per lognormal) for patients is significantly lower than for healthy individuals.

Additionally, the contrast between patients and healthy individuals, in terms of SNR/nbLog is remarkably higher for movement M4. One possible explanation for that, could be the difficulty of executing M4. Furthermore, no big difference was observed between the affected and non-affected arms for the patients, the reason behind that could be the fact patients were moving both arms at the same time, thus the affected arm impacts the non-affected arm performance.

Outcomes. For the first time, the 3D Kinematic Theory has been applied to analyse movements for stroke patients on smartwatches. The experiments have proved that it is an efficient non-invasive biomarker to assess stroke patients' progress. Further work can be done on the design of experimental scenarios by focusing on analytic movements.

3.2 Kinematic Signature in People with Parkinson's and Psoriatic Arthritis: Potential of the Sigma-Lognormal Approach

Context. Functional mobility, defined as one's ability to accomplish basic activities of daily living, is traditionally assessed using questionnaires or clinical performance tests [164]. These approaches are mainly based on subjective assessment, somehow limiting their ability to assess changes. In research labs, mobility can be assessed objectively using diverse high-end equipment [98, 164]. Yet, advances in technology, including but not limited to inertial measurement units (IMU), increase the potential for objective functional mobility appraisal outside traditional laboratories, including the clinic and the home [95]. However, these so-called wearable systems work on different basic principles, which may require to rethink some of the traditional variables used to describe mobility. For example, gait is often characterized using stride length, calculated by the displacement of the foot. With IMU, such metric requires a double integration of the aligned acceleration signal, resulting in significant integration errors. To overcome these limitations, modelling approaches can be used to characterize movement signatures [127]. Among these, the Sigma-Lognormal model, based on the Kinematics Theory, aims at characterizing the velocity profile during a pointing task. It has been extensively used to assess scripted 2D signature. Yet, mobility tasks also follow some sort of signature, though in a less controlled context. For example, turning while walking involves a specific cranio-caudal sequence where the head initiates the movement, rotating towards the new desired direction, followed by the trunk and the pelvis, until body is fully realigned [73]. In Parkinson's disease, this signature is modified due to an increased axial coupling [146]. In other words, turning while walking can be seen as a pointing task in the orientation domain, which signature varies according to the ability of a person to perform the turn safely. Similarly, gait can be seen as the foot following a specific movement signature to enable a shift in the center of mass, leading to body's displacement. This section presents the potential of the Sigma-Lognormal model to assess turn and gait.

212   R. Plamondon et al.

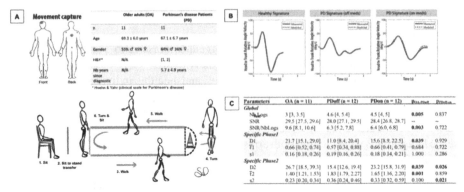

Fig. 2. Sigma-lognormal model to characterize the turn signature. (A) Experimental protocol. Participants were equipped with 17 inertial sensors. Head and trunk sensors were used to assess the turn. A total of 22 participants performed a timed-up and go where participant stands up, walks for 3m, turns around, and comes back to its initial seated position. The turn phase was manually segmented for analysis. (B) Representative turn signature for a healthy individual and a PD patient, on/off medication. (C) Sigma-lognormal parameters analysis. Phase 1 corresponds to the turn initiation by the head, while phase 2 relates to the command given to the trunk to realign with the head.

Turn signature with the Sigma-Lognormal Model. Fifteen healthy older adults (OA) and 14 Parkinson's disease participants (PD) performed a timed-up and go while equipped with IMUs (Fig. 2A). Relative orientation of the head to the trunk was calculated and derived to obtain relative orientation velocity [85, 86]. This signal was then modelled using the sigma-lognormal approach, and the resultant parameters, analyzed [83, 84].

Figure 2B illustrates the ability of the model to reproduce the signature for all participants and conditions. The overall mean signal over noise ratio (SNR) of 28.6 confirms the fit of the model with the turn signature. The various sigma-lognormal parameters (D, t and s) were then analyzed to assess (i) the ability of the model to discriminate between older adults and early Parkinson's disease, and (ii) its sensitivity to change through analysis of the PD on/off medication trials. Results have shown that the SNR/nbLogs ratio, defined as the quality of the model over the number of logs re-quired to fit the signal, have significantly changed between OA and PD (OA: 9.6 [8.1, 10.6]; PD: 6.3 [5.2, 7.8], p = 0.003). These results support the idea that motor control deteriorates with Parkinson's disease. Detailed analysis of the Sigma-Lognormal parameters also revealed a significant change between OA and PD in the D1 parameter, associated with the amplitude of the command given by the neuromuscular system to initiate the turning task (OA: 21.7 [15.1, 29.0]; PD: 11.0 [8.4, 20.4], p = 0.039). Impact of medication was also captured in the D parameters, with D1 showing a tendency to increase and D2 revealing a significant increase in command's amplitude engaging the trunk into the motion (Fig. 2C). These results confirm the usability of the Sigma-Lognormal model to assess turn signature. This study reveals the model's potential to be used in the orientation domain, on complexed tasks involving multiple segments.

Gait Signature Using the Sigma-Lognormal Model. Gait has been studied extensively, though most studies concentrate on controlled laboratory conditions [77]. Nowadays, there is an increased interest in evaluating gait in natural environments. To do so, IMUs are often used due to their portability and low cost [164]. Though these systems can detect temporal parameters accurately (e.g. cadence), they still struggle to estimate spatial information like stride length [155]. This study investigates the potential of using the Sigma-Lognormal model to (i) characterize gait, and (ii) estimate stride length. Twenty-four healthy individuals (mean age: 31 ± 10 years old) and 20 persons with psoriatic arthritis (mean age: 54 ± 9 years old) performed 2-min walking trials on a treadmill at slow, normal, and fast speeds. Participants were instrumented with 39 markers to enable full-body motion capture (OptiTrack by Natural Point, Corvallis, OR, USA). Each trial was segmented into strides, to be further analyzed. Velocity of the foot in the direction of motion was processed using the Sigma-Lognormal approach. Figure 2A illustrates the ability of the model to reconstruct a stride. The overall mean SNR of 78.5 confirms the representativity of the model. Linear regression was then performed on Sigma-Lognormal parameters (D, μ, σ) from the first two strokes to determine the ability of the model to estimate stride length. The obtained linear regression model resulted in an excellent fit ($R^2 = 0.9769$). Mean error of 0.0007cm also confirms the potential of the approach to estimate stride length. Using a Bland & Altman approach, the 95% limits of agreement were determined to be ± 9 cm. In other words, the regression model estimates stride length with an accuracy of ± 9cm in 95% of the cases. To improve these results, analysis was performed using the median stride for each individual, per speed. This approach reduced the limits of agreement to [-5.5, 4.2] cm. This study thus demonstrated the ability of the Sigma-Lognormal model to characterize gait and revealed its potential to estimate stride length.

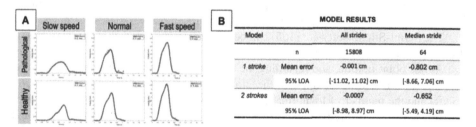

Fig. 3. Sigma-Lognormal model to characterize the gait. (A) Representative gait signature for healthy and pathological individuals at slow, normal and fast speeds. (B) Models precision results

3.3   Contribution of Lognormality in the Identification of Kinematic Biomarkers in the Identification and Early Differential Diagnosis of Parkinson's Disease

Context. Parkinson's disease (PD) affects an estimated 6 000 000 people worldwide [140], making it the second most common neurodegenerative disease, only behind Alzheimer's disease.

The objective of designing an effective diagnostic method has not been reached yet, hindering research and development efforts for better treatments and proper management. Indeed, various disorders including atypical parkinsonian syndromes, hereditary parkinsonism, as well as secondary parkinsonism due to external causes such as drugs or infections, can often be mistaken for PD, especially during the first years of symptomatic disease progression. One clinicopathologic study found only 26% accuracy for a clinical diagnosis of PD proposed at the first consultation visit to a neurologist, in cases that received diagnostic confirmation by autopsy [1].

The search for biomarkers has been a main focus of PD research for several decades. An appropriate, easily measurable biomarker would allow early detection of the disease, at a time when clinical diagnosis can be uncertain, monitor progression as well as treatment response. Various genetic, biochemical, and multimodal imaging biomarkers have been explored with promising results [36], but cost, access, and data reproducibility often limit widespread applicability. In addition, deep phenotyping of motor and non-motor features of PD has been developed, using clinical scales, kinematic platforms, and body-worn sensors for data acquisition, combined with different data mining methods. Physiological eye, limb, or axial (posture and gait) movements or tasks have been recorded, in attempts to capture a neuromuscular signature that would reflect the pathological alterations that distinctly affect motor control in PD and related disorders.

These quantitative approaches offer the salient advantage of assessing the entire neuronal network recruited to prepare and execute a motor command, and multiple relevant motor features simultaneously. Several handwriting and geometric tasks have been evaluated, discriminating PD patients from healthy participants [34, 98, 147]. However, the applicability of these signals in early disease as tools to differentiate PD from other parkinsonian syndromes remains to be determined.

Study Parameters. One of the main purposes of this study is to assess whether the Lognormality Principle and the Sigma-Lognormal model can be used as a diagnosis tool for detection and differentiation of PD and atypical Parkinsonian syndromes.

The Script-Studio software [105] can be used to extract six neuromotor parameters from a pen stroke, and two global parameters.

At this point in time, and regarding the amount of data gathered, it has been found more pertinent to focus mainly on the global parameters: the Signal to Noise Ratio (SNR) and the number of lognormal impulses (nbLog) required to reconstruct the pen stroke. One last main study parameter is the SNR divided by the number of lognormal im-pulses required: The SNR/nbLog, which gives a general overview of the quality of reconstruction and fine motor control of the patient. A high SNR/nbLog ratio tends to indicate a good reconstruction and a patient in good control of its fine motricity.

Method. *Participants.* Building on prior experience [26], we collected data on four blocks of tasks involving distinct neuromuscular programs implicated in ocular pursuit and saccades, hand graphics, arm movements, and vocal sounds, according to the kinematic theory of rapid human movements performed in 2D and 3D. The objective of this study is to collect data for at least 30 patients in each of the three groups (PD, related parkinsonian syndromes and healthy patients.) Patients between age 50–75 with a clinical diagnosis of PD (N = 10) or related Parkinsonian syndromes (N = 1) were recruited within the first 6 years of motor symptoms, and compared to age-matched healthy participants (N = 3). All provided informed consent. Patients were tested in the practically-defined OFF state, at least 12 h following the last intake of antiparkinsonian medication.

Tasks. Parkinsonian signs were assessed using a validated scale by a qualified neurologist. Eye movements were recorded with a standard eye tracker system. Following a visual or auditory cue, participants were instructed to make 30 linear strokes on a WACOM tablet using an electronic pen, repeatedly connect two or three (triangular) dots as quickly as possible, and to draw cursive connected "*ℓℓℓℓℓℓ*" and a spiral. They were asked to hold the tablet horizontally with arms stretched for 10 s, and to make triangle-shaped movements of the arms in the horizontal and vertical plane for 10 s while still holding the tablet with built-in accelerometer and gyroscope. They were asked to sustain a vowel or repeat 3 alternating vowels for 4 s, and this sequence was repeated 5 times. Velocity profiles were generated, and position signal data fed into the Sigma-Lognormal estimator. The lognormal parameters were calculated using low-pass filtered signals.

Results. Preliminary analysis for this pilot study reveals flagrant differences in SNR, number of lognormal impulses (and thus SNR/nbLog ratio) between healthy and PD patients on the "*ℓℓℓℓℓℓ*" tests. The comparison with the atypical group (typical vs atypical PD) also seems promising, though not reliable at this stage with the limited number of participants.

We cannot draw conclusions for this study until we reach a higher number of participants in all three study groups. Furthermore, a more complete analysis including all study parameters (fine and global) could prove to be an insightful discriminating tool. Lastly, a variety of tests aiming at different motor control skills could better differentiate symptoms between PD, related Parkinsonian syndromes, and healthy patients.

4 Performances

4.1 Deep Reinforcement Learning for ECG Modelling Using Lognormals

Context. In a recent study [109], we discussed the development of a model-driven approach for the analysis of the electrocardiogram (ECG) signals. This approach is motivated by the need to improve our capacity to understand the dynamics of complex systems represented in high dimensional space using comparatively sparse experimental data. This combination results in ill-posed problems that we can attempt to regularize by informing (constraining) our analysis using prior knowledge. We can operationalize this idea by embedding pre-existing knowledge in models used for inference. Further, by using biophysically-relevant models with parameters representing latent variables of interest, the inverse modelling process allows investigating processes that may not be experimentally accessible.

Previous models proposed for the ECG have mostly been limited to forward modelling and relied on systems of differential equations [24, 133]. Although very interesting, these oscillatory models operate near chaotic regimes, which makes them notoriously difficult to fit during inverse modelling. Alternatively, the PQRST complex of the ECG has been modelled by fitting a pair of Gaussian equations for each component of this complex [9]. This approach is valuable for applications relying on high-quality fitting (e.g., signal compression), but the absence of biophysical motivation for this model is limiting.

Method. Here, we propose to model the PQRST complex as a set of lognormal equations. The motivation for adopting the lognormal is well-established in the context of the Kinematic Theory [118–120, 124]. The P, Q, R, S and T components of the ECG are associated with subsequent waves of depolarization and repolarization generated by the propagation of action potentials through gap junctions across the network of myocardial cells constituting the different structure of the heart (i.e., the sinoatrial node, the walls of the atria, the atrioventricular node, the His-Purkinje system, and the walls of the ventricles). We modelled each wave of the PQRST complex with one lognormal, except for the T wave that we decomposed in two lognormals (T + and T-) because its shape was not sufficiently well captured by a single lognormal.

For inverse modelling, we used a prototype-based approach (O'Reilly & Plamondon, 2010), where a prototype was used (Fig. 4) as an initialization condition for a deep reinforcement learning approach using as a reward the difference in signal-to-noise ratio (SNR) between two consecutive steps of the iterative learning algorithm [109]. We constrained this optimization process in a box. The envelope of all solutions compatible with these constraints can be calculated [108], allowing us to validate that this envelope encompasses the PQRST complexes observed in our dataset. We also enforced model-plausibility constraints to ensure that the model obtained from the fitting operation is plausible according to our knowledge of the targeted system. In our case, the order of the waves in the PQRST complex must be conserved. Thus, we enforced that the peaks of the lognormal equations modelling each of these components are not allowed to move temporally in a way that would inverse their order. Such an alteration of the temporal ordering of components is common in lognormal modelling, with significantly higher SNR being sometimes achievable by moving components in positions that are not plausible in a physiological sense but that model sources of noise accurately.

We validated our approach with a dataset of 150 ECG recordings collected from 40 infants between 1 week and 24 months of age. We divided these recordings into 9212 60-s segments of uninterrupted ECG recordings. Heartbeats were automatically detected using the Python library HeartPy. We rejected 803 segments (8.72%) because heartbeats could not be detected (i.e., a BadSignalWarning error was raised by HeartPy or less than 20 beats were detected). We made beats comparable by epoching and normalizing the beat duration as follows. Considering three subsequent R peaks occurring at time t_1, t_2, and t_3, the epoched and normalized version of the peak corresponding to t_2 is obtained by linearly interpolating the ECG between t_2-α and $t_2 + \alpha$ over 500 regularly spaced samples, with $\alpha = (t_3$-$t_1)/2$. This approach interpolates the EEG signal roughly (exactly when t_3-$t_2 = t_2$-t_1) from t_1 to t_3 on 500 points, with t_2 in the middle of that window. Note that this approach is slightly different than what we used in [105]. This deviation is adopted to correct the fact that the method in [105] concatenating two windows interpolated on $[t_1, t_2]$ and $[t_2, t_3]$ could introduce a slight distortion in the shape of the R peak when the cardiac rhythm is accelerating or decelerating. We mapped these 500-point epochs to a $[-1, 1]$ interval and refer to the variable along that dimension as the normalized time. For each segment, we computed a mean beat by averaging across these epochs. We characterized the stability of the PQRST profile within a segment by computing the following signal-to-noise ratio between every beat and the mean beat. We rejected every segment that has a mean SNR across all its PQRST lower than 5 dB (N = 578; 6.3%). Such low SNR indicates PQRST complexes that are not similar across the recordings due to issues like R peak detection and various sources of artifacts.

We used the Stable_baseline3 and OpenAI Gym Python packages to train the reinforcement learning model and to apply it for parameter inference. The details of this procedure can be found in [109]. Parameters learned on time-normalized ECG signals can be mapped to corresponding values on the original time scale using the following relationship: $\{\mu^*, \sigma^*, t_0^*, D^*\} = \{\mu + log(\alpha), \sigma, \alpha t0, \alpha D\}$. The code used for the analyses is available at https://github.com/lina-usc/ecg_paper (accessed on 19 June 2023).

Results. We extracted the PQRST complexes for all segments (N = 1,008,784 PQRST complexes). We excluded from further analyses beats fitted with an SNR < 5 dB (8. 8%). The fitting SNRs are generally lower than for fitting movement kinematics, with an average of 10.11 dB. For example, an average SNR of 20.75 dB was reported for a prototype-based lognormal modelling of the speed of triangular motion [106]. We believe this lower fitting accuracy for ECG signals is partly due to systematic offsets in the resting potentials. Such systematic offsets significantly contribute to the modelling error and can be observed at a steady state for electric potential but not for the speed of human movements.

As a proof of concept, we validated that modelling parameters are sensitive to a factor expected to have a significant effect on ECG: age. We evaluated the significance of the relationship between age and modelling parameters using the Kendall rank correlation coefficient. We used this non-parametric test to account for the non-normality of the data. Out of 24 parameters, 14 showed a statistically significant relationship with age at p_{adj} < 0.05 with a conservative Bonferroni adjustment for 24 independent tests (Table 1).

Table 1. Kendall correlation coefficients and associated p-values for the relationships between model parameters and age. Bold red values indicate statistical significance as p_{adj} < 0.05.

	D		μ		σ		t_0	
	τ	p_{adj}	τ	p_{adj}	τ	p_{adj}	τ	p_{adj}
P	0.135	0.764	.245	2.28e-03	-0.0842	4.31	-0.374	6.04e-08
Q	-0.00487	10.5	0.178	0.110	5.10e-04	23.8	-0.322	7.07e-06
R	0.0669	6.88	0.377	4.59e-08	-0.113	1.71	-0.452	1.36e-11
S	-0.158	0.288	0.188	0.0673	0.0332	14.3	0.397	5.87e-09
T+	0.292	7.61e-05	0.382	2.92e-08	0.249	1.80e-03	0.377	4.37e-08
T-	-0.302	3.48e-05	0.422	4.22e-10	0.248	1.86e-03	0.232	5.26e-03

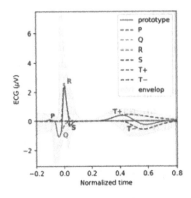
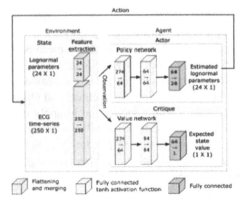

Fig. 4. Left: Prototype for the PQRST complex. The shaded region shows the envelope defined by the bounding box constraints on the value of the parameters. Right: Schematic of the deep reinforcement learning model implemented for parameter estimations. Reproduced from [109].

Discussion. We expect the fitting accuracy from an approach such as [9] to be higher than what was obtained with our model, although we did not explicitly compare accuracies. Published values may not be comparable because they were obtained on a different dataset, with different preprocessing, targeting different populations. Furthermore, our approach uses only 24 parameters, whereas the approach using pairs of normal equations in [9] uses 35. This approximative 50% increase in modelling parameters is expected to provide more flexibility to improve fitting accuracy. More importantly, we aimed to develop a biologically relevant model rather than obtain maximal fitting accuracy. High fitting accuracy is desirable for some applications, such as the signal compression application mentioned in [9]. However, for physiological interpretability, the biological relevance of the model and the preservation of component order are more important and should be prioritized even when it results in some loss in fitting accuracy. These arguments should be familiar to anyone who pondered on the issue of model overfitting.

Outcomes. As demonstrated by these initial results, the proposed model is sensitive to factors influencing the ECG signal. Given the interpretability of this model in terms of the convolution of a large number of coupled subsystems, this model-driven approach to the analysis of ECG is poised to offer a more principled way to analyze these biosignals.

4.2 Kinematic Theory, Muscle Fatigue and Optimality: Contribution to the Biomechanics of the Upper limb

Context. The laboratory of Simulation and Movement Modelling (Montréal, Canada) is recognized for its research on upper-limb biomechanics. Particularly, it focused on 1) shoulder fatigue [65, 66], a component of the injury production mechanism [32], and, more recently, 2) predictive simulation using the optimal control theory [100]. Both applications were recently studied in line with the Kinematic Theory (KT) of rapid human movements. Existing tools like visual analog scales, questionnaires, and electromyography (EMG) have provided valuable insights into shoulder fatigue prevention but remain limited or complicated to use in clinics, sports, or occupational environments.

Differentiating between central and peripheral shoulder fatigue is also critical for tailoring appropriate recovery interventions. KT, which models the neuromotor impulse response through lognormal functions, offers a robust framework for detecting pathologies. This theory provides an idealized model of motor control, where changes in the neuromuscular system are manifested through modifications in parameters defined by this theory. A relevant tool that relies on KT must be sensitive to shoulder fatigue, and its parameters should be reliable. The objectives of two recent papers [80, 81] were to assess if shoulder fatigue might change KT central and peripheral parameters and their test-retest reliability.

Invariants commonly observed in human movements provide valuable insights into movement generation and control mechanisms. According to KT, the velocity profile's invariance derives from the human system's complexity and the interconnection of its numerous subsystems. It results in an asymmetrical bell-shaped velocity profile of the end-effector, as observed in rapid human movements. Concurrently, optimal control theory suggests that a system operates in the most efficient manner possible, considering both cost function and constraints. Interestingly, no identified cost function has been able to reproduce the speed profile suggested by KT. The objectives were twofold: 1) to assess various cost functions by expressing them in terms of parameters derived from KT, and 2) to propose a novel cost function that aligns coherently with KT velocity profiles.

Shoulder Fatigue Assessment. Twenty healthy participants performed two sessions of handwriting tasks on a tablet put vertically at shoulder height, both pre- and post-fatigue of the shoulder (50% of maximum voluntary contraction in concentric at 90°/s till 9/10 on Borg CR10 scale). In one session, the fatigue was induced through internal rotation, and in the other, through external rotation. The writing tasks involved basic strokes, triangles, and horizontal and vertical oscillations. Parameters from these strokes were determined following the Sigma-Lognormal model. Both intra-subject and inter-subject changes in parameters due to fatigue were evaluated using U-Mann-Whitney tests. An additional 20 participants perform two sessions of pre-fatigue strokes only. Intraclass correlation coefficients (ICC) were calculated from the 40 participants to quantify the parameter reliability. We also reported the standard errors of measurement and minimal detectable changes.

Central and peripheral parameters were significantly modified after fatigue, but responses were subject-specific. Still, when considering our sample, parameters that describe the motor program execution increased significantly after fatigue. Reliabilities of the KT main parameters were moderate to excellent for all tests. Particularly, the parameters that best explained shoulder fatigue exhibited good to excellent reliability, accompanied by low standard errors of measurement. Overall, the setup and handwriting tests were appropriate for shoulder fatigue detection. Further research is required to detect lower levels of shoulder fatigue and determine its feasibility in clinical, sports, and occupational environments.

Optimal Control and Kinematic Theory. Common cost functions (least squared velocity, acceleration, and jerk, as well as minimal time: $\int t2 \, dt$) were expressed as functions of the lognormal parameters: μ and σ that are the log-time delay and response time, respectively. We found that minimizing the least squared velocity, acceleration, and jerk amounts to maximize μ and σ, which is not "physiological". In-deed, previous studies proposed boundaries of μ and σ for handwriting [111]. In contrast, minimizing time corresponds to minimizing μ and σ. Consequently, we proposed a cost function composed of minimal jerk, kinetic energy (i.e., weighted squared velocity), and time. Such a cost function admits a minimum within the μ and σ boundaries. We simulated arm movement in the horizontal plane by minimizing this cost function. We could predict an asymmetrical bell-shaped velocity profile of the end-effector like the one expected by KT. The asymmetry comes from the minimum time, while the concavity of the deceleration is mainly explained by the kinetic energy. The proposed cost function needs further validation; weights could be identified using inverse optimal control.

KT has paved the way for fresh perspectives, promising to deepen our comprehension of the mechanisms underlying human motion generation and its adaptation during fatigue-inducing tasks.

4.3   Objective Analysis of Surgical Performance thanks to a Simulator Augmented by Artificial Vision

Context. Surgical skill assessment is essential for the continuous improvement of surgeons. However, current methods such as evaluation using scoring systems like the OSATS [8] require at least one expert evaluator. This limits the frequency of assessments and makes them prone to bias and variability.

Many methods have been proposed in the past years for the automatic and objective evaluation of surgeons. Those methods use various data acquisition devices to capture surgical movements, such as cameras [63, 64, 72], surgical robots [52, 110], accelerometers [165], EMG sensors [148], among others. The data acquired is usually paired with metrics evaluation algorithms or machine learning based techniques to assess surgical skills [166].

The Leap Motion Controller (LMC) (Ultraleap Ltd, Bristol, UK) provides a low-cost solution to capture relevant hand movement data in three dimensions (3D) through its integrated hand-tracking software and presents a potential method to acquire kinematic data for surgical skill evaluation.

To analyze complex patterns using kinematic data, we have exploited the Sigma-Lognormal model which has shown validity in many fields of application [126] using the Lognometer, a system that integrates this model to allow the acquisition and analysis of precise 2D handwriting movements of varying complexity [49].

The aim of this study was to validate the use of the LMC to accurately capture dominant hand movements and assess its potential to be used as a data acquisition tool for surgical performance evaluation.

Methods. Three subjects participated in the data acquisition: one left-handed male, one right-handed male and one right-handed female. Two different tasks were performed for 30 repetitions each, on the Lognometer. The Lognometer comprises a digital pen and tablet (Cintiq 13HD, Wacom Co., Kazo, Japan), and captures the position of the tip of the pen at a 300 Hz frequency.

The task execution was simultaneously recorded with the LMC, which saves infrared video files and 3D positions of various hand markers with a variable acquisition frequency (60–90 Hz). The central palm marker coordinates were used to evaluate velocity profiles in this study, a good compromise between tracking stability, precision, and proximity to the end-effector.

The first task was the drawing of a single stroke with the pen on the tablet after a visual stimulus and aimed to verify the reliability of the LMC to capture fast movements. The second task was to draw a continuous line connecting three targets to form a triangle and aimed to verify the capability of the LMC to accurately reproduce velocity profiles from the recorded 3D coordinates for more complex movements. Even though 2D pen strokes on the Lognometer were compared with 3D recordings on the LMC, most of the movement was along the 2D plane of the Lognometer tablet. The position data from each device were used to obtain velocity profiles that were aligned and compared one-by-one. Normalized Cross-Correlation was used to obtain a Pearson's correlation coefficient, quantifying the similarity between the two signals between −1 and 1.

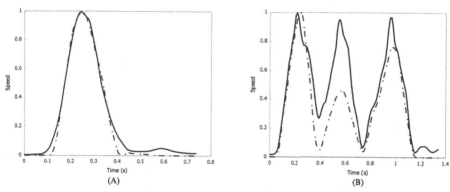

Fig. 5. Velocity profiles from the Lognometer (dotted line) and LMC (full line) for a repetition of the single pen stroke task (A) and the three-target triangle task (B).

Results. In total, 180 movements were recorded and compared. Figure 5 shows the superimposed velocity profiles from both devices for an example recording of each task. For the single pen stroke task, average Pearson correlation coefficients of 0.90 ± 0.13, 0.91 ± 0.17 and 0.98 ± 0.03 were obtained for subjects 1, 2 and 3 respectively. Four repetitions out of 30 were partially cut for subjects 1 and 2, due to the movement being too rapid for proper hand detection by the LMC. Excluding these outliers, the average Pearson correlation coefficients were 0.94 ± 0.04 and 0.98 ± 0.01 for subjects 1 and 2 respectively. For the three-target triangle task, the average Pearson correlation coefficients were 0.87 ± 0.03, 0.84 ± 0.03 and 0.91 ± 0.01 for subjects 1, 2 and 3 respectively. There were no detection interruptions for all repetitions of this task across subjects.

Discussion. This study analyzed the LMC's potential to be used in complex hand tracking movement analysis in a surgical evaluation context. The data acquisition protocol was robust, and the resulting recordings were of high quality when compared to a reference Lognometer.

With outliers removed, the Pearson correlation coefficients obtained from the single pen stroke task were very strong, with a total average across the three subjects of 0.97 ± 0.03, signifying a close adequation as observed on Fig. 5A.

For the more complex three-target triangle task, the average Pearson correlation coefficient of 0.87 ± 0.04 across the three subjects was lower than the coefficient of the simpler pen stroke task, but still represents a significant similarity between the two velocity profiles. As seen on Fig. 5B, the velocity profiles for the triangle task show similarities in peak timing. However, differences in amplitude and shape were observed: the second peak measured by the LMC was much higher, and less smooth. This may be due to the fact that, unlike the Lognometer that captures movements of the tip of the pen on a single 2D plane, the LMC captures 3D hand movement data, including pronation, supination and varying hand placement along the movement, thereby changing the shape and amplitude of some parts of the velocity profile due to additional movements being detected.

Momentary loss of detection was also observed in certain recordings for the single pen stroke task, as the LMC software cannot detect hands moving at a very high speed. No loss of detection was observed for the triangle task, since this task requires higher accuracy which is translated in a slower drawing speed: the slower movement allows for reliable detection of the hand.

To fully assess the possibility to use the LMC to track 3D hand movements, its data acquisition should be compared with devices also capable of 3D tracking. However, even when compared with reference 2D data, similar speed profiles were achieved which confirms the potential of the Leap Motion Controller for the purpose of surgical skill evaluation. This data could be evaluated through the Sigma-Lognormal model, to further compare the movements captured from both devices [116]. The lognormal parameters extracted from the model could also be used as metrics to classify different levels of expertise based on the quality of their movements.

Outcomes. The Ultraleap LMC is a promising tool to capture 3D kinematic data, which could potentially be used to assess surgical performance and analyze complex movements through the Sigma-Lognormal model.

4.4 Kinematic Reconstruction of Static Calligraphic Traces from Curvilinear Features

Context. Most of the existing works are aimed either at a precise analysis of the kinematics of a digitized input or at the segmentation of a handwriting trace into components for biometric or pattern recognition purposes. On the other hand, our specific aim is perceptually and artistically driven, and we seek to infer a physiologically plausible motion from an input trace, the kinematics of which may be unavailable, such as when using vector graphics inputs, or may be degraded or unreliable due to the poor quality of a digitization device, such as when using low-cost tablets or trackpads. The motivation for this approach is grounded on the hypothesis that the visual perception of marks made by a drawing hand triggers activity in the motor areas of the brain [61, 93], and further induces an approximate mental recovery of the likely movements and gestures underlying the artistic production [62, 114]. We argue that this is particularly true for certain art forms such as expressed in calligraphy [60] and graffiti art [14, 99], in which the mastery of a skillful movement in large part determines the aesthetic quality of the resulting artefact.

In our proposed method, we first represent an input trace as a series of closely fitted circular arcs. We then exploit this spatial and structural geometric representation to infer the kinematics of a likely generative movement—as would be performed by a skilled human expert or artist, as predicted by the Lognormality Principle. To do so, we rely on the Kinematic Theory of rapid human movements [127], a family of models of reaching and handwriting motions, in which a movement is described as the result of the parallel and hierarchical interaction of a large number of coupled neuromuscular components. The resulting method allows the reconstruction of physiologically plausible velocity profiles for the geometric trace of an input movement given as an ordered sequence of points.

Method. Our first step is to take advantage of the duality between curvature and symmetry axes [92] in order to extract more robustly curvilinear shape features (CSFs), such as those based upon extrema (of some curvature measure or approximation) along a handwriting or drawing trace. The method is also directly adaptable to open contours, to contours with breaks in curvature, and can further be used to identify loops where a trace overlaps itself. Each CSF is also explicitly paired with corresponding contact circles and a pair of curvilinear support regions: contour traces on each side of an identified contact circle or extremum, where curvature is approximately monotonic. We have introduced, defined and described how to retrieve CSFs in recent works [13, 16, 17].

In between each contact circle segment, as a second step, we fit Euler spirals to the trace of the support regions. Euler spirals or clothoids are a useful type of curves in which curvature varies linearly with arc length, permitting the description of variably curved segments which may contain an inflection. To select initial parameter values of each Euler spiral segment, we use a secant method described by Levien [91]. We proceed to refine this initial fit with a least squares optimisation based on the classic Gauss-Newton method. Once spirals are optimally fitted, we can identify inflection points and obtain a final segmentation of the entire trace as a set of circular arcs. More details can be found in [17]. This representation of the input trace, as a series of circular arcs, is now ready to be exploited together with the Signal Lognormal ($\Sigma \Lambda$) model [105, 117].

An important practical assumption is typically made when initiating the $\Sigma \Lambda$ model: handwriting movements are mostly made with rotations of the elbow or wrist. The corollary is then that the curvilinear evolution of a drawing stroke can be approximated by a circular arc. This has for consequence to simplify the computation of the angular evolution of a stroke as represented by the $\Sigma \Lambda$ model.

Each stroke is to be represented via aiming target locations. The initial set of aiming targets (aka "virtual targets") consists of three types of feature points or features for short: from CSF analysis (i) recovered curvature maxima loci, and from Euler spiral analysis (ii) inflections, and (iii) splits (of wide angled circular arcs). We can either directly used these loci or find their nearest neighbors, on the original input trace, which leads to slightly more accurate reconstructions. An initial estimation of the trajectory parameters is performed using these virtual targets.

To improve the reconstruction, we adopt an iterative refinement scheme in which we adjust the curvature and time overlap parameters together with the target positions in order to minimize the difference between the reconstructed and original trajectories. We optimize the quality of the reconstruction by maximizing an error criterion based on a signal-to-noise ratio or SNR [17]. Because we do not take into consideration the kinematics of the input, we evaluate the quality of the reconstruction using the SNR computed between the reconstructed and input trajectory. Our proposed method consistently produces accurate (> 15dB SNR) reconstructions of the input, while providing flexibility for the use of additional constraints that can be exploited in order to generate interactive stylizations and variations.

Discussion. The $\Sigma\Lambda$ model directly reflects the characteristics of a smooth human movement at the planning and neuromotor level. We therefore expect and observe that parameter perturbations result in variations of a trace that are similar to the one that would be seen in multiple instances of handwriting or drawing made by one or more subjects. We have found that applying the perturbation with a variance inversely proportional to the temporal overlap parameters improves the legibility of the variations. This is equivalent to imposing a higher precision requirement at trajectory locations with higher curvature, which are known to be the most informative [53]. This is also related to the "minimum intervention principle" [151], Suggesting that human movement variability is higher where it does not interfere with the performance required for a task.

The smooth kinematics produced by the $\Sigma\Lambda$ model can be exploited to generate expressive brush renderings of the trajectory. We have designed and applied a brush model that builds upon the assumption that the amount of paint deposited is inversely proportional to the speed of the drawing tool. We can also sweep a texture along the generated trajectory with width also inversely proportional to speed [16], which generates patterns that are highly evocative of some instances of calligraphy as well as graffiti made with markers or spray paint. The trajectory generated by the reconstruction, as well as the brush rendering parameters can be edited in real time with an intuitive user interface [16]. Also, the resulting kinematics reproduce natural human-like movements that can be exploited to create stroke animations of the input as well as to generate smooth motion paths for virtual characters or even humanoid robots [15]. Another related application of the $\Sigma\Lambda$ parametrization is to perform kinematic smoothing of a given trajectory [17].

5 Techniques

5.1 Separation Algorithm and Evaluation Applied to the Delta-Lognormal Model

Context. The present paper proposed a novel algorithm to extract lognormal parameters from handwriting gesture. The proposed algorithm is based on the branch and bound method combined with the interval arithmetic. The general idea is to exploit intervals arithmetic to bound the Delta-Lognormal function and its gradients and use the bounded functions in several ways in a branch and bound global optimization. The goal is to output the global and specific timing properties of a handwriting gesture in a unique bounding box. New tools could then exploit the confident interval of the bounding box to address the wide range of applications where the model can serve. The temporal properties extracted from the pointing gesture, allows to reconstruct the velocity profile of the gesture and represent the planning and timing used to accomplish the pointing gesture. The new algorithm produces a unique high-quality solution with a processing time sufficiently short for practical applications. The accuracy of the extracted parameters that constitute the bounding box is quantified automatically.

Methodology. Before starting to detail the proposed algorithm, some definitions and notations need to be presented. An interval is denoted by a variable in upper case as presented in (1).

$$X = \left[\underline{x}, \bar{x} \right] \tag{1}$$

An interval vector or box is denoted by a variable in uppercase in bolt (2).

$$\mathbf{X^I} = (X_1, X_2, \ldots X_n) = \left(\left[\underline{x}_1, \bar{x}_1 \right], \left[\underline{x}_2, \bar{x}_2 \right], \ldots \left[\underline{x}_n, \bar{x}_n \right] \right) \tag{2}$$

The Basic interval arithmetic operations and the one-variable transcendental functions operations are described in [19, 101].

Definition 1: The natural interval extension of a given function $f(x_1, x_2, \ldots x_n)$ of n variables is given by the interval function $F(X_1, X_2, \ldots X_n)$, which is obtained by replacing the real variable x with the corresponding interval variable X.

Fundamental Theorem. Let $F(X_1, X_2, \ldots X_n)$ be the natural interval extension of $f(x_1, x_2, \ldots x_n)$ then $f(X_1, X_2, \ldots X_n) \subseteq F(X_1, X_2, \ldots X_n)$, and for all intervals, $Y\_k \subset X\_k, for k1 \ldots . . n, f(Y\_1, Y\_2, \ldots Y\_n) \subseteq F(Y\_1, Y\_2, \ldots Y\_n)$,
where $f(Y_1, Y_2, \ldots Y_n)\{f(x_1, x_2, \ldots x_n) : x_k \in Y_k for k = 1, ..n\}$.

This theorem due to Moore [109] was extended and proved by Hansen [70] We use this theorem to bound de Delta-Lognormal function as a specific sequence of interval arithmetic operations.[19].

The global optimization problem that is considered is the following:

Minimize $f(p) subject to p \in \mathbf{P^I}$, where f is a 7 dimensional continuously differentiable function subject to p $\mathbb{R}^N \rightarrow \mathbb{R}$ and $\mathbf{P^I} \subseteq \mathbb{R}^N$ is a 7 dimensional interval vector. Thus,

$$\mathbf{P^I} = \left\{ \left[\underline{D}_1, \overline{D}_1 \right], \left[\underline{\mu}_1, \overline{\mu}_1 \right], \left[\underline{\sigma}_1, \overline{\sigma}_1 \right], \left[\underline{D}_2, \overline{D}_2 \right], \left[\underline{\mu}_2, \overline{\mu}_2 \right], \left[\underline{\sigma}_2, \overline{\sigma}_2 \right], \left[\underline{t}_0, \overline{t}_0 \right] \right\} \text{ is}$$

the bounding space.

The objective function and it's gradient are respectively:

$$f\left(\mathbf{P^I}\right) \in F\left(\mathbf{P^I}\right) = \left[\underline{F}\left(\mathbf{P^I}\right), \overline{F}\left(\mathbf{P^I}\right) \right] = \int \left(v_t(t) - \Delta\Lambda\left(t; \mathbf{P^I} \right) \right)^2 dt \tag{3}$$

$$f'\left(\mathbf{P^I}\right) \in \nabla F\left(\mathbf{P^I}\right) = F'\left(\mathbf{P^I}\right) = \frac{\partial f\left(\mathbf{P^I}\right)}{\partial \mathbf{P}_i^I} i = 1..7, \tag{4}$$

Λ is the lognormal impulse response function. Now that we have these definitions and notations, the proposed algorithm is called IAB&BPE which stands for Interval Arithmetic Branch and Bound $\Delta\Lambda$ Parameter Extractor. IAB&BPE is formulated as follows:

IAB&BPE:

1. Set the initial parameter P^I **initial rule.**
2. Set the working list $L_1 := \{ P^I \}$, the final list $L_2 := \{\}$
   and the upper bound $\tilde{f} = f(m(P^I))$
While $(L_1 \neq \{\})$
3. Select optimal box P from L_1 **Selection rule**
4. Bisect P^I into P_i^I sub boxes $i = 1..2$ **Splitting rule**
For $i = 1$ to 2
5. Compute the bound $f(m(P_i^I)), \underline{F}(P_i^I)$ **Bounding rule**
6. If $\left(\left(\underline{F}(P_i^I) < \tilde{f} \right) \text{and} \left(0 \in \nabla F(P_i^I) \right) \right)$ **Discarding rule**
7. $\tilde{f} = min\{\tilde{f}, f(m(P_i^I))\};$ **Update upper bound for f^***
8.   If P_i^I satisfy the ending criterion   **Termination rule**
     $L_2 += \{\underline{F}(P_i^I), P_i^I, \nabla F(P_i^I)\};$
9.   Else $L_1 += \{\underline{F}(P_i^I), P_i^I, \nabla F(P_i^I)\};$ **Storing rule**
10. Return L_2, f^*

The details concerning the different rule can be found in [22].

Tests and Results. The algorithm has been tested using real and synthetic human gestures. We developed a database comprising 9000 and 500 synthetics and real human gestures respectively. The real gestures were acquired with a Wacom Intuos2 digitizer, sampled at 200 Hz. The first experiment consists in testing the algorithm with synthetic gestures. In this experiment, the algorithm was tested in its ability to retrieve the global Delta-Lognormal parameters representing each synthetic gesture. For the 9000 synthetics gestures, the algorithm always finds the solution, not only the base line target within an accuracy of $\varepsilon = 10^{-6}$, but also a confidence interval including the target value. The second experiment has been conducted using data collected from human gestures. In this experiment, parameters that are considered as solutions for a gesture must have an accuracy of at least 25 dB SNR. For this criterion, the proposed algorithm converges for all cases studied. Figure 6 shows an example of a human pen tip movement and its corresponding original and reconstructed velocity profiles. Both the original and its chosen reconstructed are found in the bounding box returned by the algorithm.

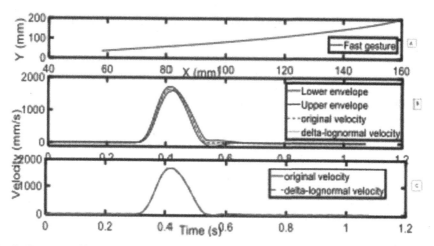

Fig. 6. Example of human Handwriting strokes extracted by IAB&BPE: A. the (x, y) position of the pen tip movement of a writer, B. the real and reconstructed velocity profile with a 31dB SNR enclosing their envelopes, C. the reconstructed velocity profile.

Outcomes. In this paper we have shown that an interval arithmetic branch and bound algorithms can extract the Delta-Lognormal parameter with less computational costs. The effectiveness of the proposed algorithm is quite remarkable. This algorithm exploits the natural interval extension and the fundamental theorem of interval arithmetic to compute the bounding operations of the Delta-Lognormal function.

5.2 Analysis of Three-Dimensional Movements with the Sigma-Lognormal Model

Context. The Kinematic Theory of rapid human movements [118–120, 123, 124] describes movements as a sequence of elementary strokes, which are planned in the brain with specific execution times and distances to cover, and are then executed by the neuromuscular system with lognormal speed. For one-dimensional movements, the Delta-Lognormal model [122] considers two strokes in opposed direction, an agonist and an antagonist movement. For two-dimensional movements, the Sigma-Lognormal model [117] considers a vectorial sum of strokes, which overlap in time. To estimate the parameters of the strokes, the Robust XZERO algorithm [41] is generally used to extract the lognormal parameters from the velocity profile, complemented with an estimation of the start and end angle of each stroke [105]. In the following, we review a recent generalization of the Sigma-Lognormal model to three dimensions [59, 144], which naturally extends the model with two additional angles.

Model. In the 3D Sigma-Lognormal model [59], each stroke has 8 parameters,

$$s_{3D} = (t_0, D, \mu, \sigma, \theta_s, \theta_e, \phi_s, \phi_e) \qquad (5)$$

where t_0 is the starting time, D is the distance to cover, μ and σ are the parameters of the lognormal speed, θ_s and ϕ_s are the starting angles, and θ_e and ϕ_e are the ending angles.

When compared with the 1D and 2D models, the same lognormal speed

$$|\vec{v}(t)| = \frac{D}{\sqrt{2\pi} \cdot \sigma(t - t_0)} \exp\left(-\frac{[\ln(t - t_0) - \mu]^2}{2\sigma^2}\right) \tag{6}$$

is considered for each stroke. When compared with the 2D model, the angles θ_s, θ_e are complemented with an additional pair of angles ϕ_s, ϕ_e to extend into three dimensions. The distance travelled at time t is

$$d(t) = \int_0^t |\vec{v}(\tau)| d\tau = \frac{D}{2}\left[1 + \operatorname{erf}\left(\frac{\ln(t - t_0) - \mu}{\sigma\sqrt{2}}\right)\right] \tag{7}$$

and the angles at time t are

$$\theta(t) = \theta_s + (\theta_e - \theta_s)\frac{d(t)}{D} \tag{8}$$

$$\phi(t) = \phi_s + (\phi_e - \phi_s)\frac{d(t)}{D} \tag{9}$$

considering a pivoting movement. The three velocity components are calculated as

$$v_x(t) = \sum_{i=1}^{n} |\vec{v_i}(t)| \sin(\phi_i(t)) \cos(\theta_i(t)), \tag{10}$$

$$v_y(t) = \sum_{i=1}^{n} |\vec{v_i}(t)| \sin(\phi_i(t)) \sin(\theta_i(t)), \tag{11}$$

$$v_z(t) = \sum_{i=1}^{n} |\vec{v_i}(t)| \cos(\phi_i(t)) \tag{12}$$

and the final movement is a vectorial sum over a sequence of n individual strokes $\vec{v}(t) = \sum_{i=1}^{n} \vec{v_i}(t)$.

Parameter Estimation. The 8 parameters of the 3D Sigma-Lognormal model are estimated from an observed trajectory as follows. First, the trajectory is preprocessed by stopping the movement at the beginning and the end during 200ms (which leads to a more stable estimation of the first and the last stroke), interpolating the velocity profile with cubic splines and resampling at 200 Hz (which leads to a normalization of the sampling rate and supports parameter estimation for acquisition devices with a low sampling rate), and removing noise introduced by the acquisition device with a low-pass filter.

Afterwards, strokes are estimated iteratively, one stroke at the time. They are detected in the speed profile with respect to a minimum area under curve and the Robust XZERO algorithm [42] is used to estimate the parameters of the lognormal speed. Afterwards, the estimation of the angular parameters is based on characteristic times of the lognormal function, including the time of maximum speed and the inflection points. They are used to estimate the velocity components in the three dimensions and calculate the angles with trigonometric functions. For more details, we refer to [59].

The model quality is measured by means of the signal-to-noise ratio (SNR)

$$SNR = 10 \cdot \log \left(\frac{\int_{t_s}^{t_e} |\vec{v_o}(\tau)|^2 d\tau}{\int_{t_s}^{t_e} |\vec{v_o}(\tau) - \vec{v_r}(\tau)|^2 d\tau} \right) \tag{13}$$

comparing the observed velocity $\vec{v_o}$ with the reconstructed velocity $\vec{v_r}$ of the analytical 3D model.

Experimental Results. The 3D extension of the Sigma-Lognormal model has been tested on two action recognition datasets, HDM05 [104] and UTKi-nect [160], as well as an Air-Writing dataset [29]. For the HDM05 dataset, we consider a common subset of 249 motion samples from 11 actions performed by 5 subjects, recorded with a Vicon motion caption suit at 120 Hz. The UTKinect dataset contains 199 samples of 10 actions performed by 10 subjects, recorded with a Kinect camera at 30 Hz. For the Air-Writing dataset, we consider a common subset of 100 words written by 5 subjects in the air, recorded by a Leap camera at 60 Hz.

Table 2 shows the SNR results for the three datasets. For the two action recognition datasets, a high-quality SNR is achieved that is clearly above 15dB, which is generally considered as a quality threshold for kinematic analysis. Although the Air-Writing results are below this threshold, the reconstructed trajectories could be used in a word recognition experiment without significantly impacting the classification accuracy [59].

Table 2. SNR results of the 3D Sigma-Lognormal model in dB.

Database	HDM05	UTKinect	Air-Writing
SNR	18.52 ± 4.09	20.21 ± 4.40	12.52 ± 2.02

Outcomes. With a natural extension of the Sigma-Lognormal model to three dimensions we were able to reconstruct a variety of 3D movements, recorded with different acquisition devices, with a good model quality. The results are encouraging and open up promising possibilities to use the Kinematic Theory in three dimensions, for example in biomedical contexts or in robotics.

5.3 Comparison of Symbolic and Connectionist Algorithms to Correlate the Age of Healthy Children with Sigma-Lognormal Neuromotor Parameters

Context. Motor control, a crucial skill that is progressively acquired during childhood, profoundly influences a children's ability to learn and live well. Traditional methods of measuring motor control maturity, such as administered motor ability tests or behavior-based questionnaires, often require significant human or material resources [23, 57] and can be influenced by cultural differences. This study proposes a convenient and culturally neutral approach using handwriting, a typical fine motor control task. Employing the Kinematic Theory of rapid human movements [118–120, 123, 124] and its Sigma-Lognormal model [106], we extract specific parameters from children's handwriting strokes on a tablet. Both this Theory and model have been used in various biomedical applications, including analyzing graphomotor performances in kindergarten children [45], assessing stroke risk [127], and identifying Attention-Deficit/Hyperactivity Disorder (ADHD) in children [79]. In this study, we extend this research and propose the use of a tablet-based system [45] to estimate motor control maturity in children, leveraging the Kinematic Theory. The Sigma-Lognormal model modelized the velocity profile of movements into lognormal functions, with each function capturing distinct kinematics related to neuromuscular commands. From each lognormal function, six parameters are derived: $\{t_0, D, \mu, \sigma, \theta_{start}, \theta_{end}\}$. Additionally, three parameters (SNR, nbLog, SNR/nbLog) were employed to evaluate the reconstruction.

Method and Experiments

Participants. We aimed to develop a model correlating Sigma-Lognormal parame-ters with motor control maturity in neurotypical children. A total of 513 children, aged 6 to 13 years, from three schools in the south-shore of Montréal participated in the tests. Children with reported neurological, psychological, or motor disorders were excluded.

Sigma-Lognormal Tests. Participants performed two tests: the simple stroke test and the triangular drawing test. For the simple stroke test, participants drew a straight line, and for the triangular drawing test, they drew a triangle crossing three round targets. The movements were recorded using a tablet [49].

Data Transformation. To facilitate model training, the one-hot encoding was used to represent the orientation of stroke drawings. Clockwise angles were converted to match counterclockwise angles.

Experiments. Different approaches were explored: training models on individual movements, calculating mean movement parameters per participant, and using all movements together. Models such as Recurrent Neural Network (RNN), Multilayer Perceptron (MLP), Ordinary Least Squares (OLS), Ridge Regression (RR), Huber Regression (HR), Support Vector Regression (SVR), XGBoost (XGB), Random Forest (RF), and K-Nearest Neighbors Regression (KNN) were tested and compared using nested cross-validation.

Results. In addition to assessing the regression model's performance using the coefficient of determination (R2), mean absolute error (MAE), and root mean squared error (RMSE) were computed to compare mean errors. The mean absolute percentage error (MAPE) was also used to evaluate errors relative to the participants' age.

The results, shown in Tables 3 and 4, point out significant differences in performance between the two tests. The models for the triangular test outperformed the models for the simple stroke test. The lower performances in the simple stroke test may be at-tributed to the test's simplicity, as even the youngest children were able to perform it well. On the other hand, the triangular test better differentiated age-related gains in performance. Nested cross-validations were performed, and one-way ANOVA analysis showed that the neural networks performed significantly better than other models, particularly with full trials.

Discussion and Future Work. The Sigma-Lognormal model proved effective in estimating the evolution of motor control maturity with efficiency and accuracy. Even simple linear regression yielded decent results when the movements were modeled using

Table 3. Regression model's performance for the triangular tests.

Data	Model	RMSE	MAE	MAPE	R2
Mean trial	OLS	1.290	1.032	0.113	0.476
	HR	1.280	1.027	0.112	0.484
	RR	1.239	0.986	0.108	0.517
	KNN	1.365	1.136	0.126	0.416
	RF	1.302	1.060	0.116	0.468
	XGB	1.268	1.029	0.113	0.493
	SVR	**1.210**	**0.971**	0.107	**0.539**
	MLP	1.278	1.010	0.110	0.486
	GRU	1.252	0.978	**0.106**	0.505
Full trials	OLS	1.385	1.166	0.128	0.400
	HR	1.382	1.162	0.128	0.403
	RR	1.386	1.167	0.128	0.399
	KNN	1.453	1.237	0.140	0.341
	RF	1.393	1.178	0.130	0.393
	XGB	1.364	1.149	0.127	0.418
	SVR	1.319	1.094	0.120	0.456
	MLP	1.244	0.991	0.108	0.515
	GRU	**1.196**	**0.937**	**0.102**	**0.548**

Table 4. Regression model's performance for the simple stroke tests.

Data	Model	RMSE	MAE	MAPE	R2
Mean trial	OLS	1.516	1.220	0.133	0.283
	HR	1.514	1.218	0.133	0.285
	RR	1.484	1.206	0.132	0.313
	KNN	1.521	1.285	0.139	0.279
	RF	1.460	1.215	0.133	0.335
	XGB	1.478	1.230	0.135	0.318
	SVR	**1.450**	**1.191**	**0.130**	**0.343**
	MLP	1.487	1.214	0.132	0.310
	GRU	1.501	1.222	0.133	0.297
Full trials	OLS	1.553	1.334	0.147	0.249
	HR	1.583	1.367	0.150	0.220
	RR	1.585	1.369	0.151	0.218
	KNN	1.616	1.392	0.156	0.186
	RF	1.541	1.324	0.146	0.261
	XGB	1.518	1.299	0.143	0.283
	SVR	1.497	1.270	0.140	0.302
	MLP	1.485	1.199	0.133	0.309
	GRU	**1.425**	**1.125**	**0.123**	**0.365**

the Sigma-Lognormal model. Handwriting, as a daily activity, can be easily acquired and analyzed for health monitoring purposes.

Among the algorithms compared, GRU and SVR performed best, highlighting the advantages of neural networks in customizing data structures to fit specific needs. However, symbolic algorithms, such as SVR, performed well and offered explanations within the context of the Kinematic Theory. Feature selection was not investigated in this study, but it may impact the performance of different models [71].

Future work includes studying the kinematics of additional tests and analyzing the original time series of movement kinematics. Symbolic algorithms may not be suitable for the larger dimensions of the original data, and larger neural networks may be preferred. Exploring self-supervised learning [163] and pre-training techniques could optimize model performance with long sequential data. Additionally, investigating the combination of symbolic models (Sigma-Lognormal) and connectionist models (such as VAEs) could provide interesting insights and improve performance. This approach could enhance the understanding of human body motions involved in handwriting.

Outcomes.
Our study presents a novel approach using the Sigma-Lognormal model and neuro-muscular tests to predict motor control maturity in children. The complex triangular test, analyzed with the Sigma-Lognormal model, offers parameters for simple linear regression that accurately predict motor control maturity. Neural networks excel in this task, but symbolic models show promises. Future research should compare alternative tests and assess test-retest reliability. This approach has potential for detecting neurodevelopmental issues for children based on their motor control development.

6 Childhood

6.1 Interest of Kinematic Theory and its Lognormal Models in Assessing Graphomotor Skills in Kindergarten and First Grade Students in France and in Québec

Context. From a cognitive point of view, tracing letters with hand implies at least three steps of processing: retrieving from memory the allograph (shape) of each letter, programming the gesture allowing to trace each allograph and controlling the execution of the corresponding motor sequence [3, 103]. Successfully implementing and operating these processing steps requires acquiring and mobilizing a set of underlying skills such as visuo-motor coordination (allowing the pencil guidance according to the visual context) and graphomotor control (allowing programming and adjusting the motor realization of a graphic gesture). Moreover, strongly dependent on lessons in school, learning to write letters by hand is also highly constrained by the development of gross and fine motor maturation allowing a dual function of (i) gripping the pen and (ii) using the hand, forearm and arm working in synergy to move it and trace the letter [44, 69, 149].

The evaluation of handwriting and their underlying skills in young students is generally carried out through a set of measures mostly standardized like motoric tests (fine and gross evaluation scales, [131, 153]), visuo-motor tests [113, 142] and even handwriting variables allowing to assess the legibility of a produced letter as well as the kinematics of its production [2]. Nevertheless, regarding the graphomotor control (i.e. motor programming and execution of a gesture implied in tracing or writing by hand [35]), it is clear that few tests make it possible to evaluate this skill independently of letter production, as other underlying skills can be approached and described independently of the written tasks which mobilize them.

Accordingly, the objective of this article is to show how the Kinematic Theory, based on lognormal models [118–121 and above], can constitute a relevant objective developmental measure of graphomotor control of pen movements in French and Quebeckers children, according to (i) grade level of students, from kindergarten to grade 1 and/or (ii) a longer kindergarten prestation at school in France (3 years), compared to Quebec (1 year).

Method. *Participants*: Ninety-four students, including 47 French students and 47 Quebec students, of French mother tongue, participated in this study. French students were enrolled in five primary schools in the cities of Créteil, Orléans and Chateauroux. This French sample consisted of 27 students (including 15 girls) in kindergarten (average age = 5.32 years, ET = 0.23) and 20 students (including 11 girls) in the first year (average age = 6.48 years, ET = 0.18). Quebec students were enrolled in three primary schools in the cities of Chicoutimi and Sherbrooke. Developed according to the same criteria as the French sample, the Quebec sample consisted of 27 kindergarten students (including 15 girls) (average age = 5.35 years, ET = 0.23) and 20 first-year students (including 11 girls) (average age = 6.43 years, ET = 0.18). Each French student was matched with a Quebecker student of the same age (to the nearest month), the same sex, the same cognitive abilities (work memory and non-verbal intelligence, as assessed by background measures not detailed here).

Measures: A series of 4 main measures, leading to 12 variables, have been elaborated in order to assess handwriting abilities and their underlying motoric, visuo-motor and graphomotor skills. (i) Motoric skills were evaluated through two tests selected from the NP-MOT scale [153] to probe the different facets of fine and gross motor skills. Fine motor skills were assessed by a fingertip tapping task designed to evaluate finger dexterity (i.e. motor speed and rapid motor programming) for the left and right hand. This test was supplemented with another evaluation dedicated to gross motor skills and consisting in walking in a straight line, jumping from a height of 20 cm and standing on one foot with your eyes open. (ii) Visuo-motor skills were evaluated by two complementary tests, one measuring the ability to guide the pencil as quickly as possible between two lines of a course (Visuo-Motor Precision, subtest of the NEPSY: [78]), the other consisting in copying a series of figures more and more complex (Visuo-Motor Integration (VMI) test: [11]). (iii) Graphomotor control skills were assessed by asking the four groups of students to produce 30 pen strokes by hand, according to the protocol used in [116]. This allowed us to extract lognormal models as the main components of the Kinematic Theory. This theory, developed and tested by Plamondon [118, 119, 121, 122] and Plamondon et al., [117, 124, 126–128] is based on the assumption that all controlled movements, be they simple or complex, are made up of basic primitives (Lognormal function) that reflect the impulse responses of the neuromuscular systems involved in their production.

Figure 7 show the reconstruction of a specific stroke trace written with a pen by a kindergarten pupil, by using Script Studio software. The extraction shows here the existence of six lognormal functions, formalized by three general parameters: (i) nbLog: number of lognormal functions required to reconstruct the signal. This parameter represents the writer's fluidity of movement. The higher the nbLog, the less fluid the movement; (ii) SNR: signal-to-noise ratio between the original speed profile and the reconstructed speed profile, computed in decibels (dB). This is a measure of the quality of the sigma-lognormal reconstruction. The higher the SNR, the better the reconstruction; (iii) SNR/nbLog: performance criterion. The ability to reconstruct a movement's speed profile with lognormals can be interpreted as an indicator of motor control quality, as the lognormal speed profile corresponds to complete motor control [126]. The higher the SNR/nbLog, the closer the movement to ideal lognormal behavior. These three parameters, by evaluating the quality of the curve-fitting, reflect the general state

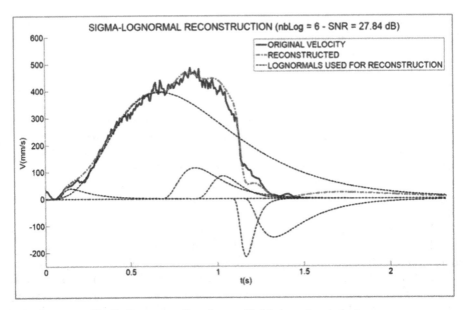

Fig. 7. Reconstruction of a specific kindergarten stroke trace

of the neuromotor system. As the Fig. 7 shows, the lognormal modeling means that the movement as produced by the pupil was based on a sequence of six successive commands, with: nbLog = 6; SNR dB) = 27.83; SNR/nbLog = 4.64. By opposite, normal adults in perfect control of their movements would have performed the stroke by using two lognormals. Indeed, if children use more lognormals than adults to execute a given stoke, this number decreases as they gradually master handwriting [45]. Accordingly, in this study, we focus on the 3 general parameters; nbLog, SNR and SNR/nbLog by seeking to understand to what extent these parameters vary significantly with the Grade and Country of students, under the effect of the development of maturation and different school learning. (iv) Finally, handwriting skills were elicited by the production of familiar letter allographs. Students were asked to write their firstname several times within 30 s, using their usual handwriting. This task is frequently used to assess handwriting, as it features the best known and doubtless most automatized letter sequence, allowing researchers to focus more purely and specifically on motor aspects [2, 5, 6, 130]. The accuracy and fluency of letters production was assessed by the 4 following variables: % of legible (recognizable) letters, letter accuracy fluency (legible letters per min), pen movement speed, number of pen pauses per letters and mean pause duration.

Apparatus: The graphomotor task (tracing 30 strokes) and handwriting task (firstname written recall) were both performed on a pen-display tablet (Wacom Cintiq Pro 13) connected to a laptop piloted by Eye and Pen© software [4]. The children wrote directly on the surface of the tablet using a stylus (Wacom Intuos 3 Grip Pen). This tablet records data at a sampling rate of 200 Hz, with a spatial resolution of 200 lines per millimeter, and the software records the timing, position, and status of the pen tip on the tablet screen in real time.

Results. Performances of the four groups of students were analyzed by running a two-ways MANOVA in order to determine e the main effects of the Grade (Kindergarten versus Grade 1) and Country (France versus Quebec) factors, on the 12 variables evaluating fine and gross motricity, visuo-motor integration, graphomotor control and handwriting skills. The multivariate effect of Grade was statistically significant. More precisely, the performance of the group of Grade 1 students, except for the number of pauses per letter, were significantly higher than those of kindergarten for all the other measurements, including the 3 lognormal general parameters: nbLog (Kindergarten: 6.36, Grade 1: 5.10; $p < .01$); SNR (Kindergarten: 26.68, Grade 1: 27.03; $p < .01$), SNR /nbLog (Kindergarten: 5.33, Grade 1: 6.35; $p < .002$). The multivariate effect of Country was also statistically significant. However, the effects for each of the variables are more contrasted. Thus, the group of French students (all grades combined) obtains a significantly higher score than that of Quebecker students for the task of gross motor maturation, the test of Visuo-Motor Integration as well as the % of legible letters in the first name written recall task. On the other hand, in the case of the pen movement speed and the fluency per legible letters score, it is the Quebecker students who attest higher performances than those of the French students. No other significant difference appears between the students of the two countries for the other measures, including those carried out by the analysis of general lognormal parameters.

Discussion. If we focus here on the analysis of the general lognormal parameters, results revealed significant differences on nbLog, SNR and SNR/nbLog between children in kindergarten and first graders. The mean value of nbLog was statistically lower for children in first grade than for children in kindergarten, and consistent with this, the mean values of SNR and SNR/nbLog were higher. Indeed, when first graders want to draw a line, they have more fluidity than kindergarten pupils, as reflected in a lower nbLog. Moreover, the quality of stroke reconstruction is better in Grade 1 than in kindergarten, as SNR and SNR/nbLog were significantly higher for the first graders, owing to improved neuromotor control and lognormality with age. It can be then argued that children's motor control improves as they grow older, as predicted by the Principle of Lognormality and the Kinematic Theory.

Moreover, the results of this study bring out two important facts. First, the extraction of Lognormal parameters from a relatively simple task (e.g., drawing 30 strokes) makes it possible to highlight coherent developmental differences between kindergarten and first grade, and this, in consistency with the effects observed for the other skills, actually motor and visuo-motor, involved in the development of handwriting. In this sense, the "stokes tracing task", independent of the tracing of letters, combined with the extraction of lognormal models, could be an interesting avenue to explore, in order to constitute a standardized and predictive test, in the long term.

Second, interestingly, lognormal parameters are here sensitive to grade level but not to country of schooling, unlike other abilities like gross motor maturation or visuo-motor integration. This result suggests that Lognormal modeling probably makes it possible to approach rather the neuromotor component of graphomotor control, which should be, as well as finger tapping performance, more strongly dependent on proximo-distal maturation than on school training.

Outcomes. Finally, if Kinematic Theory and its Lognormal models seems to represent an interest for assessing graphomotor control in young pupils, it remains to assess to what extent the fluidity of the gesture, when drawing a series of stokes, could be related to the dynamics of drawing letters and words, and more particularly to the frequency and duration of pen stops (pauses), supposed to indicate difficulties in controlling the execution of the strokes making up a letter [37, 112]. The presence of such a relation between strokes and letters could be investigated by applying the lognormal modeling to the production of letters of the alphabet and of the firstname, in addition to the production of a series of strokes.

6.2 The use of the Lognormality Principle for the Characterization and Analysis of Graphomotor Behaviours Involving Young Learners in a School Context

Context. Children learnings suppose successful mobilizations of specific graphmotor gestures (GG) as pointing, drag and drop and handwriting since their beginning at kindergarten around 2–3 years old. Earliest mastery of each of these GG in various contexts is fundamental because they are involved by most of the scholar tasks that must be executed into tangible or digital ecosystems. The lognormality of adult's expert graphomotor behaviors and a tendency to a gradual migration to this optimal lognormal behavior through development and training have been established and validated thanks to the sigma-lognormal modeling of GG of kindergarten apprentice scripters and adults [136]. However, the GGs considered had been acquired in a strict clinical framework by considering psychomotor tasks quite different from real school tasks. This raises the question of the possibility of extending these conclusions to the cases of GG specific to school constraints, carried out and acquired in the less strict context of tasks of a school nature. To answer this question, we have conducted experiments in a school context for nearly a decade with the aim of answering the following questions: Is the reconstructive power of sigma-lognormal modeling, that was observed in strict clinical cases of rapid plotting of simple trajectories, robust enough to withstand the school environment noise and its constraints? Does considering the sigma-lognormal modeling of realistic and more complex traces than those considered in the clinical case makes it possible to distinguish levels of expertise in terms of levels of motor control acquired thanks to school training?

Methodology. To answer these questions, we exploited types of graphomotor gestures carried out in school activities collected during several experiments conducted on school time in fifteen schools from primary to secondary between 1997 and 2019.

These GGs were carried out by more than a thousand all-comers, aged 3 to 14 years and enrolled from the first year of kindergarten to the third class of middle school. Some of them were made in a tangible environment in paper-and-pencil on paper mode. They were acquired online as described in [46] thanks to several models of Calcomp and Wacom digitizers, driven by the Dekat'tras application, placed as a plotting support. Others were made and acquired online directly in a digital learning environment based on the platform Copilotr@ce [140]. Some of these school GGs were produced using an ink pen or non-ink writing tool, while others were produced by finger.

Various activities including spontaneous or constrained scribbling [136–138] for 20 s, tracing on predefined trajectories, copying isolated patterns from alphabets [45] or cursive words, writing common isolated words such as first name, days of the week under various conditions [139], were offered to students.

For each of the types of graphomotor gestures acquired, the batch processing procedure of the ScriptStudio tool exploiting the Robust X-Zero approach [105] was used to perform sigma-lognormal modeling of curvilinear velocity profiles and approximation in 2D space of the trajectory executed by the pupils. Two global kinematic parameters were then extracted. The first of these parameters, called nbLog, is an integer value. It specifies the number of lognormals needed to reconstruct the speed and trajectory with a signal-to-noise ratio defining the value of the second parameter extract-ed. This one is called SNR. From these two parameters a third: the SNR/nbLog ratio, was estimated for each type of GG considered. Then, acceptable rates of good reconstruction, i.e., with an SNR greater than or equal to 15dB, were established. Next, the distribution of SNR was determined for each grade level represented in the cohort of students who participated in the collection of the type of GG considered. Finally, the behavior of each of these three parameters according to grade level and, for some, according to the constraints imposed by the task to be carried out, was tested by means of statistical tests.

Main Results. A great majority of GGs acquired under real conditions at school, whether on graphic or touch tablets and all models of equipment combined, has been rebuilt with an SNR greater than or equal to the minimum threshold of 15 dB. This, in spite of their complexity, duration, continuous or not and the grade level of the pupils whose produced them.

This first observation makes it possible to validate the robustness of Sigma-Lognormal modeling (SLM) for use for the analysis of real childish graphomotor behaviors in the school context. This robustness is verified although the school context is more prone to disruptions in the operating conditions of the SLM than clinical environments are. The use of SLM is also possible from the first years of schooling and throughout primary and secondary schooling. This, by directly considering GG produced along usual pedagogical activities.

The second observation relates to the distribution of SNR values according to the degree of experience in the implementation of school GG translated by the pupils' grade levels. Regardless of the type of GG considered, it turns out that the higher the educational level, the higher the rates of high SNR values and the lower the rates of low values of SNR. Conversely, in the case of a low educational level the rates of low SNR values are higher.

Discussion. These results therefore argue in favor of the validation of the possibility of observing the principle of migration to lognormality according to effects of school trainings from kindergarten up to at least end of middle school and this, for most GGs taught and mobilized by the school.

Based on such results, it becomes possible to set up individual monitoring of the progression of the pupils' level of motor control during their school cursus thanks to the observation of the evolution of the SNR for each type of school GG.

By virtue of the Principle of Lognormality it is possible to postulate that at equivalent SNR level for an analogous type of graphomotor gesture, the higher is the number of lognormals the more this ratio tends towards 0 which reflects a lower quality of motor control of the graphomotor gesture mobilized during the proposed task. Conversely, the lower is the number of lognormals, the higher this ratio will be, which will reflect a better motor control capability of the GG during the task.

Outcomes. The non-conservation of high SNR as so as inconsistent SNR/nbLog ratios between various constrained situations of scribbling and writing words while SNR remain high tend to show that the global parameters SNR and SNR/nbLog can play role of gauges of shortcomings in automating the planning and execution procedure of the types of GG concerned.

Therefore, a non-invasive and transparent monitoring of motor control growing seems feasible by comparing the values of these three global parameters directly through various real pedagogical situations at school. Such monitoring should also help teachers to decide on objective and quantifiable bases whether to continue, maintain or strengthen the use of some pedagogical approaches to learn school GGs.

However, to achieve such tools, solutions to quickly compute those parameters are needed.

6.3 Lognormality in Children with Mild Traumatic Brain Injury: a Pilot Study

Context. Pediatric traumatic brain injury (TBI) is a public health burden and the leading cause of disability worldwide [159]. Each year, millions of children sustain TBI, with mild traumatic brain injuries (mTBI) and concussions accounting for more than 90% of all TBI cases. Previous studies have shown that 15–30% of children with mTBI continue to experience PCS for several months following injury, which in turn can result in functional deficits and declines in quality of life [10, 102, 162]. However, there is currently a lack of accurate objective and developmentally appropriate tools to sensitively assess fine motor skills after mTBI. This pilot study investigates whether the Sigma-Lognormal model proposed by the Kinematic Theory can be used to detect a difference between simple handwriting gestures performed by children at different times after experiencing mild traumatic brain injury (MTBI) [48, 50].

Method. Participants included children and adolescent who presented to the two tertiary care pediatric hospital (i.e., Montreal Children's Hospital and CHU Sainte-Justine). 90 children and adolescent were initially recruited to the sub-study, but complete data was only available in 32 participants, aged 6 to 18 years old, with mild brain injury.

Each participant had to draw fast single strokes, one at a time, following a visual reaction time protocol. After the test, every participant should have produced 30 valid strokes. The trials were recorded at 100 Hz using a tablet digitizer (Wacom Intuos2). Every stroke had to begin from a starting point located at the middle a guide sheet, and to end at one of the sides of the sheet, as depicted in the Fig. 8.

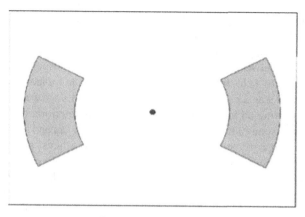

Fig. 8. The guide sheet

The direction side was set depending of the laterality of the participant. They were asked to produce handwriting strokes on a digital tablet at 1 month and 3 months after sustaining the injury. The Sigma-Lognormal model was used to analyze the executed movements.

The classification was done using the evolution of each parameter over time for each subject. To determine if the change in parameters is evolving positively, there has to be a significant statistical difference between the 1- and 3- months mean post-injury. Participants were considered as having an improved neuromotor system state when there was a decrease in the mean value of the following parameters: all rescaled t_0, first t_0, σ, number of rejected strokes, D and nbLog. Similarly, participants had a better neuromotor system state after 3 months post-injury if there was an increase of the mean value of the following parameters: μ, SNR and SNR/nbLog.

To measure the somatic, cognitive, emotional, and fatigue/sleep-related symptoms present in each participant, parents were asked to complete the Post-Concussion Symptom Inventory (PCSI) [167] to document their child's symptoms. The parent-report version of the PCSI consists of 26 items, where responses are rated for severity on a 7-point Likert scale (i.e., from 0 to 6; 0 = Not a problem, 6 = Severe problem). We examined how the number of reported symptoms, as endorsed on the parent PCSI, progressed over time. Specifically, the total score obtained on the parent PCSI (i.e., total number of symptoms) for each participant was compared at 1-month and 3-months post-injury. To this end, the children were placed in 4 different categories according to the evolution of their condition: Improvement, Deterioration, Stabilization and No judgement.

Results. This model showed significant differences between the set of traits produced by participants when comparing their results at 1 and 3 months post-injury. Of the 32 participants, 28 of them have significant differences for at least 1 lognormal parameter. We notice an improvement in the quality of the traits achieved over time. For example, there were 17 participants who had a significant difference, with the Bonferroni correction, for the SNR/nbLog. Only four of the participants showed no significant change during this period.

By examining PCSI quality-of-life questionnaires including the child's responses as well as those of the parents 1 month, 3 months after sustaining a concussion, the child's state of health were analysed to see how quality of life had changed during this period. There was a match between the parents' and the children's responses for 19 of the 32 children. In the case of 4 children, no judgement can be made for lack of data. In the case of 3 children, there was a contradiction between the child's answers and those of the parents, one stipulating an improvement and the other a deterioration. In the case of 6 children, there was a contradiction between the child's answers and those of the parents, one stipulating an improvement or deterioration, while the other stipulates a stable state.

Comparing the results of the PCSI questionnaire with those of the pencil line test, the results match for 9 out of 32 children. For the rest of children, however, the results did not match. For the 9 children where there was a match, 6 were improving, 2 were deteriorating and 1 was stable. In the other cases, there was a contradiction be-tween the child's and parent's answers, where one of the two answered that the child's condition had remained stable over this period of time. For the children for whom there was no correspondence between the results of the pencil line test and the PCSI questionnaire, for 7 children, the pencil line indicated an improvement in the child's condition, whereas the PCSI questionnaire indicated the opposite. For 9 children, the pencil test pointed out a stabilisation whereas the PCSI questionnaire indicated stability, the inverse for 2 and one case was non conclusive.

Outcomes. By comparing the results of the PCSI answers and the Sigma-Lognormal analysis, a concordance was observed between the two tests for only nine (32%) of the participants. This is not surprising as the PCSI questionnaire and Sigma-Lognormal parameters assess different aspects of functioning, and thus, are likely to yield different patterns of results. First, post-concussive symptoms were documented using subjective parents' reports on questionnaire, and it has been previously suggested that parents of children with mTBI may tend to over-report symptoms of their children on questionnaires [18]. Second, the Sigma-Lognormal analysis is an objective methodology based on the Lognormality Principle. It could be used to ponder subjective reports and provide unbiased data to confirm or infirm the evolution of the mTBI. In this perspective, these preliminary results will serve as a basis for further research into the benefits of using the Sigma-Lognormal model for the assessment of the integrity of neuromotor systems after traumatic brain injury in children.

6.4 Kinematic Analyses of Rapid Pencil Strokes Produced by Children with ADHD

Context. Most children with ADHD (Attention Deficit Disorder with or without Hyper-activity) have problems with gross and/or fine motor skills [75]. Children with ADHD often have greater difficulty planning and programming their movements effectively than their non-ADHD peers [47, 142, 161]. A proper assessment of the motor and grapho-motor skills of children, whether they have ADHD or not, seems relevant to guide intervention in the face of these problems and to better understand the nature of motor difficulties in ADHD. The kinematic analysis of writing movements can be used to study the factors involved in motor control and fine motor skills [41, 42, 106, 120, 125,

157]. When a person writes on a digitizer, the coordinates of their pencil movement are transformed into a velocity profile from which an analysis can reconstruct the movement with its corresponding sequence of lognormals. This theory uses the stroke to understand how motor control processes movement execution. According to the Kinematic Theory, when someone controls its movement, their velocity profiles will tend to approximate lognormality [126].

In the present study, the Sigma-Lognormal model was used to obtain a detailed description of children's pencil stroke velocity profiles. The first objective was to assess whether the parameters obtained from Sigma-Lognormal modeling of the fast pen stroke velocity profiles could effectively differentiate between children with and without ADHD. The hypothesis states that the quality of handwriting movement would be inferior in children with ADHD, particularly those with more severe symptoms. The second aim was to investigate the correlation between the lognormal motor behavior of children with ADHD and their performance on other assessments of graphomotor and fine motor skills. The anticipated hypothesis was that lognormal parameters would exhibit a relationship with measures of handwriting speed and accuracy, as well as fine motor skills. Lastly, the potential of lognormal parameters to enhance the accuracy and specificity of ADHD diagnosis was examined, with the expectation that these parameters would successfully distinguish between children with and without ADHD.

Methodology. 24 children aged 8 to 11 years took part in this study: 12 with ADHD and 12 without. The children took several psychometric tests: the Wechsler Intelligence Scale for Children – 4th Edition (WISC-IV¼ [156], the Pen Stroke Test (PST) on digitizer, the BHK (Échelle d'évaluation rapide de l'écriture chez l'enfant) [28], the Purdue Pegboard [150], the Finger Tapping Test (FTT) [143] and the TWISC-IV- Coding subtest [156]. The questionnaires completed by the parents assessed the presence of inattention and hyperactivity/impulsivity behaviours and of developmental coordi-nation disorders.

An optimal algorithm was used to extract the Sigma-Lognormal model parameters from the PST. For each child, the mean value of the following parameters for the 30 strokes was used in the analyses [79]. The signal-to-noise ratio (SNR) between the original velocity profile and the reconstructed velocity profile measures the quality of the Sigma-Lognormal reconstruction. The number of lognormal functions required to reconstruct the original velocity profile (nbLog) represents the fluidity of movement of the participant. Other parameters can be obtained from analyzing the participants' graphomotor behavior. Two parameters represent the neuromotor action plan. Time required (t_0; in seconds) for the brain to produce a motor command. The amplitude of the movement (D) associated with each motor command, in millimeters, is the distance planned to be covered by the pen for each lognormal.

Results. Independent measures t-tests carried out on the PST parameters revealed a significant inter-group difference on SNR/nbLog. This parameter indicated significantly poorer quality of motor control in the ADHD group. Mean nbLog was significantly higher for the ADHD group ($t = 3.475$; $p = 0.002$), which indicated that more lognormals were required to reconstruct the pen stroke signal and that the children's movements were less fluid. A significant inter-group difference was found also in terms of t_0. This parameter was greater for the ADHD group, indicating a longer delay for command preparation ($t = -3.607$; $p = 0.002$). In addition, the D parameter was significantly smaller the ADHD group (t = 2.306; p = 0.031), which reflects a smaller movement amplitude in their action plans. No significant difference was observed on the other parameters. Variability in values obtained for the PST parameters was calculated for each child and the groups were then compared. Mean SNR/nbLog variability was greater for the ADHD group (t = -2.975; p = .007) This suggests that the ADHD group had greater variability in motor control across pen strokes. Intra-individual variability was not significantly different between groups on any other parameter. The area under the ROC curve (AUC) was calculated to assess the capacity of PST parameters to discriminate between the ADHD and control groups [68]. An AUC of 1 indicates a perfect diagnostic test, whereas an AUC of .5 indicates a test performing at chance level, that is, unable to discriminate between two groups (Hajian- Tilaki, 2013). The AUC was 0.87 for SNR/nbLog; 0.84 for t_0; 0.91 for nbLog; and 0.79 for D. In other words, these four parameters discriminated between the two groups. The AUC for nbLog was significantly greater than the AUC for D (p = 0.032), indicating that nbLog can better discriminate between the two groups than D. A correlation was found between t_0 and writing speed as measured by the BHK in the ADHD group (r = -0.67; p = 0.018) indicating that the faster a child wrote, the shorter the motor command production delay (t_0). In the ADHD group, nbLog was negatively associated with performance on the WISC-IV Coding subtest (r = -0.64; p = 0.024) and the FTT (r = -0.64; p = 0.026). As such, the number of lognormals needed to reconstruct the strokes was associated with lower scores on these two tests. In the ADHD group, a correlation was observed between D and the FTT (r = 0.81; p = 0.002) indicating that greater amplitude of movement on the PST was associated with faster motor speed. In the control group, a significant correlation was found between SNR and the total score on the BHK (r = -0.80; p = 0.002) indicating that higher SNR is associated with more controlled handwriting. Finally, a significant correlation was found for the control group between SNR and the scores on the Purdue Pegboard task (r = 0.59; p = 0.043) indicating that higher SNR is associated with better manual dexterity.

Outcomes. This study explored the usefulness of the PST in evaluating fine motor skill impairment in children with ADHD. The Kinematic Theory of rapid human movements and the Sigma-Lognormal analysis allowed the use of objective parameters obtained from reconstructing fast pen stroke movements as indicators of child motor control capacity [79, 116]. A significant difference emerged between children with and without ADHD on four PST parameters: SNR/ nbLog, nbLog, t_0 and D. Moreover, children with ADHD demonstrated greater intra-individual variability in quality of motor control (SNR/nbLog). This suggests that children with ADHD are less able than peers without ADHD to control a single stroke. The results indicate that children with ADHD may have a graphomotor skill impairment at the level of motor planning, as reflected by longer t_0 and smaller D, as well as, at the execution level. The PST, based on the Sigma-Lognormal analysis, shows promise as it may offer a fast and effective way of detecting motor skills problems in children with ADHD and may contribute to refining ADHD diagnosis. Together, the findings suggest that it may be important to include assessment of motor and graphomotor skills in the clinical evaluation of children with ADHD.

6.5 Screening for Developmental Problems in Preterm Born Children: Utility of the Pen Stroke Test During the Preschool Period

Context. Yearly in Canada, about 8% of all live births occur prematurely, i.e. before 37 weeks of gestational age (GA). Among these preterm births, approximately 90% occur between 29 and 36 weeks' GA. Children born at 29–36 weeks' GA display physiological immaturity and instability making their developing brain vulnerable to various insults related to preterm birth complications and treatments [21, 134], thus increasing the risk for developmental problems, including attention deficit and hyperactivity disorders, developmental coordination disorders or difficulties with writing skills [7, 33, 76, 145, 154]. In kindergarten, 34–40% of children born between 29–36 weeks' GA have ≥1 area of vulnerability for school readiness (i.e., the developmental abilities and behavior necessary to meet school demand) due to NDD, a red flag for future learning challenges [94]. Rehabilitation services, if timely implemented, can optimize academic achievement by addressing educational needs prior to school [31, 74]. In this perspective, early identification of children born between 29–36 weeks' GA at highest risk of learning challenges is crucial.

We previously recruited 241 children born between 29–36 weeks' GA to test a developmental screening protocol combining biological and clinical markers assessed from birth to 4 months CA to identify those at higher risk of NDD at 2 years CA. Now that this cohort is growing beyond the toddler years, longitudinal follow-up is necessary as 2-year outcomes may not be sufficient to predict long-term neurodevelopment [45]. Moreover, the dynamic process of brain development may uncover emerging signs of dysfunctions that could be identified. To this end, a non-invasive, rapid, unexpensive and easily available screening instrument is necessary. The Pen Stroke Test [45, 79] (PenStroke), developed by R. Plamondon, responds to these criteria, but needs to be validated first.

The PenStroke consists in producing handwriting strokes on a computerized interface which are then analyzed using the sigma-lognormal model [105, 117]. This model provides 2 parameters describing the general state of the neuromotor system and the quality of the modeling: the number of lognormals (nbLog) and the measure of the quality of the sigma-lognormal reconstruction, or the Signal-to-Noise Ratio (SNR). A stroke that approaches the 'perfect' model is made up of 2 lognormals; the higher the nbLog, the lesser is the motor control. In contrary, the higher is the SNR, the better is the fitting and the motor control. Evidence supports the utility of the PenStroke parameters to discriminate levels of graphomotor performance achieved by children aged 3 to 5 years [19]. Performing the PenStroke as screening measures prior to school entry could improve the clinical discrimination of preterm children born at 29–36 weeks' GA at risk of NDD. However, the screening accuracy of this tool in preterm preschool children needs to be determined.

The overarching aim of our research program is to improve early identification of NDD in preterm children born at 29–36 weeks' GA. The current study specifically aims to examine the concurrent accuracy of the PenStroke in identifying NDD at age 4.5 years.

We hypothesize that the PenStroke parameters will correlate with neurodevelopmental skills at 4.5 years of age and will enhance our developmental screening protocol in predicting neurodevelopment prior to school entry.

Methods. We are currently conducting a prospective longitudinal follow-up study of an established cohort. All participants from the initial cohort (n = 241) were recruited at the Centre Hospitalier Universitaire Sainte-Justine (CHUSJ). Children aged 4.5 yrs old (±3 mo) still enrolled in the initial study (217/241 children), in which inclusion criteria were birth between 29–36 6/7 wks' GA and admission for ≥48 h in the NICU, are eligible, but those under child protection services (for consent issues) are excluded. Recruitment will run between March 2023 and May 2027 as children of our cohort reach 4.5 years old. Data are collected at a 4.5-year-old visit at CHUSJ research center. The PenStroke is first administered and then followed by a neurodevelopmental assessment. Both are conducted by trained research assistants blinded to participant's history. For the PenStroke, three simple movements on a digitizer (Wacom Cintiq 13HD, digitized at 200 Hz) are completed. The first 2 movements consist of making 30 rapid pen strokes, each time, between a starting zone, identified by a black point, and an arrival zone displayed in gray. The first time, a sound cue (at 1 kHz for 500 ms) emitted by the computer is the go signal for the child to execute the movement and the second time, a green visual stimulus is used as the cue. The third movement consists in drawing a triangle 30 times by connecting three points displayed on the screen. These tests generate optimal parameters to express the quality of the neuromotor control of the upper limb. A global optimal algorithm is used to extract the sigma-lognormal model parameters (nbLog and SNR). The whole process is synchronized with Sign@medic, an in-house program. The neurodevelopmental assessment includes 9 standardized tests covering intellectual functioning, attention, language, motor skills, behavior, and adaptive functioning. For this study, NDD will be defined as 2 or more test scores (out of 9) that fall 1 standard deviation below the mean. Concurrent accuracy of the PenStroke will be determined by Receiver Operating Characteristic curves.

Preliminary Results. To date, from the 23 families contacted, 19 accepted to participate (83%) and 12 visits have been completed at a mean age of 4.4 years old (+/− 0.2). Data collection was complete for all assessed participants. For all 12 participants, we were able to reconstruct the recorded movements produced by the children using the Sigma-Lognormal model and to extract the parameters. Figures 9A and 9B show 2 examples of the reconstruction with the auditory stimulus: 9A from a child with a better motor control than the one pictured in 9B. Overall, the ratios between the SNR and the nbLog seem to vary between participants as shown in Fig. 10, supporting the use of the Sigma-Lognormal model to characterize preschool children motricity. Next steps will involve further data collection and the analysis of the associations between the Penstroke parameters and the neurodevelopmental profile of the participants.

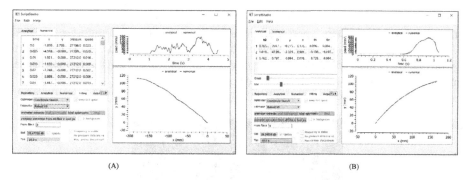

Fig. 9. (A) Reconstruction with auditory stimulus, (B) Reconstruction with auditory stimulus

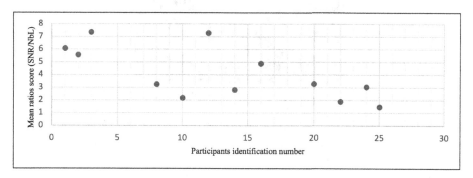

Fig. 10. Mean performance of the participants with the auditory stimulus

Expected Outcomes. Integrating the PenStroke at 4.5 years old to our developmental screening protocol could enhance the clinical discrimination of preterm children born at 29–36 weeks' GA at risk of NDD before school entry and optimize support prior to school entry.

6.6   Exploring the Benefits of Virtual Reality Lognormality Analysis for Diagnosing ADHD in Children

Context. At least 15% of the children with learning problems experience anxiety, dependency and depression, leading to loss of motivation and, in the worst cases, dropping out of school. Treatment of these cases is often costly and there is a shortage of professionals to provide follow-up care. It is estimated that it costs a minimum of $60,000 per child in Canada to carry out these diagnoses and their follow-ups.

A New Tool. To tackle these problems, the AeoVR team (https///aleovr.com) is developing an educational tool in the form of virtual reality (VR) experiences that aim to support the development of school-aged children with learning disabilities. The spin-off company proposes a set of adapted challenges, a series of virtual reality games based on exercises used by Ortho pedagogy clinics. For example, to increase participation and motivation, interactive and immersive exercises to stimulate fun and motivate learning are used. The system offers a personalized and adapted environment to foster academic development in an appropriate virtual world based on monitored stimuli. Detailed reports are provided to track progress and facilitate communication between the various parties involved. Figure 11 shows the basic VR data capture.

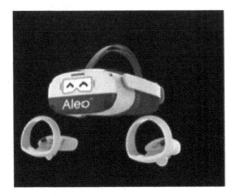

Fig. 11. VR data capture system

A Proof of Concept for VR Lognormality Study. Among the various improvements that AleoVr is exploring, stands the integration of a 3D lognormality analysis package to evaluate, characterize and monitor the child performances. A preliminary study has been run that check this hypothesis. The right-hand $x(t)$, $y(t)$, $z(t)$coordinates of 13 participants aged between 19 and 63 were recorded. Each of the volunteers had to touch: 1. A cup on a table at about 1m from the floor, 2. The corner of table located approximately at 1m from floor, 3. A chair at approximately 30 cm from floor, 4. A tree house visible in the distance which was requiring an extension of the arm of approximately 30 cm above the eye level, 5. Their left shoulder whose distance was depending on the size of the participant. Each movements had to be repeated twice.

The ten gestures per participant were reproduced using the 3D Sigma-Lognormal extractor [59, 145] and the quality of the reconstruction was computed as a feasibility measure. The SNR were always above 15dB, (the accepted threshold for considering a movement as made up of lognormals) with a mean value of 23.4 ± 3.2 dB.

Expected Outcomes. These very preliminary results confirm that the 3D Sigma-Lognormal model can be used to extract neuromotor parameter from complex 3D movements collected with a VR system and that it could be exploited for developing objective numerical metrics to study these gestures.

7   Conclusion

Looking back and ahead at the numerous applications that involve lognormality, it becomes more and more implicit that this emergent property stands among the universal behaviour that has emerged through the evolution of species, the central limit theorem slowly but surely acting as a growth force. Lognormals have been found and used as hidden primitives in numerous applications dealing with healthy and non-healthy subjects, ranging handwriting analysis and recognition [20, 51], signature verification [37, 38, 58], signal processing [43, 67], human-machine interfaces [87, 90, 96, 152] and biomarker definition [84] as well as for speech processing [25, 27]) and for Turing tests [88, 89]. We have summarized in this special session a subset of these applications, focusing on those presented in French at ACFAS 2023. Many other studies are going on in e-Security, e-Learning and e-Health [126, 129], and new fields are also expected to develop providing for examples a new set of functions for 2D and 3D smoothest curve modelling, anthropomorphic arm design, exoskeletons and prosthetics control, human-like movements modelling of virtual reality objects. Moreover, applications for fish [55, 141], farming [40] and robots [38, 39, 97, 132] are under investigations. By extending the range and significance of the Lognormality Principle these applications may, in the long run, cement lognormality as a fundamental law of nature.

Acknowledgements. The ACFAS colloquium was financially supported by the Département de Génie Électrique, Polytechnique Montréal and Institut TransMedTech. The authors thank the team members involved in their specific project as reported in each section:

Section 3.1: Alicia Fornès (Universitat Autònoma de Barcelona, UAB), Asma Bensalah (UAB), Maria Cristina Carmona Duarte (Universidad de Las Palmas de Gran Canaria, ULPGC), Jialuo Chen Tormos (UAB), Miguel Angel Ferrer Ballester (ULPGC), Andreas Fischer (University of Applied Sciences and Arts, Western Switzerland, HES-SO-UASAW), Josep Lladóos (UAB), Cristina Martín (Guttman Institute, Neurorehabilitation Institute, Badalona, Spain, GINI), Eloy Opisso (GINI), Anna Scius-Bertrand (HES-SO UASAW), Réjean Plamondon (Polytechnique Montréal), Josep Maria Tormos (GINI).

Section 3.2: Karina Lebel (UdeS – Université de Sherbrooke), Thierry Daviault (UdeS), Patrick Boissy (UdeS), Roua Walha (UdeS), Nathaly Gaudreault (UdeS), Christian Duval (Université du Québec à Montréal), Pierre Blanchet (CHUM, Université de Montréal), Réjean Plamondon (PM).

Section 3.3: Romeo Salameh (UdeM- Université de Montréal), Guillaume Seguin de Broin (PM), Maria Cristina Carmona Duarte (Las Palmas University, Gran Canarie, Spain), Karina Lebel (UdeS - Université de Sherbrooke), Vanessa Bachir (UdeM), Réjean Plamondon (PM), Pierre Blanchet (Centre Hospitalier de l'Université de Montréal).

Section 4.1 : Christian O' Reilly (University of South Carolina,USA, USC), Dee-pa Tilwani (USC.), Jessica Bradshaw (USC).

Section 4.2: Mickael Begon (UdeM - Université de Montréal), Anaïs Laurent (PM), Ben Braithwaite (PM), Réjean Plamondon (PM).

Section 4.3: Youssef Beloufa (PM), Aymeric Guy (Life Engine Technologies Inc, LET.), Catherine Forest-Nault (LET.), Louis Marceau (LET.), Olivier Desbiens (PM) Réjean Plamondon, (PM).

Section 4.4: Frédéric Fol Leymarie (University of London -Goldsmiths), Daniel Berio (Goldsmiths, University of London, UK.), Réjean Plamondon (PM).

Section 5.1: Simon Pierre Boyogueno-Bidias (PM) , Jean-Pierre David (PM), Yvon Savaria (PM), Réjean Plamondon (PM).

Section 5.2: Andreas Fischer (University of Applied Sciences and Arts Western Switzerland, HES-SOS), Roman Schindler (HES-SOS, University of Fribourg, Swit-zerland.), Manuel Bouillon (HES-SOS University of Fribourg, Switzerland.), Réjean Plamondon (PM).

Section 5.3: Zigeng Zhang (PM), Christian O' Reilly (University of South Carolina), Réjean Plamondon (PM).

Section 6.1: Denis Alamargot (Université Poitiers, France), Marie-France Morin (UdeS - Université de Sherbrooke), Nadir Faci (PM), Réjean Plamondon (PM).

Section 6.2: Céline Rémi (Université des Antilles, Guadeloupe, UA), Jimmy Na-geau (UA), Jean Vaillant (UA), Réjean Plamondon (PM), Emma-nuel Biabiany (UA).

Section 6.3 : Nadir Faci (PM), Naddley Désiré (SickKids Hospital Toronto), Miriam Beauchamp (UdeM - Université de Montréal), Isabelle Gagnon (Université McGill), Réjean Plamondon (PM).

Section 6.4: Raphaëlle Fortin (UdeM - Université de Montréal), Patricia Laniel (UdeM), Nadir Faci (PM), Miriam Beauchamp (UdeM), Réjean Plamondon (PM) Bruno Gauthier (UdeM).

Section 6.5: Marie-Noëlle Simard (UdeM - Université de Montréal), Thuy Mai Luu (CHU Ste-Justine, UdeM), Mathieu Dehaes (UdeM), Anne Gallagher (Université de Montréal), Anik Cloutier (CHU Sainte-Justine), Réjean Plamondon (PM).

Section 6.6: Caroline Bazinet (AleoVr), Alexis Maher (AleoVr), Charles Tétreault (AleoVr), Catherine Bazinet (AleoVr) , Andreas Fischer (University of Applied Sciences and Arts Western Switzerland, HES-SO) , Réjean Plamondon (PM).

Study 4.1 was supported by a pilot grant from the Carolina Autism & Neurodevelopment Center at the University of South Carolina (PI: C.O'R.). The ECG was collected under a National Institute of Mental Health grant (PI: J.B.; No: K23MH120476) and a National Institute on Deafness and Other Communication Disorders grant (PI: J.B., No: DC017252). The study presented in section 6.5 was funded by the Fondation des Étoiles. Its authors would like to thank all participants and their families.

References

1. Adler, C.H., et al.: Low clinical diagnostic accuracy of early vs advanced Parkinson disease: clinicopathologic study. Neurology **83**, 406–412 (2014)
2. Alamargot, D., Morin, M.-F.: Does handwriting on a tablet screen affect students' graphomotor execution? A comparison between grades two and Nine. Hum. Mov. Sci. **44**, 32–41 (2015). https://doi.org/10.1016/j.humov.2015.08.011
3. Alamargot, D., Morin, M.-F.: Approche cognitive de la production écrite: Principaux résultats et apports pour l'apprentissage et l'enseignement à l'école. Approche Neuropsychologique des Apprentissages chez l'Enfant (ANAE) **163**, 713721 (2019)
4. Alamargot, D., Chesnet, D., Dansac, C., Ros, C.: Eye and pen: a new device for studying reading during writing. Behav. Res. Methods **38**(2), 287–299 (2006). https://doi.org/10.3758/BF03192780
5. Alamargot, D., Morin, M.-F., Simard-Dupuis, É.: Handwriting in signing deaf middle-school students and relationship with text composition and spelling. Read. Writ. **31**, 10171038 (2018). https://doi.org/10.1007/s11145-018-9824-y
6. Alamargot, D., Morin, M.-F., Simard-Dupuis, É.: Handwriting delay in dyslexia: children at the end of primary school still make numerous short pauses when producing letters. J. Lean. Disabil. **53**(3), 163–175 (2020). https://doi.org/10.1177/0022219420903705
7. Arpi, E., Ferrari, F.: Preterm birth and behaviour problems in infants and preschool-age children: a review of the recent literature. Dev. Med. Child Neurol. **55**, 788–796 (2013). https://doi.org/10.1111/dmcn.12142
8. Asif, H., et al.: Objective structured assessment of technical skill (OSATS) in the surgical skills and technology elective program (SSTEP): comparison of peer and expert raters. Am. J. Surg. **223**(2), 276–279 (2022). https://doi.org/10.1016/j.amjsurg.2021.03.064
9. Awal, M., et al.: Design and optimization of ECG modeling for generating different cardiac dysrhythmias. Sensors **21**(5), 1638 (2021). https://doi.org/10.3390/s21051638

10. Barlow, K.M.: Postconcussion syndrome: a review. J. Child Neurol. **31**, 57–67 (2016)
11. Beery, K.E., Buktenica, N.A., Beery, N.A.: The Beery-Buktenica Developmental Test of Visual-Motor Integration: Administration, Scoring, and Teaching Manual, 6th edn. NCS Pearson, Minneapolis (2010)
12. Bensalah, A., Chen, J., Fornés, A., Carmona-Duarte, C., Lladós, J., Ferrer, M.Á.: Towards stroke patients' upper-limb automatic motor assessment using smartwatches. In: Del Bimbo, A., et al. Pattern Recognition. ICPR International Workshops and Challenges. ICPR 2021, LNCS, vol. 12661, pp. 476–489. Springer, Cham (2021). https://doi.org/10.1007/978-3-030-68763-2_36
13. Berio, D., Fol Leymarie, F., Asente, P., Echevarria, J.: StrokeStyles: stroke-based segmentation and stylization of fonts. ACM Trans. Graph. **41**(3), 1–21 (2022). Article #28, https://doi.org/10.1145/3505246
14. Berio, D., Akten, M., Fol Leymarie, F., Grierson, M., Plamondon, R.: Calligraphic stylisation learning with a physiologically plausible model of movement and recurrent neural networks. In: ACM Proceedings of 4th International Conference on Movement Computing (MOCO), London, UK (2017). https://doi.org/10.1145/3077981.3078049
15. Berio, D., Calinon, S., Fol Leymarie, F.: Learning dynamic graffiti strokes with a compliant robot. In: Proceedings of IEEE/RSJ International Conference on Intelligent Robots and Systems (IROS), Daejeon, South Korea, pp. 3981–3986 (2016).
16. Berio, D., Fol Leymarie, F., Plamondon, R.: Expressive curve editing with the sigma lognormal model. In: Diamanti, O., Vaxman. A. (eds.), Proceedings of Eurographics, Delft, The Netherlands, pp. 33–36 (2018)
17. Berio, D., Fol Leymarie, F., Plamondon, R.: Kinematics reconstruction of static calligraphic traces from curvilinear shape features. In: Plamondon, R., Marcelli, A., Ferrer, M.A. (eds.) The Lognormality Principle and its Applications in e-Security, e-Learning and e-Health. World Scientific Publishing, Series in Machine Perception and Artificial Intelligence (88), Ch. 11, pp. 237–268 (2021)
18. Bernard, C.O., Ponsford, J.A., McKinlay, A., McKenzie, D., Krieser, D.: Predictors of post-concussive symptoms in young children: injury versus non-injury related factors. J. Int. Neuropsychol. Soc. **22**(8), 793–803 (2016)
19. Bidias, S.P., David, J.-P., Savaria, Y., Plamondon, R.: On the use of interval arithmetic to bound delta-lognormal rapid human movements. In: Proceedings International Conference on pattern Recognition and Artificial Intelligence: Workshop on the Lognormality Principle and its Applications, Montréal, Canada, pp. 738–742 (2018)
20. Bhattacharya, U., Plamondon, R., Dutta Chowdhury, S., Goyal, P., Parui, S.K.: A sigma-lognormal model-based approach to generating large synthetic online handwriting samples databases. Int. J. Doc. Anal. Recogn. (IJDAR). **20**(71), 1–17 (2017)
21. Boyle, E.M., et al.: Neonatal outcomes and delivery of care for infants born late preterm or moderately preterm: a prospective population-based study. Arch Dis Child Fetal Neonatal Ed **100**, F479-485 (2015). https://doi.org/10.1136/archdischild-2014-307347
22. Boyoguéno-Bidias, S.P.: Extracteur de paramètres Delta-Lognormaux globalement optimaux par séparation et évaluation exploitant l'arithmétique par intervalles : thèse doctorat, Polytechnique Montréal (2022)
23. Cancer, A., Minoliti, R., Crepaldi, M., Antonietti, A.: Identifying developmental motor difficulties: a review of tests to assess motor coordination in children. J. Funct. Morphol. Kinesiol. **5**(1), 16 (2020). https://doi.org/10.3390/jfmk5010016
24. Cardarilli, G.C., Di Nunzio, L., Fazzolari, R., Re, M., Silvestri, F.: Improvement of the cardiac oscillator based model for the simulation of bundle branch blocks. Appl. Sci. **9**(18), 3653 (2019). Article 18. https://doi.org/10.3390/app9183653
25. Carmona-Duarte, C., Ferrer, M.A., Plamondon, R., Gómez-Rodellar, A., Gómez-Vilda, P.: Sigma-lognormal Modeling of Speech. Cogn. Comput. **13**(2), 488–503 (2021)

26. Carmona-Duarte, C., Ferrer, M.A., Gómez-Vilda, P., Van Gemmert, A.W.A., Plamondon, R.: Evaluating Parkinson's disease in voice and handwriting using the same methodology. In: The Lognormality Principle and its Applications in e-Security, e-Learning and e-Health, pp. 161–175 (2020). https://doi.org/10.1142/9789811226830_0007

27. Carmona-Duarte, C., Gomez, P., Ferrer, M.A., Plamondon, R., Londral, A.: Study of several parameters for the detection of amyotrophic lateral sclerosis from articulatory movement. Loquens. 4(2), 038 (2017)

28. Charles, M., Soppelsa, R., Albaret, J.M.: BHK échelle d'évaluation rapide de l'écriture chez l'enfant [BHK Concise Evaluation Scale for Children's Handwriting]. ECPA (2004)

29. Chen, M., AlRegib, G., Juang, B.-H.: Air-writing recognition – part ii: detection and recognition of writing activity in continuous stream of motion data. IEEE Trans. Hum.-Mach. Syst. 46(3), 436–444 (2016)

30. Cinnera, A.M., Morone, G.: Motor recovery in stroke rehabilitation supported by robot-assisted therapy. In: Assistive Technologies for Assessment and Recovery of Neurological Impairments, pp. 304–321 (2022). https://doi.org/10.4018/978-1-7998-7430-0.ch015

31. Cioni, G., Inguaggiato, E., Sgandurra, G.: Early intervention in neurodevelopmental disorders: underlying neural mechanisms. Dev. Med. Child Neurol. 58(Suppl 4), 61–66 (2016). https://doi.org/10.1111/dmcn.13050

32. Côté, J.N.: Adaptations to neck/shoulder fatigue and injuries. Adv. Exp. Med. Biol. 826, 205–228 (2014)

33. Cserjesi, R., et al.: Functioning of 7-year-old children born at 32 to 35 weeks' gestational age. Pediatrics Pediatrics 130(4), e838–846 (2012). https://doi.org/10.1542/peds.2011-2079

34. Dankovičová, Z., Drotár, P., Gazda, J., Vokorokos, L.: Overview of the handwriting processing for clinical decision support system. In: IEEE 14th International Scientific Conference on Informatics, p. 6367 (2017). https://doi.org/10.1109/INFORMATICS.2017.8327223

35. Danna, J., Longcamp, M., Nalborczyk, L. Velay, J-L., Commengé, C., Jover, M.: Interaction between orthographic and graphomotor constraints in learning to write. Learn. Instr. 80, 101622 (2022)

36. Delenclos, M., Jones, D.R., McLean, P.J., Uitti, R.J.: Biomarkers in Parkinson's disease: advances and strategies. Parkinsonism Rel. Disord 22, S106–S110 (2016)

37. Diaz, M., Fischer*, A., Ferrer, M.A., Plamondon, R.: Dynamic signature verification system based on one real signature. IEEE Trans. Cybern. 48(1), 228–239 (2018)

38. Diaz, M., Ferrer, M.A., Impedovo, D., Malik, M.I., Pirlo, G., Plamondon, R.: A perspective analysis of handwritten signature technology ACM Comput. Surv. 51(6), 39 (2019)

39. Diaz, M., Quintana, J.J., Ferrer, M.A., Carmona-Duarte, C., Wolniakowski A., Miatliuk, K.: Lognormality of velocity profiles in rapid robotic arm movements. In: 19th International Graphonomics Conference (IGS2019), Cancun, México, June 9–12 (2019)

40. Diaz, M., et al.: Studying the principle of lognormality in livestocks. In: Plamondon, R., Marcelli, A., Ferrer, M.A. (eds.) The Lognormality Principle and its applications in e-security, e-learning and e-health, World Scientific, Series in Machine Perception Artificial Intelligence, ISBN: 978-081-122-682-2, vol. 88, pp. 397–398 (2021). https://doi.org/10.1142/9789811226830

41. Djioua, M., Plamondon, R.: A new algorithm and system for the characterization of handwriting strokes with delta-lognormal parameters. IEEE Trans. Pattern Anal. Mach. Intell. 31(11), 2060–2072 (2009)

42. Djioua, M., Plamondon, R.: A new algorithm and system for the extraction of delta-lognormal parameters. Technical Report, EPM-RT-2008-04, École Polytechnique de Montréal (2008)

43. Djioua, M., & Plamondon, R. (2008). A new methodology to improve myoelectric signal processing using handwriting. In: Proceedings International Conference on Frontiers in Handwriting Recognition, Montreal, ICFHR'2008, pp. 112–117

44. Douret, L., Auzias, M.: Le développement de l'organisation motrice et temporo-spatiale de l'écriture chez l'enfant. Approche Neuropsychologique des Apprentissages chez l'Enfant (ANAE) **5**, 2935 (1993)

45. Duval, T., Rémi, C., Plamondon, R., Vaillant, J., O'Reilly, C.: Combining sigma-lognormal modeling and classical features for analyzing graphomotor performances in kindergarten children. Hum. Mov. Sci. **43**, 183–200 (2015). https://doi.org/10.1016/j.humov.2015.04.005

46. Duval, T, Rémi, C., Plamondon, R., O'Reilly, C.: On the use of the sigma-lognormal model to study children handwriting. In: 16th Biennial Conference of the Graphonomics Society (IGS 2013), Japan, pp. 26–29 (2013)

47. Eliasson, A.-C., Ro€sblad, B., Forssberg, H.: Disturbances in programming goal-directed arm movements in children with ADHD. Dev. Med. Child Neurol. **46**(1), 19–27 (2004). https://doi.org/10.1111/j.1469-8749.2004.tb00429.x

48. Faci, N., Désiré, N., Beauchamp, M.H., Gagnon, I., Plamondon, R.: Lognormality in children with mild traumatic brain injury: a preliminary pilot study. In: Proceedings of ICPRAI 2018. ICPRAI 2018 First International Workshop on the Lognormality Principle and its Applications, Montréal, Canada, pp. 790–794 (2018)

49. Faci, N., Boyogueno Bidias, S.P., Plamondon, R., Bergeron, N.: An interactive tablet-based system to run neuromuscular tests. In: Plamondon, R., Marcelli, A., Ferrer, M.A. (eds.) The Lognormality Principle and Its Applications in E-Security, e-Learning and e-Health, World Scientific Publishing, Series in Machine Perception and Artificial Intelligence, vol.88, pp 269–288 (2021). https://doi.org/10.1142/9789811226830_0012

50. Faci, N., Désiré, N., Beauchamp, M.H., Gagnon, I., Plamondon, R.: Lognormality in children with mild traumatic brain injury: a preliminary pilot study. In Plamondon, R., Marcelli, A., Ferrer, M.A. (eds.) The Lognormality Principle and its Applications in e-Security, e-Learning and e-Health. World Scientific Publishing, Series in Machine Perception and Artificial Intelligence, vol. 88, pp. 143–160 (2021)

51. Faundez-Zanuy, M., Fierrez, J., Ferrer, M.A., Diaz, M., Tolosana, R., Plamondon, R.: Handwriting biometrics: applications and future trends in e-security and e-health. Cogn. Comput. **12**, 940–953 (2020)

52. Fawaz, H.I., Forestier, G., Weber, J., Idoumghar, L., Muller, P.-A.: Accurate and interpretable evaluation of surgical skills from kinematic data using fully convolutional neural networks. Int. J. Comput. Assist. Radiol. Surg. **14**(9), 1611–1617 (2019). https://doi.org/10.1007/s11 548-019-02039-4

53. Feldman, J., Singh, M.: Information along contours and objcct boundaries. Psychol. Rev. **112**(1), 243–252 (2005)

54. Ferrer, M.A., Diaz, M., Carmona-Duarte, C., Plamondon, R.: iDelog: iterative dual spatial and kinematic extraction of sigma-lognormal parameters. IEEE Trans. Pattern Anal. Mach. Intell. (PAMI). **42**(1): 114–125 (2020)

55. Ferrer, M., et al.: From operculum and body tail movements to different coupling of physical activity and respiratory frequency in farmed gilthead sea bream and European sea bass. Insights on aquaculture biosensing. Comput. Electron. Agric. **175**(105531), 1–9 (2020). ISSN 0168–1699

56. Ferrer, M., Diaz, M., Quintana-Hernandez, J., Carmona-Duarte, C., Plamondon, R.: A multilognormal analysis of 3D human movements. IEEE Trans. Pattern Anal. Mach. Intell. 13, March 2023

57. Fahr, A., Keller, J.W., Balzer, J., Lieber, J., van Hedel, H.J.A.: Quantifying age-related differences in selective voluntary motor control in children and adolescents with three assessments. Hum. Mov. Sci. **77**, 102790 (2021). https://doi.org/10.1016/j.humov.2021.102790

58. Fischer, A., Plamondon, R.: Signature verification based on the kinematic theory of rapid human movements. IEEE Trans. Hum. Mach. Syst. **47**(2), 169–180 (2017)

59. Fischer, A., Schindler, R., Bouillon, M., Plamondon, R.: Modeling 3d movements with the kinematic theory of rapid human movements. In: Plamondon, R., Marcelli, A., Ferrer, M. (eds.), The Lognormality Principle and its Applications in e-Security, e-Learning and e-Health, chapter 15, pp. 327–342. World Scientific (2021)

60. Fong, W.C.: Why Chinese painting is history. Art Bull. **85**(2), 258–280 (2003)

61. Freedberg, D., Gallese, V.: Motion, emotion and empathy in esthetic experience. Trends Cogn. Sci. **11**(5), 197–203 (2007)

62. Freyd, J.J.: Representing the dynamics of a static form. Mem. Cognit. **11**(4), 342–346 (1983)

63. Funke, I., Mees, S.T., Weitz, J., Speidel, S.: Video-based surgical skill assessment using 3D convolutional neural networks. Int. J. Comput. Assist. Radiol. Surg. **14**(7), 1217–1225 (2019). https://doi.org/10.1007/s11548-019-01995-1

64. Goldbraikh, A., D'Angelo, A.-L., Pugh, C.M., Laufer, S.: Video-based fully automatic assessment of open surgery suturing skills. Int. J. Comput. Assist. Radiol. Surg. **17**(3), 437–448 (2022). https://doi.org/10.1007/s11548-022-02559-6

65. Goubault, E., Martinez, R., Bouffard, J., Dowling-Medley, J., Begon, M., Dal Maso, F.: Shoulder electromyography-based indicators to assess manifestation of muscle fatigue during laboratory-simulated manual handling task. Ergonomics **65**(1), 118–133 (2022)

66. Goubault, E., Verdugo, F., Pelletier, J., Traube, C., Begon, M., Dal Maso, F.: Exhausting repetitive piano tasks lead to local forearm manifestation of muscle fatigue and negatively affect musical parameters. Sci. Rep. **11**(1), 8117 (2021)

67. Guerfali, W., Plamondon, R.: Signal processing for the parameter extraction of the delta lognormal model. In: Research in Computer and Robot Vision, pp. 217–232, World Scientific 1995

68. Hajian-Tilaki, K.: Receiver operating characteristic (ROC) curve analysis for medical diagnostic test evaluation. Caspian J. Intern. Med. **4**(2), 627–635 (2013)

69. Hamstra-Bletz, L., Blöte, A.W.: Development of handwriting in primary school: a longitudinal study. Percept. Mot. Skills **70**(3), 759770 (1990)

70. Hansen, E., Walster, G.W.: Global Optimization Using Interval Analysis: Revised and Expanded. CRC Press, Boca Raton (2003)

71. Heaton, J.: An empirical analysis of feature engineering for predictive modeling. Southeast-Con **2016**, 1–6 (2016). https://doi.org/10.1109/SECON.2016.7506650

72. Hira, S., et al.: Video-based assessment of intraoperative surgical skill. Int. J. Comput. Assist. Radiol. Surg. **17**(10), 1801–1811 (2022). https://doi.org/10.1007/s11548-022-02681-5

73. Hong, M., Perlmutter, J.S., Earhart, G.M.: A kinematic and electromyographic analysis of turning in people with parkinson disease. Neurorehabil. Neural Repair **23**(2), 166–176 (2009). https://doi.org/10.1177/1545968308320639

74. Hughes, A.J., Redsell, S.A., Glazebrook, C.: Motor development interventions for preterm infants: a systematic review and meta-analysis. Pediatrics **138**, (2016). https://doi.org/10.1542/peds.2016-0147

75. Kaiser, M.L., Schoemaker, M.M., Albaret, J.M., Geuze, R.H.: What is the evidence of impaired motor skills and motor control among children with attention deficit hyperactivity disorder (ADHD)? systematic review of the literature. Res. Dev. Disabil. **36C**, 338–357 (2015). https://doi.org/10.1016/j.ridd.2014.09.023

76. Kerstjens, J.M., et al.: Developmental delay in moderately preterm-born children at school entry. J. Pediatr. **159**, 92–98 (2011). https://doi.org/10.1016/j.jpeds.2010.12.041

77. Kieves, N.R.: Objective gait analysis: review and clinical applications. Vet. Clin. North Am. Small Anim. Pract. **52**(4), 857–867 (2022). https://doi.org/10.1016/j.cvsm.2022.03.009

78. Korkman, M., Kirk, U., Kemp, S.: NEPSY-II : Bilan neuropsychologique de l'enfant. Seconde édition. Pearson Canada Assessment, Toronto (2012)

79. Laniel, P., Faci, N., Plamondon, R., Beauchamp, M.H., Gauthier, B.: Kinematic analysis of fast pen strokes in children with ADHD. Appl. Neuropsychol. Child 9, 125–140 (2020). https://doi.org/10.1080/21622965.2018.1550402

80. Laurent, A., Plamondon, R., Begon, M.: Central and peripheral shoulder fatigue pre-screening using the sigma-lognormal model: a proof of concept. Front. Hum. Neurosci. 14, 171 (2020)

81. Laurent, A., Plamondon, R., Begon, M.: Reliability of the kinematic theory parameters during handwriting tasks on a vertical setup. Biomed. Sig. Process. Control 71, 103157 (2022)

82. Lawhern, V.J., Solon, A.J., Waytowich, N.R., Gordon, S.M., Hung, C.P., Lance, B.J.: Eegnet: A compact convolutional network for EEG-based brain-computer interfaces (2016). CoRR, abs/1611.08024. http://arxiv.org/abs/1611.08024. arXiv:1611.08024

83. Lebel, K., Nguyen, H., Duval, C., Plamondon, R., Boissy, P.: Capturing the cranio-caudal signature of a turn with inertial measurement systems: methods, parameters robustness and reliability. Front. Bioeng. Biotech. 5, 51 (2017). https://doi.org/10.3389/fbioe.2017.00051

84. Lebel, K., Duval, C., Nguyen, H., Plamondon, R., Boissy, P.: Turn cranio-caudal signature assessment from inertial systems for mobility deficit identification in Parkinson's disease patients. Parkinsonism Relat. Disord. 46, E24–E25 (2018)

85. Lebel, K., Duval, C., Nguyen, H.P., Plamondon, R., Boissy, P.: Cranio-caudal kinematic turn signature assessed with inertial systems as a marker of mobility deficits in Parkinson's disease. Front. Neurol. 9, 22 (2018). https://doi.org/10.3389/fneur.2018.00022

86. Lebel, K., Duval, C., Plamondon, R., Faci, N., Boissy, P.: Sigma-Lognormal modelling to assess mobility deficits: the case of turn signature assessed with inertial measurement units (IMUs). In: Plamondon, R., Marcelli, A., Ferrer, M.Á., (eds.) The Lognormality Principle and its Applications in e-Security, e-Learning and e-Health. World Scientific Publishing Series in Machine Perception and Artificial Intelligence, vol. 88, pp. 177–193 (2020). https://doi.org/10.1142/9789811226830_0008

87. Leiva, L.A., Martín-Albo, D., Plamondon, R., Vatavu, R.-D.: KeyTime: super-accurate prediction of stroke gesture production times. In: Proceedings of the 2018 CHI Conference on Human Factors in Computing Systems, vol. 2018 (2018)

88. Leiva, L., Diaz, M., Ferrer, M.A., Plamondon, R.: Human or machine? it is not what you write, but how you write It. In: Proceedings of ICPR 2020. 25th International Conference on Pattern Recognition, ICPR 2020, Milan, Italy, pp. 2612–2619 (2021)

89. Leiva, L., Vatavu, R.D., Martin Albo, D., Plamondon, R.: Omnis pracdictio: estimating the full spectrum of human performance with stroke gestures. Int. J. Hum. Comput. Stud. 142, 102466 (2020)

90. Leiva, L., Martin Albo, D, Plamondon, R., Vidal, E.: Gestures à go go: authoring synthetic human-like gestures using the kinematic theory of rapid movements. In: Proceedings of CHI 2015. CHI 2015, Seoul, Korea, pp.1–10 (2015)

91. Levien, R.: From spiral to spline: optimal techniques in interactive curve design, Ph.D. thesis, EECS Department, University of California, Berkeley (2009)

92. Leyton, M.: Symmetry-curvature duality. Comput. Vis. Graph. Image Process. 38(3), 327–341 (1987)

93. Longcamp, M., Anton, J.L., Roth, M., Velay, J.L.: Visual presentation of single letters activates a pre-motor area involved in writing. Neuroimage 19(4), 1492–1500 (2003)

94. Louis, D., et al.: School readiness among children born preterm in Manitoba. Canada. JAMA Pediatr 176, 1010–1019 (2022). https://doi.org/10.1001/jamapediatrics.2022.2758

95. Mancini, M., et al.: Continuous monitoring of turning in Parkinson's disease: rehabilitation potential. NeuroRehabilitation 37(1), 3 (2015). https://doi.org/10.3233/NRE-151236

96. Martin-Albo, D., Leiva, L.A., Huang, J., Plamondon, R.: Strokes of insight: user intent detection and kinematic compression of mouse cursor trails. Inf. Process. Manage. **52**(6), 989–1003 (2016)

97. Miatliuk, K., Wolniakowski, A., Diaz, M., Ferrer, M.A.: Universal robot employment to mimic human writing. In: 20th International Carpathian Control Conference, ISBN: 978-1-7281-0702-8, pp. 1–5, 26–29 May 2019. https://doi.org/10.1109/CarpathianCC.2019.876 6027, Kraków-Wieliczka, Poland

98. Nadeau, A., et al.: A 12-week cycling training regimen improves upper limb functions in people with Parkinson's disease. Front. Hum. Neurosci. **12**(351), 1–10 (2018). https://doi.org/10.3389/fnhum.2018.00351

99. Mediavilla, C.: Calligraphy: From Calligraphy to Abstract Painting. Scirpus Publications, Wommelgem (1996)

100. Michaud, B., Bailly, F., Charbonneau, E., Ceglia, A., Sanchez, L., Begon, M.: Bioptim, a python framework for musculoskeletal optimal control in biomechanics. IEEE Trans. Syst. Man Cybern. **53**(1), 321–332 (2023)

101. Moore, R.E.: Interval analysis. Prentice-Hall, Englewood Cliffs (1966)

102. Moran, L.M., et al.: Quality of life in pediatric mild traumatic brain injury and its relationship to postconcussive symptoms. J. Pediatr. Psychol. **37**(7), 736–744 (2011)

103. Morin, M.-F., Bara, F., Alamargot, D.: Apprentissage de la graphomotricité à l'école : Quelles acquisitions? Quelles pratiques? Quels outils? Scientia Paedagogica Experimentalis, LIV **1–2**, 4782 (2017)

104. Müller, M., Röder, T., Clausen, M., Eberhardt, B., Krüger, B., Weber, A.: Documentation mocap database HDM05, Technical Report, CG-2007-2, Universität Bonn (2007)

105. O'Reilly, C., Plamondon, R.: Development of a sigma-lognormal representation for on-line signatures. Pattern Recogn. Spec. Issue Front. Handwriting Recogn. **42**(12), 3324–3337 (2009)

106. O'Reilly, C., Plamondon, R.: Prototype-based methodology for the statistical analysis of local features in stereotypical handwriting tasks. In: International Conference on Pattern Recognition, IEEE, Istanbul, Turkey, pp.1864–1867 (2010)

107. O'Reilly, C., Plamondon, R., Landou, M.K., Stemmer, B.: Using kinematic analysis of movement to predict the time occurrence of an evoked potential associated with a motor command. Eur. J. Neurosci. **37**(2), 173–180 (2013). https://doi.org/10.1111/ejn.12039

108. O'Reilly, C., Plamondon, R.: A globally optimal estimator for the delta-lognormal modeling of fast reaching movements. IEEE Trans. Syst. Man Cybern. Part B (Cybernetics) **42**, 1428–1442 (2012). https://doi.org/10.1109/TSMCB.2012.2192109

109. O'Reilly, C., Oruganti, S.D.R., Tilwani, D., Bradshaw, J.: Model-driven analysis of ECG using reinforcement learning. Bioengineering **10**(6), 696 (2023)

110. Oğul, B.B., Gilgien, M., Özdemir, S.: Ranking surgical skills using an attention-enhanced siamese network with piecewise aggregated kinematic data. Int. J. Comput. Assist. Radiol. Surg. **17**(6), 1039–1048 (2022). https://doi.org/10.1007/s11548-022-02581-8

111. Pan, Z., Talwar, S., Plamondon, R., Van Gemmert, A.W.: Characteristics of bi-directional unimanual and bimanual drawing movements: The application of the delta-lognormal models and sigma-lognormal model. Pattern Recogn. Lett. **121**, 97–103 (2019)

112. Paz-Villagrán, V., Danna, J., Velay, J.-L.: Lifts and stops in proficient and dysgraphic handwriting. Hum. Movement Sci. **33**, 381–394 (2014). https://doi.org/10.1016/j.humov.2013.11.005

113. Pfeiffer, B., Moskowitz, B., Paoletti, A., Brusilovskiy, E., Zylstra, S.E., Murray, T.: Developmental test of visual-motor integration (VMI): an effective outcome measure for handwriting interventions for kindergarten, first-grade, and second-grade students? Am. J. Occup. Ther. **69**(4), 1–7 (2015). https://doi.org/10.5014/ajot.2015.015826

114. Pignocchi, A.: How the intentions of the draftsman shape perception of a drawing. Conscious. Cogn. **19**(4), 887–898 (2010)

115. Plamondon, R., Djioua, M., O'Reilly, C.: La Théorie cinématique des mouvements humains rapides : développements récents. Traitement du Signal, Numéro Spécial : Le Document Écrit. **26**(5), 377–394 (2009)

116. Plamondon, R., O'Reilly, C., Rémi, C., Duval, T.: The lognormal handwriter: learning, performing and declining. Front. Psychol. Cogn. Sci. **2013**, 1–14 (2013)

117. Plamondon, R., Djioua, M.: A multi-level representation paradigm for handwriting stroke generation. Hum. Mov. Sci. **25**(4–5), 586–607 (2006)

118. Plamondon, R.: A kinematic theory of rapid human movements. Part I. movement representation and generation. Biol. Cybern. **72**(4), 295–307 (1995a). https://doi.org/10.1007/BF0 0202785

119. Plamondon, R.: A kinematic theory of rapid human movements: part II: movement time and control. Biol. Cybern. **72**(4), 309–320 (1995). https://doi.org/10.1007/BF00202786

120. Plamondon, R.: A kinematic theory of rapid human movements: Part III: kinetic outcomes. Biol. Cybern. **78**, 133–145 (1998)

121. Plamondon, R.: The lognormality principle: a personalized survey. In: Plamondon, R., Marcelli, A., Ferrer, M.A. (eds.), The Lognormality Principle and its applications in e-security, e-learning and e-health, World Scientific Publishing, Series in Machine Perception and Artificial Intelligence, vol. 88, pp 1–39 (2021)

122. Plamondon, R., Guerfali, W.: The generation of handwriting with delta-lognormal synergies. Biol. Cybern. **78**(2), 119–132 (1998). https://doi.org/10.1007/s004220050419

123. Plamondon, R., Feng, C., Djioua, M.: The convergence of a neuromuscular impulse response towards a lognormal, from theory to practice. (Technical Report EPM-RT-2008–08) (2008)

124. Plamondon, R.: A kinematic theory of rapid human movements part V. Movement representation and generation. Biol. Cybern. **72**, 295–307 (1995)

125. Plamondon, R., Feng, C., Woch, A.: A kinematic theory of rapid human movements: part IV: a formal mathematical proof and new insights. Biol. Cybern. **89**, 126–138 (2003)

126. Plamondon, R., Li, X., Djioua, M.: Extraction of delta-lognormal parameters from handwriting strokes. J. Front. Comput. Sci. China **1**(1), 106–113 (2007)

127. Plamondon, R., Marcelli, A., Ferrer, M.A. (eds.) The lognormality principle and its applications in e-security, e-learning and e-health. World Sci. Publ. Ser. Mach. Percept. Artif. Intell. **88**, 415 (2021)

128. Plamondon, R., O'Reilly, C., Galbally, J., Almaksour, A., Anquetil, E.: Recent developments in the study of rapid human movements with the Kinematic theory: applications to handwriting and signature synthesis. Pattern Recogn. Lett. **35**(1), 225–235 (2014). https://doi.org/10.1016/j.patrec.2012.06.004

129. Plamondon, R., O'Reilly, C., Ouellet-Plamondon, C.: Strokes against stroke—strokes for strides. Pattern Recogn. **47**(3), 929–944 (2014). https://doi.org/10.1016/j.patcog.2013.05.004

130. Plamondon, R., Pirlo, G., Anquetil, E., Rémi, C., Teuling, H-L., Nakagawa, M.: Personal digital bodyguards for e-security, e-learning and e-health: a prospective survey. Pattern Recogn. **81**, 633–659 (2018). https://doi.org/10.1016/j.patcog.2018.04.012

131. Pontart, V., Bidet-Ildei, C., Lambert, E., Morisset, P., Flouret, L., Alamargot, D.: Influence of handwriting skills during spelling in primary and lower secondary grades. Front. Psychol. **4**, 19 (2013). https://doi.org/10.3389/fpsyg.2013.00818

132. Provincial council for maternal and child health. Final report of the neonatal follow-up clinics. vol. 47 (2015)

133. Quintana, J.J., Ferrer, M.A., Diaz, M., Feo, J.J., Wolniakowski, A., Miatliuk, K.: Uniform vs. lognormal kinematics in robots: perceptual preferences for robotic movements. Appl. Sci. **12**(23), 12045 (2022). ISSN: 2523–3963

134. Quiroz-Juárez, M.A., Jiménez-Ramírez, O., Vázquez-Medina, R., Breña-Medina, V., Aragón, J.L., Barrio, R.A.: Generation of ECG signals from a reaction-diffusion model spatially discretized. Sci. Rep. **9**(1), 19000 (2019). https://doi.org/10.1038/s41598-019-554 48-5

135. Raju, T.N.: Developmental physiology of late and moderate prematurity. Semin. Fetal Neonatal. Med. **17**, 126–131 (2012). https://doi.org/10.1016/j.siny.2012.01.010

136. Rémi, C., Nagau, J., Vaillant, J., Dorville, A., Plamondon, R.: Multimodal acquisition and analysis of children handwriting for the study of the efficiency of their handwriting movements: the @MaGma challenge. In: 16th International Conference on Frontiers in Handwriting Recognition, pp.459–464. Niagara Falls, United States (2018)

137. Rémi, C., Vaillant, J., Plamondon, R., Prévost, L., Duval, T.: Exploring the kinematic dimensions of kindergarten children's scribbles. In: 17th Biennial Conference of the International Graphonomics Society, 79–82. Guadeloupe (2015)

138. Rémi, C., Nagau, J., Vaillant, J., Plamondon, R.: Preliminary study of t0, a sigma-lognormal parameter extracted from young childrens controlled scribbles. In: Proceedings of the 18th International Graphonomics Society Conference, Italy, pp.93–97 (2017)

139. Rémi, C., Nagau, J., Vaillant, J., Plamondon, R.: Could sigma-lognormal modeling help teachers to characterize the kinematic efficiency of pupils' cursive procedures of handwriting? In: Plamondon, R., Marcelli, A., Ferrer, M.A. (eds.) The Lognormality Principle and its Applications in e-Security, e-Learning, and e-Health, pp. 87–116. World Scientific Publishing Company, Series in Machine Perception and Artificial Intelligence, vol. 88 (2021). https://doi.org/10.1142/9789811226830_0004

140. Rémi, C., Nagau, J., Copilotrace: a platform to process graphomotor tasks for education and graphonomics research. In: Carmona-Duarte, C., Diaz, M., Angel Ferrer, M., Morales, A. (eds.) 20th International Conference of the International Graphonomics Society 2022, LNCS, vol. 13424, pp. 129–143. Springer, Heidelberg (2022), https://doi.org/10.1007/978-3-031-19745-1_10

141. Rocca, W.A.: The burden of Parkinson's disease: a worldwide perspective [Comment]. Lancet Neurol. **17**, 928–929 (2018)

142. Rosell-Moll, E., et al.: Use of accelerometer technology for individual tracking of activity patterns, metabolic rates and welfare in farmed gilthead sea bream (Sparus aurata) facing a wide range of stressors. In: Aquaculture, ISSN 0044–8486, vol. 539, pp. 1–10, 30 (2021)

143. Rosenblum, S., Epsztein, L., Josman, N.: Handwriting performance of children with attention deficit hyperactive disorders: a pilot study. Phys. Occup. Ther. Pediatr. **28**(3), 219–234 (2008). https://doi.org/10.1080/01942630802224934

144. Schatz P. (2011) Finger Tapping Test. In: Kreutzer J.S., DeLuca J., Caplan B. (eds) Encyclopedia of Clinical Neuropsychology. Springer, New York, NY, 1050–1051

145. Schindler, R., Bouillon, M., Plamondon, R., Fischer*, A.: Extending the sigma-lognormal model of the kinematic theory to three dimensions. In: Proceedings of ICPRAI 2018. ICPRAI 2018 First International Workshop on the Lognormality Principle and its Applications, Montréal, Canada, 748–752 (2018)

146. Shah, P., Kaciroti, N., Richards, B., Oh, W., Lumeng, J.C.: Developmental outcomes of late preterm infants from infancy to kindergarten. Pediatrics **138** (2016). https://doi.org/10.1542/peds.2015-3496

147. Sica, M., et al.: Continuous home monitoring of Parkinson's disease using inertial sensors: a systematic review. PLoS ONE **16**(2), e0246528 (2021). https://doi.org/10.1371/journal.pone.0246528

148. Smits, E.J., et al.: Standardized handwriting to assess bradykinesia, micrographia and tremor in Parkinson's disease. PLoS ONE **9**(5), e97614 (2014)

149. Soangra, R., Sivakumar, R., Anirudh, E.R., Reddy Y.S.V., John, E.B.: Evaluation of surgical skill using machine learning with optimal wearable sensor locations. PLOS ONE **17**(6) (2022). https://doi.org/10.1371/journal.pone.0267936

150. Steinhart, S., Weiss, P.L., Friedman, J.: Proximal and distal movement patterns during a graphomotor task in typically developing children and children with handwriting problems. J. Neuroeng. Rehabil. **18**, 178 (2021). https://doi.org/10.1186/s12984-021-00970-9

151. Tiffin, J.: Purdue Pegboard Examiner Manual. Science Research Associates, Chicago (1968)

152. Todorov, E.: Optimality principles in sensorimotor control. Nat. Neurosci. **7**(9), 907–915 (2004)

153. Ungurean O.-C., Vatavu R.-D., Leiva L.A., Plamondon, R.: Gesture input for users with motor impairments on touchscreens: empirical results based on the kinematic theory. In: Proceedings of the 2018 CHI Conference on Human Factors in Computing Systems (2018)

154. Vaivre-Douret, L., Paquet, A.: L'évaluation standardisée développementale des fonctions neuro-psychomotrices: présentation de la batterie normée française NP-MOT. Neurophysiol. Clin. **49**(6), 421 (2019)

155. Vohr, B.: Long-term outcomes of moderately preterm, late preterm, and early term infants. Clin. Perinatol. **40**, 739–751 (2013). https://doi.org/10.1016/j.clp.2013.07.006

156. Walha, R., et al.: The accuracy and precision of gait spatio-temporal parameters extracted from an instrumented sock during treadmill and overground walking in healthy subjects and patients with a foot impairment secondary to psoriatic arthritis. Sensors **21**(18), 6179 (2021). https://doi.org/10.3390/s21186179

157. Wechsler, D.: WISC-IV: Échelle d'intelligence de Wechsler pour enfants [Wechsler Intelligence Scale for Children, 4th ed. (WISC-IV)]. Toronto, ON: PsychCorp (2004)

158. Woch, A., Plamondon, R., O'Reilly, C.: Kinematic characteristics of bidirectional delta-lognormal primitives in young and older subjects. Hum. Mov. Sci. **30**(1), 1–17 (2011). https://doi.org/10.1016/j.humov.2009.10.006

159. Wolniakowski, A., Quintana, J.J., Diaz, M., Miatliuk, K., Ferrer, M.A.: Towards human-like kinematics in industrial robotic arms: a case study on a UR3 robot. In: Procceding of the 54th International Carnahan Conference on Security Technology (ICCST), University of Hertfordshire, Hatfield, UK, pp. 1–5, 1–3, September 2022. https://doi.org/10.1109/ICCST49569.2021.9717393

160. World Health Organization. Neurological disorders: public health challenges: World Health Organization (2006)

161. Xia, L., Chen, C. Aggarwal, J.: View invariant human action recognition using histograms of 3d joints. In: Proceedings of IEEE Conference on Computer Vision and Pattern Recognition Workshops (CVPRW), pp. 20–27 (2012)

162. Yan, J.H., Thomas, J.R.: Arm movement control: differences between children with and without attention deficit hyperactivity disorder. Res. Q. Exerc. Sport **73**(1), 10–18 (2002). https://doi.org/10.1080/02701367.2002.10608987

163. Zemek, R., Osmond, M.H., Barrowman, N., on behalf of PERC Concussion Team.: In: Predicting and preventing postconcussive problems in paediatrics (5P) study: protocol for a prospective multicentre clinical prediction rule derivation study in children with concussion. BMJ Open **2013**(3), e003550 (2013). https://doi.org/10.1136/bmjopen-2013-003550

164. Zerveas, G., Jayaraman, S., Patel, D., Bhamidipaty, A., Eickhoff, C.: A transformer-based framework for multivariate time series representation learning. In: Proceedings of the 27th ACM SIGKDD Conference on Knowledge Discovery & Data Mining, pp. 2114–2124 (2021). https://doi.org/10.1145/3447548.3467401

165. Zhou, H., Hu, H.: Human motion tracking for rehabilitation—a survey. Biomed. Sig. Proc. Control **3**(1), 1–18 (2008). Article 1. WorldCat.org. https://doi.org/10.1016/j.bspc.2007.09.001

166. Zia, A., Sharma, Y., Bettadapura, V., Sarin, E.L., Essa, I.: Video and accelerometer-based motion analysis for automated surgical skills assessment. Int. J. Comput. Assist. Radiol. Surg. **13**(3), 443–455 (2018). https://doi.org/10.1007/s11548-018-1704-z

167. Sady, M., Vaughan, C.G., Gioia, G.A.: Psychometric characteristics of the postconcussion symptom inventory in children and adolescents. Arch Clin. Neuropsychol. **29**(4), 348–63 (2014). https://doi.org/10.1093/arclin/acu014. Epub 2014 Apr 15

Author Index

A. Parziale et al. (Eds.): IGS 2023, LNCS 14285, pp. 259–260, 2023.
https://doi.org/10.1007/978-3-031-45461-5

Printed in the United States
by Baker & Taylor Publisher Services